Lecture Notes in Computer Science   10980

Commenced Publication in 1973
Founding and Former Series Editors:
Gerhard Goos, Juris Hartmanis, and Jan van Leeuwen

More information about this series at http://www.springer.com/series/7409

Florian Kerschbaum · Stefano Paraboschi (Eds.)

Data and Applications Security and Privacy XXXII

32nd Annual IFIP WG 11.3 Conference, DBSec 2018
Bergamo, Italy, July 16–18, 2018
Proceedings

 Springer

Editors
Florian Kerschbaum
University of Waterloo
Waterloo, ON
Canada

Stefano Paraboschi
Università degli Studi di Bergamo
Dalmine
Italy

ISSN 0302-9743   ISSN 1611-3349 (electronic)
Lecture Notes in Computer Science
ISBN 978-3-319-95728-9   ISBN 978-3-319-95729-6 (eBook)
https://doi.org/10.1007/978-3-319-95729-6

Library of Congress Control Number: 2018947573

LNCS Sublibrary: SL3 – Information Systems and Applications, incl. Internet/Web, and HCI

Printed on acid-free paper

This Springer imprint is published by the registered company Springer Nature Switzerland AG
The registered company address is: Gewerbestrasse 11, 6330 Cham, Switzerland

Preface

This volume contains the papers selected for presentation at the 32nd Annual IFIP WG 11.3 Conference on Data and Applications Security and Privacy (DBSec 2018), held in Bergamo, Italy, during July 16–18, 2018.

In response to the call for papers of this edition, 50 submissions were received, and all submissions were evaluated on the basis of their significance, novelty, and technical quality. The Program Committee, comprising 36 members, performed an excellent task and with the help of additional reviewers all submissions went through a careful anonymous review process (three or more reviews per submission). The Program Committee's work was carried out electronically, yielding intensive discussions. Of the submitted papers, 16 full papers and five short papers were selected for presentation at the conference.

The success of DBSec 2018 depended on the volunteering effort of many individuals, and there is a long list of people who deserve special thanks. We would like to thank all the members of the Program Committee and all the external reviewers, for all their hard work in evaluating the papers and for their active participation in the discussion and selection process. We are very grateful to all people who gave their assistance and ensured a smooth organization process, in particular Sara Foresti for her efforts as DBSec 2018 general chair; Sabrina De Capitani di Vimercati (IFIP WG11.3 chair) for her guidance and support; and Enrico Bacis and Marco Rosa (publicity chairs) for helping with publicity. A special thanks goes to the keynote speakers, who accepted our invitation to deliver a keynote talk at the conference.

Last but certainly not least, thanks to all the authors who submitted papers and all the conference attendees. We hope you find the proceedings of DBSec 2018 interesting, stimulating, and inspiring for your future research.

June 2018

Florian Kerschbaum
Stefano Paraboschi

Organization

Program Committee

Frederik Armknecht	Universität Mannheim, Germany
Vijay Atluri	Rutgers University, USA
Frédéric Cuppens	Telecom Bretagne, France
Nora Cuppens-Boulahia	IMT Atlantique, France
Sabrina De Capitani di Vimercati	University of Milan, Italy
Giovanni Di Crescenzo	Vencore Labs, USA
Sara Foresti	University of Milan, Italy
Joaquin Garcia-Alfaro	Telecom SudParis, France
Stefanos Gritzalis	University of the Aegean, Greece
Ehud Gudes	Ben-Gurion University, Israel
Yuan Hong	Illinois Institute of Technology, USA
Sushil Jajodia	George Mason University, USA
Sokratis Katsikas	Center for Cyber and Information Security, NTNU, Norway
Alex Liu	Michigan State University, USA
Peng Liu	The Pennsylvania State University, USA
Giovanni Livraga	University of Milan, Italy
Ashwin Machanavajjhala	Duke University, USA
Brad Malin	Vanderbilt University, USA
Catherine Meadows	NRL, USA
Martin Olivier	University of Pretoria, South Africa
Andreas Peter	University of Twente, The Netherlands
Silvio Ranise	FBK-Irst, Italy
Indrajit Ray	Colorado State University, USA
Kui Ren	State University of New York at Buffalo, USA
Pierangela Samarati	University of Milan, Italy
Scott Stoller	Stony Brook University, USA
Tamir Tassa	The Open University of Israel, Israel
Mahesh Tripunitara	University of Waterloo, Canada
Jaideep Vaidya	Rutgers University, USA
Lingyu Wang	Concordia University, Canada
Wendy Hui Wang	Stevens Institute of Technology, USA
Attila A. Yavuz	Oregon State University, USA
Ting Yu	Qatar Computing Research Institute, Qatar
Nicola Zannone	Eindhoven University of Technology, The Netherlands

Additional Reviewers

Alhebaishi, Nawaf
Bacis, Enrico
Behnia, Rouzbeh
Bernau, Daniel
Bezawada, Bruhadeshwar
Boehler, Jonas
Borbor, Daniel
Bui, Thang
Bösch, Christoph
Fischer, Andreas
Fuhry, Benny
Kar, Diptendu Mohan
Lei, Xinyu
Majumdar, Suryadipta

Makri, Eleftheria
Oqaily, Alaa
Ozmen, Muslum Ozgur
Rindal, Peter
Rosa, Marco
Siena, Alberto
Thang, Hoang
Tueno, Anselme
Venkatesan, Sridhar
Voloch, Nadav
Wang, Han
Weggenmann, Benjamin
Xie, Shangyu
Zhang, Bo

Contents

Administration

Modeling and Mitigating the Insider Threat of Remote Administrators
in Clouds.. 3
  Nawaf Alhebaishi, Lingyu Wang, Sushil Jajodia, and Anoop Singhal

Blockchain-Based Auditing of Transparent Log Servers............... 21
  *Hoang-Long Nguyen, Jean-Philippe Eisenbarth, Claudia-Lavinia Ignat,
  and Olivier Perrin*

Probabilistic Event Graph to Model Safety and Security
for Diagnosis Purposes 38
  *Edwin Bourget, Frédéric Cuppens, Nora Cuppens-Boulahia,
  Samuel Dubus, Simon Foley, and Youssef Laarouchi*

Access Control Policies

Enabling the Deployment of ABAC Policies in RBAC Systems.......... 51
  Gunjan Batra, Vijayalakshmi Atluri, Jaideep Vaidya, and Shamik Sural

Policy Languages and Their Suitability for Trust Negotiation........... 69
  Martin Kolar, Carmen Fernandez-Gago, and Javier Lopez

Role of Apps in Undoing of Privacy Policies on Facebook 85
  Vishwas T. Patil, Nivia Jatain, and R. K. Shyamasundar

Towards Adaptive Access Control............................. 99
  *Luciano Argento, Andrea Margheri, Federica Paci, Vladimiro Sassone,
  and Nicola Zannone*

Privacy-Preserving Access and Computation

Oblivious Dynamic Searchable Encryption on Distributed Cloud Systems ... 113
  Thang Hoang, Attila A. Yavuz, F. Betül Durak, and Jorge Guajardo

Privacy-Preserving Planarity Testing of Distributed Graphs 131
  Guy Barshap and Tamir Tassa

Image Pixelization with Differential Privacy....................... 148
  Liyue Fan

Integrity and User Interaction

Data Integrity Verification in Column-Oriented NoSQL Databases 165
Grisha Weintraub and Ehud Gudes

A Novel Hybrid Password Authentication Scheme Based on Text
and Image 182
Ian Mackie and Merve Yıldırım

"It's Shocking!": Analysing the Impact and Reactions to the A3:
Android Apps Behaviour Analyser 198
Majid Hatamian, Agnieszka Kitkowska, Jana Korunovska,
and Sabrina Kirrane

Security Analysis and Private Evaluation

FlowConSEAL: Automatic Flow Consistency Analysis of SEAndroid
and SELinux Policies 219
B. S. Radhika, N. V. Narendra Kumar, and R. K. Shyamasundar

On Understanding Permission Usage Contextuality in Android Apps 232
Md Zakir Hossen and Mohammad Mannan

Private yet Efficient Decision Tree Evaluation 243
Marc Joye and Fariborz Salehi

Fixing Vulnerabilities

Breaking and Fixing the Security Proof of Garbled Bloom Filters 263
Cédric Van Rompay and Melek Önen

USBlock: Blocking USB-Based Keypress Injection Attacks 278
Sebastian Neuner, Artemios G. Voyiatzis, Spiros Fotopoulos,
Collin Mulliner, and Edgar R. Weippl

Networked Systems

Virtually Isolated Network: A Hybrid Network to Achieve High
Level Security 299
Jia Xu and Jianying Zhou

Fingerprinting Crowd Events in Content Delivery Networks:
A Semi-supervised Methodology 312
Amine Boukhtouta, Makan Pourzandi, Richard Brunner,
and Stéphane Dault

Assessing Attack Impact on Business Processes by Interconnecting
Attack Graphs and Entity Dependency Graphs   330
    *Chen Cao, Lun-Pin Yuan, Anoop Singhal, Peng Liu, Xiaoyan Sun,
    and Sencun Zhu*

Author Index   349

Administration

Modeling and Mitigating the Insider Threat of Remote Administrators in Clouds

Nawaf Alhebaishi[1,2(✉)], Lingyu Wang[1], Sushil Jajodia[3], and Anoop Singhal[4]

[1] Concordia Institute for Information Systems Engineering, Concordia University, Montreal, Canada
{n_alheb,wang}@ciise.concordia.ca
[2] Faculty of Computing and Information Technology, King Abdulaziz University, Jeddah, Saudi Arabia
[3] Center for Secure Information Systems, George Mason University, Fairfax, USA
jajodia@gmu.edu
[4] Computer Security Division, National Institute of Standards and Technology, Gaithersburg, USA
anoop.singhal@nist.gov

Abstract. As today's cloud providers strive to attract customers with better services and less downtime in a highly competitive market, they increasingly rely on remote administrators including those from third party providers for fulfilling regular maintenance tasks. In such a scenario, the privileges granted for remote administrators to complete their assigned tasks may allow an attacker with stolen credentials of an administrator, or a dishonest remote administrator, to pose severe insider threats to both the cloud tenants and provider. In this paper, we take the first step towards understanding and mitigating such a threat. Specifically, we model the maintenance task assignments and their corresponding security impact due to privilege escalation. We then mitigate such impact through optimizing the task assignments with respect to given constraints. The simulation results demonstrate the effectiveness of our solution in various situations.

1 Introduction

The widespread adoption of cloud leads to many unique challenges in terms of security and privacy [13]. As the cloud service market becomes more and more competitive, cloud providers are striving to attract customers with better services and less downtime at a lower cost. The search for an advantage in cost and efficiency will inevitably lead cloud providers to follow a similar path as what has been taken by their tenants, i.e., outsourcing cloud maintenance tasks to remote administrators including those from specialized third party maintenance providers [9]. Such an approach may also lead to many benefits due to resource sharing, e.g., the access to specialized and experienced domain experts,

© IFIP International Federation for Information Processing 2018
Published by Springer International Publishing AG, part of Springer Nature 2018. All Rights Reserved
F. Kerschbaum and S. Paraboschi (Eds.): DBSec 2018, LNCS 10980, pp. 3–20, 2018.
https://doi.org/10.1007/978-3-319-95729-6_1

the flexibility (e.g., less need for full-time onsite staff), and the lower cost (due to the fact such remote administrators are shared among many clients).

However, such benefits come at an apparent cost in terms of increased security threats. Specifically, the remote administrators must be provided with necessary privileges, which may involve direct accesses to the underlying cloud infrastructure, in order to complete their assigned maintenance tasks. Armed with such privileges, a dishonest remote administrator, or an attacker with the stolen credentials of an administrator, can pose severe insider threats to both the cloud tenants (e.g., causing a large scale leak of confidential user data) and the provider (e.g., disrupting the cloud services or abusing the cloud infrastructure for illegal activities) [12]. On the other hand, cloud providers are under the obligation to prevent such security or privacy breaches caused by insiders [14], either as part of the service level agreements, or to ensure compliance with security standards (e.g., ISO 27017 [19]). Therefore, there is a pressing need to better understand and mitigate such insider threats.

Dealing with the insider threat of remote administrators in clouds faces unique challenges. First, there is a lack of public access to the detailed information regarding cloud infrastructure configurations and typical maintenance tasks performed in clouds. Evidently, most existing works on insider attacks in clouds either stay at a high level or focus on individual nodes instead of the infrastructure [9,20,32] (a more detailed review of related work will be given in Sect. 6). Second, cloud infrastructures can be quite different from typical enterprise networks in terms of many aspects of security. For instance, multi-tenancy means there may co-exist different types of insiders with different privileges, such as administrators of a cloud tenant, those of the cloud provider, and third party remote administrators. Also, virtualization means a more complex attack surface consisting of not only physical nodes but also virtual or hypervisor layers. To the best of our knowledge, there is a lack of any concrete study in the literature on the insider attack of remote administrators in cloud data centers.

In this paper, we take the first step towards understanding and mitigating such insider threats. Specifically, we first model the maintenance tasks and their corresponding privileges. We then model the insider threats posed by remote administrators assigned to maintenance tasks by applying the existing k-zero day safety metric as follows; remote administrators possess elevated privileges due to the assigned maintenance tasks, and those privileges correspond to initially satisfied security conditions, which are normally only accessible by external attackers after exploiting certain vulnerabilities. Such model allows us to formulate the mitigation of the insider threats of remote administrators as an optimization problem and solve it using standard optimization techniques. We evaluate our approach through simulations and the results demonstrate the effectiveness of our solution under various situations. In summary, the main contribution of this paper is twofold:

- To the best of our knowledge, this is the first study on the insider threat of remote administrators in cloud infrastructures. As cloud providers leverage third parties for better efficiency and cost saving, our study demonstrates the need to also consider the security impact, and our model provides a way for quantitatively reasoning about the tradeoff between such security impact with other related factors.

- By formulating the optimization problem of mitigating the insider threat of remote administrators through optimal task assignments, we provide a relatively effective solution, as evidenced by our simulation results, for achieving the optimal tradeoff between security and other constraints using standard optimization techniques.

The remainder of this paper is organized as follows. Section 2 presents a motivating example and discusses maintenance tasks and privileges. In Sect. 3, we present our models of task assignment and insider threat. Section 4 formulates the optimization problem and discusses several use cases. Section 5 gives simulation results. Section 6 discusses related work. Section 7 concludes the paper.

2 Preliminaries

This section gives a motivating example and discusses maintenance tasks and privileges.

2.1 Motivating Example

A key challenge to studying security threats in cloud data centers is the lack of public accesses to detailed information regarding hardware and software configurations deployed in real cloud data centers. Existing work mainly focus on either high level frameworks and guidelines for risk and impact assessment [1,21,28], or specific vulnerabilities or threats in clouds [15,30], with a clear gap between the two. To overcome such a limitation, we choose to devise our own fictitious, but realistic cloud data center designs, by piecing together publicly available information gathered from various cloud vendors and providers [5], as shown in Fig. 1.

To make our design more representative, we devise this configuration based on concepts and practices borrowed from major cloud vendors and providers. For example, we borrow the multi-layer concept and some hardware components, e.g., Carrier Routing System (CRS), Nexus (7000, 5000, 2000), Catalyst 6500, and MDS 9000, from the cloud data center design of Cisco [7]. We synthesize various concepts of the VMware vSphere [18] for main functionality of hardware components in our cloud infrastructure (e.g., authentication servers, DNS, and SAN). We also assume the cloud employs OpenStack as its operating system [24]. The infrastructure provides accesses to both cloud users and remote administrators through the three layer design. Layer 1 connects the cloud to the internet and includes the authentication servers, DNS, and Neutron Server. Layer 2 includes the rack servers and compute nodes. Layer 3 includes the storage servers. OpenStack components run on the authentication servers, DNS server (a Neutron component provides address translation to machines running the

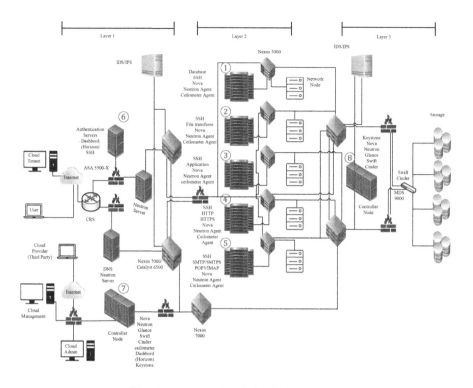

Fig. 1. An example of cloud data center

requested services), and compute nodes (Nova to host and manage VMs, Neutron to connect VMs to the network, and Ceilometer to calculate the usage) to provide cloud services.

Such a cloud data center may require many maintenance tasks to be routinely performed to ensure the normal operation of the hardware and software components. Such maintenance tasks may be performed by both internal staff working onsite and remote administrators, including those from specialized third party providers. In our example, assume the cloud provider decides to rely on third party remote administrators for the regular maintenance of the five compute nodes (nodes #1–5 in Fig. 1), the authentication servers (node #6), and the two controllers (nodes #7 and 8). Table 1, shows the maintenance tasks need to be performed on those nodes. For simplicity, we only consider three types of tasks here (more discussions about maintenance tasks will be given in next section).

In such a scenario, the cloud provider would naturally raise security concerns due to the fact that necessary privileges must be granted in order to allow the third party remote administrators to perform their assigned maintenance tasks. For instance, the task *read log files* needs certain read privilege to be granted, whereas modifying configuration files and installing a new system would demand much higher levels of privileges. Such privileges may allow a dishonest remote administrator, or attackers with stolen credentials of a remote administrator,

Table 1. An example of required maintenance tasks

Node number (in Fig. 1)	Maintenance tasks		
	Read log files	Modify configuration files	Install a new system
1	×	×	
2	×		×
3	×	×	×
4		×	×
5	×		×
6	×	×	
7	×		
8	×		

to launch an insider attack and cause significant damage to the cloud provider and its tenants. Even though the cloud provider may (to some extent) trust the third party maintenance provider as an organization, it is in its best interest to understand and mitigate such threats from individual administrators. However, as demonstrated by this example, there are many challenges in modeling and mitigating such insider threats.

- First, as demonstrated in Table 1, there may exist complex relationships between maintenance tasks and corresponding privileges needed to fulfill such tasks, and also relationships between different privileges (e.g., a root privilege implies many other privileges). Those relationships will determine the extent of an insider threat.
- Second, the insider threat will also depend on which nodes in the cloud infrastructure are involved in the assigned tasks, e.g., an insider with privileges on the authentication servers (node #6 in Fig. 1) or on the compute nodes (nodes #1–5) may have very different security implications.
- Third, the extent of the threat also depends on the configuration (e.g., the connectivity and firewalls), e.g., an insider having access to the controller node #8 would have a much better chance to compromise the storage servers than one with access to the other controller node #7).
- Finally, while an obvious way to mitigate the insider threat is through assigning less tasks to each remote administrator such as to limit his/her privileges, our study will show that the effectiveness of such an approach depends on other factors and constraints, e.g., the amount of tasks to be assigned, the number of available remote administrators, constraints like each administrator may only be assigned to a limited number of tasks due to availability, or a subset of tasks due to his/her skill set, etc.

Clearly, how to model and mitigate the insider threat may not be straight-forward even for such a simplified example (we will give the solution for this example scenario in Sect. 4.2), and the scenario might become far more complex in practice than the one demonstrated here. The remainder of the paper will tackle those challenges.

2.2   Remote Administrators, Maintenance Tasks, and Privileges

A cloud provider may hire different types of administrators to perform mainte-nance tasks onsite or through remote accesses [9]. First, *hardware administra-tors* have physical access to the cloud data center to perform maintenance on the physical components. Second, *security team administrators* are responsible for maintaining the cloud security policies. Third, *remote administrators* (RAs) perform maintenance tasks on certain nodes inside the infrastructure. The first two types can be considered relatively more trustworthy due to their limited quantity and the fact they work onsite, and directly for the cloud provider. The last type is usually considered riskier due to two facts, i.e., they work through remote access which is susceptible to attacks (e.g., via stolen credentials), and they may be subcontracted through third party companies which means less control by the cloud provider. In this paper, we focus on such remote admin-istrators (RAs), even though our models and mitigation solution may equally work for dealing with other types of users if necessary.

There exists only limited public information about the exact maintenance tasks performed at major cloud providers. We have collected such information from various sources, and our findings are summarized on the left-hand side of Table 2, which shows sample maintenance tasks mentioned by Amazon Web Service [2], Google Cloud [3], and Microsoft Azure [4]. As to privileges required for typical maintenance tasks, Bleikertz et al. provided five sample privileges required for maintaining the compute nodes in clouds [9], which we will borrow for our further discussions, as shown on the right-hand side of Table 2.

Table 2. Maintenance tasks in popular cloud platforms (left) and the privileges (right)

Maintenance Task	AWS [2]	GCP [3]	Azure [4]	Privilege	Restriction
Review Logs	×	×	×	No privilege	No access
Hard Disk Scan		×	×	Read	Cannot read VM-related data
Update Firmware	×	×	×	Write_L1	The restriction of read privilege
Patch Operating System	×	×	×		applies, software modification restricted
Update Operating System	×	×	×		to trusted repository
System Backup	×	×	×	Write_L2	Bootloader, kernel, policy enforcement,
Upgrades System	×	×	×		maintenance agent, file system
Maintain Automated Snapshots	×				snapshots, package manager transaction logs,
Bug Fix	×	×	×		and certain dangerous system parameters
Update Kernel	×	×		Write_L3	No restriction

Table 3. Maintenance tasks and privileges for the running example

Task number	Node number (in Fig. 1)	Task description	Privilege
1	4 (*http*)	Read log files for monitoring	Read
2	4 (*http*)	Modifying configuration files	Write_L1
3	4 (*http*)	Patching system files	Write_L3
4	3 (*app*)	Read log files for monitoring	Read
5	3 (*app*)	Modifying configuration files	Write_L1
6	3 (*app*)	Update kernel	Write_L3
7	1 (*DB*)	Read log files for monitoring	Read
8	1 (*DB*)	Modifying configuration files	Write_L1
9	1 (*DB*)	Update kernel	Write_L3
10	1 (*DB*)	Install new systems	Write_L2

To simplify our discussions, our running example will be limited to ten maintenance tasks on three compute nodes with corresponding privileges on such nodes, as shown in Table 3. Later in Sect. 4.2, we will expand the scope to discuss the solution for our motivating example which involves all the eight nodes.

3   Models

This section presents out threat model and models of the maintenance task assignment and insider threat.

3.1   Threat Model and Maintenance Task Assignment Model

Our work is intended to assist the cloud provider in understanding and mitigating the insider threat from dishonest remote administrators or attackers with stolen credentials of a remote administrator. To this end, we assume the majority of remote administrators is trusted, and if there are multiple dishonest administrators (or attackers with their credentials), they do not collude (a straightfoward extension of our models by considering each possible combination of administrators as one insider can accommodate such colluding administrators, which is considered as future work). We assume the third party provider is trusted as an organization and will collaborate with the cloud provider to implement the intended task assignment. We assume the cloud provider is concerned about certain critical assets inside the cloud, and it is aware of the constraints about task assignments such as the number of remote administrators, their availability and skill set, etc. Finally, as a preventive solution, our mitigation approach is intended as a complementary solution to existing vulnerability scanners, intrusion detection systems, and other solutions for mitigating insider threats.

   The cloud provider assigns the maintenance tasks to remote administrators (RAs) based on given constraints (e.g., which tasks may be assigned each RA), and consequently the RA will obtain privileges required by those tasks. This can be modeled as follows (which has a similar syntax as [27]).

Definition 1 (Maintenance Task Assignment Model). *Given*

- *a set of remote administrators RA,*
- *a set of maintenance task T,*
- *a set of privileges P,*
- *the remote administrator task relation $RAT \subseteq RA \times T$ which indicates the maintenance tasks that are allowed to be assigned to each remote administrator, and*
- *the task privilege relation $TP \subseteq T \times P$ which indicates the privileges required for each task,*

a maintenance task assignment is given by function $ta(.) : RA \to 2^T$ that satisfies $(\forall ra \in RA)(ta(ra) \subseteq \{t \mid (ra, t) \in RAT\}$ (meaning a remote administrator is only assigned with the tasks to which he/she is allowed), and the corresponding set of privileges given to the remote administrator is given by function $pa(ra) = \bigcup_{t \in ta(ra)} \{p \mid (t, p) \in TP\}$.

3.2 Insider Threat Model

We given an overview of our model for the insider threat, which will be demonstrated through an example shown in Fig. 2. First, we borrow the resource graph concept [31] to represent the causal relationships between different resources inside the given cloud configuration. Second, we map the privileges given to RAs through maintenance task assignments (Definition 1) to exploits of corresponding resources in the resource graph. Third, we apply the k-zero day safety metric [33] to quantify the insider threat of each RA through his/her k value. Finally, we take the average (and minimum) of all RAs' k values as the average (and worst) case indication of insider threat.

Figure 2 shows an example resource graph for our running example (the dashed lines and shades can be ignored and will be discussed later in Sect. 4.2; also, only a small portion of the resource graph is shown here due to space limitations). Each triplet inside an oval indicates a potential zero day or known exploit in the format <service or vulnerability, source host, destination host> (e.g. <Xen, RA, 4> indicates an exploit on Xen), and the plaintext pairs indicate the pre- or post-conditions of those exploits in the format <condition, host> where condition can be either a privilege on the host (e.g., <W1,4> means the level 1 write privilege and <R,4> means the read privilege which are both explained in Sect. 2.2), the existence of a service on the host (e.g., <Xen,4>), or a connectivity (e.g., <0,4>means attacker can connect to host 4 and <4,4> means a local exploit on host 4). The edges point from pre-conditions to an exploit and then to its post-conditions, which indicate that any exploit can be executed if and only if all of its pre-conditions are satisfied, whereas executing an exploit is enough to satisfy all its post-conditions.

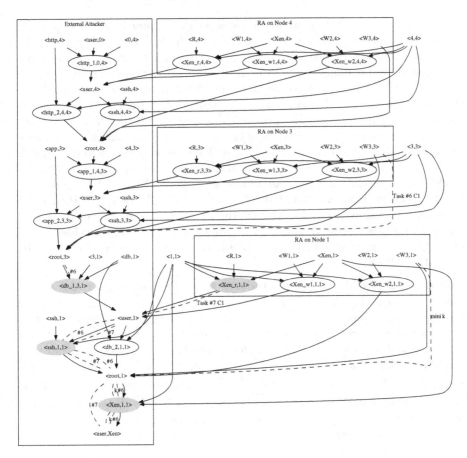

Fig. 2. Modeling insider threat using the resource graph

In Fig. 2, the left-hand side box indicates the normal resource graph which depicts what an external attacker may do to compromise the critical asset <user, Xen>. The right-hand side boxes depict the insider threats coming from RAs assigned to each of the three compute nodes. The gray color exploits are what captures the consequences of granting privileges to remote administrators. For example, an RA with the level 1 write privilege <W1,4> can potentially exploit Xen (i.e., <Xen_w1,4,4>) to escalate his/her privilege to the user privilege on host 4 (i.e., <user,4>), whereas a higher level privilege <W2,4> can potentially lead to the root privilege <root,4> through an exploit <Xen_w2,4,4>, and the highest privilege <W3,4> can even directly lead to that privilege. Those examples show how the model can capture the different levels of insider threats as results of different privileges obtained through maintenance task assignments.

Next, given the maintenance task assignment for each RA, we can obtain all the possible paths he/she may follow in the resource graph, starting from all the initially satisfied conditions (e.g., <Xen,4>) and those implied by the task assignment (e.g., <W1,4>) to the critical asset (i.e., <user,Xen>). To quantify the relative level of such threats, we apply the k-zero day safety metric (k0d) [33] which basically counts the number of zero day exploits (known exploits are not counted, and exploits of the same service are only counted once) along the shortest path. The metric value of each RA provides an estimation for the relative level of threat of each RA, since a larger number of distinct zero day exploits on the shortest path means reaching the critical asset is (exponentially, if those exploits are assumed to be independent) more difficult. For example, an RA with privilege <W3,1> would have a k0d value of 1 since only one zero day exploit <Xen,1,1> is needed to reach the critical asset, whereas an RA with <W2,1> would have a k value of 2 since an additional exploit <Xen_w2,1,1> is needed. Finally, once we have calculated the k values of all RAs based on their given maintenance task assignments, we take the average (and minimum) of those k values as the average (and worst) case indication of the overall insider threat of the given maintenance task assignments. The above discussions are formally defined as follows.

Definition 2 (Insider Threat Model). *Given the maintenance task assignment (i.e., RA, T, P, RAT, TP, ta, and pa, as given in Definition 1) let $C_r = \bigcup_{ra \in RA} pa(ra)$ be the set of privileges implied by the assignment and E_r be the set of new exploits enabled by C_r. Denote by $G(E \cup E_r \cup C \cup C_r, R)$ the resource graph (where E and C denote the original set of exploits and conditions, respectively, and R denote the edges) and let k0d(.) be the k zero day safety metric function. We say $k0d(ra)$, $\frac{\sum_{ra \in RA} k0d(ra)}{|RA|}$, and $min(\{k0d(ra) : ra \in RA\})$ represent the insider threat of ra, the average case insider threat of the maintenance task assignment, and the worst case insider threat of the maintenance task assignment, respectively.*

4   The Mitigation

In this section, we formulate the optimization-based solution for mitigate the insider threat during maintenance task assignment and discuss several use cases.

4.1   Optimization-Based Mitigation

Based on our definitions of the maintenance task assignment model and the insider threat model, we can define the problem of optimal task assignment as follows. Note the remote administrator task relation RAT basically gives the constraints for optimization since it states which tasks may be assigned to which RA (in some cases the constraints may also be modeled differently for convenience, e.g., as the maximum number of tasks for each RA).

Definition 3 (The Optimal task assignment problem). *Given a resource graph G, the remote administrators RA, maintenance tasks T, privileges P, the remote administrator task relation RAT, and the task privilege relation TP, find a maintenance task assignment function ta which maximizes the insider threat $\frac{\sum_{ra \in RA} k0d(ra)}{|RA|}$ (or $min(\{k0d(ra) : ra \in RA\})$).*

Theorem 1. *The Optimal task assignment problem (Definition 3) is NP-hard.*

Proof: First, calculating the $k0d$ function is already NP-hard w.r.t. the size of the resource graph [33]. On the other hand, we provide a sketch of a proof to show the problem is also NP-hard from the perspective of the maintenance task assignment. Specifically, given any instance of the well known NP-complete problem, exact cover by 3-sets (i.e., given a finite set X containing exactly $3n$ elements, and a collection C of subsets of X each of which contains exactly 3 elements, determine whether there exists $D \subseteq C$ such that every $x \in X$ occurs in exactly one $d \in D$), we can construct an instance of our problem as follows. We use X for the set of maintenance tasks, and C for the set of RAs, such that the three elements of each $c \in C$ represent three tasks which can be assigned to c. In addition, no RA can be assigned with less than three tasks, and an RA already assigned with three tasks can choose any available task to be assigned in addition. We can then construct a resource graph in which the critical asset can be reached through any combination of four privileges. It then follows that, the insider threat is maximized if and only if there exists an exact cover D due to the following. If the exact cover exists, then every RA $d \in D$ is assigned with exactly three tasks and therefore the k value of every RA, and hence the insider threat, will be equal to infinity since the critical asset cannot be reached with less than four privileges; if the cover does not exist, then to have every task assigned, we will have to assign at least one RA with more than three tasks, and hence the k value will decrease. □

In our study, we use the genetic algorithm to optimize the maintenance task assignments by maximizing k. Specifically, the resource graph is taken as input to the optimization algorithm, with the (either average case or worst case) insider threat value k as the fitness function. We try to find the best task assignment for maximizing the value k within a reasonable number of generations. The constraints can be given either through defining the remote administrator task relation RAT in the case of specific tasks that can be assigned to each RA, or as a fixed number of tasks for each RA. Other constraints can also be easily applied to the optimization algorithm. In our simulations, we choose the probability of 0.8 for crossover and 0.2 for mutation based on our experiences.

4.2   Use Cases

We demonstrate our solution through several use cases with different constraints. The first three use cases are based on the five remote administrators and ten maintenance tasks presented in Table 3 and the last use case is based on the motivating example shown in Sect. 2.1.

- Use Case A: In this case, each RA should be assigned with two tasks. The three tables shown in Table 4 show three possible assignments and the corresponding k values. Also, Fig. 2 shows an example path (dashed lines) for tasks assigned to RA C_1 based on the top table, and also the shortest path yielding the

Table 4. Maintenance tasks assignments for use case A

User	A₁	B₁	C₁	D₁	E₁
Tasks Number	4 1	5 10	6 7	8 3	9 2
k	3	1	2	2	1
$\bar{k}$			1.8		
Minimum k			1		

User	A₂	B₂	C₂	D₂	E₂
Tasks Number	6 9	4 3	7 10	8 1	5 2
k	1	3	1	2	3
$\bar{k}$			2		
Minimum k			1		

User	A₃	B₃	C₃	D₃	E₃
Tasks Number	4 1	5 2	6 7	8 3	9 10
k	3	3	2	2	1
$\bar{k}$			2.2		
Minimum k			1		

minimum k value. We use the GA to find the optimal task assignment that meets the constraint given in this case, as shown in the last table, the maximal average of k values among all RAs is $\bar{k} = 2.2$. It can also be seen that the minimum k value among all RAs is always $k = 1$ in this special case.

– Use Case B: In this case, each RA should be assigned with at least one task. The optimal task assignment under this constraint is (RA1{8,9,10}, RA2{4,5}, RA3{3}, RA4{1,2}, and RA5 {6,7}). This relaxed constraint improves the average of k from 2.2 in the previous example to 2.8, which shows relaxing the constraint may increase k (which means less threat).

– Use Case C: In this case, each RA can handle a fixed subset of tasks. In our example, we assume RA1 can be assigned to any task requiring the read privilege, RA2 to tasks requiring write level 1 privilege, RA3 to tasks requiring write level 1 and 2, RA4 to tasks requiring write level 3, and RA5 can be assigned to any task. After applying our solution, the optimal assignment yields the maximal average of k values to be $k = 2.2$.

– Use Case D: This case shows the optimal maintenance task assignment for tasks discussed in our motivating example in Sect. 2.1. We have eight RAs and each RA can handle maximum two tasks. The upper table in Table 5 shows the 15 maintenance tasks to be assigned. In Table 5, the four tables on the bottom show four different tasks scenarios assigned to RAs and each table shows different average k. The bottom table on the right side shows the optimal task assignment in term of the average $k = 3.125$.

5   Simulations

This section shows simulation results on applying our mitigation solution under various constraints. All simulations are performed using a virtual machine equipped with a 3.4 GHz CPU and 4GB RAM in the Python 2.7.10 environment under Ubuntu 12.04 LTS and the MATLAB R2017b's GA toolbox. To generate a large number of resource graphs for simulations, we start with seed graphs with realistic configurations similar to Fig. 1 and then generate random resource graphs by injecting new nodes and edges into those seed graphs. Those resource graphs were used as the input to the optimization toolbox where the fitness function is to maximize the average or worst case insider threat value k (given in Definition 2) with various constraints, e.g., the number of available RAs and

Table 5. Maintenance task assignments for use case D (the motivating example)

Task#	Maintenance task	Task#	Maintenance task
1	Read log files for node 1	2	Modify configuration file for node 1
3	Read log files for node 2	4	Install a new system for node 2
5	Read log files for node 3	6	Modify configuration file for node 3
7	Install a new system for node 3	8	Modify configuration file for node 4
9	Install a new system for node 4	10	Read log files for node 5
11	Install a new system for node 5	12	Read log files for node 6
13	Modify configuration file for node 6	14	Read log files for node 7
15	Read log files for node 8		

User	RA1	RA2	RA3	RA4	RA5	RA6	RA7	RA8
Tasks Number	14 / 5	1 / 9	4 / 15	8 / 12	2 / 10	3 / 11	7 / 13	6
k	1	3	2	3	2	3	2	3
$\bar{k}$				2.375				
Minimum k				1				

User	RA1	RA2	RA3	RA4	RA5	RA6	RA7	RA8
Tasks Number	1 / 9	2 / 10	3 / 11	4 / 12	5 / 13	6 / 14	7 / 15	8
k	3	2	3	3	3	1	2	5
$\bar{k}$				2.75				
Minimum k				1				

User	RA1	RA2	RA3	RA4	RA5	RA6	RA7	RA8
Tasks Number	1 / 4	2 / 7	3 / 9	5 / 10	6 / 11	15 / 12	13 / 14	8
k	3	2	4	4	3	2	1	5
$\bar{k}$				3				
Minimum k				1				

User	RA1	RA2	RA3	RA4	RA5	RA6	RA7	RA8
Tasks Number	1 / 12	2 / 7	3 / 9	5 / 10	6 / 11	14 / 15	4 / 13	8
k	3	2	4	4	3	1	3	5
$\bar{k}$				3.125				
Minimum k				1				

maintenance tasks and how many task may be assigned to each RA. We repeat each simulation on 300 different resource graphs to obtain the average result.

The objective of the first two simulations is to study how the average case insider threat (i.e., the average of k values among all RAs) may be improved through our mitigation solution under constraints on the number of tasks and RAs, respectively. In Fig. 3, the number of available RAs is fixed at 500, while the number of maintenance tasks is varied between 500 and 2,000 along the X-axis. The Y-axis shows the average of k among all RAs. The solid lines represent the results after applying our mitigation solution under constraints about the maximum number of tasks assigned to each RA. The dashed lines represent the results before applying the mitigation solution.

Results and Implications: From the result, we can make the following observations. First, the mitigation solution successfully reduces the insider threat (increasing the average of k values) in all cases. Second, the results before and after applying the solution decrease (meaning increased insider threat) following similar linear trends, as the number of maintenance tasks increases until each RA reaches its full capacity. Finally, the result of maximum four tasks per RA after applying the solution is close to the result of maximum ten tasks per RA before applying the solution, which means the mitigation solution may allow more (more than double) tasks to be assigned to the same number of RAs while yielding the same level of insider threat.

In Fig. 4, the number of maintenance tasks is fixed at 2,500 while the number of RAs is varied between 400 and 1,000 along the X-axis. The Y-axis shows the average of k among all RAs. The solid lines represent the results after applying the mitigation solution and the dashed lines for the results before applying the solution. All the lines start with sufficient numbers of RAs for handling all the tasks since we only consider one round of assignment. We apply the same constraint as in previous simulation.

Results and Implications: Again we can see the mitigation solution successfully reduces the insider threat (increasing the average of k values) in all cases. More interestingly, we can observe the trend of the lines as follows. The dashed lines all follow a similar near linear trend, which is expected since a larger number of RAs means less insider threat since each RA will be assigned less tasks and hence given less privileges. On the other hand, most of the solid lines follow a similar trend of starting flat then increasing almost linearly before reaching the plateau. This trend indicates that, the mitigation solution can significantly reduce the insider threat when the number of RAs is within certain ranges past which it becomes less effective (because each RA already receives minimum privileges). The trend of 4 tasks per RA is slightly different mostly due to the limited number of RAs (Fig. 4).

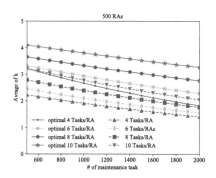
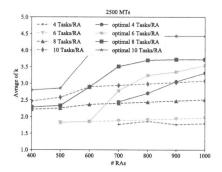

Fig. 3. Average of k among 500 RAs before and after applying the mitigation solution

Fig. 4. Average of k among different number of RAs before and after the solution

The objective of the next two simulations is to study how the worst case insider threat (i.e., the minimum k values among all RAs) behaves under the mitigation solution. Figures 5 and 6 are based on similar X-axis and constraints as previous two simulations, whereas the Y-axis shows the minimum k among all RAs (averaged over 300 simulations).

Results and Implications: In Fig. 5, we can see that the minimum k values also decrease (meaning more insider threat) almost linearly as the number of tasks increases. In contrast to previous simulation, we can see the minimum k values are always lower than the average k values, which is expected. In Fig. 6, we can see the minimum k values also increase almost linearly before reaching the plateau as the number of RAs increases. In contrast to previous simulation, we can see the increase here is slower, which means the worst case results (minimum k values) are more difficult to improve with a increased number of RAs.

Also, we can see that the worst case results reach the plateau later (e.g., 900 RAs for 8 tasks per RA) than the average case results (700 RAs).

6   Related Work

The insider threat is a challenging issue for both traditional networks and clouds. Ray and Poolsapassit proposed an alarm system to monitor the behavior of malicious insiders using the attack tree [25]. Mathew et al. used the capability acquisition graphs (CAG) to monitor the abuse of privileges by malicious insiders [23]. Sarkar et al. proposed DASAI to analyze if a process contains a step that meet the insider attack condition [29]. Chinchani et al. proposed a graph-based model for insider attacks and measure the threat [11]. Althebyan and Panda proposed predication and detection model for insider attacks based on knowledge gathered by the internal users during work time in the organization [6]. Bishop et al. presented insider threat definition based on security policies and determine source of risk [8]. Roy et al. studied an employee assignment problem to find an optimal tasks assigned to the employee based on constraints in role-based access control [26].

There is lack of work focusing on the cloud security metrics in general and for insider attacks especially. Our previous work focus on applying threat modeling to cloud data center infrastructures with a focus on external attackers [5]. Gruschka and Jensen devise a high level attack surface framework to show from where the attack can start [16]. The NIST emphasizes the importance of security measuring and metrics for cloud providers in [1]. A framework is propose by Luna et al. for cloud security metrics using basic building blocks [22].

Besides threat modeling, mitigating insider attackers in clouds is also a challenging task. There are many works discuss securing the cloud from insider attack by limiting the trust on the compute node [32]. Li et al. focuses on supporting users to configure privacy protection in compute node [20]. Closest to our work, Bleikertz et al. focus on securing the cloud during maintenance time by limiting the privilege grant to the remote administrator based on the tasks assigned

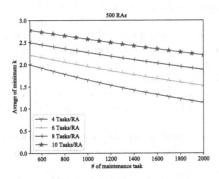

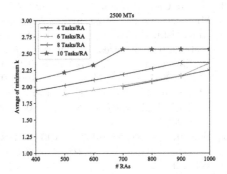

Fig. 5. Minimum k for 500 RAs

Fig. 6. Minimum k for varying # of RAs

to that administrator [9]. We borrow their categorization of the privileges. Our mitigation approach is also inspired by the network hardening approaches using genetic algorithms [10,17].

7   Conclusion

In this paper, we have modeled the insider threat during maintenance task assignment for cloud providers to better understand such threat posed by third party remote administrators, and we have formulated the optimal assignment problem as an optimization problem and applied standard optimization algorithm to derive a solution under different constraints. We have also conducted simulations whose results show our solution can significantly reduce the insider threat of remote administrators. Our future work will focus on following directions. First, we will improve our solution to handle more realistic scenarios, e.g., incremental assignment for streams of new maintenance tasks, and handling dynamics (joining or leaving) of RAs, giving priority or weight to tasks. Second, we will consider explicit cost models for assignments and incorporate the cost into the mitigation solution, e.g., based on the number of RAs, the amount or duration of tasks, and privileges needed.

Acknowledgements. The authors thank the anonymous reviewers for their valuable comments. This work was partially supported by the National Institutes of Standard and Technology under grant number 60NANB16D287, by the National Science Foundation under grant number IIP-1266147, and by Natural Sciences and Engineering Research Council of Canada under Discovery Grant N01035.

References

1. National Institute of Standards and Technology: Cloud Computing Service Metrics Description (2015). http://www.nist.gov/itl/cloud/upload/RATAX-CloudServiceMetricsDescription-DRAFT-20141111.pdf. Accessed 17 June 2015
2. Amazon Web Services (2018). https://aws.amazon.com/. Accessed 28 Feb 2018
3. Google Cloud Platform (2018). https://cloud.google.com/. Accessed 28 Feb 2018
4. Microsoft Azure (2018). https://azure.microsoft.com. Accessed 28 Feb 2018
5. Alhebaishi, N., Wang, L., Jajodia, S., Singhal, A.: Threat modeling for cloud data center infrastructures. In: Cuppens, F., Wang, L., Cuppens-Boulahia, N., Tawbi, N., Garcia-Alfaro, J. (eds.) FPS 2016. LNCS, vol. 10128, pp. 302–319. Springer, Cham (2017). https://doi.org/10.1007/978-3-319-51966-1_20
6. Althebyan, Q., Panda, B.: A knowledge-base model for insider threat prediction. In: 2007 IEEE SMC Information Assurance and Security Workshop, pp. 239–246, June 2007
7. Bakshi, K.: Cisco cloud computing-data center strategy, architecture, and solutions (2009). http://www.cisco.com/web/strategy/docs/gov/CiscoCloudComputing_WP.pdf
8. Bishop, M., Engle, S., Peisert, S., Whalen, S., Gates, C.: We have met the enemy and he is US. In: Proceedings of the 2008 New Security Paradigms Workshop, NSPW 2008, pp. 1–12. ACM, New York (2008)

9. Bleikertz, S., Kurmus, A., Nagy, Z.A., Schunter, M.: Secure cloud maintenance: Protecting workloads against insider attacks. In: Proceedings of the 7th ACM Symposium on Information, Computer and Communications Security, ASIACCS 2012, pp. 83–84. ACM, New York (2012)

10. Borbor, D., Wang, L., Jajodia, S., Singhal, A.: Diversifying network services under cost constraints for better resilience against unknown attacks. In: Ranise, S., Swarup, V. (eds.) DBSec 2016. LNCS, vol. 9766, pp. 295–312. Springer, Cham (2016). https://doi.org/10.1007/978-3-319-41483-6_21

11. Chinchani, R., Iyer, A., Ngo, H.Q., Upadhyaya, S.: Towards a theory of insider threat assessment. In: 2005 International Conference on Dependable Systems and Networks (DSN 2005), pp. 108–117, June 2005

12. Claycomb, W.R., Nicoll, A.: Insider threats to cloud computing: directions for new research challenges. In: 2012 IEEE 36th Annual Computer Software and Applications Conference, pp. 387–394, July 2012

13. Cloud Security Alliance. Security guidance for critical areas of focus in cloud computing v 3.0 (2011)

14. Cloud Security Alliance. Top threats to cloud computing (2018). https://cloudsecurityalliance.org/topthreats/csathreats.v1.0.pdf

15. Dahbur, K., Mohammad, B., Tarakji, A.B.: A survey of risks, threats and vulnerabilities in cloud computing. In Proceedings of the 2011 International Conference on Intelligent Semantic Web-Services and Applications, ISWSA 2011, pp. 12:1–12:6. ACM, New York (2011)

16. Gruschka, N., Jensen, M.: Attack surfaces: a taxonomy for attacks on cloud services. In: 2010 IEEE 3rd International Conference on Cloud Computing, pp. 276–279. IEEE (2010)

17. Gupta, M., Rees, J., Chaturvedi, A., Chi, J.: Matching information security vulnerabilities to organizational security profiles: a genetic algorithm approach. Decis. Support Syst. **41**(3), 592–603 (2006). Intelligence and Security Informatics

18. Hany, M.: VMware VSphere in the Enterprise. http://www.hypervizor.com/diags/HyperViZor-Diags-VMW-vS4-Enterprise-v1-0.pdf. Accessed 05 Feb 2015

19. ISO Std IEC. ISO 27017. Information technology- Security techniques- Code of practice for information security controls based on ISO/IEC 27002 for cloud services (DRAFT) (2012). http://www.iso27001security.com/html/27017.html

20. Li, M., Zang, W., Bai, K., Yu, M., Liu, P.: Mycloud: supporting user-configured privacy protection in cloud computing. In: Proceedings of the 29th Annual Computer Security Applications Conference, ACSAC 2013, pp. 59–68. ACM, New York (2013)

21. Luna, J., Ghani, H., Germanus, D., Suri, N.: A security metrics framework for the cloud. In: 2011 Proceedings of the International Conference on Security and Cryptography (SECRYPT), pp. 245–250, July 2011

22. Luna, J., Ghani, H., Germanus, D., Suri, N.: A security metrics framework for the cloud. In: 2011 Proceedings of the International Conference on Security and Cryptography (SECRYPT), pp. 245–250. IEEE (2011)

23. Mathew, S., Upadhyaya, S., Ha, D., Ngo, H.Q.: Insider abuse comprehension through capability acquisition graphs. In: 2008 11th International Conference on Information Fusion, pp. 1–8, June 2008

24. Openstack. Openstack Operations Guide. http://docs.openstack.org/openstack-ops/content/openstack-ops_preface.html. Accessed 27 Aug 2015

25. di Vimercati, S.C., Syverson, P., Gollmann, D. (eds.): ESORICS 2005. LNCS, vol. 3679. Springer, Heidelberg (2005). https://doi.org/10.1007/11555827

26. Roy, A., Sural, S., Majumdar, A.K., Vaidya, J., Atluri, V.: On optimal employee assignment in constrained role-based access control systems. ACM Trans. Manage. Inf. Syst. **7**(4), 10:1–10:24 (2016)
27. Sandhu, R.S., Coyne, E.J., Feinstein, H.L., Youman, C.E.: Role-based access control models. Computer **29**(2), 38–47 (1996)
28. Saripalli, P., Walters, B.: Quirc: a quantitative impact and risk assessment framework for cloud security. In: 2010 IEEE 3rd International Conference on Cloud Computing, pp. 280–288, July 2010
29. Sarkar, A., Khler, S., Riddle, S., Ludaescher, B., Bishop, M.: Insider attack identification and prevention using a declarative approach. In: 2014 IEEE Security and Privacy Workshops, pp. 265–276, May 2014
30. Shaikh, F.B., Haider, S.: Security threats in cloud computing. In: 2011 International Conference for Internet Technology and Secured Transactions (ICITST), pp. 214–219, December 2011
31. Sheyner, O., Haines, J., Jha, S., Lippmann, R., Wing, J.M.: Automated generation and analysis of attack graphs. In: Proceedings of the 2002 IEEE Symposium on Security and Privacy, pp. 273–284 (2002)
32. Sze, W.K., Srivastava, A., Sekar, R.: Hardening openstack cloud platforms against compute node compromises. In: Proceedings of the 11th ACM on Asia Conference on Computer and Communications Security, ASIA CCS 2016, pp. 341–352. ACM, New York (2016)
33. Wang, L., Jajodia, S., Singhal, A., Cheng, P., Noel, S.: k-zero day safety: a network security metric for measuring the risk of unknown vulnerabilities. IEEE Trans. Dependable Secure Comput. **11**(1), 30–44 (2014)

Blockchain-Based Auditing
of Transparent Log Servers

Hoang-Long Nguyen[✉], Jean-Philippe Eisenbarth, Claudia-Lavinia Ignat,
and Olivier Perrin

Université de Lorraine, CNRS, Inria, LORIA, 54000 Nancy, France
`hoang-long.nguyen@loria.fr`

Abstract. Public key server is a simple yet effective way of key management in secure end-to-end communication. To ensure the trustworthiness of a public key server, CONIKS employs a tamper-evident data structure on the server and a gossiping protocol among clients in order to detect compromised servers. However, due to lack of incentive and vulnerability to malicious clients, a gossiping protocol is hard to implement in practice. Meanwhile, alternative solutions such as EthIKS are too costly. This paper presents *Trusternity*, an auditing scheme relying on Ethereum blockchain that is easy to implement, inexpensive to operate and resilient to malicious clients. We also conduct an empirical study of system behaviour in face of attacks and propose a lightweight anomaly detection algorithm to protect clients against such attacks.

Keywords: Authentication · Public key · Blockchain · Auditing Ethereum

1 Introduction

In order to meet user demands regarding online privacy and prevent digital snooping, identity and data theft, we can see in the last years an increase in the number of end-to-end encryption (*E2EE*) messaging services. A major challenge in any E2EE system is to prevent man-in-the-middle attack (*MITM*) where an adversary impersonates a legitimate communication participant. Thus, some E2EE systems leverage Out-of-Band (OOB) channels for client *authentication* by means of manual comparison of public key fingerprints [27] or pre-known shared passwords [5]. However, secure and easy to use OOB channel is hard to achieve in practice. Password entropy is often overlooked by users while fingerprint comparison is error-prone and cumbersome [22]. Other client authentication solutions rely on trusted third parties, i.e. *key servers* to distribute and authenticate public keys among clients. Many popular E2EE services such as WhatsApp [21] adopt centralized key servers as they are easy to use and straightforward to implement.

Published by Springer International Publishing AG, part of Springer Nature 2018. All Rights Reserved
F. Kerschbaum and S. Paraboschi (Eds.): DBSec 2018, LNCS 10980, pp. 21–37, 2018.
https://doi.org/10.1007/978-3-319-95729-6_2

However, a centralized key server becomes a system single point of failure being vulnerable to attacks from adversaries or surveillance agencies. Therefore, secure and autonomous client authentication remains a major challenge for E2EE.

Rather than preemptively verify the exchanged keys, by using the *Key transparency* approach [13, 17, 26], clients can verify if the key server behaves correctly during communication. The general idea is to turn the key server to a *transparent log server* using an *authenticated data structure* [18] that is append only and can be efficiently audited. The key server acts as a *prover* who returns public keys upon request along with compact proofs that can be verified by clients. Thus, clients do not worry about MITM attack as any attempt to modify client keys is recorded on the auditable server log.

Authenticated data structure ensures that the server cannot change user keys without being recorded. It is, however, possible for a compromised key server to *equivocate* by presenting different answers to different clients. Therefore, log clients need a way to *cross validate* the received information to ensure the key server *consistency* among clients. This process is called *auditing*. There are third-party clients (*auditors*) who *frequently* query the key server for proofs. Thus, whenever clients receive replies from the key server, they can cross check the proofs with these auditors. State of the art suggests the use of a *gossiping protocol* among log clients and auditors to exchange information and effectively blacklist any exposed compromised key server.

However, such gossiping mechanism is hard to implement in practice [3]. It is vulnerable to certain classes of failures when attackers are present in the network i.e. Sybil attack [10]. It is hard to incentivize clients to participate and bootstrap the gossiping network. Users' privacy may also be at risk [20]. So far, we are not aware of any complete gossiping protocol design in current Transparent log systems. A similar effort in Certificate Transparency [15] is being standardized though after several years, and it is still not finished. Rather than using a separate gossiping protocol, EthIKS [4] implements the transparent log server on Ethereum blockchain [23]. However, as EthIKS operation cost increases proportionally with the number of users and due to the significant increase in the price of ETH, the system does not scale to large key servers with millions of users.

Auditing is a mandatory mechanism to secure a transparent log scheme. However, proposed auditing mechanisms using gossiping are vulnerable and difficult to implement. Meanwhile, blockchain based auditing is considered too expensive to operate as demonstrated in EthIKS. To tackle this problem, we present *Trusternity*, a practical transparent log auditing scheme using blockchain that is secure, easy to implement, suitable for large scale key servers, as well as lightweight for clients. The contributions of this paper are the following:

- We design Trusternity, a secure, scalable auditing mechanism using a blockchain to ensure key server consistency. Our scheme is complete and more cost effective in comparison to state-of-the-art approaches.
- We implement a proof-of-concept for Trusternity using Ethereum and extending a state-of-the-art solution.

– We simulate an attack that deceives clients to accept a compromised blockchain and provide metrics to help detection of such attack.

2 Requirements

We now define several requirements for our auditing system.

R1 Trustless auditor: The system must be able to detect anomaly in auditing process even when clients connect to malicious auditors.

R2 Scalability: The system is scalable with unbounded number of servers and clients. For this, the system must satisfy the following sub requirements.

R2.1 *Incentive:* Auditors must be incited for their service of querying key servers and answer client requests.

R2.2 *Budget operation:* We want to reduce the operation cost of the key server when participating in the auditing process.

R2.3 *Thin client:* The auditing mechanism must not require extensive client resources so that it can be easily adopted in practice.

3 Background and Related Work

In this section, we shortly describe some background notions and related work.

3.1 Key Transparency

Key transparency brings autonomous key verification to end users in order to eliminate the need to fully trust a key server. Melara et al. introduced CONIKS [17], the first key transparency scheme which also preserves user privacy. Google Key Transparency [13] and Yahoo End-to-End [26] rely on this approach.

A CONIKS system includes three major components: (1) a CONIKS server managed by an *Identity Provider* (IP) that stores bindings between user identities and their public keys, (2) CONIKS clients which run on users' devices to manage cryptographic keys and (3) auditors who help clients to verify IPs consistency.

A CONIKS server uses a *Merkle radix tree* to map each user to his public key in a *binding*. The index path of each binding in the tree is randomized based on the user identity. At every fixed period of time (called an *epoch*), the CONIKS server signs the *root* of the Merkle tree to create a *Signed Tree Root (STR)* value. A STR_t at epoch t is also hashed together with STR_{t-1} to form a hash chain of the entire history of the key server. The server then *publishes* STR_t to all clients and auditors. When a client queries for a public key, the CONIKS server returns the chain of STR values, the binding at the leaf and an *authentication path* from the leaf to STR to prove that the binding exists in the tree. The client can cross validate STR value with any auditors to validate the CONIKS server answer.

CONIKS guarantees two security properties:

S1 No malicious keys: At every epoch t, a client looks up its own binding on the server by performing a *monitor* operation. Thus, an IP cannot insert malicious keys binding for users without being detected.

S2 Non-equivocation: After monitoring, the client queries STR_t from auditors via an *auditing* protocol. Thus, an IP cannot provide different answers to different user queries without accepting a high risk of being exposed. In case that an IP and auditors collude to equivocate a client, Melara et al. [17] shows that by choosing randomly 4 auditors, a CONIKS client can discover a malicious server with 99,7% probability.

As CONIKS data structure is very efficient and privacy-preserving, our solution extends CONIKS by replacing its auditing mechanism.

3.2 Gossiping

In CONIKS execution model, an IP and clients need to *disseminate STR* in every epoch to ensure that the key server does not equivocate different STR to different clients. CONIKS suggests a decentralized *gossiping* protocol for this purpose. In this protocol, all IPs act as auditors for each other. For example, *Alice@foo.com* can perform audit with *bar.com* while *Bob@bar.com* can audit his key server with *foo.com*.

However, such gossiping network is hard to design in practice where there are potentially millions of IPs and clients. The protocol has to be decentralized so that the system does not depend on any single trust party. Each IP needs to broadcast his STR at every epoch to all other parties and has to answer random queries from any clients. There is no incentive for IPs to provide such extra overhead of communication bandwidth or for third party auditors to query an IP and to answer to random clients.

Another limitation for the gossiping network is the epoch time. CONIKS suggests an epoch time of one hour. This period depends not only on the computational power of each key server, but also the efficiency of the gossip protocol. The longer the epoch time is, the longer it takes for a client to register or revoke its key to the system, hence the longer the vulnerability window for an attack is. Meanwhile, shorter epoch time will increase the communication traffic in the gossiping network.

Finally, a decentralized gossip protocol is still vulnerable to network partition attack. An attacker can isolate a client from honest gossiping nodes to trick the client to accept compromised results from the server. Similarly, an attacker can plague the network with a great number of malicious nodes to increase the possibility that the client will connect to his nodes (*Sybil attack*).

A good example for the challenging aspect of this situation is the standardization process for gossiping protocol in Certificate Transparency [20] where browsers, auditors and certificate authorities gossip about the root hash of Certificate Transparency log. The standard has been on discussion for several years but it is still not finalized.

To sum up, while the proposed gossiping network protocol in CONIKS and similar systems is necessary for auditing CONIKS key server, such solution is hard to implement in an efficient, scalable, Sybil resilient and incentive manner.

3.3   Blockchain

Blockchain [19] is an append-only list of *blocks* where each block is linked directly to the previous one with cryptographic hashes. A blockchain system operates using a *peer-to-peer* (P2P) architecture where peers create and exchange *transactions* to modify the *state* of the system. Those transactions can hold different data types from financial records [6] to arbitrary code execution instructions [23].

Wust et al. [25] show a methodology to determine how a blockchain system solves various technological problems. Indeed, we can simplify a set of requirements for an auditing method as follows. First, a CONIKS server needs to disseminate a *state* (which is encapsulated in a *STR*) every epoch. There should be multiple servers that can disseminate information asynchronously since a user might have different accounts at different IPs. There is also no trusted third party in the network. Wust methodology shows that blockchain – either permissioned or permissionless, depending on whether only authorized set of entities or any entities can read or write the blockchain respectively – is the suitable solution for those requirements. In this paper, we consider a generic auditing mechanism that allows any untrusted CONIKS server to participate. Therefore, we choose permissionless blockchain, in particular, Ethereum as the underlying platform.

Ethereum is one of the major permissionless blockchain systems in the world besides Bitcoin. Ethereum uses blockchain as a ledger of transactions where a sender deposits coins (money) to a receiver. The sender signs the transaction with his private key and gives the ownership of the coin to the receiver so that later the receiver can redeem the received coin for subsequent transactions. A main issue addressed by the system is how to avoid sender generating invalid transactions of double spending a coin to two different receivers. Due to the decentralized nature of the system, the two receivers might not know each other, thus blindly accept the invalid transaction.

Similar to Bitcoin and some other blockchain solutions, Ethereum resolves this issue using *Proof-of-work (POW)*. A group of *miners* participating in the system uses their computing power to solve a puzzle in a form of exhaustive search at a given *difficulty*. The first miner who solves the puzzle can create a block consisting of a set of pre-selected transactions and broadcast the solution. Other miners validate the block and move on to solve next puzzles. In the case that a sender attempts to double-spend, only transactions chosen by the winning miner will be considered valid.

In case there are multiple forks of the chain, a miner always chooses the *longest chain*, i.e. the chain with the highest accumulated difficulty, to work on the next block. Thus, after some time, the whole network will abandon shorter forks. According to this consensus rule, the longer a block stays in the blockchain, the harder it is to be discarded by other miners. An alternative fork would have to solve all puzzles starting from the mentioned block to the end of the chain. Unless there is a party who owns more than 50% of the computing power of the whole Ethereum network, it is impossible for somebody to always produce a longer chain.

We chose Ethereum as our underlying platform as, in contrast to Bitcoin, it features a Turing-complete virtual machine that can execute scripts defined by users in various *smart contracts* and submitted inside a transaction. The script, along with the transaction, is permanently included within the blockchain unless it is scripted to self destruct at some point. Users can execute functions in the script by sending other transactions to the contract with appropriate *transaction fee* and parameters. These transactions are validated and executed by all Ethereum clients. The transaction fee is calculated by an internal unit called *gas* and then paid by the sender in *ETH*. In this paper, we use an exchange rate of € 500 for 1 ETH (as in January 1st 2018).

3.4   EthIKS

EthIKS is the first contribution that proposes using a blockchain to enhance CONIKS. EthIKS implements a CONIKS server in an Ethereum smart contract. In particular, the smart contract stores the Merkle tree in the persistent storage of Ethereum. The server can update the tree by executing the smart contract, while a client can query public keys by extracting data from the blockchain storage. As EthIKS clients have the same view of the key server within the blockchain, no separate gossip protocol is needed for key server consistency.

However, EthIKS introduces several inconveniences to the original CONIKS scheme. In order to fully trust the blockchain, EthIKS clients must download and validate every single transaction from the genesis block to the most recent block which is around 100 GB. This is in contradiction with our **R2.3** requirement. Although Ethereum *light client* can significantly reduce the bandwidth amount, EthIKS must trust a third party to deliver the lightweight block header (see **R1**).

Moreover, EthIKS server operates entirely on Ethereum smart contracts. Every operation affecting the key server database has to be recorded in a transaction. EthIKS claimed that those transactions are relatively cheap (e.g. approximately € 0.0004 for an insertion, not including the mandatory transaction fee). However, for a large size key server (million users) with high key change frequency, it will introduce great additional cost for the Identity Provider. Thus, **R2.2** is not satisfied.

4   Architecture

We present the architecture design and implementation of our proposed auditing scheme. As discussed above, we choose CONIKS data structure for our transparent-log server so we focus our proposal on the auditing scheme. Similar to EthIKS, we consider blockchain as an effective piggyback channel for such purpose. We also optimize the system so that server operation cost is kept

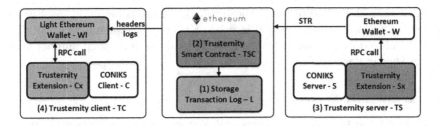

Fig. 1. Trusternity architecture

at minimum. We develop **Trusternity** [9] and depict the general architecture in Fig. 1. The architecture contains four modules: *Storage, Smart Contract, Server* and *Client*. We explain each module in detail in the following subsections.

4.1 Storage

We consider Ethereum as an immutable distributed database. Thus, we can use Ethereum to store and distribute STR to all clients. We consider *transaction log* for this purpose. A transaction Log L is a collection of *Log entry l* which is the result of the code execution in Ethereum virtual machine (EVM) and can be recomputed at anytime by re-executing the code stored in the blockchain. Therefore, storing data in log costs only 8 *gas* per byte, 80 times less than storing data inside the smart contract as in EthIKS [23]. The downside of this method is that we cannot directly access log data from smart contracts. Yet, we designed our own smart contract to address this problem.

We also consider the hybrid approach where actual data is stored in an immutable data structure provided by third party services such as IPFS [2] while the smart contract only holds a reference pointer to data location. Although this method significantly reduces the blockchain storage cost, clients have to rely on third party services. Thus, we do not use this approach.

4.2 Trusternity Smart Contract

We develop a Trusternity smart contract TSC on Ethereum[1]. Each IP is mapped by its Ethereum wallet address in a map data structure *ProviderList*. We assume that each IP only uses one address to create and sign transactions. The smart contract exposes two main functions: *Register* and *Publish*. *Register* accepts server name and related meta-data to insert into *ProviderList* then set it's *lastepoch* as 0. At each epoch, a registered server calls the *Publish* function by sending an *epoch* number and a 32 bytes STR. A key server must not be able to publish different STR for the same epoch or modify the previous ones. It also must not be able to publish STR in different sequence order to limit client

---

[1] The full source can be found at https://github.com/coast-team/trusternity-contract/blob/master/src/trusternity_log.sol.

difficulty in tracking and ordering those values. To use transaction log storage, we defined event *Published* which is fired at every *Publish* function call. The event is indexed by two *topics*, i.e. the sender address and epoch number while STR is kept in data field.

4.3   Trusternity Server

A Trusternity server TS is a transparent key server that enables auditing via Ethereum. TS consists of three components: a *CONIKS Server S*, a *Trusternity extension* for server Sx and an Ethereum wallet W. S is the original CONIKS server. A CONIKS server handles registration, look-up and monitoring keys operations. At every epoch, the server automatically recalculates its Merkle Tree database. We then developed Sx as a plugin for S. The extension allows S to communicate with W, the official Go implementation of the Ethereum protocol [1], via a RPC API. In every *epoch*, TS sends an Ethereum *transaction*, embedded with STR, to a smart contract on the blockchain network.

1. **Register:** Sx calls smart contract *Register* function.
2. **Calculate *STR*:** As defined in CONIKS.
3. **Get *lastEpoch*:** Sx checks last epoch from TSC. Though this step is optional, it helps Sx to avoid sending duplicate transactions blindly to TSC. Sx then performs a check to make sure that the server is at the correct epoch e where $e = lastepoch + 1$.
4. **Publish:** Sx calls *Publish* function and sends the new STR_e to TSC.
5. **Canonical chain confirm:** It is required to wait for a certain number of blocks γ to avoid chain reorganization [24]. Currently, we set $\gamma = 5$. After γ block, Sx checks again if the transaction is correctly included in the chain.

4.4   Trusternity Client

A Trusternity client TC is a key management software that a user runs on his computer. TC has three components: a *CONIKS client C*, a *Light Ethereum Wallet Wl* and a *Trusternity Extension* for client Cx. C performs public key registration and looks up other public keys by sending HTTP requests to S as designed in CONIKS.

We add an extension module Cx to C that handles public key auditing using Ethereum. The extension is configured to synchronize epoch time with the server and then it regularly performs look up and audits registered public keys. Unlike TS, TC uses a light Ethereum wallet that can significantly reduce local storage and network bandwidth concerning the blockchain. We also found that a light wallet for client is enough to secure Trusternity scheme. The auditing process involves three steps as follows.

1. **Register:** As defined in CONIKS.
2. **Lookup:** When TC enables auditing with Trusternity, TC periodically performs public key lookup operation with its own identity (i.e. email) and validates the authentication path.

3. **Light chain lookup:** After validating the authentication path and the public key, TC follows light wallet look up protocol to find the corresponding STR' of the server in that epoch. This value is then compared to the received STR from step 2.

4.5   Light Ethereum Wallet

In a cryptocurrency scheme, in order to fully trust the blockchain, a client must download and validate all transactions starting from the genesis block. Currently, an Ethereum wallet must download around 100 GB data. This type of client is called a full client/wallet which we run on Trusternity server. However, for a client who is not interested in cryptocurrency, it is hard to force him to download and store all transactions just to extract the log from some particular transactions published by TS.

A *light client*, on the contrary, only downloads block headers and transactions filtered with requests from the client. Ethereum light client protocol is specified in [8]. As stated in the specification, an Ethereum light client can efficiently "watch" for events that are logged by TS by filtering transactions tagged only with log topics $IP.Adr$ and e.

According to the protocol specification, using a light client does not offer full security function of a blockchain. In fact, Wl cannot check if a downloaded block header $\mathcal{H}$ is completely valid or not. Wl can only make sure that $\mathcal{H}$ contains a valid POW result. Wl also does not have access to other information in a full block such as the block state tree. As Trusternity does not use that information, we do not need the state tree. Yet, the described security limitation of Wl is a great concern. Section 5 will discuss this problem in detail.

4.6   Deployment Architecture

As Trusternity works over Ethereum, we want to make sure the system does not create undesirable impacts to the Ethereum ecosystem. We assume that there are

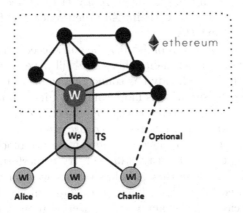

Fig. 2. Trusternity deployment with a proxy wallet

thousands of W and millions of corresponding Wl connected over Ethereum P2P network. A light client does not, or cannot, relay data like a full node, yet it consumes bandwidth from other full nodes. Thus, it reduces the network throughput.

For this reason, we propose that each TS hosts a centralized proxy service Wp that relays Ethereum block headers and relevant transactions from TS to other Wl. Wp can be replicated and balanced so that there is no bottleneck in system availability. Optionally, if needed, Wl can also participate in the public Ethereum network. We depict the deployment architecture in Fig. 2.

From a security point of view, Wl should trust Wp in the same way as Wl trusts any other full client in the public Ethereum network. The only difference here is that Wp is hosted by IP as a way to improve the availability of Trusternity without damaging the Ethereum ecosystem.

5   Security Analysis

In this section we analyze the security of Trusternity in terms of requirements defined in Sect. 2.

Trusternity uses S and C from CONIKS. Thus, we retain security requirement [S1] from CONIKS. For [S2], if we assume Ethereum blockchain is trustworthy, the auditing is then similar to that in CONIKS where auditors are Ethereum clients. However, if an adversary Adv compromises TS, it is possible that the adversary presents TC a fake blockchain. We now present several scenarios where Adv can perform such attack.

5.1   Scenarios

Let us consider a scenario where *Alice*, *Bob* and *Charlie* use a key server TS as in Fig. 2. An adversary Adv compromises TS and wants to perform MITM attack against the 3 users. Thus, besides an honest TS, Adv maintains a compromised TS' where he keeps $<Alice, PK_{Adv}>$. At epoch e, TS sends a *Publish* transaction T_e to Ethereum blockchain (*MainNet*) for *Alice* to monitor while sends T_e' from TS' to a fake blockchain. Adv then sends this fake chain to *Bob* to trick him into accepting PK_{Adv}.

As in Fig. 2, if Adv can compromise Wp, he will succeed in tricking *Bob* into accepting a compromised blockchain. Thus, *Bob* will have no way to detect the attack. However, if the user already has connection to other Ethereum nodes in MainNet as *Charlie*, the situation is more complex. First, Adv can compromise several Ethereum full nodes and find a way to redirect *Charlie* to those compromised nodes. This is sometimes referred as *eclipse attack* [16]. Secondly, if Adv can hijack *Charlie*'s network connection, he can simply block all connections to honest nodes except to Wp. Lastly, Adv can try to perform Sybil attack on MainNet. Nevertheless, we see that Adv has various ways of tricking a user to connect a compromised full node and accept a compromised blockchain.

Detecting a malicious blockchain while connecting to an untrusted full node is a mandatory step to satisfy both [S2] and [R1] requirements. We now simulate scenarios when a client is fed on a malicious blockchain and present how to detect such problem.

Recall from Sect. 3.3 that miners run a POW algorithm to solve a computing puzzle at a given block difficulty d_n of block number $n > 0$ at t_n. d_n is calculated based on d_{n-1} and the *time interval* $\Delta_{t_n} = t_n - t_{n-1}$ [7]. The calculation function is tuned so that the average block time of the Ethereum network is around 17 s. For example, d_n increases if $\Delta_{t_n} < \Delta_{t_{n-1}}$ and decreases otherwise. d_n, t_n and the accumulated difficulty $\sum_d$ of all blocks in the chain is stored in each block header. Therefore, if Adv controls all of the neighbor nodes of Wl, Adv must provide a malicious, yet valid blockchain to Wl. Assume that Wl has access to a portion of MainNet from block 0 to block $m - 1$ until Adv decides to fork into a fake chain. This can be achieved by hard coding *checkpoint blocks* in Cx. If the adversary does not have enough computing power, he cannot solve POW with the honest chain difficulty as fast as MainNet. Thus, the client will observe significant increases in block time interval and drops in block difficulty. We then conduct a simulation on a private Ethereum network to simulate this scenario and propose our method to *automatically* detect the attack on the client side.

5.2   Attack Simulation

We deploy a private Ethereum network of 40 miners on a testbed system. All miners are connected to a *bootnode* which helps bootstrapping the peer-to-peer network. We then study the distribution of MainNet mining pools [11] to have a brief understanding of a potential adversary capability. There are many mining pools who process relatively large computing power (*Hashrate*) in comparison to the rest of the network. Our simulation is based on the assumption that an adversary can compromise one of the pools and use its computing power for a brief period of time to conduct the attack. We define $p > 0$ as the capability of Adv over total computing power of MainNet. Since Adv should not have more than 50% computing power of the whole network, $p < 0.5$. Our experiment consists of two phases:

1. **Stable:** We run a fresh private Ethereum network with all 40 miners from our genesis block beginning with d_0 of block 0. We run this phase for 1 h to produce a base chain of a stable Ethereum network where all nodes are honest. Our simulation script automatically switches to the second phase after 1 h.
2. **Malicious:** Instead of keeping running all 40 miners, we only keep m miners for an additional hour where $m/40 = p$. As in [11], the biggest mining pool has around 25% of MainNet computing power. Thus, with $m = 10$, we can simulate the situation when this pool is compromised. We repeat the simulation varying m range from 1 to 19 multiple times.

We did not choose to simulate this attack on any official Ethereum test network (e.g. ropsten[2]) because our simulated attack could cause temporary forks in the network that may harm experiments from other parties.

---

[2]   https://ropsten.etherscan.io/.

5.3   Results

In all experiments, we are interested in the aberration of d and Δ_n. Figure 3 shows two sample results from our experiments with $m = 4$ and $m = 10$ respectively. $m = 10$ can be interpreted as the adversary has 25% of the total network Hashrate by compromising the biggest mining pool, i.e. ethpool [12] while $m = 4$ is when the secondary biggest pool with 10% Hashrate is compromised. d is collected directly from the chain header and is presented with a blue line. The average block time interval $\bar{t}$ is calculated as in Eq. 1 where we set $l1 = 10$. We will explain the rationale of choosing $l1$ in the next section.

$$\bar{t}_n = \frac{\sum_{i=0}^{l1-1} \Delta_{t_{n-i}}}{l1} \tag{1}$$

In both cases, we observe the immediate change in the trend of d and $\bar{t}$ when the malicious phase kicked in. $\bar{t}$ is kept below 20 s in the stable time then increased significantly after block 241. On the other hand, d experienced a dropping trend after block 241 due to the increase in time between blocks. However, it is not trivial to *automatically* distinguish between malicious attempt and an occasional fluctuation of the result.

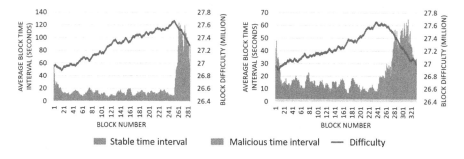

Fig. 3. Average block time interval and difficulty where $m = 4$ ($p = 10\%$) and $m=10$ ($p=25\%$) respectively

5.4   Detection of Malice

Given the presented results, we want to detect the block when the adversary forks the chain as soon as possible. Our general idea is to detect anomalies in the change of d and $\bar{t}$ over time. Several approaches of anomaly detection in multi-time series data have been proposed [14]. However, due to **R2.3**, we follow a simple approach in anomaly detection. We first analyze 4 million Ethereum blocks in MainNet. For a block i on MainNet, we observe that $\bar{t}_i$ is less than 20 s in 92% of the time. We also find that d_i never decreases continuously more than 20 times.

Algorithm 1. Detection of Malice

---

input : A block header H_i contains t_i and d_i
output: `true` if H_i is malicious, else `false`

1 *Constant: $l1$, $l2$, λ, $\langle t \rangle$;*
2 $\bar{t}_i \leftarrow$ equation 1 ;
3 $S1 \leftarrow \sum\limits_{k \leftarrow 0}^{l1-1} \bar{t}_{i-k}/\langle t \rangle$; // $l1$ `block before` i
4 $\Delta_{d_i} \leftarrow (d_i - d_{i-1}) < 0$; // `1 iff` `true`, `0 iff` `false`
5 $S2 \leftarrow \sum\limits_{k \leftarrow 0}^{l2-1} \Delta_{d_{i-k}}$;
6 **return** $(S1 > 2 * l1) \vee (S2 > l2 * \lambda)$;

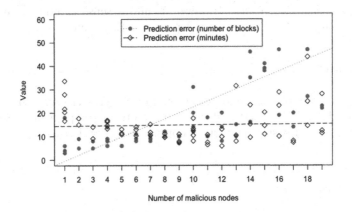

Fig. 4. Prediction error.

Assuming we start monitoring blockchain header at block i, all previous blocks are trusted. We then design an adaptive algorithm to detect the malicious in real-time manner as presented in Algorithm 1. We introduce 4 parameters:

$l1$: Number of blocks to compute average block time.
$l2$: Number of blocks to compute difficulty decrease streak.
$\langle t \rangle$: Mean of Δ_t from block 0 to the most recent trusted block.
λ: Longest decrease times of Δ_d over $l2$.

The idea of $l1$ and $l2$ is to smooth out the block time and difficulty value. If they are too small, we cannot eliminate the risk of true negativity for detection. Meanwhile, large values mean that we might not detect the attack early enough after it happens. Our aim is to keep the time required for detection at a reasonable length, i.e. ≈ 15 min. We find those values by permuting a set of possible parameters and rerun the algorithm. We achieve a result where $l1 = 10$ and $l2 = 20$. In MainNet we can set $\langle t \rangle$ at 17.5 s and 13 in our private net.

Figure 4 presents our detection result when the number of malicious miners change. The figure shows the prediction error, i.e. how much time or number of block we need after the malicious miner appears to detect the attack. Two dashed lines in Fig. 4 represent the regression line, i.e. to show the trends of prediction errors when the number of malicious participants change.

We see that the number of needed blocks increases almost linearly when the number of malicious miners increases, yet the needed time shows almost no difference ($\approx$ 15 min as intended) due to the decrease in average block time when there are more malicious miners in the network. We note that our prediction results are acquired in conjunction with analyzing past 4 million Ethereum blocks on MainNet. Thus, while we cannot guarantee 100% confidence in detecting future attacks, we have a strong base of trust in the method if the network continues to behave as in the past. Obviously, in case there are events that significantly affect block time and difficulty such as a hard fork or natural disasters, our algorithm will yield true negative results. However, it makes sense to notify users when such events happen since Trusternity depends on Ethereum.

6 Evaluation

In this section, we show a thorough evaluation of Trusternity with regard to network bandwidth overhead and operating costs in comparison to CONIKS and EthIKS. We also suggest various options to apply Trusternity into other systems.

6.1 Network Overhead

We reuse most of setup and assumptions from CONIKS and EthIKS. In particular, Trusternity client uses the eliptic-curve based VUF and signature scheme. There are total $U = 2^{32}$ users, $u = 2^{21}$ users update their keys per epoch and $k = 24$ epochs per day. Ethereum block time average is set at a lower bound of 12 s.

However, our calculation[3] shows that an Ethereum client has to download $\approx$ 0.6 KB for each header instead of only 0.2 KB per block header as in EthIKS scenario. We slightly modify EthIKS calculation to reflect this change and calculate our result for Trusternity in Table 1.

Overall, we see there are no change in look up and monitor cost compared to CONIKS since the calculation separates blockchain into auditing section. An EthIKS full client has to download all α transactions related to EthIKS. This assumption is rather complicated since we do not have the source code of EthIKS smart contract, however, α should be proportional to the number of updates to the contract per epoch. Thus, in a naive assumption, we can have $\alpha \approx u$. We also cannot compare to a EthIKS light client since the author assumes that the light version has a trusted source to query for Ethereum block header and data.

---

[3] https://github.com/coast-team/trusternity-contract/blob/master/appendix/calcul ation.md.

Table 1. Client bandwidth requirements (KB) with α is the number of transaction in each epoch

Operation	CONIKS	EthIKS	Trusternity
lookup (per binding)	1.2	7.9	1.2
monitor (per epoch)	0.7	5.2	0.7
monitor (daily)	17.6	1405	17.6
audit (per epoch)	0.1	$200.4 + \alpha * 2$	201.6
audit (daily)	2.3	$4809.6 + \alpha * 48$	4838.5

In summary, we can see that Trusternity only adds a fixed amount of bandwidth overhead per epoch of 200 KB, result in less than 5 MB per day to operate in comparison to the original CONIKS client. We calculate this number entirely based on Ethereum formal specification so the actual amount might be slightly different due to encoding, extra protocol messages or bloom filter false positive result. However, our calculation shows a clear advantage of our approach to EthIKS over network bandwidth.

6.2 Gas Cost

The transaction costs of operating Trusternity only come from the two listed functions on the smart contract. Overall, *Register* costs 63,000 *gas* and *Publish* costs 44,000 *gas*. We take the assumption from Sect. 4.1 which is $0.0004ETH$ per 20,000 *gas* and each ETH costs € 500. This results in *Register* costs € 0.63 which an IP only has to pay once when he installs Trusternity and € 0.44 for each *Publish* call per epoch or $\approx$ € 10.56 per day. Comparing our results to EthIKS, assume that we only take into account 2^{21} update mapping transactions of 12,000 *gas* per epoch, this costs $\approx$ € 6 million per day.

6.3 Final Result

We compare our implementation to the pre-defined requirements from Sect. 2. **S1** and **S2** are satisfied as we discussed in Sect. 5. Regarding **R1**, our anomaly detection algorithm can effectively detect a fork attack from a sub network of malicious Ethereum miners in less than 15 min, assuming that the malicious network only has less than 50% of the main network computing power. Thus, even with untrusted auditors, Trusternity is still able to detect malicious behaviors after a short period of time.

We also show above the improvement over network bandwidth and gas cost overhead of Trusternity over EthIKS. Our scheme adds a flat amount of € 10 per day for an Identity Provider to operate regardless of the client amounts (**R2.2**). Each Trusternity client only has to download a merely extra 5 MB every day. Although our anomaly detection algorithm requires clients to continuously monitor the downloaded Ethereum block header, the algorithm is simple enough to not cause any noticeable overhead for clients. As a result, **R2.3** is satisfied. Lastly, Trusternity operates on Ethereum, any Ethereum client can be considered an auditor, including W. Thus, **R2.1** is trivial to achieve.

7   Conclusion

We presented Trusternity, an auditing mechanism for Transparent-log key server using Ethereum which is significantly more efficient and budget than state-of-the-art approach. Our solution scales with an unbound number of log clients, cheap to operate (€ 10 per day for the server) and does not require huge network bandwidth or storage of clients. Our solution is also independent of any trusted third party by being able to detect malicious sudden change in the network. Trusternity is also easy to extend for other purposes. Other transparent log based approaches such as Certificate Transparency [15] can also benefit from our proposal. CONIKS client and server components are also replaceable with similar components, i.e. Key Transparency [13] server and clients.

References

1. Go Ethereum: Official Go implementation of the Ethereum protocol (2017). https://geth.ethereum.org/
2. Benet, J.: IPFS-content addressed, versioned, P2P file system. arXiv preprint (2014). arXiv:1407.3561
3. Birman, K.: The promise, and limitations, of gossip protocols. ACM SIGOPS Operating Syst. Rev. **41**(5), 8–13 (2007)
4. Bonneau, J.: EthIKS: using ethereum to audit a CONIKS key transparency log. In: Clark, J., Meiklejohn, S., Ryan, P.Y.A., Wallach, D., Brenner, M., Rohloff, K. (eds.) FC 2016. LNCS, vol. 9604, pp. 95–105. Springer, Heidelberg (2016). https://doi.org/10.1007/978-3-662-53357-4_7
5. Boyko, V., MacKenzie, P., Patel, S.: Provably secure password-authenticated key exchange using Diffie-Hellman. In: Preneel, B. (ed.) EUROCRYPT 2000. LNCS, vol. 1807, pp. 156–171. Springer, Heidelberg (2000). https://doi.org/10.1007/3-540-45539-6_12
6. Brito, J., Castillo, A.: Bitcoin: A primer for policymakers. Mercatus Center at George Mason University (2013)
7. Buterin, V.: Homestead hard-fork changes (2015). https://github.com/ethereum/EIPs/blob/master/EIPS/eip-2.md
8. Buterin, V.: Ethereum light client protocol (2016). https://github.com/ethereum/wiki/wiki/Light-client-protocol
9. COAST team: The Trusternity Project (2017). https://github.com/coast-team/coniks-go
10. Douceur, J.R.: The sybil attack. In: Druschel, P., Kaashoek, F., Rowstron, A. (eds.) IPTPS 2002. LNCS, vol. 2429, pp. 251–260. Springer, Heidelberg (2002). https://doi.org/10.1007/3-540-45748-8_24
11. etherchain.org: Mining statistics (2017). https://etherchain.org/statistics/miners. Accessed 28 Aug 2017

12. ethpool: The Ethereum Solo Mining Pool (2017). http://ethpool.org. Accessed 28 Aug 2017
13. Google: Key Transparency (2017). https://github.com/google/keytransparency
14. Jones, M., Nikovski, D., Imamura, M., Hirata, T.: Exemplar learning for extremely efficient anomaly detection in real-valued time series. Data Min. Knowl. Discov. **30**(6), 1427–1454 (2016)
15. Laurie, B.: Certificate transparency. Queue **12**(8), 10:10–10:19 (2014). https://doi. org/10.1145/2668152.2668154
16. Marcus, Y., Heilman, E., Goldberg, S.: Low-resource eclipse attacks on Ethereum's peer-to-peer network (2018). http://www.cs.bu.edu/~goldbe/projects/eclipseEth. pdf
17. Melara, M.S., Blankstein, A., Bonneau, J., Felten, E.W., Freedman, M.J.: Coniks: bringing key transparency to end users. In: 24th USENIX Security Symposium (USENIX Security 2015), pp. 383–398 (2015)
18. Miller, A., Hicks, M., Katz, J., Shi, E.: Authenticated data structures, generically. In: ACM SIGPLAN Notices, vol. 49, pp. 411–423. ACM (2014)
19. Nakamoto, S.: Bitcoin: A peer-to-peer electronic cash system (2008). https:// bitcoin.org/bitcoin.pdf
20. Nordberg, L.: Gossiping in CT (2014). https://tools.ietf.org/html/draft-linus-trans-gossip-ct-00
21. WhatsApp: WhatsApp Messenger (2017). https://www.whatsapp.com/. Accessed 28 Aug 2017
22. Whitten, A., Tygar, J.D.: Why Johnny can't encrypt: a usability evaluation of PGP 5.0. In: USENIX Security Symposium, vol. 348 (1999)
23. Wood, G.: Ethereum: A secure decentralised generalised transaction ledger. Ethereum Proj. Yellow Paper **151**, 1–32 (2014)
24. Wood, G.: Chain Reorganisation Depth Expectations (2015). https://blog. ethereum.org/2015/08/08/chain-reorganisation-depth-expectations/. Accessed 25 Sept 2017
25. Wüst, K., Gervais, A.: Do you need a blockchain? (2017). https://eprint.iacr.org/ 2017/375.pdf
26. Yahoo: Yahoo End-To-End (2017). https://github.com/yahoo/end-to-end
27. Zimmermann, P.R.: The Official PGP User's Guide. MIT Press, Cambridge (1995)

Probabilistic Event Graph
to Model Safety and Security
for Diagnosis Purposes

Edwin Bourget[1]([⊠]), Frédéric Cuppens[1], Nora Cuppens-Boulahia[1],
Samuel Dubus[3], Simon Foley[1], and Youssef Laarouchi[2]

[1] IMT Atlantique, Cesson-Sévigné, France
edwin.bourget@imt-atlantique.fr
[2] EDF Labs, Palaiseau, France
[3] Nokia Bell Labs, Nozay, USA

Abstract. Diagnosing accidental and malicious events in an industrial
control system requires an event model with specific capacities. Most
models are dedicated to either safety or security but rarely both. And
the latter are developed for objectives other than diagnosis and therefore
unfit for this task. In this paper, we propose an event model considering
both safety and security events, usable in real-time, with a probabilistic
measure of on-going and future events. This model is able to replace alerts
in the context of more global scenarios, including with reinforcements or
conflicts between safety and security. The model is then used to provide
an analysis of some of the security and safety events in the Taum Sauk
Hydroelectric Power Station.

1 Introduction

With the increasing interconnection of Industrial Control Systems (ICS) through
cyberspace, new challenges arise when ensuring their safety and security. Once
rather well separated, both characteristics of the system are now completely
interleaved: a cyber-attack may have consequences on an industrial process and
the response to a safety incident can inadvertently impact the security of the
system. Therefore, when an incident occurs in an ICS, it is more and more
difficult, yet essential, to understand what is happening in order to select the
appropriate response. The analysis of the incident is the diagnosis.

Providing explanation of purely accidental and malicious incidents is typically
done using, respectively, fault trees [1] and attack trees [2]. Risk analysis or
incident tracking can be done using more advanced methods such as Bayesian
networks [3] or Petri networks [4] However, they can in practice be viewed as a
refinement of fault and attack trees.

There exist several models dedicated to one characteristic, either safety or
security, but they are hardly adaptable to the other one. The reason is that
safety and security have their different semantics and using one for the other

F. Kerschbaum and S. Paraboschi (Eds.): DBSec 2018, LNCS 10980, pp. 38–47, 2018.
https://doi.org/10.1007/978-3-319-95729-6_3

is not always meaningful. Therefore, the propagation of the incident is different and most models cannot represent both. A small number of models exist that can represent both safety and security at the same time, such as BDMP [5,6] or the FIGARO language [7]. However, they were not originally developed for diagnosis purposes and therefore, lack essential features considered in this paper, such as real-time monitoring or alert instantiation, towards achieving this objective.

According to [8], diagnosis can be divided into three sub problems: detecting the problem, locating it and determining its scope. Detecting the problem means having the knowledge that a safety or a security incident is happening. Locating the problem is knowing what components are at fault or targets of an attack. Determining its scope is being able to identify the affected subsystems. In a nutshell, it means explaining what is happening. In order to do so, a model of what can happen is required. Risk analysis models based on fault and attack trees are suited for that. Then, mapping the ongoing situation to the model allows for finding the roots of the problem or generating hypotheses on evolutions of the problem, such as the objective of an attacker or the next components to fail. Sometimes, though, the ongoing situation might not completely fit the model. Therefore, a measure of the variation of the incident from the model should be provided. Being able to reason beyond the scope of the system is an important part of diagnosis and is what we provide with our model.

The objective of this paper is to lay the foundations of a way to model safety and security in order to perform diagnosis of incidents in ICS. We propose a model to represent safety and security events, draw logical connections between them in order to generate complete scenarios and a probabilistic component to compute the likelihood of both the complete scenarios and the elementary events.

The paper is organised as follows: Sect. 2 introduces the LAMBDA language for describing security attacks and upon which the proposed model, described in Sect. 3, is based. Section 4 illustrates the capabilities of the model on a use case. Section 5 compares the proposed model to existing research and Sect. 6 gives insights on future uses and evolutions of the model.

2   Background

LAMBDA [9] is a language used to describe security attacks. It is based on the general concept that an attack can succeed if a set of conditions (called *preconditions*) is satisfied, and will have effects (called *postconditions*) on the system if it succeeds. It is also described by a *scenario*, being the different actions needed to be combined to perform the attack. Attacks described in LAMBDA can be of any granularity going from elementary steps that an attacker needs to carry out to progress towards his objective, to the description of a complete scenario.

CRIM [10] is a correlation engine that draws connection between attacks described in LAMBDA: if a postcondition of an attack A_1 matches with a precondition of an attack A_2, then the realisation of A_1 favours the realisation of A_2. That is A_1 enables the attacker to then perform A_2. In this particular example, the attack graph generated would have a connection from A_1 to A_2.

Unfortunately, LAMBDA does not fit to model safety events. Indeed, every attack is to be described by a scenario, being a set of actions. When modelling safety, a component failure, like the one of a hard-drive, can happen without being the result of a particular action: it is its regular wear. Moreover, LAMBDA in itself is devoid of any probabilistic evaluation. [11] proposes a modification of LAMBDA to overcome this issue but it only computes a mean time to success (MTTS) and this is not sufficient for a complete evaluation of the likelihood of an incident.

Nonetheless, we will base the model we present in Sect. 3 on a heavily modified version of LAMBDA in order to reuse its event-tracking ability and the pre/postconditions modelling, as well as CRIM.

3   The Model

In this section, we present our model. First we define the events, then we construct scenarios out of events, and we finally compute the probabilities required for diagnosis.

3.1   The Event

In the model we propose, the system in which incidents happen is represented by a set of variables. This set is called the *system state*. We define an event as a modification in the system state. Therefore, an event is the result of the occurrence of an attack or an accidental failure.

An event is characterised by its attributes: a set of preconditions, a set of postconditions, the nature of the event, a realisation process and a detection process.

The **preconditions set** and the **postconditions set** are inherited from LAMBDA. They are composed of predicates combined with the logical connectives ∧, ∨ and ¬. The former set is used to describe the value that the variables of the system state must have for the event to be feasible. The later set is used to describe the value that the variables of the system state will have after the event has occurred.

The **nature** of the events is a label used to quickly know the type of the event: so far, we only used safety and security but any other type of events could potentially be added, such as countermeasures or regular events whose occurrence is part of the industrial process.

We define the **realisation process** as a probability distribution function (PDF). It is used to describe the evolution of the occurrence probability of the event over time, given that all of the conditions for the event to happen are met. Any PDF can be used, even custom ones. This is where the difference in modelling security and safety events lies in our model. Indeed, their realisation process is different and is represented, in this model through the PDF. With this approach, the model can therefore acknowledge for any kind of propagation: when modelling a specific event, one simply has to use its most appropriate PDF.

The **detection process** is used to link the modelled event to an alert $\mathcal{A}$ collected by the SCADA or SIEM system. It is used to inform the model that the event has been realised in order to update the system state and trigger instantiation of said alert $\mathcal{A}$.

Figure 1 gives the model of the failure of a hard-drive. The PDF associated with the event is a Weibull distribution. The distributions and their parameters are chosen by the experts modelling the system, but can be derived from sizeable return on experience. For instance, when it comes to hard-drive failures, [12] has determined that the Weibull distribution is much more suited than the exponential distribution. Modelling this event with a PDF allows us to compute the mean time to failure of the event (5 years) or the probability of failure after ninety days (7.52×10^{-9}) for instance.

Name	Hard-drive failure
Preconditions	$\neg failed(HardDrive)$
Postconditions	$failed(HardDrive)$
Nature	safety
Realisation	Weibull distribution ($lambda = 5.516$, $k = 4$)
Detection	server operating system raises alert

Fig. 1. Hard-drive failure

3.2 The Attack Graph

After the set of elementary events have been defined, it can be used by CRIM to correlate the dependencies between the events and generate event graphs corresponding to complete scenarios. CRIM says that events A and B are correlated if $Post(A)$, the postconditions of A, and $Pre(B)$, the preconditions of B, are correlated. And this happens when at least one of the predicates of $Post(A)$ and one of the predicates of $Pre(B)$ are unifiable through a most general unifier (mgu) [13]. If such an mgu is found, a directed connection from A to B is present in the event graph output by CRIM. CRIM tries to correlate every pair of events and then generates its event graph displaying the logical dependencies between the events, as illustrated in Fig. 4.

3.3 Recombining PDF

Once the logical dependencies have been established between the different events and a scenario has been selected, its PDF can be computed. To do so, the local PDF associated with each event needs to be recombined in order to express the global PDF of the scenario. There exists three different situations: the sequence, the AND, and the OR.

On a side note, we will assume that the random variables associated with two events are always independent. It means that, the time taken to realise one event has no influence on the time taken to realise another event.

The Sequence. Let us consider that events A and B happen in sequence. C^1 corresponds to "A happens then B happens". A, B, and C are respectively associated with the PDF f_A, f_B, and f_C. The probability that C happens in a given timespan $\mathcal{I}$ given that nothing has happened yet is actually the probability that both A and B happen in $\mathcal{I}$. This can be written:

$$f_C : \mathbb{R} \to \mathbb{R}$$
$$x \mapsto \int_{-\infty}^{+\infty} f_A(t) f_B(x - t) dt$$

In other words, f_C is the convolution of f_A and f_B: $f_C = f_A * f_B$.

The AND. Let us consider that both events A and B need to happen for C to happen. A and B are respectively associated with the PDF f_A and f_B, the CDF F_A and F_B (the cumulative distribution function evaluated at x is the probability that the event will be realised at x), and with random variables X and Y. The probability that A and B happen in a given timespan $\mathcal{I}$ can therefore be written $P(X \in \mathcal{I}, Y \in \mathcal{I})$. X and Y being independent, we have:

$$P(X \in \mathcal{I}, Y \in \mathcal{I}) = P(X \in \mathcal{I})P(Y \in \mathcal{I})$$

If we call g the PDF associated with the event "A and B has happened", we obtain:

$$g = f_A F_B + F_A f_B$$

The OR. The case of the OR is similar to the one of the AND, with the difference that the AND is the set intersection when the OR is the set union. The resulting PDF, using the same notations as the AND case is:

$$g = f_A + f_B - f_A F_B - F_A f_B$$

The nature of the calculus used to obtain the PDF corresponding to the three situations make it so that they can be done in any order. For instance, the PDF associated with $(A \, or \, B) \, or \, C$ is the same as $A \, or \, (B \, or \, C)$.

3.4   Perspectives of the Probabilistic Recombinations

In this paragraph, we illustrate how to recombine the distributions with a generic example. Let us consider three events A, B and C respectively associated with PDF f_A, f_B and f_C and with their cdf F_A, F_B and F_C. We use the same events calculus algebra as LAMBDA [9] to combine the events: "$A;B$" represents A in sequence with B and "$A\&B$" means that both A and B must happen.

---

[1] C is not a LAMBDA event. It is just an abstraction used to compute the PDF associated to a set of events. It has no meaning outside of the scope of the probabilistic calculations.

Let us consider the situation $A; (B\&C)$. Using the formulas demonstrated in the precedent paragraph, we obtain the distribution function g associated with this situation: $g = f_A * (f_B F_C + F_B f_C)$.

Distribution g can then be used to evaluate the mean time that it will take for a composition of events to occur, or to compute the probability that this composition will happen in any given duration. The recombination formulas we provide in this section are valuable tools for the diagnosis. Indeed, where a system expert can realistically provide accurate distributions for elementary events, it becomes much more arbitrary for more complex events. By decomposing a complex event in elementary ones, then defining PDF for these elementary events and recombining them to have the one of the complex event, we obtain an accurate description of the realisation process of this event. The PDF can then be used as a metric and combined with other ones, such as the impact, in order to give comprehensive feedback to a decision-maker who is looking for the most appropriate response, for example.

4   The Use Case

The case study is based on an actual power station: Taum Sauk Hydroelectric Power Station [14–16]. For our study, we will consider the upper and the lower reservoir, the pump, the Operator Control Center (OCC) and the two automatons Common PLC (Common_PLC) and Upper Reservoir PLC (UR_PLC). OCC, Common_PLC and UR_PLC are in the same network Operator Control Network (OCNet). When the water level in the upper reservoir overcomes a certain threshold, sensors send this information to the PLCs that forward the information to the OCC that can turn off the pump. If for whatever reason the pump does not stop, other sensors sends the information to the two PLCs who directly trigger a hard stop on the pump. If the water level keep rising, it will eventually overtop the reservoir, erode the relief upon which it is built and will cause a massive breach as it happened in december 2005 [14–16].

Following the methodology of our model, in order to get the scenarios, one must first describe all of the elementary attacks or failures. In this paper we will present two elementary events in Figs. 2 and 3: an intruder gaining access to the OCNet and an attacker compromising the communication link between the Common PLC and the Pump.

After defining all of the events identified by the safety and security experts, they are fed to the correlation engine that outputs scenarios. Several scenarios can lead to the failure of the upper reservoir. For the sake of this article, we have selected one displayed on Fig. 4. The graph output by CRIM corresponding to the selected scenario is displayed in Fig. 4. It describes that one can cause the overtopping by intercepting all stop orders sent to the pump while it is active. Three sources can produce the stop orders: the Common PLC, the Upper Reservoir PLC and the Operator Control Center. All of the orders can be intercepted if one compromises the communication links between the order sources and the pump. Finally, all of the communication links can be compromised if one has

Name	Access Operator Control Network
Preconditions	encryption(OC_Net, null)
Postconditions	remoteAccess(A, OC_Net)
Nature	attack
Realisation	exponential distribution ($1/\lambda = 3years$)
Detection	IDS detects unknown IP address

Name	Compromise Common PLC communication link
Preconditions	remoteAccess(A, OC_Net) & vulnerable(Common_PLC, cve-2004-1234)
Postconditions	manInTheMiddle(A, Common_PLC, Pump)
Nature	attack
Realisation	exponential distribution ($1/\lambda = 10min$)
Detection	IDS detects ARP spoofing

Fig. 2. Access to the Operator Control Network

Fig. 3. Compromising of the communication link

access to the Operator Control Network. For reference, all of the probability distributions are chosen exponential, except for the event "Pump does not stop" which is a Dirac delta function. The parameters are displayed next to the name of the corresponding event.

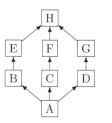

- A: Access OC net; $1/\lambda = 3years$
- B: Compromise Common_PLC com. link; $1/\lambda = 8min$
- C: Compromise UR_PLC com. link; $1/\lambda = 8min$
- D: Compromise OCC com. link; $1/\lambda = 10min$
- E: Send false order (Common_PLC); $1/\lambda = 5min$
- F: Send false order (UR_PLC) ; $1/\lambda = 5min$
- G: Send false order (OCC); $1/\lambda = 7min$
- H: Pump does not stop

Fig. 4. Scenario output by CRIM

We will consider various cases where several alerts have been raised. The cases and the probabilistic results are displayed in Table 1. Only the MTTS is shown but, as in the precedent paragraph, the probability of occurrence after any duration can be computed. As a matter of fact, we have plotted the probability that event H happens for case 6 in Fig. 6. All of the computations can be done beforehand or in real-time.

Table 1. MTTS associated with various cases

Case	Alerts raised	MTTS
1	$\emptyset$	3y 23 min 27 s
2	A	23 min 27 s
3	A, B	21 min 13 s
4	A, B, E	20 min 54 s
5	A, C, D	14 min 54 s
6	A, B, C, D, G	7 min 30 s

Having an evaluation of the MTTS depending on the raising of various alerts is a precious asset for a decision-maker. First, it is a metric that can be recombined with others, like the impact, in order to have an accurate assessment of the risk. Moreover, a safety/security supervisor might want to define a threshold under which the deployed countermeasures are different. Indeed, an impending undesired event may call for a response more effective, but with more negative side-effects.

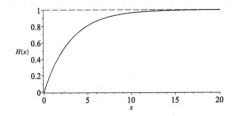 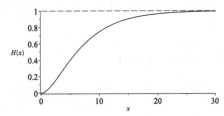

Fig. 5. Evolution of the probabilities in case 1

Fig. 6. Evolution of the probabilities in case 6

With several different cases over one scenario, we have shown that the model adapts to real-time scenarios: the probabilities of the undesired events evolve over the realisation of subsequent ones. This is important because, for example, the choices of the attacker may change which are the most probable scenarios. And the appropriate response may differ depending on what parts of the system are at risk. Safety and security supervisors obtain precious information from the model in the form of probabilistic evaluations of the evolution of the failure/compromise rate.

5   Related Work

In this section, we will discuss about existing models that give a probabilistic evaluation of the duration until an incident occurs. Models that give a probabilistic evaluation of a choice the system or the environment makes is out of the scope of this study.

FIGARO [7] is a versatile object language used to populate knowledge bases, later on used to model safety and security events through two kinds of rules: occurrence and interaction rules.

After the model has been defined using the FIGARO language, it is fed to the KB3 platform: a calculus engine. KB3 can not be used in real time to monitor the evolution and propagation of ongoing incidents. By using CRIM, our model is able to track which events have occurred. Their realisation changing the probabilities of possible undesired events, it is an important part of diagnosis.

[17] proposed a model based on Markov chains to compute MTTS (named MTTF in the paper). This model can only consider exponential distributions, which is understandable for security but not for safety. Moreover, with a model based on Markov chains, it can only consider transitions present in the model.

It is therefore impossible of analysing interleaved scenarios, since the scenarios will be modelled as disjoint Markov chains.

Bayesian networks is a popular model for safety modelling [18]. Notably, [19] had an interesting take on the matter. Like in our approach, they associated a random variable to each node of their Bayesian network. The random variable models the probability of failure of a component for a given duration. They also use the distributions associated with the random variable to compute failure rates for a scenario. However, they have to discretize the timespan they consider for their scenario, when we have a purely continuous approach, providing more accurate results.

6   Conclusions

In this paper, we presented an incident model responding to the needs and respecting the constraints of diagnosis. We proposed a graphical model of safety and security incidents, usable in real-time if need be, and able to track the realisation of events and updating itself accordingly. The model, considering concurrent events, is thus able to get the context in which alerts are raised, locating the problem. Through PDF embedded in each event, the model allows for a probabilistic evaluation of possible future events, as well as an estimation of the likelihood of occurrence of an event. This feature gives us both the possible reach of the incident and a way to measure the appropriateness of the model to the situation. We have illustrated the capacities of the model on an industrial use case.

With this usecase we have presented that it is possible to compute the likelihood of one scenario. Since the model acknowledges for several scenarios, one can compute which is the most probable one, given a set of alerts. Or which are the five most probable one, with the information that the undesired events associated with these scenarios are safety or security events. Moreover, with the model keeping track of past events, it is able to give the origin of a scenario, and whether it was caused by failures, attacks, or both. The model is also able to evaluate the likelihood of an event by comparing its realisation time with references values in the form of a PDF that describes the realisation time. All of this is valuable information that helps to the diagnosis of an event, as well as represents a precious aid when deciding of the appropriate response to an incident.

The model is modular and easily extendible. That will incidentally be the object of future works in order to add a measure of the impact of an incident and its propagation to be able to assess the risk, as well as countermeasures.

References

1. Vesely, W.E., Goldberg, F.F., Roberts, N.H., Haasl, D.F.: Fault tree handbook. Report, DTIC Document (1981)
2. Bruce, S.: Attack trees. Dr. Dobb's J. **24**, 21–29 (1999)
3. Frigault, M., Wang, L., Singhal, A., Jajodia, S.: Measuring network security using dynamic Bayesian network. In: Proceedings of the 4th ACM Workshop on Quality of Protection, 1456368, pp. 23–30. ACM (2008)

4. Kumar, S., Spafford, E.: A pattern matching model for misuse intrusion detection (1994)
5. Bouissou, M., Bon, J.L.: A new formalism that combines advantages of fault-trees and Markov models: Boolean logic driven Markov processes. Mater. Reliab. Eng. Syst. Saf. **82**(2), 149–163 (2003)
6. Piètre-Cambacédès, L., Bouissou, M.: Beyond attack trees: dynamic security modeling with Boolean logic driven Markov processes (BDMP). In: Proceedings of the 2010 European Dependable Computing Conference, vol. 1827752, pp. 199–208. IEEE Computer Society (2010)
7. Bouissou, M., Villatte, N., Bouhadana, H., Bannelier, M.: Knowledge modelling and reliability processing: presentation of the figaro language and associated tools. Report, Electricite de France (EDF), December 1991
8. Pernestl, A.: A Bayesian approach to fault isolation with application to diesel engine diagnosis. Thesis (2007)
9. Cuppens, F., Ortalo, R.: LAMBDA: a language to model a database for detection of attacks. In: Debar, H., Mé, L., Wu, S.F. (eds.) RAID 2000. LNCS, vol. 1907, pp. 197–216. Springer, Heidelberg (2000). https://doi.org/10.1007/3-540-39945-3_13
10. Cuppens, F., Miège, A.: Alert correlation in a cooperative intrusion detection framework. In: Proceedings 2002 IEEE Symposium on Security and Privacy, pp. 202–215 (2002)
11. Kanoun, W., Cuppens-Boulahia, N., Cuppens, F., Dubus, S., Martin, A.: Success likelihood of ongoing attacks for intrusion detection and response systems. In: 2009 International Conference on Computational Science and Engineering, vol. 3, pp. 83–91 (2009)
12. Schroeder, B., Gibson, G.A.: Disk failures in the real world: what does an MTTF of 1,000,000 hours mean to you? In: Proceedings of the 5th USENIX Conference on File and Storage Technologies, 1267904. USENIX Association 1 (2007)
13. Cuppens, F., Autrel, F., Miège, A., Benferhat, S.: Recognizing malicious intention in an intrusion detection process. In: HIS, pp. 806–817 (2002)
14. Rogers, J., M. Watkins, C.: Overview of the Taum Sauk Pumped Storage Power Plant Upper Reservoir Failure, Reynolds County, MO (2008)
15. Team, F.T.S.I.: Report of findings on the overtopping and embankment breach of the upper dam - Taum Sauk pumped storage project, Report, 28 Apr 2006
16. Before the public service commission state of Missouri - staff's initial incident report. Report, October 2007
17. Dacier, M., Deswarte, Y., Kaâniche, M.: Quantitative assessment of operational security: models and tools. In: Katsikas, S.K., Gritzalis, D. (eds.) Information Systems Security, pp. 179–186. Chapman & Hall, London (1996)
18. Weber, P., Medina-Oliva, G., Simon, C., Iung, B.: Overview on Bayesian networks applications for dependability, risk analysis and maintenance areas. Eng. Appl. Artif. Intell. **25**(4), 671–682 (2012)
19. Boudali, H., Dugan, J.B.: A new Bayesian network approach to solve dynamic fault trees (2005)

Access Control Policies

Enabling the Deployment of ABAC Policies in RBAC Systems

Gunjan Batra[1]([✉]), Vijayalakshmi Atluri[1], Jaideep Vaidya[1], and Shamik Sural[2]

[1] MSIS Department, Rutgers Business School, Newark, USA
{gunjan.batra,atluri,jsvaidya}@rutgers.edu
[2] Department of Computer Science and Engineering, IIT Kharagpur,
Kharagpur, India
shamik@cse.iitkgp.ernet.in

Abstract. The flexibility, portability and identity-less access control features of Attribute Based Access Control (ABAC) make it an attractive choice to be employed in many application domains. However, commercially viable methods for implementation of ABAC do not exist while a vast majority of organizations use Role Based Access Control (RBAC) systems. In this paper, we present a way in which organizations having a RBAC system can deploy an ABAC policy. Thus, we propose a method for the translation of an ABAC policy into a form that can be adopted by an RBAC system. We compare the cost of enforcement in ABAC and RBAC with respect to time taken to evaluate an access request, and experimentally demonstrate that RBAC is significantly better in this respect. Since the cost of security management is more expensive under RBAC when compared to ABAC, we present an analysis of the different management costs and present mitigation approaches by considering various administrative operations.

1 Introduction

Role-Based Access Control (RBAC) has been a well accepted standard for access control for more than three decades. Most businesses today use RBAC to assign access to the network and systems based on job title or defined role. However, a primary limitation of RBAC is its significant dependence on user identity for mapping it to a set of roles. As an alternative, the Attribute Based Access Control (ABAC) model has been developed. In ABAC, subject requests to perform operations on objects are granted or denied based on assigned attributes of the subject, assigned attributes of the object, environment conditions, and a set of policies that are specified in terms of those attributes and conditions [8]. As such, ABAC can comprehensively handle various factors affecting access control decisions like location, time, server load, etc., and also facilitates inter-domain accesses. Furthermore, use of user and object attributes for defining access control makes ABAC more portable across organizational domains. Indeed the flexibility, portability and *identity-less* access control features make ABAC very

© IFIP International Federation for Information Processing 2018
Published by Springer International Publishing AG, part of Springer Nature 2018. All Rights Reserved
F. Kerschbaum and S. Paraboschi (Eds.): DBSec 2018, LNCS 10980, pp. 51–68, 2018.
https://doi.org/10.1007/978-3-319-95729-6_4

attractive to be employed in many application domains, including cloud computing, web services, collaborative and coalition based systems, as it is feasible to make access control decisions without any prior knowledge of the subject. As a result, many organizations are now moving to ABAC, which is a non-identity based model and is highly dynamic and flexible. Indeed, Gartner predicts that by 2020, 70% of enterprises would use ABAC as the dominant mechanism to protect critical assets, up from less than 5% today [8].

ABAC is also advantageous from a security management perspective. Since ABAC allows for the creation of access policies based on the existing attributes of the users and objects, rather than the manual assignment of roles, ownership or security labels, it minimizes the need for manual intervention in configuring and deploying access control. More specifically, if an employee changes roles or leaves the company, an administrator must manually change access rights accordingly perhaps within several systems. As organizations expand and contract, partner with external entities, and modernize systems, this method of managing user access becomes increasingly difficult and inefficient [8]. On the other hand, such organizational changes effectively do not incur any manual cost under an ABAC system as no changes need to be made to the access control configuration. As such, the administrative cost of ABAC is significantly lower as compared to that of RBAC (or even that of discretionary access control (DAC)).

Despite many organizations wanting to adopt ABAC as their method of access control, there do not yet exist many commercial ABAC implementations. Some vendors such as Axiomatics, do offer ABAC implementations as dynamic authorization solutions, however, ABAC implementations have not yet been incorporated into any of the popular operating systems, or applications such as DBMS, etc. As such, organizations wanting to adopt ABAC, need to implement it on their own, which can often be error-prone and unreliable. Since RBAC is widely deployed in almost all commercially available OS and application systems, our basic idea in this paper is to propose an approach that can help realize an ABAC policy using a RBAC system. Essentially, we translate the ABAC policies into an equivalent RBAC configuration so that a user gains access to a resource in RBAC if and only if that user has the specified access under ABAC.

There are a number of benefits for taking this path to enforcing access control. First, our approach is an alternative where ABAC can simply be realized with a readily available RBAC implementation. Second, it is well known that when an access request is submitted by a user, the enforcement in ABAC is much more expensive in terms of time and processing power than that in RBAC. We experimentally show that this is indeed true. As a result, with our approach, one can enjoy the benefits of ABAC (such as flexibility, etc.) as well as the benefits of RBAC (efficient authorization enforcement). Due to this, one may still want to go on our proposed path, even if an ABAC implementation were to be available in future. Third, as ABAC paradigm is more suited for cloud environments due to its fine-grained property. Therefore, our proposed approach is a solution for the organizations that have an RBAC system in place and would like to be a part of cloud or another data sharing environment.

However, while RBAC administration and maintenance are considered less costly when compared to DAC, as mentioned earlier, it is more expensive when compared to ABAC. Recognizing this fact that the maintenance cost in RBAC is significantly higher than that of ABAC, we propose methods to handle such changes effectively by considering the different change scenarios such as addition/deletion of users and objects, changes to ABAC policies including addition/deletion of subject/object attributes, addition/deletion of ABAC rules.

The rest of this paper is organized as follows. In Sect. 2, we provide a brief overview of ABAC and RBAC. In Sect. 3, we discuss the problem of converting an ABAC policy to RBAC. The idea is to cover all the authorizations of ABAC model and build an equivalent RBAC model. We also examine how the number of policy rules in ABAC relates to the number of roles in RBAC. In Sect. 4 we experimentally compare the cost of enforcement in an ABAC system to the cost of enforcement in RBAC once the ABAC policies are implemented in the RBAC system. In Sect. 5, we discuss the management cost by considering the administrative operations in this system and ways to make it more efficient. In Sect. 6, we discuss related work. Finally, in Sect. 7, we conclude the paper and discuss future research directions.

2   Preliminaries

In this section, we briefly present the attribute based access control (ABAC) model [1,12] and the Role Based Access Control model [7], upon which all of the following work is based. In ABAC, the authorization to perform an operation (e.g.,read/write/modify) is granted based on the attributes of the requesting user, requested object, and the environment in which a request is made. In RBAC, the authorization to perform an operation is based on role of a user requesting permission to access and object.

2.1   RBAC

The basic components of RBAC are as follows:

Users $(\mathcal{U})$: Represents a set of authorized users/subjects. Each member of this set is denoted as u_i, for $1 \leq i \leq |\mathcal{U}|$.

Objects $(\mathcal{O})$: Represents a set of resources to be protected. Each member of this set is denoted as o_i, for $1 \leq i \leq |\mathcal{O}|$.

ROLES $(\mathcal{R})$: Represents a set of roles. Each member of this set is denoted as r_i, for $1 \leq i \leq |\mathcal{R}|$.

$\mathcal{OPS}$: Represents a set of operations. Each member of this set is denoted as op_i, for $1 \leq i \leq |\mathcal{OPS}|$.

$\mathcal{PRMS}$: Represents the set of Permissions $\mathcal{PRMS} \subseteq \{(o\text{-}op) \mid o \in \mathcal{O} \land op \in \mathcal{OPS}\}$.

$\mathcal{UA}$: User Role assignment relation, $\mathcal{UA} \subseteq \mathcal{U} \times \mathcal{R}$ is a many-to-many mapping of user to role assignments. We use a $m \times n$ binary matrix to represent $\mathcal{UA}$.

$\mathcal{PA}$: Permission Role assignment relation, $\mathcal{PA} \subseteq \mathcal{PRMS} \times \mathcal{R}$ is a many-to-many mapping of permission to role assignments.

2.2 ABAC

The basic components of ABAC are as follows:

Users ($\mathcal{U}$): Represents a set of authorized users/subjects. Each member of this set is denoted as u_i, for $1 \leq i \leq |\mathcal{U}|$.

Objects ($\mathcal{O}$): Represents a set of resources to be protected. Each member of this set is denoted as o_i, for $1 \leq i \leq |\mathcal{O}|$.

Environment ($\mathcal{E}$): Represents a set of environment conditions, independent of users and objects. Each member of this set is denoted as e_i, for $1 \leq i \leq |\mathcal{E}|$.

$\mathcal{U_A}$: Represents a set of user attribute names. Members of these sets are represented as ua_i, for $1 \leq i \leq |\mathcal{U_A}|$, Each ua_i is associated with a set of possible values it can acquire. For instance, if a user attribute *Position* is associated with the values {*Manager, Associate, Customer*}, then for every $u \in \mathcal{U}$, value of the attribute *Position* can be either *Manager, Associate* or *Customer*.

$\mathcal{O_A}$: Represents a set of object attribute names. Members of these sets are represented as oa_i, for $1 \leq j \leq |\mathcal{O_A}|$. Each oa_i is associated with a set of possible values it can acquire. For instance, if an object folder with records of customers has object attribute *Region* associated with a set of values {*EastCoast, West-Coast*}, then for every $o \in \mathcal{O}$, *Region* can be either *EastCoast* or *WestCoast*.

For the sake of simplicity, in this paper, we ignore environmental attributes.

$\mathcal{U_C}$: Represents a set of all possible user attribute conditions denoted as uc_j, for $1 \leq j \leq |\mathcal{U_C}|$. Members of this set are represented as equalities of the form $n = c$, where n is a user attribute name and c is either a constant or *any*. For instance if user attribute *Position* has possible values {*Manager, Associate, Customer*} and user attribute *Region* has possible values as {*EastCoast, WestCoast*}, then $\mathcal{U_C}$ will be a set comprising of {*Position = Manager*}, {*Position = Associate*}, {*Position = Customer*}, {*Position = any*}, {*Region = EastCoast*}, {*Region = WestCoast*}, {*Specialty = any*}. Note here, that the condition $n = any$ does not have to be explicitly chosen. It is set only if at least one other condition for n is present. We use the notation $\mathcal{U_C}.u_i$ to express the user attribute condition set of a user u_i.

$\mathcal{O_C}$: Represents a set of all possible object attribute conditions denoted as oc_k, for $1 \leq k \leq |\mathcal{O_C}|$. Members of this set are represented as equalities of the form $n = c$, where n is an object attribute name and c is either a constant or *any*. For instance if object attribute *Region* has possible values {*EastCoast, WestCoast*} and object attribute *RecordOf* has possible values {*Manager, Associate, Customer, Staff*}, then $\mathcal{O_C}$ will be a set comprising of {*Region = EastCoast*},

$\{Region = WestCoast\}$, $\{Region = any\}$, $\{RecordOf = Manager\}$, $\{RecordOf = Customer\}$, $\{RecordOf = Associate\}$, $\{RecordOf = Staff\}$, $\{RecordOf = any\}$. For an attribute name n, if the value of c is any, then the attribute n is not relevant for making the corresponding access decision. Therefore, as above, the condition $n = any$ does not have to be explicitly chosen. It is set only if at least one other condition for n is present. We use the notation $\mathcal{O}_C.o_i$ to express the object attribute condition set of an object o_i. ABAC Policy base Π_A: This represents a set of access rules in the ABAC system. Each member of this set is denoted as π_i, for $1 \leq i \leq |\Pi|$, where π is a quadruple of the form $\langle uc, oc, ec, op \rangle$. If a user makes a request to access an object, the policy base is searched for any rule through which the user can gain access. If such a rule exists, then access is granted, otherwise it is denied.

In $\mathcal{U}_C$ and $\mathcal{O}_C$ we have represented the attribute conditions as equalities, however, our approach is flexible to include the complex attribute condition constructs (inequalities, negation, subset, etc.) by converting them to their corresponding list of attributes conditions. In the following, we define the mapping between users and user attribute conditions as well as objects and object attribute conditions.

Table 1. $\mathcal{U}\mathcal{A}\mathcal{R}$

User (u)	Region = EastCoast(uc_1)	Position = Manager(uc_2)	Region = WestCoast(uc_3)	Position = Associate(uc_4)
u_1	0	1	1	0
u_2	0	0	1	1
u_3	1	1	0	0
u_4	1	0	0	1

$\mathcal{U}\mathcal{A}\mathcal{R}$: User attribute relation $\mathcal{U}\mathcal{A}\mathcal{R} \subseteq \mathcal{U} \times \mathcal{U}_C$ is a many-to-many mapping of users and user attribute conditions. We use a $m \times n$ binary matrix to represent $\mathcal{U}\mathcal{A}\mathcal{R}$, where $\mathcal{U}\mathcal{A}\mathcal{R}[i,j] = 1$, if user u_i satisfies an attribute condition uc_j. As shown in the example in Table 1, user u_1 is an $Manager$ whose region is $WestCoast$.

Table 2. $\mathcal{O}\mathcal{A}\mathcal{R}$

Object (o)	Region = WestCoast (oc_1)	Region = EastCoast (oc_2)	Recordof = Customer (oc_3)
o_1	1	0	1
o_2	0	1	1

Table 3. Policy (Π_A)

Attributes	Permission
uc_3, uc_4, oc_1, oc_3	op_1
uc_2, uc_3, oc_1, oc_3	op_1
uc_1, uc_2, oc_2, oc_3	op_1
uc_1, uc_4, oc_2, oc_3	op_1
uc_2, uc_3, oc_1, oc_3	op_2
uc_1, uc_2, oc_2, oc_3	op_2

$\mathcal{OAR}$: Object attribute relation, $\mathcal{OAR} \subseteq \mathcal{O} \times \mathcal{O_C}$ is a many-to-many mapping of objects and the set of all attributes conditions, where we again use a $m \times n$ binary matrix to represent $\mathcal{OAR}$. $\mathcal{OAR}[i,j] = 1$ if an object o_i satisfies an object attribute condition oc_j. Table 2 shows an example where object o_1 is the *recordof Customer* in *WestCoast region*.

3   ABAC to RBAC Translation

This section presents our methodology to translate the ABAC policy configuration to an equivalent one in RBAC. Towards this end, we first formally define the *optimal ABAC to RBAC translation problem* and then present our approach.

3.1   Problem Formulation

Intuitively, our goal is to discover RBAC roles from ABAC policy base in such a way that the set of RBAC roles is minimum and at the same time the authorizations are the same as those under ABAC. In the following, we formalize the definition of the ABAC to RBAC translation problem.

$\mathcal{A}$: An authorization a having the form of $\langle u, o, op \rangle$ denotes that the user u is allowed to perform an operation op on the object o, where $u \in \mathcal{U}$, $o \in \mathcal{O}$, and $op \in \mathcal{OPS}$. We use $u.a$, $o.a$ and $op.a$ to denote the user, object and operation associated with a. We denote the set of all authorizations as $\mathcal{A}$. For each operation $op_i \in \mathcal{OPS}$, we define $\mathcal{A}_{op_i} \subseteq \mathcal{A}$ such that for every $a \in \mathcal{A}_{op_i}$, $op.a = op_i$. For example, if $\mathcal{OPS} = \{read, write\}$, we have $\mathcal{A}_{read}$ and $\mathcal{A}_{write}$ such that $\mathcal{A}_{read} \cup \mathcal{A}_{write} = \mathcal{A}$.

Given an ABAC policy base Π_A, we say $\mathcal{A}$ covers π if for every user u and object o combination where u is allowed to perform operation op on o, there exists an authorization $a = \langle u, o, op \rangle \in \mathcal{A}$. (In the following subsection, we provide an algorithm on how to derive such $\mathcal{A}$ from Π.) Similarly, given an RBAC policy Π_R, we say $\mathcal{A}$ covers Π_R if for every user u and object o combination where u is allowed to perform operation op on o in Π_R, there exists an authorization $a = \langle u, o, op \rangle \in \mathcal{A}$. Now we are ready to formally define the optimal ABAC to RBAC translation problem.

Problem Statement. Given an ABAC policy Π_A, Users $\mathcal{U}$, Objects $\mathcal{O}$, User Attribute relation ($\mathcal{UAR}$), and Object Attribute relation ($\mathcal{OAR}$), the ABAC to RBAC translation problem is to identify a RBAC policy Π_R that includes a set of Roles $\mathcal{R}$, $\mathcal{PA}$ and $\mathcal{UA}$ such that the set of authorizations $\mathcal{A}$ derived from Π_A and Π_R are equal and the number of roles $|\mathcal{R}|$ is minimum.

3.2   Approach

In this section, we discuss how we develop a system that will translate ABAC policies in a manner that they can be implemented by an RBAC. The $\mathcal{UAR}$, $\mathcal{OAR}$ and ABAC policy base Π_A is fed to an ABAC-RBAC Translator which

---

Algorithm 1. Generating $\mathcal{A}$ and $\mathcal{UPA}$

Require: $\mathcal{UAR}, \mathcal{OAR}, \Pi_A$
  INITIALIZE $\mathcal{A} = \emptyset$
  for all $(u_i\text{-}o_j)$ combinations in $\mathcal{UAR}$ and $\mathcal{OAR}$ **do**
    for all π_k in Π_A **do**
      if $\pi_k \subseteq \mathcal{U_C}.u_i \bigcup \mathcal{O_C}.o_j$ **then**
        $\mathcal{A} \leftarrow \mathcal{A} \bigcup (u_i, o_j, op_k.\pi_k)$
      end if
    end for
  end for
  INITIALIZE $\mathcal{UPA}$ of size $M \times N$ such that $M = 1, \ldots, |U|; N = 1, \ldots, |u_i - o_i|$ in $\mathcal{A}$
  for all a_l in $\mathcal{A}$ **do**
    $\mathcal{UPA}(u_i.a_l, o_j.a_l\text{-}op_k.a_l) \leftarrow 1$
  end for

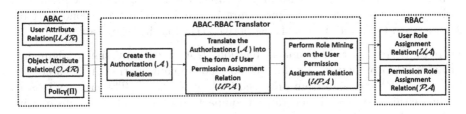

Fig. 1. Approach for Deployment of ABAC in RBAC

generates Π_R, which includes $\mathcal{R}$ and the corresponding $\mathcal{UA}$ and $\mathcal{PA}$ that form the RBAC policy. The detailed process for translation is described below and has been shown in Fig. 1.

Steps for ABAC to RBAC translation:

Step 1. Construct the set of Authorizations $\mathcal{A}$ from the User Attribute Relation $(\mathcal{UAR})$, Object Attribute Relation $(\mathcal{OAR})$ and the ABAC policy base (Π_A): For each user(u_i)-object(o_j) combination from $\mathcal{UAR}$ and $\mathcal{OAR}$, we check if their corresponding attribute conditions$(\mathcal{U_C}.u_i$ and $\mathcal{O_C}.o_i)$ form a superset of any of the given ABAC rules in Π_A. For every such superset occurence, we include the set comprising of user(u_i), object(o_j) and the operation$(op_k.\pi_k)$ in $\mathcal{A}$. The procedure is automated in the first part of Algorithm 1. As an example, given $\mathcal{UAR}$ in Table 1, $\mathcal{OAR}$ in Table 2 and Π in Table 3, the derived $\mathcal{A}$ is shown in Table 4.

Step 2. Derive User Permission Assignment $(\mathcal{UPA})$ from $\mathcal{A}$: The $\mathcal{UPA}$ is defined as an $M \times N$ matrix, where $M = |\mathcal{U}|$ comprising of a row for each user, and $N = |\mathcal{O}\text{-}op|$, comprising of a column for each object and operation combination in $\mathcal{A}$. Using $(\mathcal{A})$, we derive $(\mathcal{UPA})$ as follows: We consider all the Users in $(\mathcal{A})$ and associate the objects with permissions to form PRMS$(o\text{-}op)$ in RBAC.

Table 4. $\mathcal{A}$

User	Object	Permission
u	o	op_i
u_1	o_1	op_1
u_2	o_1	op_1
u_3	o_2	op_1
u_4	o_2	op_1
u_1	o_1	op_2
u_3	o_2	op_2

Table 5. $\mathcal{UPA}$

	o_1-op_1	o_1-op_2	o_2-op_1	o_2-op_2
u_1	1	1	0	0
u_2	1	0	0	0
u_3	0	0	1	1
u_4	0	0	1	0

There is a row in $\mathcal{UPA}$ for each user and a column for each PRMS(o-op). For each row, if the (o-op) is true for that user, the corresponding cell is filled with 1, otherwise with 0. The procedure is automated in the second part of Algorithm 1. Given $\mathcal{A}$ in Table 4, the derived $\mathcal{UPA}$ is shown in Table 5.

Step 3. Derive User Assignment Relation ($\mathcal{UA}$) and Permission Assignment Relation ($\mathcal{PA}$) by performing Role Mining: For the automation of this step, we have used DEMiner algorithm proposed by Uzun et al. [3]. The primary reason to choose this is because it generates a compact set of roles which are disjoint in their permissions. As a result, it makes administration of access requests much easier, which is in sync with the idea of this work. When a user requests for a specific permission, there will be a single role with that specific permission, thus making the access control decision faster and efficient. This is the reason why we choose this algorithm as the benchmark. It reduces the administrative cost, as the roles generated are non overlapping and the access request decision is evaluated faster than any other role mining algorithm that produces overlapping roles.

We performed slight modification to the DeMiner algorithm by sorting the users in the $\mathcal{UPA}$ in decreasing order of the number of $\mathcal{PRMS}$ before applying the algorithm on our dataset. This helped improve the efficiency and effectiveness of the algorithm in terms of time and the number of roles created. Considering our example once again, given $\mathcal{UPA}$ in Table 5, the derived $\mathcal{UA}$ and $\mathcal{PA}$ are shown in Tables 6 and 7, respectively.

Theorem 1. *Let $\mathcal{A}$ be the set of authorizations covered by Π_A and $\mathcal{R}$. If $|\Pi_A|$ is the minimum number of ABAC rules required to cover $\mathcal{A}$ and $|\mathcal{R}|$ is the minimum number of roles required to cover $\mathcal{A}$, then $|\Pi_A| \geq |\mathcal{R}|$.*

Proof. Let 'k' be the minimum number of ABAC Rules $|\Pi_A|$, where $\Pi_A = \{\pi_1, \pi_2, \pi_3 \dots \pi_k\}$ that cover a set of authorizations $\mathcal{A}$ and let 'n' be the minimum number of RBAC roles $\mathcal{R}$ that cover the same set of authorizations $\mathcal{A}$ is $\mathcal{R} = \{r_1, r_2, r_3, \dots r_n\}$.

Table 6. $\mathcal{U}\mathcal{A}$

	r_1	r_2	r_3	r_4
u_1	1	1	0	0
u_2	1	0	0	0
u_3	0	0	1	1
u_4	0	0	1	0

Table 7. $\mathcal{P}\mathcal{A}$

	$o_1\text{-}op_1$	$o_1\text{-}op_2$	$o_2\text{-}op_1$	$o_2\text{-}op_2$
r_1	1	0	0	0
r_2	0	1	0	0
r_3	0	0	1	0
r_4	0	0	0	1

Because 'k' is the minimum number of rules, each rule covers atleast one unique authorization. So, if we map each of the policy rules π_i in ABAC to a role r_j in RBAC (where both π_i and r_j cover same set of authorizations in $\mathcal{A}$), we will get exactly 'k' roles. We have shown the same in Example 1 described below. Therefore, for every rule we can create one corresponding role which will cover same set of authorizations. So, we can infer that in all possible cases, the count of roles to express a set of authorizations $\mathcal{A}$ will never be more than the count of rules. In the worst case, $|\Pi_A|$ and $|\mathcal{R}|$ will be equal.

So far, we know that, for 'n' to be the minimum roles required to express $\mathcal{A}$, 'k' has to be equal to 'n' or greater than 'n'. Else we cannot say that 'n' is the minimum number of roles (i.e. $k \geq n$). To check if 'k' could be less than or equal to 'n', we conjecture that, we can map the authorizations expressed by a single role in RBAC to a single rule in ABAC. We use a simple counter example to disprove the above conjecture. We can see in Example 2 below, that for 2 RBAC roles, we need atleast 6 ABAC rules to express the same authorizations. We need 5 ABAC rules: π_1, π_2, π_3, π_4 and π_5 to describe authorizations of r_1 and one ABAC rule π_6 to describe authorizations of r_2. Note that it is impossible to describe role r_1 by a single ABAC rule as r_1 covers the set users which satisfy no common attribute condition(s).

In case we have common attributes between users or objects in the role, for example in role r_2, user u_1 and u_4 have a common attribute uc_4, then one ABAC rule could cover the same authorizations of r_2, i.e. π_6 (this will give access to both u_1 and u_4 to o_3 to perform op_1 as both u_1 and u_4 satisfy user attribute condition uc_4). Hence, we need at least 6 ABAC Rules to express the authorizations covered by 2 roles. Thus, Example 2 is a testimony to that fact that it is possible to have an RBAC role where no single ABAC rule can express the authorizations of that particular single role.

To conclude, the number of Policy Rules in ABAC is always greater than or equal to the number of Roles in RBAC, i.e., $|\Pi_A| \geq |\mathcal{R}|$.   □

Example 1: An ABAC rule π_1: $\langle uc_1, oc_1, read \rangle$ gives users u_1 and u_2 (both having attribute uc_1), *read* access on object o_1(having attribute oc_1); i.e. two authorizations $\mathcal{A}_1$ and $\mathcal{A}_2$, where $\mathcal{A}_1 = \langle u_1, o_1, read \rangle$ and $\mathcal{A}_2 = \langle u_2, o_1, read \rangle$. The corresponding role r_1 will be assigned to users(u_1, u_2) and will be granted permission (o_1,*read*).

Table 8. $\mathcal{A}$

User	Object	Permission
u_1	o_1	op_1
u_1	o_2	op_1
u_1	o_3	op_1
u_2	o_1	op_1
u_2	o_2	op_1
u_3	o_1	op_1
u_3	o_2	op_1
u_4	o_3	op_1

Table 9. $\mathcal{UA}$

	r_1	r_2
u_1	1	1
u_2	1	0
u_3	1	0
u_4	0	1

Table 10. $\mathcal{PA}$

	$o_1\text{-}op_1$	$o_2\text{-}op_1$	$o_3\text{-}op_1$
r_1	1	1	0
r_2	0	0	1

Table 11. $\mathcal{UAR}$

User	uc_1	uc_2	uc_3	uc_4
u_1	1	0	0	1
u_2	0	1	0	0
u_3	0	0	1	0
u_4	0	0	0	1

Table 12. $\mathcal{OAR}$

Object	oc_1	oc_2	oc_3
o_1	1	0	0
o_2	0	1	0
o_3	0	0	1

Example 2: An RBAC system which has two roles r_1 and r_2 giving authorizations $\mathcal{A}$ (Table 8) to four users(u_1, u_2, u_3, u_4). The $\mathcal{UA}$ relation is given in Table 9 and $\mathcal{PA}$ relation is in Table 10. The users and objects satisfy the attribute conditions as shown in the User Attribute Relation $\mathcal{UAR}$ (Table 11) and Object Attribute Relation $\mathcal{OAR}$ (Table 12). In total, atleast 6 ABAC policy rules are required to cover the authorizations of both the roles. They are as follows:

π_1: $\langle\, uc_1\, \rangle$, $\langle\, \text{Any}\, \rangle$ π_4: $\langle\, uc_3\, \rangle$, $\langle\, oc_1\, \rangle$

π_2: $\langle\, uc_2\, \rangle$, $\langle\, oc_1\, \rangle$ π_5: $\langle\, uc_3\, \rangle$, $\langle\, oc_2\, \rangle$

π_3: $\langle\, uc_2\, \rangle$, $\langle\, oc_2\, \rangle$ π_6: $\langle\, uc_4\, \rangle$, $\langle\, oc_3\, \rangle$

4   Experimental Comparison of Access Request Evaluation Cost in ABAC and RBAC

In order to compare the time taken for *access request* (AR) evaluation, the same ABAC and RBAC policy, we need to first create two equivalent policies and compare the time taken to evaluate the same set of access requests. This is done as follows. First, a synthetic ABAC policy base (Π_A) is created. For creating synthetic ABAC Policies we used the data generator used by Talukdar et al. [12]. Next, using the ABAC policy base and the User Attribute relation ($\mathcal{UAR}$) and Object Attribute Relation ($\mathcal{OAR}$), the ($\mathcal{UPA}$) relation is created, on which

Role Mining is done on the $(\mathcal{UPA})$ relation to create the User Assignment $(\mathcal{UA})$ and Role Assignment $(\mathcal{PA})$ relation. Any Role Mining algorithm could be used, as long as it completely covers the given $\mathcal{UPA}$. In this particular case, we use the DEMiner algorithm proposed by Uzun et al. [3].

For each set of experiments, we have compared the access request evaluation time for both ABAC and RBAC. The experiments are performed on a Intel Core i7 2.60 GHz machine with 8.00 GB memory running 64-bit Windows 10. Since we are interested in seeing how the access request evaluation cost changes with respect to different parameters, we run fours sets of experiments where one parameter is varied while keeping the rest constant. Specifically, we examine the following four different scenarios: (1) increasing the rule size, (2) increasing the number of attributes in ABAC rules, (3) increasing the number of users and objects, and (4) increasing the count of positive authorizations. Here positive authorizations imply access requests that should be granted, while negative authorizations imply access requests that should be rejected. To compare the efficiency of ABAC and RBAC, we have evaluated the time taken to evaluate access requests for 100 user-object pairs. For the first three cases, we take 50 random positive authorizations and 50 random negative authorizations. For the last case, we have increased the count of positive authorizations and reduced the count of negative authorizations by keeping total access requests at 100. Further these access request evaluations were run three times and the time was averaged over all of these runs.

The key parameters are the number of users $(\mathcal{U})$, objects $(\mathcal{O})$, user attributes $(\mathcal{U}_C)$, object attributes $(\mathcal{O}_C)$, number of rules given (Π_A) to the ABAC system. In Tables 13, 14 and 15, the first column $|\mathcal{U}|$ is count of users, the second column $|\mathcal{O}|$ is count of objects, third column $|\mathcal{U}_C|$ is count of user attribute conditions, fourth column $|\mathcal{O}_C|$ is count of object attribute conditions, fifth column $|\Pi_A|$ is count of ABAC policy rules, $|\mathcal{R}|$ is the number of RBAC roles discovered after role mining, $AvgRT_{\text{ABAC}}$ is the average run time for ABAC and $AvgRT_{\text{RBAC}}$ is the average run time for RBAC. In Table 16, there are two additional columns for count of Positive Authorizations and Negative Authorizations.

For all the experiments, we observe that the count of roles $|\mathcal{R}|$ discovered after role mining is much less than the count of ABAC policy rules $|\Pi_A|$ for the same set of authorizations. We can also observe that the run time for access request evaluation for ABAC is significantly greater than the run time for access request evaluation for RBAC. Next we see the individual effects of varying the parameters while keeping all others constant.

Varying Number of ABAC Rules: Table 13 and Fig. 2 show the results obtained for access request evaluation time of ABAC and RBAC, while increasing the count of ABAC Rules, but keeping all other parameters constant. We have varied the ABAC rule count between 500, 1000, and 2000. We observe that the count of RBAC roles discovered was 200 in all the three cases. The average access request evaluation time for RBAC remains roughly the same, whereas the access request evaluation time for ABAC increases linearly. This is due to the fact that

Table 13. Increasing rule size

$|\mathcal{U}|$	$|\mathcal{O}|$	$|\mathcal{U}_C|$	$|\mathcal{O}_C|$	$|\Pi_A|$	$|\mathcal{R}|$	$AvgRT_{\text{ABAC}}$ (in ms)	$AvgRT_{\text{RBAC}}$ (in ms)
200	200	500	500	500	200	19.385	0.032
200	200	500	500	1000	200	35.227	0.032
200	200	500	500	2000	200	69.108	0.032

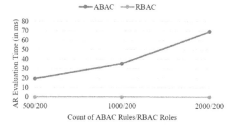

Fig. 2. Increasing rule size　　　　**Fig. 3.** Increasing attribute size

Table 14. Increasing attribute size

$|\mathcal{U}|$	$|\mathcal{O}|$	$|\mathcal{U}_C|$	$|\mathcal{O}_C|$	$|\Pi_A|$	$|\mathcal{R}|$	$AvgRT_{\text{ABAC}}$ (in ms)	$AvgRT_{\text{RBAC}}$ (in ms)
200	200	500	500	500	200	19.385	0.032
200	200	1000	1000	500	200	35.381	0.032
200	200	2000	2000	500	200	73.894	0.033

Table 15. Increasing User/Object Size

$|\mathcal{U}|$	$|\mathcal{O}|$	$|\mathcal{U}_C|$	$|\mathcal{O}_C|$	$|\Pi_A|$	$|\mathcal{R}|$	$AvgRT_{\text{ABAC}}$ (in ms)	$AvgRT_{\text{RBAC}}$ (in ms)
300	300	150	150	50	41	0.656	0.008
400	400	150	150	50	41	0.705	0.008
500	500	150	150	50	41	0.658	0.009

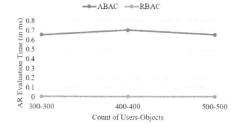

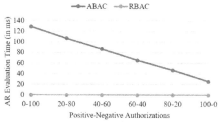

Fig. 4. Increasing User Object Size　　　　**Fig. 5.** Increasing Positive Authorizations

Table 16. Increasing Positive Authorisations

$|\mathcal{U}|$	$|\mathcal{O}|$	$|\mathcal{U}_C|$	$|\mathcal{O}_C|$	$|\Pi_A|$	$|\mathcal{R}|$	Positive accesses	Negative accesses	$AvgRT_{\text{ABAC}}$ (in ms)	$AvgRT_{\text{RBAC}}$ (in ms)
200	200	2000	2000	500	200	0	100	128.640	0.032
200	200	2000	2000	500	200	20	80	106.464	0.031
200	200	2000	2000	500	200	40	60	86.615	0.032
200	200	2000	2000	500	200	60	40	65.242	0.032
200	200	2000	2000	500	200	80	20	46.610	0.031
200	200	2000	2000	500	200	100	0	25.495	0.032

the size of $\mathcal{UA}$ and $\mathcal{PA}$ remain the same for the three cases, whereas the count of ABAC rules to be checked for granted access doubles each time.

Varying Number of User and Object Attributes: Table 14 and Fig. 3 show the results obtained for access request evaluation time of ABAC and RBAC, while increasing the count of Users Attributes and Objects Attributes for ABAC policy rules, while keeping all other parameters constant. We have increased both user and object attribute counts for ABAC rules using values 500, 1000 and 2000 for both. We observe that the count of RBAC roles discovered was 200 in all three cases. The average access request evaluation time for RBAC remains roughly the same, whereas the access request evaluation time for ABAC increases linearly. This is because of the fact that the size of $\mathcal{UA}$ and $\mathcal{PA}$ relation remains the same for the three cases, whereas the count of attributes to be checked for granting access in each rule increases.

Varying Number of Users and Objects: Table 15 and Fig. 4 show the results obtained for access request evaluation time of ABAC and RBAC, while increasing the count of Users and Objects, but keeping all other parameters constant. Again, we observe that the average access request evaluation time in ABAC is almost 75 times that of RBAC.

Varying Number of Positive Authorizations: Table 16 and Fig. 5 show the results obtained for access request evaluation time of ABAC and RBAC, while varying the count of positive authorizations, but keeping all other parameters constant. Out of the 100 random user-object access requests we predetermine the number of accesses that would evaluate to be positive (granted). These positive access requests were varied between the values 0, 20, 40, 60, 80, and 100, with the remaining requests used being negative requests. We observe that the average access request evaluation time in RBAC is roughly the same as earlier, however the average access request evaluation time in ABAC has reduced linearly. An ABAC system checks each policy rule, one by one, to see if it can grant the access. When an access request is granted, no further policy rules need to be checked; whereas, when an access request is denied the ABAC system keeps on checking all the policy rules it has.

The overall results indicate the fact that evaluation of access requests in RBAC is significantly faster across the board in all cases than those of ABAC.

5   Maintenance Cost Comparison in ABAC and RBAC

In this section, we discuss the configuration and the maintenance cost while dealing with various changes to the ABAC policy and the cost of translating them into an equivalent RBAC policy. The list of operations that can be performed on the original ABAC policy system is as follows:

1. Addition/Deletion of Rules
2. Addition/Deletion of Users/Objects
3. Addition/Deletion of User/Object Attributes
4. Addition/Deletion of Attributes in ABAC Rules

We know that in ABAC, the initial configuration cost is the sum of number of attributes of users, objects and the policy rules, i.e., $|\mathcal{U}_C| + |\mathcal{O}_C| + |\Pi_A|$. Whereas, when we implement ABAC in an RBAC system, the initial config-uration cost will be the sum of the number of user role assignments and role permission assignments, i.e., $|\mathcal{U}\mathcal{A}| + |\mathcal{P}\mathcal{A}|$. The maintenance cost of the above mentioned operations will be negligible in case of an ABAC system as every access request is evaluated at the time of enforcement. However, if we wish to deploy the ABAC policies using an RBAC system with our approach, the maintenance cost for some operations vary from making changes to the RBAC system directly to performing the entire ABAC-RBAC translation again. In the following, we have identified the maintenance cost associated with each change operation. While Fig. 6 provides the overview of how these changes are handled, the exact approach for each change is discussed in detail. To discuss the way these change operations are handled, we have divided them into two types based on the type of effort required. Specifically, some changes require the ABAC-RBAC translation to be done all over. On the other hand, due to the additional information that we maintain, they do not require such translation to be done again, but lend itself to make the relevant changes to the RBAC policy directly. In the following subsections, we elaborate on these cases, and discuss what addi-tional information need to maintained. It turns out that, very few cases require performing the ABAC-RBAC translation all over again.

5.1   Changes Requiring Direct Modification to the RBAC Policy

Addition of Users: When a new user is added to the system, the $\mathcal{U}\mathcal{P}\mathcal{A}$ changes which would require performing role mining all over again. However, if we keep the user attributes required for that role, we can avoid this expensive step, as we can simply derive which role to assign to the user. Therefore, we create a Role User Attribute Assignment Relation $\mathcal{R}\mathcal{U}\mathcal{A}$, which is a many-to-many map-ping of roles to user attribute conditions, i.e., $\mathcal{R}\mathcal{U}\mathcal{A} \subseteq \mathcal{R} \times \mathcal{U}_C$. We use a $m \times n$

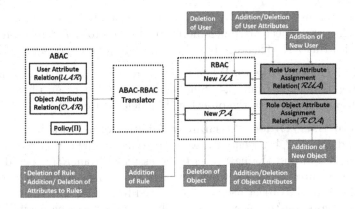

Fig. 6. Management of Administrative Operations on the system

binary matrix to represent $\mathcal{RUA}$, where $\mathcal{RUA}[i,j] = 1$, if user attribute condition uc_j is present in all the users assigned to a role r_j.

For example, we created a $\mathcal{RUA}$ in Table 17 using Tables 1 and 6. Notice that role r_1 in $\mathcal{RUA}$, has $uc_3 = 1$ as uc_3 is present in both the users assigned to r_1 (u_1 and u_2). Basically, attribute conditions assigned to a role are the set of maximum possible common attribute conditions of users in a given role. When a new user is added we can now simply select the roles to be assigned to this user by checking if user has the user attributes necessary for the role. A new row will be added to $\mathcal{UA}$ to reflect this.

Table 17. $\mathcal{RUA}$

Role	uc_1	uc_2	uc_3	uc_4
r_1	0	0	1	0
r_2	0	1	1	0
r_3	1	0	0	0
r_4	1	0	0	1

Table 18. $\mathcal{ROA}$

Role	oc_1	oc_2	oc_3	op_1	op_2
r_1	1	0	1	1	0
r_2	1	0	1	0	1
r_3	0	1	1	1	0
r_4	0	1	1	0	1

Addition of Objects: Similar to the case of adding a new user, in this case we maintain a Role Object Attribute Assignment Relation $\mathcal{ROA}$ which is a many-to-many mapping of roles to object attribute conditions (O_c) and operations ($\mathcal{OPS}$), i.e., $\mathcal{ROA} \subseteq \mathcal{R} \times (\mathcal{O}_c \cup \text{OPS})$. We again use a $m \times n$ binary matrix to represent $\mathcal{ROA}$, where $\mathcal{ROA}[i,j]=1$, if object attribute condition oc_j (or op) is present in all the objects (or operations) assigned to a role r_j. Table 18 shows $\mathcal{ROA}$ created using Tables 2 and 7. The attribute conditions assigned to a role are the set of maximum possible common set of object attribute conditions and permissions in a given role. When a new object is added, we select the roles that contain the permissions to perform an operation on the object by checking if the object has the object attributes necessary for the role. $\mathcal{PA}$ relation will be updated with this $\mathcal{PRMS}(o\text{-}op)$ by adding a corresponding column to it.

Deletion of Users/Objects: When a user is removed, the row corresponding to that user is deleted from $\mathcal{UA}$. Similarly, on deletion of an object, all the permissions associated with the object will be deleted from $\mathcal{PA}$.

Addition of User/Object Attributes: Addition of new attributes to a user requires updates to $\mathcal{UA}$. Essentially, we need to delete the earlier record of this user from $\mathcal{UA}$ and find the new roles to be assigned from $\mathcal{RUA}$ based on this new set of attributes. Similarly, when new attributes to an object are added, the row pertaining to the object needs to be deleted from $\mathcal{PA}$, and a new row need to be added based on this new set of attributes after checking eligibility using $\mathcal{ROA}$.

Addition of Rules: Upon adding an ABAC rule, since the $\mathcal{UPA}$ changes accordingly, we need to redo the ABAC-RBAC translation step to generate the new $\mathcal{UA}$ and $\mathcal{PA}$. However, there is an alternative to avoid this expensive step. Instead, one can add a new role corresponding to this new ABAC rule by examining the users and objects satisfying this new rule and reflect that in $\mathcal{UA}$ and $\mathcal{PA}$. While this is somewhat a manual process, this avoids redoing the translation every time a new ABAC rule is added. However, in this case, the translation step can be performed after a batch of ABAC rules are added. Note, however, that this action might create redundant roles in the system.

5.2   Changes Requiring Redoing of ABAC-RBAC Translation

Deletion of Rules: On deleting an ABAC rule, the $\mathcal{UPA}$ changes, and as a result the step of ABAC-RBAC translation has to be redone, which generates new $\mathcal{UA}$ and $\mathcal{PA}$.

Addition/Deletion of Attributes to ABAC Rules: Since addition or deletion of attributes to a ABAC rule essentially creates a new rule, it results in a new $\mathcal{UPA}$. Therefore, it requires redoing of the ABAC-RBAC translation step.

6   Related Work

There have been attempts in past to integrate ABAC and RBAC. Authors have proposed methods to unify both the models to get benefits of both. Kuhn et al. [10] discussed incorporating attributes into roles to combine the best of ABAC and RBAC and provide an effective access control. Also, Al-Kahtani et al. [11] proposed a model to dynamically assign users to roles using attribute based rules. Further, Jin et al. [9] proposed RABAC: Role-centric Attribute based Access Control where they extend RBAC with user and object attributes and also add a Permission Filtering Policy (PFP) to their model. All these focus on extending RBAC rather than using the basic RBAC that is available in most commercial implementations today.

Huang et al. [5] have proposed a model to integrate ABAC and RBAC at two levels: aboveground and underground. The aboveground level is RBAC model with environment constraints added to it and the underground level uses attribute-based policies for user-role assignment and role-permission assignment. Their work is different from that of ours as they focus on a top-down model to integrate ABAC and RBAC.

To the best of our knowledge, there have been no attempts to address this problem of deployment of an ABAC policy in a RBAC system. The NIST report on ABAC [1] mentions that "while it is possible to achieve ABAC objectives using ACLs or RBAC, demonstrating access control (AC) requirements compliance is difficult and costly due to the level of abstraction required between the AC requirements and the ACL or RBAC model. Another problem with ACL or RBAC models is that if the AC requirement is changed, it may be difficult to identify all the places where the ACL or RBAC implementation needs to be updated." Our approach attempts to draw the benefits from ABAC as well as RBAC by automatically translating a ABAC policy into RBAC.

7   Conclusions and Future Work

In this paper we demonstrate how ABAC can be deployed using an RBAC system. Our evaluation shows that the access request evaluation cost of RBAC is always less than the cost of the ABAC system implementing the same policy. However, since RBAC's maintenance cost is higher than that of ABAC, we also discuss several mitigation strategies to minimize the cost of various administrative operations that cause changes to ABAC. In future, we plan to implement this deployment approach while enforcing segregation of duty constraints [2]. In this work, we assumed there were no environmental conditions in ABAC. In future, we would like to include the environmental conditions as well and see how they translate into a context aware RBAC model.

Acknowledgments. Research reported in this publication was supported by the National Institutes of Health under award R01GM118574, by the National Science Foundation under awards CNS-1564034 and CNS-1624503 and by the National Academies of Sciences, Engineering, and Medicine under the PAK-US Science and Technology Cooperation Program. The content is solely the responsibility of the authors and does not necessarily represent the official views of the agencies funding the research. We would also like to thank Dr. Emre Uzun for his comments.

References

1. Hu, V.C., Ferraiolo, D., Kuhn, R., Schnitzer, A., Sandlin, K., Miller, R., Scarfone, K.: Guide to Attribute Based Access Control (ABAC) definition and considerations. In: NIST Special Publication, 800-162 (2014)
2. Jha, S., Sural, S., Atluri, V., Vaidya, J.: Enforcing separation of duty in attribute based access control systems. In: ICISS, pp. 61–78 (2015)
3. Uzun, E., Lorenzi, D., Atluri, V., Vaidya, J., Sural, S.: Migrating from DAC to RBAC. In: DBSec, pp. 69–84 (2015)
4. Vaidya, J., Atluri, V., Guo, Q.: The role mining problem: finding a minimal descriptive set of roles. In: SACMAT, pp. 175–184 (2007)
5. Huang, J., Nicol, D., Bobba, R., Huh, J.: A framework integrating attribute-based policies into role-based access control. In: SACMAT, pp. 187–196 (2012)
6. Hu, V., Kuhn, R., Ferraiolo, D.: Attribute-based access control. In: IEEE, pp. 85–88 (2015)
7. Sandhu, R., Coyne, E., Feinstein, H., Youman, C.: Role-based access control models. In: IEEE Computer, pp. 38–47 (1996)
8. Fisher, B., Brickman, N., Burden, P., Jha, S., Johnson, B., Keller, A., Kolovos, T., Umarji, S., Weeks, S.: Attribute Based Access Control. In: NIST Special Publication 1800-3 (2017)
9. Jin, X., Sandhu, R., Krishnan, R.: RABAC: role-centric attribute-based access control. In: MMM-ACNS, pp. 84–96 (2012)
10. Kuhn, D., Coyne, E., Weil, T.: Adding attributes to role-based access control. IEEE Comput. **43**, 79–81 (2010)
11. Al-Kahtani, M., Sandhu, R.: A model for attribute-based user-role assignment. In: IEEE, pp. 353–362 (2002)
12. Talukdar, T., Batra, G., Vaidya, J., Atluri, V., Sural, S.: Efficient bottom-up mining of attribute based access control policies, pp. 339–348. IEEE (2017)

Policy Languages and Their Suitability for Trust Negotiation

Martin Kolar, Carmen Fernandez-Gago[(⊠)], and Javier Lopez

Network, Information and Computer Security Lab,
University of Malaga, 29071 Malaga, Spain
{kolar,mcgago,jlm}@lcc.uma.es

Abstract. Entities, such as people, companies, institutions, authorities and web sites live and exist in a conjoined world. In order to live and enjoy social benefits, entities need to share knowledge, resources and to cooperate together. The cooperation brings with it many new challenges and problems, among which one is the problem of trust. This area is also important for the Computer Science. When unfamiliar entities wish to cooperate, they do not know what to expect nor whether they can trust each other. Trust negotiation solves this problem by sequential exchanging credentials between entities, which have decided to establish a trust relationship in order to reach a common goal. Entities specify their own policies that handle a disclosure of confidential information to maintain their security and privacy. Policies are defined by means of a policy language. This paper aims to identify the most suitable policy language for trust negotiation. To do so, policy languages are analysed against a set of criteria for trust negotiation that are first established.

1 Introduction

Entities in our world, in order to live and enjoy the benefits of our civilisation, need to cooperate together and share many resources, such as knowledge, services, products and jobs. This sharing or exchanging requires fair conditions for all parties, so that everybody can use shared resources equally and receive fair consideration for each contribution. One of the biggest issues is trust. Entities need to know who they can trust when cooperating, to prevent deception and abuse. They need to be sure the others are going to behave as expected [1]. Trust is usually built up over a long period of time, as entities get to know each other better. In this case, the main constructor of trust is experience, which is gained with each interaction and if the output is positive, trust increases. This way trust is built step by step. An entity supposes that others generally do not change too much over time, so its previous experience with them is also relevant for the future. An entity expects others to provide similar outputs in the future, as they have provided in the past. This expectation, positive or negative, is de facto trust.

© IFIP International Federation for Information Processing 2018
Published by Springer International Publishing AG, part of Springer Nature 2018. All Rights Reserved
F. Kerschbaum and S. Paraboschi (Eds.): DBSec 2018, LNCS 10980, pp. 69–84, 2018.
https://doi.org/10.1007/978-3-319-95729-6_5

However, trust cannot always be established in this natural way. Nowadays with online environments, our communication capabilities have been widely extended and the number of participating entities is enormous. Because there are so many of them, their anonymity tend to increase. However, entities still need to be sure about the provision of their resources, information, etc. to other parties [2]. For this reason suitable approaches for establishing trust and maintaining confidence should be used. Trust negotiation establishes trust without the need of a direct previous experience with an entity. It is a credentials exchange process between two entities resulting in the establishment of trust [4,5], where entities authenticate themselves by disclosing their private information. This information may be signed by an authority assuring their genuineness and authenticity. Generally, entities involved in trust negotiations need to control access over their data. This can be achieved by a definition of policies in a policy language. Policy languages provide a suitable way to express various types of policies and cover by them diverse aspects of trust negotiation, such as security and privacy. During trust negotiation, policies are read and evaluated in order to make credential disclosure decisions.

For the purpose of this paper, policy languages are observed for their suitability of usage for trust negotiation. This requires analysing the trust negotiation criteria that comprise a set of requirements needed to efficiently handle trust negotiation. The policy languages are analysed by classifying their attributes. Then, the attributes are checked against the identified criteria and if a match is found, the language is marked as supporting the criterion. The more criteria the policy language supports, the more suitable it is. Some criteria may be more important than others and some may even be essential. As a result, one or more policy languages suitable for trust negotiation can be identified. This paper identifies the general criteria for trust negotiation and analyses and classifies policy languages according to the selected criteria. It is important to carefully select the possibly suitable languages for trust negotiation that are to be classified. This classification is helpful to make a decision, which policy language should be chosen for a trust negotiation model. An engineer designing such model can view attributes of the analysed languages and thus select the most suitable language according to his needs.

The remainder of this paper is organised as follows: In Sect. 2, related work on trust, trust negotiation, policy languages and their classification is presented. Section 3 describes and explains the general concepts of trust negotiation and Sect. 4 identifies and presents the trust negotiation criteria. In Sect. 5, policy languages are analysed and matched against the criteria identified in Sect. 4. Finally, Sect. 6 concludes the paper and outlines future work.

2   Related Work

Entities experience trust on an everyday basis as they relate to each other and make decisions. Gambetta [1] defines trust as a subjective probability, by which an individual A expects another individual B to perform a given action, on which its welfare depends. This definition supposes that the trustor is dependent on the trustee and the trustee is reliable. According to Jøsang [2], there are two common definitions of trust called *reliability trust* and *decision trust*. Reliability trust can be interpreted as the reliability of something or somebody and decision trust as a magnitude of willingness of one entity to be dependent on another in a given scenario. The entity should feel relatively secure and comfortable about the other, even though it must accept possible negative consequences. Grandison and Sloman [3] define trust related to a given context: "Trust is the firm belief in the competence of an entity to act dependably, securely, and reliably within a specified context." From these definitions it is clear that the area of trust is quite diverse and it is difficult to define a single, standard and general trust definition covering all possible aspects and scenarios.

Trust establishment is a process of creating trust between two entities. Winsborough [4] claims that the mainstream approaches presume that the entities already know each other. Two standard approaches are used: *Identity-based*, when an entity is authenticated based on its known identity and *capability-based*, when an entity possesses capabilities needed by the requester. However, this approach does not work well in open systems, e.g. online environments, where the entities are anonymous and their attributes are unknown. In this case, trust negotiation can be used. It belongs to the trust-based decision-model concept [7] and is a process of incrementally establishing trust by exchanging credentials, one by one between two entities. The exchange process continues until the required trust level is reached [4,5]. Credentials are private resources of an entity that contain sensitive information and can lead to identify the entity or to disclose facts about it. According to Winsborough [4] credentials or property-based digital credentials are the on-line analogues of paper credentials that people carry in their wallets. They appear to be well suited to establish trust in open systems. Credentials can also authenticate other entities, their properties and relationships. Yu et al. offer another definition [6], which states that digital credentials are verifiable, unforgeable digitally signed assertions. They are signed by a credential issuer about the properties of the parties mentioned in the credential. They can also contain a public key of one or more of the parties they mention, so these parties can prove that the credentials describe them.

Policies are defined in policy languages and they are essential for trust negotiation, because they control access to credentials and protect the security and privacy of entities. In many cases policy languages are implementation dependent and there are no standard metrics to analyse and evaluate the effectiveness of these languages or to compare them [11]. Further attempts to classify policy languages have been made. Kasem and Meier [10] present an overview of languages that are suitable for security and privacy. They classify their attributes into four main categories, such as *type, intention of use, scope* and *design and implementation details*. The work in [11] classifies policy languages into the following categories: *sophisticated access control languages, web privacy policy languages, enterprise privacy policy languages* and *context sensitive languages*. Seamons et al. [12] present a classification that is aimed at trust negotiation.

They propose many criteria that can be useful for trust negotiation, such as *credential combinations, sensitive policies, transitive closure* and so on. This work is similar to ours. The difference is that we chose different criteria for the language comparisons and we include more languages.

The first trust-based negotiation-model was TrustBuilder and TrustBuilder2 is its enhanced version [8,9]. Another trust-based negotiation-model is PROTUNE and it is rule-based [25]. Trust negotiation is classified as a sub-class of the trust-based decision-model concept [7]. The models can use various negotiating strategies. PROTUNE uses a cooperative default strategy, where all the relevant and releasable information are disclosed at each step. TrustBuilder allows the entities to choose the most suitable strategy for their needs. They can choose for example the eager or the parsimonious strategy [4].

This paper aims to identify trust negotiation criteria and to classify policy languages against them. Kasem and Meier classified PPL, A-PPL, P2U, PRML, SecPAL4P, XPref and XACML [13,14,16,17,21,24,27] as security or privacy languages, which makes them good candidates for the analysis. Seamons et al. chose for their classification of trust negotiation languages such as PSPL, TPL, X-Sec and the language of the KeyNote trust management system [28–31], which makes them also good candidates. The other languages that seem to be valid for trust negotiation, are PlexC, the language of the Cassandra trust management system, X-TNL, ASL and HiPoLDS [18–20,22,26]. In the following, the language of Cassandra and the language of KeyNote will be referred as Cassandra and KeyNote, respectively. All these languages have been selected, because they have proven useful for keeping privacy of entities, the appropriate access control handling or for other models of credentials exchange.

3   General Concepts of Trust Negotiation

Trust negotiation belongs to the trust-based decision-model concept that uses defined rules and policies to control access to credentials and resources [7]. It can be defined as a process of incrementally establishing trust by exchanging credentials between two entities, while they may be complete strangers to each other [4,5]. The entities share their credentials iteratively one by one. The first entity discloses one credential to the other one and thus builds a basic trust in the second entity and then the second entity discloses one credential to the first one achieving the same effect. The exchange process continues until the required trust level is reached.

The basic concept of the trust negotiation is depicted in Fig. 1. It shows two entities trying to establish trust in each other. Entity (1) requests a credential from another entity (2). If entity (2) is willing to do so, it discloses a credential to entity (1) and by this action entity (1) might be willing to disclose another credential to entity (2). This way the entities exchange their credentials and build up trust in each other. The negotiation process continues until the desired level of trust is reached and the entities are willing to disclose new credentials. Once sufficient trust has been built, the trust negotiation successfully terminates.

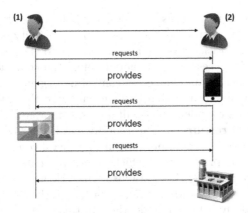

Fig. 1. Trust negotiation basic concept

If an entity is not willing to disclose more credentials, depending on the negotiation strategy, it may be asked to provide alternative credentials or the whole
negotiation process is terminated without being successful.

4 Trust Negotiation Criteria

The criteria are a set of requirements that will guide the whole process of trust
negotiation. We identified, analysed and collected the generally accepted requirements for trust negotiation from the literature. We were looking for the important criteria that are needed to accomplish or that can simplify the process of
establishing trust between two entities. The requirements are defined quite generally as they should cover wide areas that can be further divided and can be
mapped to diverse existing policy languages. Entities possess credentials and
various resources that may contain private and sensitive data. For that reason,
the requirements must ensure that the resources are protected and the conditions
under which they can be accessed must be clearly defined. A set of requirements
may form a policy that is a statement of intent to guide decisions and achieve
rational outcomes. Entities in trust negotiation must be able to specify their own
policies defining access to their private resources. For example, some negotiation
strategies, such as the eager strategy, use a concept of locked and unlocked credentials, where only the unlocked credentials can be disclosed and the locked
credentials may become unlocked after receiving new credentials from the other
entity [4]. The following requirements can be identified for trust negotiation:

- **Privacy of resources.** This is an important requirement of trust negotiation. An entity must be confident that access to its private data will not be
  abused. It should not be possible to obtain the protected resources through
  a swindle, e.g. by providing forged credentials. The private data must not be
  intentionally modified by a third party. The access policy itself can lead to
  facts about obtaining access to credentials, so it should be protected.

- **Access control to resources.** This requirement partially covers the need for privacy, which is natural as it comes from a proximity of this criterion to the previous one. Entities need to manage access to their private data, such as credentials. The access control should define the conditions under which resources can be accessed. The access control management should be simple but efficient enough and it should be transparent to the entity, so the entity can be sure that its confidentiality will not be compromised.
- **Usage control of resources.** This requirement is referred as usage control, however it is understood more broadly, like a general compliance. It partially covers the need for privacy too, which comes from its nature. As entities exchange their credentials, they establish trust. However, an entity may discover that the other one is not playing according to the rules, e.g. it is providing false information or forged credentials. In this case the entity may decide to stop the process of building trust and terminate the trust negotiation. The entity may mark the other one as a cheater and may refuse to cooperate with it in the future.
- **Exchange of resources.** This criterion is very important for trust negotiation and also for a policy language in order to allow definitions of policies suitable for the exchange process and to support trust negotiation efficiently. The principle of trust negotiation means to exchange credentials that are the private and confidential resources of their owning entities. An entity must be provided with a secure and straightforward way of passing its credentials to another entity. An entity may use credentials and certificates exchange with an authority to verify their authenticity.
- **Authority.** Trust negotiation may require access to an authority for the validation of credentials. In case of doubts during a trust negotiation, entities can independently communicate with a local or global authority where they can verify credentials provided from the other entity involved. The rejection of credentials has implications. The use of authorities is not mandatory for all scenarios in trust negotiation, however sometimes it can be very helpful.
- **Information granularity.** Credentials exchanged during trust negotiations may comprise various information levels. The information contained in a credential may be too detailed and for the actual needs it would be enough to disclose only a part or a more general, less detailed version. For example, rather than disclosing the exact location information by providing the GPS coordinates, the region or the city name would be provided instead. It may be useful to support information granularity for trust negotiation, because the credential confidentiality levels can be controlled during their disclosure and thus protect the security and privacy of their owner.
- **Context sensitivity.** Trust negotiation should take place in the context of an intended goal. Entities have diverse capabilities and they possess various skills in different fields. For this reason, the trust built is context-sensitive and it should only be used for the defined goal or for goal-related purposes.

– **Roles.** Roles are related to context sensitivity. Entities play various roles that may determine attributes of the entities and the purpose of the entity in trust negotiation. Roles can also determine the access control to the resources of an entity.

One of the most important requirements is the exchange of resources, which is implicit in the nature of trust negotiation, where credentials are exchanged between entities. Other important requirements are privacy of resources and access control to resources that handle privacy and protection of sensitive data. Context sensitivity is important too, if the intended trust relationship is considered to be established for a specific purpose. The rest of the requirements may enrich and simplify trust negotiation in specific scenarios.

5 Analysis of Policy Languages

The analysis of potentially suitable policy languages for trust negotiation is presented here. The languages were chosen if their attributes seemed to be helpful, e.g. they supported security or privacy. The languages will be analysed to classify their features and then these features will be checked against the trust negotiation criteria identified in Sect. 4. If a match is found with a particular criterion, the language is marked supporting trust negotiation.

5.1 Privacy of Resources

The maximum privacy preservation would be to not disclose any credentials or resources to anyone. This approach is not desirable as for trust negotiation information exchange is essential. Privacy preservation contradicts the requirement of exchanging resources. Therefore, it is important to find a trade-off between the two. To preserve privacy, it is important to disclose credentials sequentially and alternately, as they are received from the other negotiator. This approach is used by P2U [17], PlexC [18], Cassandra [19], X-TNL [20], HiPoLDS [26] and PSPL [28]. They can be configured to initially exchange fewer confidential credentials and as trust builds, more confidential ones are disclosed, thereby protecting privacy. However, we do not consider X-TNL, HiPoLDS and Cassandra to satisfy this privacy criterion as they neither explicitly provide any expressions of privacy policies nor include the preservation of privacy in their design. Other languages such as PPL [14], A-PPL [16], P2U, PlexC, XPref [21], SecPAL4P [24], PRML [27] and PSPL do support the definition of privacy policies. They can be used to define the accepted maximum confidentiality level and in that way control the exposure of credentials. Each language takes a different approach. Some languages, such as PPL, A-PPL, P2U and PRML use privacy specification elements, where policies express the privacy relationships among them. Other languages, such as XPref and SecPAL4P allow entities to specify their privacy preferences, which handle the way of treating their sensitive information by a service. PlexC ensures privacy by a minimisation of the over-exposure problem. When an entity reaches the desired acceptable exposure area, the credentials disclosure risk is minimised and its privacy is preserved. This provides the best approach for privacy, because it tries to keep the exposure within desired boundaries. This is also done through a given feedback, if the boundaries are exceeded. Other languages do not provide a feedback about privacy abuse. PSPL focuses on privacy preservation of clients and servers by avoiding unnecessary disclosures. The rest of the languages, such as XACML, ASL, TPL, X-Sec and KeyNote do not provide any privacy-preserving features.

5.2 Access Control to Resources

Access control is supported by all policy languages, because each one provides a data protection and an authorised access. This criterion is given by the nature and proposed operation of policy languages. Only credentials with a certain confidentiality level can be disclosed to preserve privacy and only to the authorised entity. The attribute-based access control (*ABAC*) is a basic one and is supported by XACML [13], PPL [14] and A-PPL [16]. These languages define access rights through attribute-combining policies with the use of Boolean logic and use triggers, which are events filtered by conditions, related to an obligation. This paradigm is suitable for defining disclosure policies with respect to negotiators. It combines entity attributes with Boolean logic to implement an exchange model. The values, such as the credential confidentiality level or a list/number of disclosed and received credentials should be defined. The role-based access control (*RBAC*) represents another approach to access control. Disclosure policies are defined based on the entities' roles. However, complete strangers may interact with each other and if they do not take on any roles, it is impossible to make control decisions based on them. The role-based access control is used by PRML, TPL and Cassandra, where entities are mapped into roles e.g. based on issued credentials by third parties. When an entity requests permission to perform an action, its role is checked against a policy in order to permit access. Yet another approach to access control are the privacy policies used by P2U, PlexC, XPref and SecPAL4P. Access to a sensitive resource is determined based on the entity's privacy preferences. They are highly suited to trust negotiation, because an entity can maintain its desired disclosure level to protect its privacy. KeyNote uses a compliance checker that controls the disclosure of credentials. The compliance checker is an appealing solution, because it handles the disclosure decisions on behalf of the entity. A similar approach is to use personalised access rights with respect to an authorised entity. PSPL defines a client-server access control, X-TNL uses disclosure and certificate policies, ASL defines policies and authorisations managing the access control decisions, HiPoLDS defines policy domains describing a global system architecture and X-Sec manages access control to web documents. The languages, such as PlexC, X-TNL, SecPAL4P, PSPL, TPL, X-Sec, Cassandra and KeyNote make use of authorities to handle access control decisions.

5.3   Usage Control of Resources

During trust negotiation, the entities involved exchange of credentials. The problem is that once credentials have been disclosed, their owner loses control over them. Access control policies define under which conditions credentials can be disclosed. Usage control policies specify how the disclosed credentials can be used by the recipient. Usage control policies are not mandatory for trust negotiation, however, they can improve an entity's privacy in the case that it obtains a credible feedback about its credentials usage. PlexC uses an *exposure control loop* that provides a periodical exposure feedback to entities about the conceded access paths to their resources and how they are being shared. This feedback is then used to adjust the entity policies over time in order to prevent over-exposure in the future. It is called exposure polymorphism [18]. Over-exposure is classed as when too many credentials are disclosed and their overall confidentiality is too high. PlexC may catch this situation and accordingly revise policies to prevent too many disclosures in a future trust negotiation. However, the exposure control is dynamic, non-trivial and some input values, such as the credential use after the disclosure, may be unknown. Therefore, PlexC tends to revise the policies continuously and to catch small changes in feedback. The rest of the languages neither control nor monitor credentials once they have been disclosed.

5.4   Exchange of Resources

Generally, policy languages supporting this criterion can be considered as usable for trust negotiation. The exchange of resources is a must for trust negotiation, because it is a given consequence of the process itself. Entities exchange credentials during trust negotiation and it is important that the exchange process is gradual and balanced to preserve privacy. Resources may be exchanged in large and distributed networks, such as the Internet. PlexC and Cassandra permit a trust negotiation scenario to be easily implemented in these networks. The languages, P2U, PlexC, Cassandra, X-TNL, HiPoLDS and PSPL are suitable for trust negotiation, because they allow rules for credentials exchange to be defined and controlled. Credentials are exchanged sequentially and alternately, which ensures a balanced privacy exposure of both parties. Each language can be used with a negotiation strategy that handles the exchange process, calculates the established trust from the credentials received and controls the disclosure of credentials based on their confidentiality. The strategy is not defined in the language itself, but rather in the system using the language. The Cassandra trust management system uses a strategy similar to the "Parsimonious Strategy" [4]. It handles the exchange process itself through agents thereby removing this responsibility from the user. PlexC and Cassandra are designed to process trust negotiations in large networks, which introduces security and privacy issues. PlexC reduces them by the over-exposure control and Cassandra follows well-defined conditions, defined by the local access control policies. The languages, P2U, HiPoLDS and PSPL use a different approach to exchange resources. P2U facilitates a user data sharing and negotiation over various applications, HiPoLDS uses reference monitors to control the exchange process among policy domains and PSPL exchanges credentials and declarations between clients and servers. The rest of the languages, XACML, PPL, A-PPL, XPref, ASL, SecPAL4P, PRML, TPL, X-Sec and KeyNote do not support this criterion and thus are not suitable for trust negotiation. However, TPL is extensible and provides other suitable criteria for trust negotiation, such as access control, authority and roles, so it could be extended to include this criterion.

5.5   Authority

Trust negotiation may require the presence of one or more authorities. A trusted certification authority serves to issue and verify credentials, which, in turn makes the negotiators more confident about the credentials' authenticity. A general authority is referred as it may stand for different types of authorities, however, the analysed languages do not specify the exact type of a certification authority. It is supported by a few languages, such as X-TNL, SecPAL4P, PSPL, TPL and X-Sec. This is the basic use of authority and it can be helpful for entities involved in trust negotiation to verify the validity and the genuineness of credentials. X-TNL, TPL and X-Sec allow authorities to be organised into categories. In X-TNL and X-Sec, credentials and declarations form certificates that are collected into X-Profiles. TPL organises certificates into certification profiles and is able to automatically collect missing certificates from peer servers. Some languages, such as PlexC, SecPAL4P, Cassandra and KeyNote support a delegation of trusted decisions or actions, where the trustee can act on behalf of the trustor. These languages are designed for large decentralised networks, such as the Internet. Delegation of authority is useful here, because the requester and the authoriser may not have established a trust relationship. A disclosure decision of a trustor may be inspired by a disclosure decision of a trustee. The delegation of authority, trusted decisions or actions is also suitable for trust negotiation, because it allows entities to delegate disclosure decisions to trusted parties, such as security agents. The Cassandra trust management system uses trusted agents to control the credentials exchange process. These agents take responsibility for actions and decisions that are delegated to them by trustors. The rest of the policy languages, XACML, PPL, A-PPL, P2U, XPref, ASL, HiPoLDS and PRML do not support this criterion.

5.6   Information Granularity

Credentials possess various confidentiality levels depending on, for example, their importance. When a credential is disclosed, its owner's privacy is automatically compromised, as far as the confidentiality allows. PlexC allows information about an entity to be disclosed with different accuracy levels. The degree of information provided can be defined by policies. For example, an entity can provide its precise position with GPS coordinates, or less accurately by disclosing only a region or a city name. Additionally, rules can be defined based on the current time or location. For example, the access to resources can be permitted, only when the entity is located in a certain region or for a certain period of time. Data can be shared with more or less precision so as to preserve privacy. PlexC may revise the disclosure policies to provide less precise and therefore less confidential information, when the entity during trust negotiation reaches the over-exposure area. The revision of policies is controlled by PlexC automatically. The rest of the languages do not explicitly support any form of different accuracy levels. They understand credentials disclosure as a binary operation, so a credential is either disclosed completely or not at all. If an entity wants to provide less confidential information, it must do so for itself e.g. by dividing the credential into parts.

5.7 Context Sensitivity

Entities that want to establish trust with each other, do so to accomplish a common goal, for a specific purpose. Each entity possesses different knowledge, abilities, skills and resources, for which the entity can be trusted to successfully participate in reaching the goal. The entity might not be trusted for another purpose, because different attributes would be required. Therefore, trust negotiation examines important attributes for the intended purpose, for which the entity can be trusted. One approach is to define purpose-dependant conditions, under which credentials can be shared or disclosed. This is the case of PPL, A-PPL, P2U, PlexC and XPref. On the other hand, PRML defines such conditions in order to control data operations, i.e. what operation on which data can be performed. This approach is more general, because it allows an entity to define its own purpose-dependant data operations. All these languages allow the purpose for the credentials exchange to be defined during the trust negotiation. If a credential is demanded for a different purpose then this is specified in the disclosure policy and the access may be denied. Concretely, PPL and A-PPL define authorisation types that can use resources only for a particular set of purposes, P2U uses the *purpose-relevance-sharing* principle, where only the relevant resources to the specific purpose and context of use are shared, PlexC defines context-dependant policies that influence the access traces to private data and XPref and PRML specify a purpose object for the same reasons. Unlike the others, PPL and A-PPL allow a hierarchy of the purpose elements to be created, so that Boolean logic can be applied to them, which improves and simplifies the purpose-relevant access decisions. For example, the parent-purpose element may specify that a credential may be disclosed only for establishing trust and its child-purpose element may specify in which context. The credential will be disclosed if both of the conditions are satisfied. Some languages, such as A-PPL, P2U and XPref, allow a retention value to be defined, which specifies the duration of access to a resource. This feature improves security and privacy of the resource owner. After the defined time period, the resource will be deleted. The rest of the languages are not context sensitive and do not allow purpose-relevant conditions to be specified.

5.8 Roles

As mentioned earlier, entities take part in trust negotiations to reach a common goal. Only those entities with suitable attributes become trusted to accomplish it. Entities may take on roles that are associated with their attributes, e.g. a certain role requires that an entity possesses certain features. These roles can be specified by some languages, such as XACML, PPL, A-PPL, PlexC, ASL, HiPoLDS, PRML, TPL and Cassandra. Some of them, such as XACML, PPL and A-PPL already contain some specific, predefined roles that entities can have and that control access to their resources. However, all these languages allow entities to define a new role and to perform a particular action based on it. In PlexC, roles can be assigned to a group with given permissions, which simplifies the permission management and is useful for large networks. Cassandra supports auxiliary roles that can express some attributes of their owner and can be used without an active role. HiPoLDS defines roles by assigning policy domain attributes to policy domains representing entities. PlexC, TPL and Cassandra can use an authority to issue and verify certificates about the assigned roles. The languages, ASL, PRML and Cassandra can form a hierarchy of roles. This enables a role combination to be easily defined in order to perform an action or disclose a credential. As occurs for the context sensitivity, Boolean logic is applied when forming the hierarchy of the roles. PRML allows a role to extend over multiple other roles and to inherit their permissions. Unlike the others, Cassandra supports a role retention, which means that a role validity period can be defined. After its expiration the role is no longer valid and in consequence, obtaining credentials during trust negotiation can be refused. This feature improves the security and privacy of negotiators.

5.9 Analysis Summary

After the policy languages analysis is performed in Sect. 5 we can summarise our findings in Table 1. A partially supported criterion is defined as a criterion that was found as a secondary effect of other criteria supported by the language, but was not explicitly mentioned in the literature nor its presence was intended or designed by the authors of the language.

Each of the languages was originally designed to solve another type of problem. Some of them already included some form of trust negotiation in their design, such as P2U, PlexC, X-TNL, HiPoLDS, PSPL and Cassandra. The best one for trust negotiation seems to be PlexC, as it is the only one to support all of the identified criteria in Sect. 4. PlexC takes an interesting approach. It introduces the exposure control problem and claims that there is an area of acceptable exposure. Entities try to eliminate the over-exposure of their data and tend to transform it into the most acceptable exposure that does not expose them to a major risk. For trust negotiation this means that only a minimal set of credentials will be disclosed to reach the required level of trust. The other highly recommended languages are P2U and Cassandra. P2U focuses on the purpose of data sharing, so the context is important. It simply defines the data provider,

Table 1. Supported trust negotiation criteria'

Language	Privacy of resources	Access control to resources	Usage control of resources	Exchange of resources	Authority	Information granularity	Context sensitivity	Roles
XACML		×						×
PPL	×	×					×	×
A-PPL	×	×					×	×
P2U	×	×		×			×	
PlexC	×	×	×	×	×	×	×	×
Cassandra	*	×		×	×			×
X-TNL	*	×		×	×			
Xpref	×	×					×	
ASL		×						×
SecPAL4P	×	×			×			
HiPoLDS	*	×		×				×
PRML	×	×					×	×
PSPL	×	×		×	×			
TPL		×			×			×
X-Sec		×			×			
KeyNote		×			×			

Legend: (×): supported
(*): partially supported

the data consumer and the relevant policies for the data exchange. Cassandra acts as a local service and it is completely decentralised. It supports roles and actions that are performed over these roles. In this way each entity has total control over its resources and policies in trust negotiation.

The languages, X-TNL, HiPoLDS, PSPL and TPL support the criteria only partially. They can be used for a special or simple case of trust negotiation, but they lack its general support. All the languages except TPL support the exchange of resources, which is essential. TPL supports access control, authority and roles, but can be further extended to the exchange of resources. X-TNL although originally designed for trust negotiation, lacks some criteria, such as roles, context sensitivity and partial privacy of resources. HiPoLDS and PSPL were designed for different purposes, but their capabilities could also be used for trust negotiation. PSPL is an expressive and extendible language. The remainder of the languages, XACML, PPL, A-PPL, XPref, ASL, SecPAL4P, PRML, X-Sec and KeyNote serve specific purposes that are not concerned with trust negotiation. XACML is an attribute-based access control system, PPL and A-PPL are extensions over XACML with data handling and protection capabilities, XPref and SecPAL4P serve for users to define their privacy preferences, PRML merges the corporate privacy policies and the data handling policies, ASL serves for expressing authorisations, X-Sec protects web documents and KeyNote handles authorisations in decentralised environments.

6 Conclusion

In this paper we have analysed policy languages to check their suitability for trust negotiation. In order to do so, we have first identified the following criteria: privacy of resources, access control to resources, usage control of resources, exchange of resources, authority, information granularity, context sensitivity and roles. We believe them to be quite a complete list of general criteria for trust negotiation regardless that they can be refined in the future for specific purposes.

Then, the policy languages have been analysed against them. From this analysis, it has emerged that only PlexC is fully suited for trust negotiation. PlexC was found to be the only one from all the languages analysed that supports all of the identified criteria for trust negotiation. Due to its completeness and flexibility, PlexC is a good candidate to be used in the Internet of Things (IoT) trust negotiation scenarios.

A subset of the chosen languages were suitable in part, because they generally support the exchange of resources, but lack the other possible criteria demanded by trust negotiation. The rest of the languages are not suitable, because they lack the essential criterion for trust negotiation, which is the exchange of resources and other possibly important requirements too.

In the future work, the identified criteria will be divided into more fine-grained criteria, if needed for specific purposes, that could match the analysed policy languages more precisely. The current criteria are quite broad, so it is a good idea to make another identification of more specialised criteria important or useful for trust negotiation. They will form a subclass of the currently identified criteria. In addition, other criteria although not directly related to trust negotiation could be taken into consideration, such as the languages syntax and user-friendliness.

Acknowledgements. This research has been supported by the European project "European Network for Cyber-security (NECS)" - the European Unions Horizon 2020 research and innovation programme under the Marie Sklodowska-Curie grant agreement No. 675320 and the Spanish Ministry of Economy and FEDER through the project PRECISE (TIN2014-54427-JIN).

References

1. Gambetta, D.: Can We Trust Trust? Gambetta, D. (ed.) Trust: Making and Breaking Cooperative Relations, pp. 213–238. B. Blackwell, Oxford (1990)
2. Jøsang, A., Ismail, R., Boyd, C.: A Survey of trust and reputation systems for online service provision. Decis. Support Syst. **43**, 618–644 (2007)
3. Grandison, T., Sloman, M.: A survey of trust in internet applications. Commun. Surveys Tuts. (2000)
4. Winsborough, W.H., Seamons, K.E., Jones, V.E.: Automated trust negotiation. In: DARPA Information Survivability Conference and Exposition, DISCEX 2000, Proceedings, vol. 1, pp. 88–102 (2000)

5. Winsborough, W.H., Li, N.: Towards practical automated trust negotiation. In: Proceedings Third International Workshop on Policies for Distributed Systems and Networks, pp. 92–103 (2002)
6. Yu, T., Winslett, M.: A unified scheme for resource protection in automated trust negotiation. In: 2003 Symposium on Security and Privacy, pp. 110–122 (2003)
7. Moyano, F.: Trust engineering framework for software services. Ph.D. thesis, Lenguajes y Ciencias de la Computacin, Universidad de Mlaga (2015)
8. Winslett, M., Yu, T., Seamons, K.E., Hess, A., Jacobson, J., Jarvis, R., Smith, B., Yu, L.: Negotiating trust in the web. IEEE Internet Comput. 6(6), 30–37 (2002)
9. Lee, A.J., Winslett, M., Perano, K.J.: TrustBuilder2: a recongurable framework for trust negotiation. No. SAND2007-1928C. Sandia National Laboratories (SNL-CA), Livermore, CA (United States) (2007)
10. Kasem-Madani, S., Meier, M.: Security and privacy policy languages: a survey, categorization and gap identification. arXiv preprint arXiv:1512.00201 (2015)
11. Kumaraguru, P., et al.: A survey of privacy policy languages. In: Workshop on Usable IT Security Management (USM 07): Proceedings of the 3rd Symposium on Usable Privacy and Security. ACM (2007)
12. Seamons, K.E., et al.: Requirements for policy languages for trust negotiation. In: 2002 IEEE Proceedings of the Third International Workshop on Policies for Distributed Systems and Networks (2002)
13. Parducci, B., Lockart, H.: eXtensible Access Control Markup Language (XACML) 3.0. Committee Specification 01, 10 August 2010
14. Ardagna, C.A., et al.: Primelife policy language. In: W3C Workshop on Access Control Application Scenarios. W3C (2009)
15. Trabelsi, S., et al.: PPL engine: a symmetric architecture for privacy policy handling. In: W3C Workshop on Privacy and Data Usage Control, vol. 4, no. 5 (2010)
16. Azraoui M., et al.: A-PPL: an accountability policy language. In: Garcia-Alfaro, J., et al. (eds.) DPM/QASA/SETOP -2014. LNCS, vol. 8872, pp. 319–326. Springer, Cham (2015). https://doi.org/10.1007/978-3-319-17016-9_21
17. Iyilade, J., Vassileva, J.: P2U: a privacy policy specification language for secondary data sharing and usage. In: 2014 IEEE Security and Privacy Workshops (2014)
18. Gall, Y.L., Lee, A.J., Kapadia, A.: PlexC: a policy language for exposure control. In: Proceedings of the 17th ACM Symposium on Access Control Models and Technologies (2012)
19. Becker, M.Y., Sewell, P.: Cassandra: distributed access control policies with tunable expressiveness. In: Fifth IEEE International Workshop on Policies for Distributed Systems and Networks, POLICY 2004, Proceedings. IEEE (2004)
20. Bertino, E., Ferrari, E., Squicciarini, A.: X-TNL: an XML-based language for trust negotiations. In: Proceedings POLICY 2003, IEEE 4th International Workshop on Policies for Distributed Systems and Networks (2003)
21. Agrawal, R., Kiernan, J., Srikant, R., Xu, Y.: XPref: a preference language for P3P. Computer Networks (2005)
22. Jajodia, S., Samarati, P., Subrahmanian, V.S.: A logical language for expressing authorizations. In: Proceedings, 1997 IEEE Symposium on Security and Privacy (Cat. No. 97CB36097) (1997)
23. Clark, J., DeRose, S.: XML Path Language (XPath) Version 1.0. W3C Recommendation (1999)
24. Berker, M.Y., Malkis, A., Bussard, L.: A Framework for Privacy Preferences and Data-Handling Policies. Technical Report MSR-TR-2009-128 (2009)
25. Bonatti, P.A., De Coi, J.L., Olmedilla, D., Sauro, L.: A rule-based trust negotiation system. IEEE Trans. Knowl. Data Eng. 22(11), 1507–1520 (2010)

26. Dell'Amico, M., et al.: HiPoLDS: A Hierarchical Security Policy Language for Distributed Systems. Inf. Secur. Tech. Rep. **17**, 81–92 (2013)
27. PRML: Privacy Rights Markup Language Specification Version 0.9. Zero-Knowledge Systems (2001)
28. Bonatti, P., Samarati, P.: Regulating service access and information release on the web. In: 7th ACM Conference on Computer and Communications Security, Athens, Greece, November 2000
29. Herzberg, A., Mass, Y., Mihaeli, J., Naor, D., Ravid, Y.: Access control meets public key infrastructure, or: assigning roles to strangers. In: Proceeding 2000 IEEE Symposium on Security and Privacy, S&P 2000, Berkeley, CA, pp. 2–14 (2000)
30. Bertino, E., Castano, S., Ferrari, E.: On specifying security policies for web documents with an XML-based language. In: Sixth ACM SACMAT, Chantilly, Virginia (2001)
31. Blaze, M., Feigenbaum, J., Ioannidis, J., Keromytis, A.: The KeyNote Trust-Management System Version 2. RFC 2704, September 1999

Role of Apps in Undoing of Privacy Policies on Facebook

Vishwas T. Patil$^{(\boxtimes)}$, Nivia Jatain, and R. K. Shyamasundar

Information Security R&D Center,
Department of Computer Science and Engineering,
Indian Institute of Technology Bombay, Mumbai 400076, India
ivishwas@gmail.com, jatain.nivia@gmail.com, shyamasundar@gmail.com

Abstract. Facebook allows its users to specify privacy settings for the information they share with other users and Apps. Apps seek a set of permissions from the user at the time of installation. There is no check that is performed to evaluate any possible adverse implications of App's permissions on the *in-force* privacy settings of an user. In this paper, we have investigated Facebook's platform for access to users' data by Apps and Advertisers. By signing up with Facebook, users implicitly trust the platform, which they believe can be held accountable in case of a breach. However, similar expectation of accountability from Apps is hard to imagine and difficult to ensure. At times, Apps have as much access to user data as Facebook and such a common access to user data undermines provenance of data leakage. Recently, though Facebook has reduced the extent of data access for Apps by deprecating certain APIs, a systematic design approach is missing for platform-wide access policy specification and conformance. We have presented several scenarios where App permissions are violating user privacy policies. Our findings have been presented with the help of experiments using Facebook Developer Platform.

Keywords: Social network · Privacy · Linkability

1 Introduction

Facebook is the largest social network. Maintaining 1.5 billion daily active users, their connections and updates in real-time is a tremendous engineering feat. However, it appears that the guiding principles in the evolution of Facebook's data platform have been: real-time response [2] and features to users, app developers, and advertisers. The recent revelations [3] have forced Facebook to acknowledge that data privacy is an important *feature!* The platform's design choices, for speed and features, will hinder it from coherently enforcing privacy policies anytime soon in the near future.

© IFIP International Federation for Information Processing 2018
Published by Springer International Publishing AG, part of Springer Nature 2018. All Rights Reserved
F. Kerschbaum and S. Paraboschi (Eds.): DBSec 2018, LNCS 10980, pp. 85–98, 2018.
https://doi.org/10.1007/978-3-319-95729-6_6

Facebook's platform allows users to establish and organize their relationships with other users using social relationship categories like "Friends", "Close Friends", "Family", etc. An update in user's personal life is more relevant to members of "Family" than "Friends" and the platform does such a prioritization intelligently. Similarly, among the categories of relationships further prioritization of updates is done based on the interests of the users that are at the other end of the connection. That is, a friend from school falls in sub-category school and likewise a friend from university. Furthermore, friends from school who have interest in history are distinguished from the friends who have interest in finance. Such a segmentation of categories helps the platform to build relevant audiences for a user's updates. Users are given a control to decide which segment should see what updates. Facebook organizes all these information about its users and their interactions as a graph – called social graph. Users (nodes) are free to form new relationship (edge) and update the old ones. Social graph is a continuously evolving graph and this type of organization of users and their data helps Facebook in segmenting users with similar interests so that they can be introduced to a new post or an advertisement.

Facebook platform allows developers to write Apps, which users can install. An App serves a specific function to its users. When a user installs an App (represented by an edge between the App and the user on social graph), it signifies that user's interest in the functionality provided by that App. Thus, users get a functional convenience and Facebook automatically gets contextual insights about users. Both, the App and the platform will have an access to users' interactions within the administrative sphere of the App. Facebook can build an accurate context about an user than an App because it has other insights about the user. Thus an App, through its functional category, helps the platform to segment users in a specific category so that it can be used in profiling the users. For example, a flower delivery App can help identify users who are single, male, within a specific geographical area, and who have purchased flowers last year on Valentine's day. In order to build audiences of such type, Facebook needs to build, maintain a detailed profile for each of its users. Higher the interactions of a user, richer the profile. Connectivity and interactions are important objectives of the platform, and Facebook does it very well in its ecosystem of users, Apps, content and interactions among them. This ecosystem of interacting nodes is depicted as a pyramid, in Fig. 2), to highlight their access privileges (either explicit or implicit) on the platform. Each layer (user layer, app layer, advertisement layer) serves a different purpose and has a different access control mechanism to control access to users' information. In [21], we have analyzed privacy claims of the platform at the user level alone. In this paper, we analyze conformance of user privacy settings in the presence of Apps. **We will show that there is no coherence in policy enforcement across the layers, which undermines the privacy of its users.** We have validated our observations through experiments on Facebook's developer platform v2.12 and Facebook Audience Network. While Facebook does profiling of users for varieties of reasons, one of the trusting factors of Facebook is that it shall not divulge intentionally or for price the data that violates its committed privacy setting with its users. However, this cannot be said about the app developers or the advertisers on the app. Thus, our findings show the challenges to plug the leaks, due to apps/advertisers, Facebook should undertake.

In the following section, we present the somewhat hybrid, ad-hoc nature of access control mechanisms employed by Facebook. In Sect. 3, we analyze the platform and trace the flow of user information beyond the layers of its policy sphere. In Sect. 4, we present a few scenarios where defined privacy settings of a user are violated due to Apps. Section 5 discusses related work followed by conclusion in Sect. 6.

2   Access Control in Facebook

At the different layers of the platform, Facebook employs different types of access control mechanisms. At the user layer, user content and user attributes are protected by a discretionary access control. At the App layer, user content and user attributes are protected by capability lists. The other entities of the platform are not governed by any policy that user can influence. Also, the metadata the platform collects about user is not controlled by the user in any way. The platform organizes all of its entities and content in a graph, which has a sub-graph that can be traversed by users/Apps according to their respective permissions. The platform owner can traverse the whole graph without any restriction and acts as a proxy to its collaborators (the advertisers).

Social Graph - Reachability as the Condition for Access: Social graph in Facebook is a representation of user information on Facebook. Two user nodes have an edge between them if the users are friends with each other. Having an edge between two nodes establishes connectivity between them and in turn extends their reachability: that is, a user can access posts of her friend because there is a path present on the graph between the user and her friend's post via the friend node. Now, if the user likes her friend's post, this will be reflected in the social graph by putting an edge of type like between the user and her friend's post. Thus, each and every action or event created by Facebook's users is consumed by the social graph. The graph continuously changes its state reflecting its users' actions and interactions. Updates to social graph happen by adding/deleting nodes (or updating fields of nodes), and adding/deleting/updating the labelled edges – all such updates are due to a user's and app's *interactions* with their reachable nodes. Passive nodes like posts, photos, et al., do not interact on their own. Social graph also allows its nodes to be queried [21]. A user is allowed to compose a query by specifying a particular node (of type *root* [8]) about which the requester needs information. It is very likely that different sets of information about a node are presented based on who the requester is.

Lists as Access Policies for Users: Each user is provided with pre-defined relationship categories, called lists, along which users organize their relationships with others. Then there is a category of lists that Facebook creates for a user based on her social affiliations. And a user is also allowed to create and manage her own private lists. Given below is a typical set of labels provided to express access control policies:

- Only Me: is a label/list in which user herself is the only member
- Public: is a label, when used, the associated object is accessible publicly
- Friends: is the primary list under which all friendship relations are enlisted
- Restricted: is a list of friends to whom only Public labelled information is allowed
- Family: is a list of friends who are assigned as family members
- Close Friends: is a list of friends who are assigned as close friends
- Acquaintances: is a list of friends who are assigned as acquaintances
- Friends of friends: list of users who have friendship relation with "Friends"
- *University*: is a social list of friends who are also members of Smart List *University*
- *School*: is a social list of friends who are also members of Smart List *School*
- *Cycling*: is a Private List to which user has assigned a set of friends
- Custom: is a custom policy constructed using the label types described above.

Access control of objects in Facebook is a simple check on associated list's membership. If a requester of an object is a member of the list with which the object is protected, the requester gets access. Tagging is a positive exception to the membership check. There are two negative exceptions to the membership check: "Restricted" list and "Blocked" list. If a requester of an object is member of one of these lists, access is denied even when the requester is member of the list with which the object is protected.

In Fig. 1, User2 can reach & access Post1 because there is a path and the access policy for Post1 is set as *friends* by its owner User1. Therefore, User2 could interact with Post1 by *like* action. User1 & User2 can access Post3 because User1 is a *friend of friend* of User3 and User2 is *friend* of User3. Post2 cannot be accessed by User1 because the custom policy allows access to all

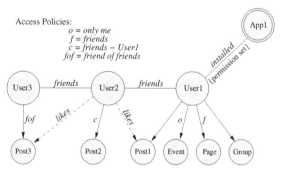

Fig. 1. Reachability and access in social graph of Facebook

friends of User2 except User1. The Event created by User1 cannot be accessed by anyone except User1 because the access policy is *only me*. Thus, labels or lists are used to control access to the content owned/posted by Facebook users.

Capabilities as Access Policies for Apps: Facebook Apps too are represented by nodes on social graph. However, Apps' traverse-ability on the social graph is limited to the immediate neighborhood of the user node consisting only the object nodes. In other words, the App can neither reach the friends of the user nor the other Apps installed by that user. What interactions the App can do in the user's neighborhood is determined by the set of permissions the user has allowed at the time of establishing the *installed* relationship with the user. There are 48 such permissions an App can obtain from its user. This is similar to capability lists in access control paradigm [16]. In later sections we shall discuss which of these permissions to an App undermines user's privacy.

The utility of social graph is not limited to representation of subjects, objects and their relationship but to also provide real-time updates about the changes in the neighborhood of the subject. Prioritization of updates according to their relevancy to a user based on users' past interactions on social graph is handled by NewsFeed algorithm; a core function of Facebook platform. How the App ecosystem helps it in achieving precision is explained below along with the other important components of platform.

3 Architecture of Facebook Platform

Figure 3 gives a schematic architecture of Facebook platform depicting the relationships between the major entities of this platform. In the following we describe the entities and their functionalities. The platform is logically divided into two: public space & private space. The entities in public space are the users and applications. They are said to be in public space because, having an account on Facebook, these types of nodes can query and interact among each other based on the access policies. Though the entities from private space can influence and have a richer view of the graph topology, they cannot perform any of the operations available to nodes in public space without being a node in the public space. Figure 2 depicts the access-hierarchy in the social graph of Facebook. The primary objective of the platform is to build accurate user profiles (behavioral, psychometric, etc.) so that advertisers can be accurately matched to their audience. The platform has been quite successful in micro-targeting users in real-time so that it artificially puts limits on advertisers while building their target audiences. An advertiser cannot compose a target audience whose size is less than 100. Similarly, an advertiser cannot request audience-tracking for audience size less than 100. To understand the design of this platform let us describe the role and functionality of its individual entities.

NewsFeed: Facebook has an intelligent algorithm to prioritize the updates to a user, which is called News-Feed. If we assume that each object/content on the social graph has a category type associated with it, like: education, finance, food, sarcasm, celebrity, etc., then a subject's interaction with these objects

Fig. 2. Access-hierarchy in the social graph

determine the probability of interest the subject may have in such categories. Each interaction of a subject with its neighborhood node improves the confidence level of subject-category mapping. The objective of NewsFeed algorithm is to increase subjects' interaction with varying categories [11] of content so that a rich user profile can be built. Such a user profile is necessary to determine relevancy of updates to the user and also to match the user with an advertiser interested in particular category [22]. If we assume the nodes in the graph are labelled with categories and edges are weighted proportional to the confidence level of the category, then we can think of an *influence* function over two nodes. A node with higher confidence value influences the confidence value of its peer. Thus the utility of NewsFeed function is incite the user to interact with content from its neighborhood and also from other influential nodes with whom the user does not have relationship (either *friend* or *follow*) yet. Higher the engagement of the user, more are the interaction, and thus higher the confidence value to categorize the user.

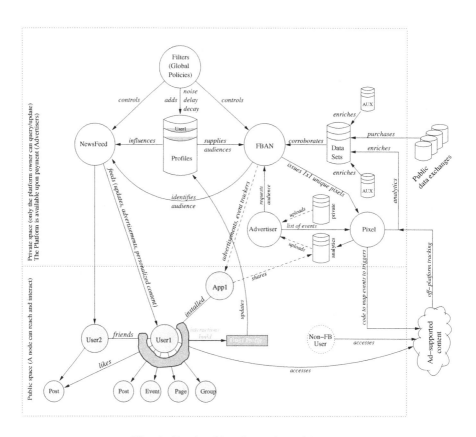

Fig. 3. Facebook's schematic architecture

Users: Users are the largest part of the platform. Their *interactions* within their reachable neighborhood and with the nodes introduced by the NewsFeed builds their individual user profiles. Users interactions with content outside the platform also helps in building the profile.

Apps: The platform gives a general purpose connectivity and interaction mechanism to the users, whereas the Apps give a context to user profile. Apps serves a specific functionality (e.g., finance, education, dating, et al.) to its users and that functionality is a stronger measure to categorize users. Apps can opt for monetization of their functionality by serving advertisements to the users via the App. Apps obtain analytics over their users interactions. The analytics information contains attributes (like mobile advertisement ID, Facebook UID, email, phone, Device info, location, etc.) that can uniquely measure interactions of App users. To advertise itself, or to persuade its existing users the App may share its analytics with advertisers to target the existing and new users.

Advertisers: Advertisers are the paid interfaces to the platform's ability to find precise audiences for a specific category/issue. Advertisers build advertisement campaigns by requesting specific audience type from the platform against a fee. To build the audience request, advertisers upload data fields that are compared against the user profiles that are built by the platform. Upon evaluating the scope of campaign targeting based on the uploaded data by the advertiser, the platform either accepts or rejects the request. Advertisers are allowed to micro-target a specific audience that is already engaged with it. Advertisers do so by defining events inside the Apps and trigger actions via Pixel for those events' realization. For example, list of users who have browsed a product but did not checkout.

Pixel: It is a micro-targeting framework https://fb.com/business/learn/facebook-ads-pixel that uniquely identifies users of the platform and also the users off-the-platform. This is a script that generates a unique tracking number each time a defined event occurs. The events could be as simple as loading a website or a user selecting a product in her cart. The unique number concatenated with cookie at user side tracks the user event by event. These user behavior analytics are shared by the platform with the advertisers so that advertisers can measure the impact of their advertising campaigns.

FBAN: Facebook Audience Network (https://fb.com/audiencenetwork) is the core component of the platform and has access to users profiles generated by the platform. It has its own data-set that is built from user tracking (analytics) and other associated platforms' meta-data information (like WhatsApp, Messenger, Instagram). It accepts audience requests from advertisers and based on the corroboration with its data-sets and user profiles, it identifies the target audience for a campaign. There exist public data-exchanges for user information, which can help enriching the profile attributes of users that come in contact with the platform.

Profiles: All individual user profiles are further enriched and attributed by the insights obtained from platform analytics and plausibly external public/private data-sets [5] (For Indian users, Facebook tried to link their Aadhaar numbers with their profiles. Aadhaar numbers are not secret but are used in various financial and public services delivery).

Filters: These determine the general access policy of the platform. For example, Facebook recently decided not to allow querying of its users (nodes) by their email/phone. This is also responsible for guiding the behavior of the platform in general. For example, to suppress a specific category of nodes appearing in the NewsFeed. Facebook had made an understanding with a large government (Project Colorful Balloons) to ensure a specific category of nodes is identified, tracked and controlled.

Having understood the roles various entities play in the Facebook ecosystem and keeping in mind those entities' access hierarchy, the question we ask is the following:

Assuming users explicitly trust Facebook to handle their private data against the free services, and assuming that Facebook desensitizes user data before making use of it for advertisement: what privacy & leakage assurances can we expect from the platform?

As Apps are only loosely coupled with the ecosystem as compared to the other entities in the ecosystem, it is difficult to assume that (smaller) Apps will strive for achieving the same level of trust with users as Facebook *may* have. In the following we present a few scenarios in which Apps violate users' privacy settings. In [21], we have presented whether Facebook users really preserve their privacy as they understand it or certain of their innocuous actions leak information contrary to their privacy settings. We would like to list those findings (at user-object layer of the platform) here:

1. Nonrestrictive change in policy of an object risks privacy of others,
2. Restrictive change in policy of an object suspends other's privileges,
3. "Share" operation is privacy-preserving,
4. Policy composition using intensional labels is not privacy-preserving,
5. "Like", "Comment" operations are not privacy-preserving.

In this paper, we extended the scope of our investigation to higher layers in the platform: that is, App layer and advertiser layer.

4   Experimental Scenarios of Access by Apps

In this section we list out our experiments using apps and advertisement facility of Facebook and highlight their potential in undermining user's privacy and security. The experiments are carried out using Facebook APIs (v2.12) and our findings are reproducible as of April 13, 2018. This sort of gap analysis in privacy policy conformance across platform is ignored [7], and precisely due to the lack of a platform-wide, coherent, privacy policy enforcement, rouge apps are tracking and siphoning off user data.

4.1   App Finds Out User's Friends

Facebook has deprecated Apps to access its user's friend list. Consider a scenario as shown in Fig. 4, in which Alice has set her list of friends to private in her privacy settings. This setting sets an expectation that Alice's friend list will not be available to others. Alice installs App1 with permission **user_posts**. This permission allows App1 to reach all of Alice's posts and their fields (comments, reactions, post privacy settings). Figure 5 is the list of posts retrieved by App1 from Alice's timeline. Figure 6 shows

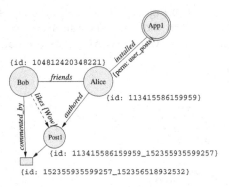

Fig. 4. Scenario: Alice has installed App1. Bob is Alice's friend

the retrieval of comment & reaction on the first post in the list shown in Fig. 5. Facebook's NewsFeed function presents updates from Alice's timeline to her friends (Bob). When a friend interacts with the post, App1 can observe it and deduce with high probability that Bob is Alice's friend. The probability of such an inference is 1 when Alice has given App1 permission to post with post's access policy as "Friends". Similarly, depending on post's permission policy setting, App1 can reason about Family et al.

```
data:Array(7)
0:{message: "Test post for comment",
   created_time: "2018-04-12T10:34:40+0000",
   id: "113415586159959_152355935599257"}
1:{message: "Post by TestApp",
   created_time: "2018-04-12T06:47:07+0000",
   id: "113415586159959_152253442276173"}
2:{message: "Vtp",
   created_time: "2018-04-10T08:29:11+0000",
   id: "113415586159959_150842215750629"}
3:{message: "Modified Post",
   created_time: "2018-04-07T07:14:44+0000",
   id: "113415586159959_148447715990079"}
4:{message: "test post",
   created_time: "2018-04-03T08:21:11+0000",
   id: "113415586159959_145280909640093"}
5:{message: "Test post for Comments",
   created_time: "2018-03-20T04:16:11+0000",
   id: "113415586159959_133157927519058"}
6:{message: "Test post for Alice",
   created_time: "2018-03-20T04:15:24+0000",
   id: "113415586159959_133157680852416"}
length:7
```

```
data:Array(1)
 0:
    created_time:"2018-04-12T10:36:14+0000"
    from:
     id:"104812420348221"
     name:"Bob Greenewitz"
     __proto__:Object
    id:"152355935599257_152356518932532"
    message:"Test comment by Bob"
    __proto__:Object
 length:1

data:Array(1)
 0:
    id:"104812420348221"
    name:"Bob Greenewitz"
    type:"WOW"
    __proto__:Object
 length:1
```

Fig. 5. List of posts retrieved by App1 from Alice's timeline

Fig. 6. Retrieval of comment & reaction on the first post in the list shown in Fig. 5

4.2   App Can Access User Objects Despite "Only Me" Policy

Consider in Fig. 4, Alice changes the access policy of her post P1 to "Only Me". This implies that only she can access this post. However, App1 can still access the post P1 even when Alice sets the policy to "Only Me", see Fig. 7.

```
created_time:"2018-04-07T07:14:44+0000"
id:"113415586159959_148447715990079"
message:"Modified Post"
privacy:
  allow:""
  deny:""
  description:"Only me"
  friends:""
  value:"SELF"
```

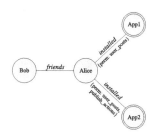

Fig. 7. Results of App1's query to Post1

Fig. 8. Scenario: Alice has installed App1 and App2. Bob is Alice's friend

4.3   App Can Find Out Other Apps Installed by the User

Consider the scenario shown in Fig. 8. Both the apps have permission **user_posts**. App2 (i.e., anshx.ananx as its real name in our experiments) has one additional permission **publish_actions** as shown in the figure. Let us assume that App2 publishes a post on Alice's timeline. App1 can observe this event and can obtain the post ID. Figure 9 shows the query composed by App1 and its result, through which App1 deduces that Alice has also installed App2. Such a knowledge is useful is various ways.

4.4   App and Advertiser Can Identify Users: Linkability

Figure 11 is the analytics report for a campaign we designed for a Page under our control. The analytics is available in real-time. The campaign was to invite users to follow our page on "Online Privacy". We could correlate the Likes (by Facebook users) on our page with the feed sequence report and find out which user has accessed the advertisement from what type of device and device OS version. This information greatly narrows down the types of attack payloads one can design to compromise a device. We could also access App user's Device Information (Fig. 10).

A summary of privacy violations & data leaks from the above scenarios is given below:

1. App finds out user's friends despite user setting it private.
2. App can access user objects with "Only Me" policy.
3. App can find out what other apps are installed by its users.
4. Linkability: App and advertiser can identify their audience from the analytics data.

```
FB.api( "/{post-id}?fields=application,created_time,message",
    function (response) {
        if (response && !response.error) {
            /* handle the result */
        }});

application:
    category:"Education"
    id:"335320743592541"
    link:"https://apps.facebook.com/anshxananx/"
    name:"anshx.ananx"
    namespace:"anshxananx"
    __proto__:Object
created_time:"2018-04-11T13:07:29+0000"
id:"108348820021337_108175360038683"
message:"Post by Anshx"
```

```
["devices"]=>
    object(Facebook\GraphNodes\GraphNode)#16 (1) {
        ["items":protected]=>
        array(1) {
            [0]=>
            object(Facebook\GraphNodes\GraphNode)#15 (1) {
                ["items":protected]=>
                array(1) {
                    ["os"]=>
                    string(7) "Android"}}}}
```

Fig. 9. Query composed by App1 and its result

Fig. 10. Retrieving App user's device information

4.5 Analysis

Given that the trust levels of Facebook and an app are not comparable, the question is how Facebook can control such data leaks? Some of the broad ways to contain these data leaks are:

1. By increasing the user's privacy policy specification scope from current user-object layers (refer Fig. 2) to all the layers of the platform, except the owner's layer. The current approach is fragmented and incoherent – that is, impact of changes at app layer on *in-force* settings at user layer is not communicated to users. The use of naturally understandable labels like "Friends", "Family" should be devised to categorize apps and advertisers, using which user can define her access policies.
2. By encrypting the analytics available to apps and advertisers such that per campaign a distinct but ciphered string is generated for each measurable event that cannot be used to track users across campaigns. Only the platform owner should link the events across campaigns. Thus, only one entity takes the accountability.
3. It appears that Facebook is trying to address this issue of linkability through the concept of scope_id. A user is assigned a unique local ID, whose scope is limited to the context (App, Page) for which it is generated. For example, App1 will generate a scope_id, which is different from the scope_id generated by App2. Thus App1 and App2 or their parent cannot link users. However, we observed that, as of now, these scope IDs are resolving to the real user ID for whom the scope IDs were generated. For example, https://fb.com/100007460080360, https://fb.com/2051781625080487, and https://fb.com/1708004396124880 reveal the actual user.

5   Related Work and Discussion

Social networks like Facebook, Twitter, Snapchat have come to prominence in last decade because of their ability to engage users online such that users can carry out their social discourse 24×7, around the world. As the users get convenience and real-time engagement with their connections for free, the platform

	A	C	D	G	H	I	J	L	N
1	Reporting Starts	Campaign Name	Region	Results	Result Indicator	Reach	Impressions	Amount Spent (INR)	Page Likes
2	01/04/18		Unknown	6	actions:like	32	32	13.18	6
3	01/04/18	Followers for Online Privacy Page	Assam	1	actions:like	7	8	2.16	1
4	01/04/18	Followers for Online Privacy Page	Haryana	2	actions:like	2	2	2.92	2
5	01/04/18	Followers for Online Privacy Page	Himachal Pradesh			1	1	0.47	
6	01/04/18	Followers for Online Privacy Page	Jammu and Kashmir			2	2	0.32	
7	01/04/18	Followers for Online Privacy Page	Maharashtra	1	actions:like	1	1	0.14	1
8	01/04/18	Followers for Online Privacy Page	Odisha			1	1	0.1	
9	01/04/18	Followers for Online Privacy Page	Punjab region	1	actions:like	1	1	2.35	1
10	01/04/18	Followers for Online Privacy Page	Rajasthan			1	1	0.22	
11	01/04/18	Followers for Online Privacy Page	West Bengal	1	actions:like	9	10	2.83	1
12	01/04/18	Followers for Online Privacy Page	Bihar			1	1	0.07	
13	01/04/18	Followers for Online Privacy Page	Madhya Pradesh			1	1	1.14	
14	01/04/18	Followers for Online Privacy Page	Uttar Pradesh			1	1	0.07	
15	01/04/18	Followers for Online Privacy Page	Jharkhand			2	2	0.39	

Fig. 11. Campaign measurement report

gets user insights. The platform recovers its operational costs by sharing the insights in plausibly privacy-preserving fashion with advertisers https://fb.com/ads/about/. The rich data-sets generated by such social networks have ushered: advertising into a real-time persuasion industry [17,24,25], communication into a precision tracking system [1,6], and social network platform into a rich user/content/relation labelling platform. All of these transformations have brought in tremendous challenges [18] in terms of privacy of users.

Privacy in social networks has been studied for quite some time and the research community had been highlighting privacy implication of connectivity [13,23] even before the Cambridge Analytica fiasco. In [12], a survey on security and privacy in social networks is presented that touches upon properties like: anonymization, de-anonymization, link predictability [10,14], information leakage, trust [20], and link privacy [19]. In [9], a privacy-preservation model for Facebook-style social network is proposed. Concepts for privacy-preservation in an app ecosystem, presented in [15] for mobile platforms, can be borrowed in Facebook's platform. Facebook's infrastructure [2] is a unique and not much is available in public. It remains interesting to see how Facebook adopts to the forthcoming European GDPR [4] regulation. The data generated across layers of Facebook platform is interlinked and once a data-tuple is associated with personal data, it becomes tainted and the tainted attributes propagate user's identity further. Under GDPR, when a Facebook user invokes her right to be forgotten/erased, it will be interesting to see how far the data deletion chain goes; since the data is linked across the ecosystem. We believe that Facebook will have to define context and scope of user information and the deletion of user data will happen within that pre-defined scope.

6   Conclusion

We presented the role Apps play in tracking and profiling users on Facebook platform. We have shown a few instances of App configurations that violated the underlying primary privacy settings of the user. Apps may use such shortcomings in policy enforcement for various reasons that can seriously undermine not only the privacy of users but also their security. From the study of ecosystem on Facebook's platform we showed that Apps potentially have as much visibility of its users' objects, connections, and interactions as Facebook itself. If a coherent access control model across layers of Facebook ecosystem is not deployed, then Facebook with its ad-hoc approach will remain a sophisticated surveillance system available to any user. People, including lawmakers, around the world are asking Facebook should it really be expanding into influencing people based on what it has captured as their profile? This conundrum is multiplied in the presence of millions of Apps on its platform. App permission management need to be made understandable and available as extensional/intensional labels similar to permission management at users layer. It is not hard to see why our recommendations based on our analysis demands expansion of the scope of user privacy policies across user layer, app layer, and beyond.

Acknowledgments. This work is carried out as part of research at ISRDC (Information Security Research and Development Center), supported by Ministry of Electronics and Information Technology, Govt. of India (15DEITY00-004). The authors would like to thank Anshu S. Anand, Abhishek Behra, Ankush Dubey for their participation in discussions and experiments.

References

1. Acar, G., Alsenoy, B.V., Piessens, F., Diaz, C., Preneel, B.: Facebook tracking through social plug-ins. Technical report, KU Leuven, June 2015
2. Bronson, N., et al.: TAO: Facebook's distributed data store for the social graph. In: USENIX ATC 13, pp. 49–60 (2013)
3. Cadwalladr, C.: 'I made Steve Bannon's psychological warfare tool': meet thedata war whistleblower (2018). The Guardian. https://www.theguardian.com/news/2018/mar/17/data-war-whistleblower-christopher-wylie-faceook-nix-bannon-trump
4. European Union: Data Protection - Rules for the protection of personal datainside and outside the EU (2018). https://ec.europa.eu/info/law/law-topic/data-protectionen
5. Facebook: Data policy (2016). https://www.facebook.com/full_data_use_policy
6. Facebook: About facebook pixel (2018). https://www.facebook.com/business/help/742478679120153
7. Facebook: Cracking down on platform abuse (2018). https://newsroom.fb.com/news/2018/03/cracking-down-on-platform-abuse/
8. Facebook: Graph API overview (2018). https://developers.facebook.com/docs/graph-api
9. Fong, P.W.L., Anwar, M., Zhao, Z.: A privacy preservation model for facebook-style social network systems. In: Backes, M., Ning, P. (eds.) ESORICS 2009. LNCS, vol. 5789, pp. 303–320. Springer, Heidelberg (2009). https://doi.org/10.1007/978-3-642-04444-1_19
10. Gilbert, E., Karahalios, K.: Predicting tie strength with social media. In: Proceedings of the SIGCHI Conference on Human Factors in Computing Systems, CHI 2009, pp. 211–220. ACM (2009)

11. International Personality Item Pool: The 3,320 IPIP items in alphabeticalorder (2018). https://ipip.ori.org/AlphabeticalItemList.htm
12. Joshi, P., Kuo, C.C.J.: Security and privacy in online social networks: a survey. In: 2011 IEEE International Conference on Multimedia and Expo, pp. 1–6, July 2011
13. Juels, A.: Targeted advertising... and privacy too. In: Naccache, D. (ed.) CT-RSA 2001. LNCS, vol. 2020, pp. 408–424. Springer, Heidelberg (2001). https://doi.org/10.1007/3-540-45353-9_30
14. Kahanda, I., Neville, J.: Using transactional information to predict link strength in online social networks. In: International AAAI Conference on Web and Social Media (2009)
15. Lee, S., Wong, E.L., Goel, D., Dahlin, M., Shmatikov, V.: Box: a platform for privacy-preserving apps. In: NSDI 13, pp. 501–514. USENIX (2013)
16. Levy, H.M.: Capability-Based Computer Systems. Digital Press, Burlington (1984)
17. Matz, S.C., et al.: Psychological targeting as an effective approach to digital mass persuasion. PNAS **114**(48), 12714–12719 (2017)
18. Michal, K., et al.: Facebook as a research tool for the social sciences: opportunities, challenges, ethical considerations, and practical guidelines. Am. Psychol. **70**(6), 543–556 (2015)
19. Mittal, P., Papamanthou, C., Song, D.: Preserving link privacy in social network based systems. CoRR abs/1208.6189 (2012)
20. Patil, V.T., Shyamasundar, R.K.: Privacy as a currency: un-regulated? In: SECRYPT 2017, vol. 4, pp. 586–595 (2017)
21. Patil, V.T., Shyamasundar, R.K.: Undoing of privacy policies on Facebook. In: Livraga, G., Zhu, S. (eds.) DBSec 2017. LNCS, vol. 10359, pp. 239–255. Springer, Cham (2017). https://doi.org/10.1007/978-3-319-61176-1_13
22. ProPublica Data Store: Facebook ad categories (2016). https://www.propublica.org/datastore/dataset/facebook-ad-categories
23. Roosendaal, A.: We are all connected to Facebook... by Facebook! In: Gutwirth, S., Leenes, R., P Hert, P., Poullet, Y. (eds.) European Data Protection. In Good Health? pp. 3–19. Springer, Dordrecht (2012). https://doi.org/10.1007/978-94-007-2903-2_1
24. Sam Biddle: Facebook uses artificial intelligence to predict your futureactions for advertisers, says confidential document (2018). https://theintercept.com/2018/04/13/facebook-advertising-data-artificial-intelligence-ai/
25. Youyou, W., Kosinski, M., Stillwell, D.: Computer-based personality judgments are more accurate than those made by humans. PNAS **112**(4), 1036–1040 (2015)

Towards Adaptive Access Control

Luciano Argento[1], Andrea Margheri[2]([✉])[ID], Federica Paci[2][ID],
Vladimiro Sassone[2][ID], and Nicola Zannone[3][ID]

[1] University of Calabria, Rende, Italy
luciano.argento@unical.it
[2] University of Southampton, Southampton, UK
{a.margheri,f.m.paci,vsassone}@soton.ac.uk
[3] Eindhoven University of Technology, Eindhoven, Netherlands
n.zannone@tue.nl

Abstract. Access control systems are nowadays the first line of defence
of modern IT systems. However, their effectiveness is often compromised
by policy misconfigurations that can be exploited by insider threats. In
this paper, we present an approach based on machine learning to refine
attribute-based access control policies in order to reduce the risks of users
abusing their privileges. Our approach exploits behavioral patterns representing how users typically access resources to narrow the permissions
granted to users when anomalous behaviors are detected. The proposed
solution has been implemented and its effectiveness has been experimentally evaluated using a synthetic dataset.

Keywords: Access control · Machine learning · Policy adaptation
Insider threat · Runtime monitoring

1 Introduction

Data are recognized as the most vital asset of an enterprise and, thus, their
protection is of paramount importance. Access control systems are typically
employed as the first line of defence for the protection of data as they guarantee
that only authorized users can gain access to sensitive resources. Over the past
few years, Attribute-Based Access Control (ABAC) [1] has gained in popularity
due to its flexibility and expressiveness, allowing the specification of fine-grained
and context-aware access control policies.

Despite this flexibility and expressiveness, ABAC (and access control in
general) has an intrinsically static nature that makes it difficult to adapt policies in order to timely response to critical events, e.g. a cyber attack. At the
same time, policies can become out-of-dated quickly, thus requiring continuous,
manual maintenance, which makes policy management and administration a
cumbersome and error-prone task. These issues can lead to policy misconfigurations that leave organizations exposed to attacks against data confidentiality
and integrity.

© IFIP International Federation for Information Processing 2018
Published by Springer International Publishing AG, part of Springer Nature 2018. All Rights Reserved
F. Kerschbaum and S. Paraboschi (Eds.): DBSec 2018, LNCS 10980, pp. 99–109, 2018.
https://doi.org/10.1007/978-3-319-95729-6_7

A study conduced by SANS in 2017 on threats against sensitive data[1] showed that insider threats are the top concern for organizations, followed by ransomware and denial of service attacks. Insider threats are current or former employees, contractors or business partners who have or had authorized access to the organization's network, system or data, and intentionally exceeds or misuses their privileges in a manner that negatively affected the confidentiality, integrity or availability of the organization's information or information system [2]. Thus, organizations need to reinforce their access control systems with procedures to identify policy misconfigurations that could be exploited by an insider threat and update the policies to prevent such exploitations.

Detecting and preventing insider threats by analyzing access control policies and monitoring user behavior have been an active area of research. Common approaches rest on rule mining techniques to discover harmful exploitable policy faults [3,4] or on monitoring systems based on behavioral models to detect insider threats [5–8]. Other works [5,9] have also exploited knowledge from access control policies to detect insider threats. However, these approaches only aim at threat detection and do not focus on the adaptation of access control policies. To date, only a few works (e.g., [10,11]) have exploited user behavior to generate and adapt access control policies. However, these approaches either require human intervention for policy update [10] or build models that do not properly discriminate behaviors of different types of users [11].

Contribution. In this paper, we propose an approach based on machine learning to dynamically refine policies to prevent misconfiguration exploitation. The proposed approach allows the refinement of access control rules according to behavioral features monitored at run-time. The designed system, named ML-AC, exploits a white-box decision learning approach whose aim is to learn behavioral profiles of users accessing resources so to accurately refine policies. There might exist different behavioral profiles, here called *classes of interaction*, that can be determined based on the analysis of contextual knowledge that concerns users and resources. Such knowledge has proven to be a valuable source of information for approaches devoted to improve insider threat detection and access control [6,12].

ML-AC uses access pattern knowledge learned at run-time to introduce controls on behavioral features into access control rules to avoid abuse of granted rights. Behavioral features refine access policies by introducing controls like frequency of access, amount of data, location, etc. By building an access control knowledge model, this work poses the basis towards machine-assisted administration procedures to support timely changing of access rights.

Paper Structure. Section 2 provides a motivating example. Section 3 provides an overview of ML-AC and details how machine learning is empowering access control. Section 4 describes the implementation and evaluation of the performance of ML-AC. Section 5 concludes the paper and outlines directions for future work.

---

[1] https://www.sans.org/reading-room/whitepapers/analyst/sensitive-data-risk-2017 -data-protection-survey-37950.

2   Motivating Example

To outline our approach, we introduce an ABAC system managing accesses to software projects within an organization where users' permissions depend on their role and on the projects they are assigned to.

Let us assume an access control policy allowing users assigned to role *junior manager* to *read* resources of type *R1*. However, only junior managers working on *ProjectA* and from *Department 1* can actually access those resources. This policy can be represented in the FACPL language [13], an XACML-like ABAC language that we use for its conciseness, as follows:

```
policy policy1 {deny-unless-permit
  rule rule1(permit
    target:
        equal ("read", action/id) && equal ("R1", resource/type)
        && equal ("Junior manager", subject/role)
        && equal ("Department1", subject/department)
        && equal ("ProjectA", subject/project))}
```

Intuitively, our sample policy consists of a `policy` element (*policy1*) comprising a *permit* rule (*rule1*) whose `target` defines an access condition built on attributes describing which *action* a certain *subject* can perform on a *resource*.

Let us assume that Bob, a *junior manager* of *Department 1*, attempts to *read* a resource of type *R1*, represented by the following access request (*req1*):

```
(subject/department,"Department 1")
(subject/role, "Junior manager")
(subject/project, "ProjectA")
(action/id="read")
(resource/type,"R1")
```

It is easy to observe that the attributes in the request match the rule target, thus yielding a *permit* decision.[2]

Suppose now that Bob attempts to retrieve a large amount of sensitive project documents without a plausible reason. As the previous request exemplifies, *policy1* would allow him to do so regardless of how many documents he has retrieved. This situation, however, may indicate that the junior manager is abusing his access privileges for personal interests and benefits (e.g., to sell the documents to a competitor).

These insider threats cannot be prevented by existing access control systems. The main problem lies in the fact that access control is static in the sense that the enforced access conditions do not change dynamically according to user behaviour. We argue that *contextual features*, such as the *number of accesses* and *amount of accessed data*, should be taken into account in access decision making. For instance: *Could a user perform multiple read queries in a given time window? Could a user access large amounts of data?* Failing to answer

---

[2] We overlook combining algorithm `deny-unless-permit` as it yields *permit* if the enclosed rule returns *permit*, and yields *deny* otherwise.

these questions can lead to neglect anomalous behaviour representing the abuse of granted access privileges from insider threats.

To reduce the risks of users abusing their privileges, we need to empower access control with proactive measures that adapt policies according to user behavior. Specifically, our goal is to *dynamically refine access control policies based on user behaviour monitored at run-time by narrowing granted privileges*.

To achieve this goal, we need to equip access control systems with a means to build user profiles representing how users normally access resources and use those profiles to dynamically refine access rules. This requires extracting contextual features that capture the behavior exhibited by users accessing a specific set of resources by means of a selected set of operations.

For the sake of exemplification, let us assume that contextual features `feature/NumberOfReadsPerHour` and `feature/BytesReadPerHour` are monitored by the system and can be checked via new attributes in access rules. In particular, it is observed that every hour junior managers typically access at most 14 project documents for a total 345.6 KB. This knowledge can be exploited to refine *policy1* as follows:

```
policy policy2 {deny-unless-permit
  rule rule2 (permit
    target:
        equal ("read", action/id) && equal ("R1", resource/type)
        && equal ("Junior manager", subject/role)
        && equal ("Department1", subject/department)
        && equal ("ProjectA", subject/project))}
        && less-than (feature/BytesReadPerHour, 345.6)
        && less-than (feature/NumberOfReadsPerHour, 14)
```

Intuitively, *policy2* narrows the access conditions of *policy1* through contextual features by imposing additional constraints on how much and how often resources are typically accessed by junior managers. Consider, for instance, the case where Bob attempts to access 50 project documents within 10 min. Based on the updated policy, this behavior would be deemed as anomalous and thus denied, preventing Bob to access all documents.

3   Adaptive Access Control

In this section, we introduce ML-AC, a system for adaptive access control that aims to reduce the risks of users abusing their privileges. Figure 1 presents the ML-AC architecture. It comprises the following components:

- *Authorization Server* is a standard ABAC infrastructure à la XACML based on PEP/PDP.
- *Policy Administration Point (PAP)* features the proactive policy refinement functionalities proposed in this work.
- *Monitoring System* supervises the whole system and provides the information needed to build behavioral profiles used by Policy Administration in its refinement process.

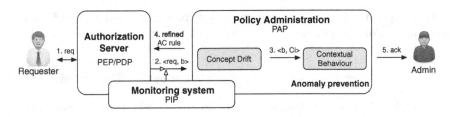

Fig. 1. The ML-AC system

Once an access request is received by the Authorization Server (step 1), it is evaluated following typical PEP/PDP evaluation frameworks. If access is granted (i.e., a *permit* decision is returned) by the Authorization Server, the request, together with the corresponding behaviour provided by the Monitoring system, is forwarded to the PAP (step 2) to determine whether it is anomalous. The PAP dynamically refines the access control policies based on the user behavior and enforce them in the Authorisation Server (steps 3–4). Administrators are informed of the changes (step 5).

Our contribution lies in the Policy Administration component. Specifically, we equip PAPs with the *Contextual Behaviour Learning* component, which is responsible to build user profiles according to the monitored behavior and refine access control policies based on those profiles. The *Concept Drift* component detects the evolution of the learned user profiles and inform the Contextual Behavior Learning component when new behaviors are detected (step 3).

In the remaining, we introduce our representation of behavioral models and present the mechanics of the Contextual Behaviour and Concept Drift components.

3.1 Behavioral Model

To build the behavioral models used to identify anomalous accesses, we introduce the notion of *user behavior*. Behaviours, denoted as b, represent how users are *utilizing* resources. They are defined in terms of the attributes forming access requests (i.e., user, resource and action) and of any contextual knowledge features that can be exploited by the access control system for decision making (e.g., working time, working location, types of activities). Formally, a behaviour is defined as:

$$b \triangleq \langle A_1^u, \ldots, A_m^u, A_1^o, \ldots, A_h^o, A_1^r, \ldots, A_k^r, \ldots A_1^c \ldots A_z^c \rangle$$

where attribute A_i^u describe users, A_k^o operations, A_y^r resources and A_z^c the context. An attribute is an expression of form $A \triangleq$ name op *value*, where op is a relational operator (e.g., $=, >$) between an attribute name and a value from the attribute's codomain. For instance, the following behaviour (we shorten attribute names for ease)

$$b_1 = \langle \texttt{role} = jnr\text{-}mng, \texttt{act} = read, \texttt{res} = R1, \texttt{\#byte} = 250, \texttt{\#read} = 10 \rangle$$

corresponds to the access request reported in Sect. 2, where #byte and #read are contextual features provided by the Monitoring System.

Behaviors are grouped into so-called *class of interaction*s. Each class represents a group of homogeneous behaviours (i.e., whose representation involves the same set of attribute name) that are considered normal. We assume that the set of initial classes are defined according to the access policy rules, hence on the basis of the controls on user, action and resource attributes. Changes at runtime to the classes are managed by the Concept Drift component (Sect. 3.3).

3.2   Contextual Behavior

Our approach builds behavioral profiles of normal accesses in the form of class of interactions. To determine to which class of interaction a given behavior belong, we relies on Random Forest (RF) [14], where each RF is used to characterize a class of interaction. Based on this matching, the knowledge on the corresponding contextual features is used to refine access control policies.

Learning Practicalities. Given a class of interactions C_i, our goal is to recognize whether a user behavior b_i is similar to those represented by C_i or not, i.e. whether b_i is anomalous. Practically, being b_i a potentially anomalous behavior, we cannot assume it will always match (the attributes of) C_i. It follows that this problem cannot be addressed as a multi-class classification (labels would be represented by the classes of interactions and our goal would be to determine if the label of a test sample b_i is C_i or another C_j, with $i \neq j$), but as a *One Class Classification* (OCC) problem [15] for each of class of interaction C_i individually.

Solutions for the OCC problem are numerous. However, being our goal to obtain learning outputs that can be used to refine policies, we opted for the white-box approach of RF. Specifically, each RF is an ensemble of *Decision Tree* (DT) each of which models the conditions on the attributes identifying the normal behaviors of a class. Each DT produces an output of the form of *antecedent* $\Rightarrow$ *consequent* rules [16]. The antecedent consists of logical conjunctions stating under which conditions a behavior can be classified as *normal* or *anomalous*, as indicated by the consequent.

It is worth noting that each DT produces its own output, leading to potential inconsistencies. For instance, let us suppose a RF with three DTs. Given a behavior b, each DT produces its own decision, e.g. $DT_1(b) = 1$, $DT_2(b) = 0$ and $DT_3(b) = 1$, where 1 and 0 denote normal and anomalous behavior, respectively. To solve this problem RF relies on a majority vote algorithm among DTs; hence b is classified as normal. Notably, a final decision can always be guaranteed by using a known RF voting solution [17].

Access Control Refinement. The DT outputs, hereafter called *ML-rules*, is used to bridge from the machine learning world to the actual refinement of access control policies. Practically, they encode the obtained knowledge in terms of additional conditions to add to the access control policy. The syntax of ML-rules is defined by the following grammar:

$$ML\text{-}rule ::= Antec \Rightarrow Consec$$
$$Antec ::= Cnd \; \{\&\& \; Cnd\} \qquad Cnd ::= \texttt{name} \; op \; \texttt{value}$$
$$Op ::= = | > | < | \leq | \geq | \; \texttt{in} \qquad Consec ::= \texttt{true} \; | \; \texttt{false}$$

where `true` (resp., `false`) identifies a normal (resp., anomalous) behavior. The antecedent consists of a conjunctive sequence of conditions, whereas the consequent is a Boolean value stating whether a behavior satisfying the antecedent is normal or anomalous. For instance, the following ML-rule represents the refinement leading from *policy1* to *policy2* of the example

$$\texttt{role} = jnr\text{-}mng \;\&\&\; \texttt{act} = read \;\&\&\; \texttt{res} = R1$$
$$\&\& \; \#\texttt{read} < 14 \;\&\&\; \#\texttt{byte} < 345.6 \qquad \Rightarrow \quad \texttt{true}$$

Therefore, ML-rules are used to transfer the contextual knowledge learned by the RFs into the access control policies. Policy refinement occurs on the basis of the conditions on the contextual features present in an ML-rule (e.g., the #read and #byte above). Practically, the access control rules to refine correspond to those matching the conditions on user, action and resource attributes present in the ML-rule. The refined rules contain the additional controls on the contextual features as per the example of *policy2*.

3.3   Concept Drift

After the behavioral models have been build, the system starts monitoring the evolution of user behaviors to detect concept drifts in order to maintain the RF models accurate over time. It follows from the RF design that concept drifts can only be detected on the contextual features.

To this aim, we rely on *Olindda* [18], a clustering-based approach similar to the one followed by BBNAC [11]. Olindda uses the well-known *k-means* algorithm (or one of its extensions, e.g. *k-modes* for categorical features) to cluster behaviors of the classes of interactions and detect the emergence of new classes (aka new clusters) based on the distance among clusters.

Figure 2(a) depicts a scenario where concept drift can be observed. For instance, given three classes of interactions C_1, C_2 and C_3, at the beginning just three groups of user behaviors, respectively the clusters A, B and D of blue-filled shapes, are identified. After a certain amount of time, the behaviors in the cluster D change to the point that concept drift is detected: the red-filled shapes. Therefore, these behaviors are used by the RF modelling the class C_3 to update its knowledge accordingly. Additionally, when behavior like those represented by red cross shapes are observed, i.e. not forming any cluster, Olindda

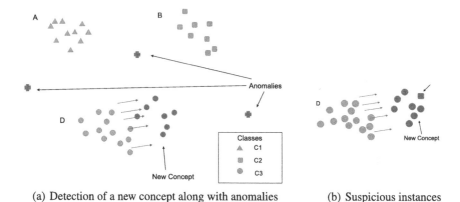

(a) Detection of a new concept along with anomalies   (b) Suspicious instances

Fig. 2. Detection of concept drift

deems them as anomalies. This is the key assurance to avoid RF to refine access control policies with conditions allowing anomalous behaviors.

Notably, emerging concepts may overlap among classes leading to difficulties in their classification. For instance, Fig. 2(b) depicts new concepts emerging from the cluster D that present similarities to both cluster D (circle shapes) and cluster B (square shape). All emerging concepts like the latter are treated as anomalies.

Divergence in Clusters. A key aspect of concept drift is the emergence of sub-clusters within an existing cluster. Given a class C_i, it may happen that a subset of its users start behaving significantly different from the remaining users, over time. This would lead to the discovery of new classes of interactions detailing different behavioral profiles.

Our approach aims to build classes of interactions that are characterized by behaviors that are very similar to each other. Therefore, in the light of the new discovered sub-clusters, we derive two new classes of interaction from C_i, namely C_i^n and C_i^o, representing behavior related to the new and old concepts, respectively. This has the consequence of introducing a new RF modelling the new class. In order to keep updating the policy refinements generated by the initial C_i, it is required a layered RF modelling able to discriminate between the two new classes. Further details are left to future work.

4   Evaluation

To evaluate the effectiveness of our approach, we have implemented it[3] and performed experiments using a synthetic dataset. The goal of the experiments is to demonstrate the benefits of combining domain context knowledge (inferred using machine learning) with knowledge based on access control rules (used to create classes of interaction) for the detection of anomalies. In particular, we

---

[3] The tool is freely available at https://github.com/cybersoton/ml-ac/.

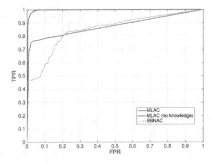

Fig. 3. Comparison among ML-AC, *BBNAC* and ML-AC$_{nok}$

assess the detection accuracy of ML-AC by analyzing the number of true and false positive. This will allows us to demonstrate how the refinement based on this detection approach will prevent anomalies to happen a priori. Note that we do not evaluate the use of machine learning to classify user behavior, being this extensively reported in the literature (e.g., [19]).

In the experiments, we compared our approach for anomaly prevention with two other approaches. We took BBNAC [11], the closest approach from the literature. To avoid bias in the experimentation, we re-implemented BBNAC in Matlab. Additionally, we performed a comparison with ML-AC$_{nok}$, a variant of ML-AC where a priori knowledge on the policy is not used. This allows us to better assess the role of contextual knowledge.

Dataset. We generated a synthetic dataset whose data instances represent user behaviors, under the assumption that there are two classes of interactions. The behaviors are represented as three-dimensional points and based on numerical features. We generated over 3000 behaviors, with almost an equal number of normal and anomalous instances. Intuitively, about 2000 behaviors were used for training, while the rest for testing.

Results. To evaluate the accuracy of the approaches, we computed the ROC curve for the three evaluated approaches (Fig. 3). The ROC curve is a graphical plot we use to evaluate how well the classifier we defined distinguishes between normal and anomalous behaviors, based on a varying discrimination threshold (i.e., the value used to deem a behavior anomalous). Specifically, it shows the true positive rate or TPR (y-axis) against the false positive rate or FPR (x-axis) with respect to different threshold settings. These performances can also be reduced to a single scalar value, called *area under the ROC curve* (AUC), which represents the probability that a classifier will rank a randomly chosen anomalous instance higher than a randomly chosen normal instance. This gives better insights on the number of false positive detected.

As can be seen in Fig. 3, ML-AC achieves the best performance. ML-AC significantly surpasses the others due to the use of a priori knowledge on the policy. This allows ML-AC to create more accurate profiles and hence to discern more precisely among groups of behaviors. Specifically, we have that the AUC drops from the 99% of ML-AC to the 87% and 85% of ML-AC$_{nok}$ and BBNAC, respectively. The main cause is that both BBNAC and ML-AC$_{nok}$ classify most of the anomalous behaviors of each class as a normal behavior of the other class.

5   Conclusion

In this paper we proposed ML-AC, an approach to refine and update access policies in order to eliminate policy misconfigurations that can be exploited by insider threats. ML-AC builds behavioral models representing the normal usage of resources and exploits these models at run-time to prevent anomalous accesses. Our approach has been implemented and validated using a synthetic dataset.

Future Work. There are a number of interesting aspects to address as future work. Firstly, we plan to conduct more extensive experiments based on real-life datasets and measure the number of refinement applied in practice to the access control policies.

Moreover, we would like to study further the presence of an adversarial attacker [20], who may try to deceive the machine learning algorithm in order to bypass security controls. ML-AC employs different machine learning algorithms to achieve its goals, therefore it may incur in the risk of being subject to adversarial attacks. The definition of class of interaction may constitute a starting point for devising strategies to hinder typical attacks such as causative and exploratory. The fact that user behaviors are split based on the classes, may make the task of deceiving ML-AC quite difficult. Many anti-adversarial algorithms have been proposed in literature, like those presented in [11] that effectively mitigate threats related to concept drift.

Another aspect concerns classes of interactions. It might not always be possible to clearly define those classes based only on the knowledge derived from the context and access control policies. There may be some classes that should be merged or split, hence we plan to design a preprocessing step to support the classes definition process.

References

1. Hu, V.C., Kuhn, D.R., Ferraiolo, D.F.: Attribute-based access control. IEEE Comput. **48**(2), 85–88 (2015)
2. Silowash, G., Cappelli, D., Moore, A., Trzeciak, R., Shimeall, T., Flynn, L.: Common sense guide to mitigating insider threats. Technical report (2012)
3. Hwang, J.H., Xie, T., Hu, V., Altunay, M.: Mining likely properties of access control policies via association rule mining. In: Foresti, S., Jajodia, S. (eds.) DBSec 2010. LNCS, vol. 6166, pp. 193–208. Springer, Heidelberg (2010). https://doi.org/10.1007/978-3-642-13739-6_13
4. Bauer, L., Garriss, S., Reiter, M.K.: Detecting and resolving policy misconfigurations in access-control systems. ACM Trans. Inf. Syst. Secur. **14**(1), 2:1–2:28 (2011)

5. Park, J.S., Giordano, J.: Role-based profile analysis for scalable and accurate insider-anomaly detection. In: Proceedings of International Conference on Performance, Computing, and Communications. IEEE (2006). 7 p

6. Maloof, M.A., Stephens, G.D.: ELICIT: a system for detecting insiders who violate need-to-know. In: Kruegel, C., Lippmann, R., Clark, A. (eds.) RAID 2007. LNCS, vol. 4637, pp. 146–166. Springer, Heidelberg (2007). https://doi.org/10.1007/978-3-540-74320-0_8

7. Legg, P.A., Buckley, O., Goldsmith, M., Creese, S.: Caught in the act of an insider attack: detection and assessment of insider threat. In: Proceedings of International Symposium on Technologies for Homeland Security, pp. 1–6. IEEE (2015)

8. Alizadeh, M., Peters, S., Etalle, S., Zannone, N.: Behavior analysis in the medical sector: theory and practice. In: Proceedings of Symposium on Applied Computing. ACM (2018)

9. Hu, N., Bradford, P.G., Liu, J.: Applying role based access control and genetic algorithms to insider threat detection. In: Proceedings of the Annual Southeast Regional Conference, pp. 790–791. ACM (2006)

10. Costante, E., Fauri, D., Etalle, S., den Hartog, J., Zannone, N.: A hybrid framework for data loss prevention and detection. In: Proceedings of IEEE Security and Privacy Workshops, pp. 324–333. IEEE (2016)

11. Frias-Martinez, V., Sherrick, J., Stolfo, S.J., Keromytis, A.D.: A network access control mechanism based on behavior profiles. In: Proceedings of Annual Computer Security Applications Conference, pp. 3–12. IEEE (2009)

12. Hummer, M., Kunz, M., Netter, M., Fuchs, L., Pernul, G.: Adaptive identity and access management contextual data based policies. EURASIP J. Inf. Secur. **2016**(1), 19 (2016)

13. Margheri, A., Masi, M., Pugliese, R., Tiezzi, F.: A rigorous framework for specification, analysis and enforcement of access control policies. IEEE Trans. Softw. Eng. (2017). https://doi.org/10.1109/TSE.2017.2765640

14. Breiman, L.: Random forests. Mach. Learn. **45**(1), 5–32 (2001)

15. Tax, D.M.J.: One-class classification: concept-learning in the absence of counter-examples. Ph.D. thesis, University of Delft (2001)

16. Quinlan, J.R.: Generating production rules from decision trees. In: Proceedings of International Joint Conference on Artificial Intelligence, pp. 304–307. Morgan Kaufmann Publishers Inc. (1987)

17. Andrzejak, A., Langner, F., Zabala, S.: Interpretable models from distributed data via merging of decision trees. In: Proceedings of Symposium on Computational Intelligence and Data Mining, pp. 1–9. IEEE (2013)

18. Spinosa, E.J., de Leon, F., Ponce, A., Gama, J.: Novelty detection with application to data streams. Intell. Data Anal. **13**(3), 405–422 (2009)

19. Nellikar, S., Nicol, D.M., Choi, J.J.: Role-based differentiation for insider detection algorithms. In: Proceedings of Workshop on Insider Threats, pp. 55–62. ACM (2010)

20. Huang, L., Joseph, A.D., Nelson, B., Rubinstein, B.I., Tygar, J.: Adversarial machine learning. In: Proceedings of Workshop on Security and Artificial Intelligence, pp. 43–58. ACM (2011)

Privacy-Preserving Access and Computation

Oblivious Dynamic Searchable Encryption on Distributed Cloud Systems

Thang Hoang[1]([✉]), Attila A. Yavuz[1], F. Betül Durak[2], and Jorge Guajardo[3]

[1] EECS, Oregon State University, Corvallis, OR, USA
{hoangmin,attila.yavuz}@oregonstate.edu
[2] École Polytechnique Fédérale de Lausanne (EPFL), Lausanne, Switzerland
betul.durak@epfl.ch
[3] Robert Bosch RTC—LLC, Pittsburgh, PA, USA
jorge.guajardomerchan@us.bosch.com

Abstract. Dynamic Searchable Symmetric Encryption (DSSE) allows search/update operations over encrypted data via an encrypted index. However, DSSE has been shown to be vulnerable to statistical inference attacks, which can extract a significant amount of information from access patterns on encrypted index and files. While generic Oblivious Random Access Machine (ORAM) can hide access patterns, it has been shown to be extremely costly to be directly used in DSSE setting.

By exploiting the distributed cloud infrastructure, we develop a series of Oblivious Distributed DSSE schemes called ODSE, which enable oblivious access on the encrypted index with a high security and improved efficiency over the use of generic ORAM. Specifically, ODSE schemes are $3\times$–$57\times$ faster than applying the state-of-the-art generic ORAMs on encrypted dictionary index in real network settings. One of the proposed ODSE schemes offers desirable security guarantees such as information-theoretic security with robustness against malicious servers. These properties are achieved by exploiting some of the unique characteristics of searchable encryption and encrypted index, which permits us to harness the computation and communication efficiency of multi-server PIR and Write-Only ORAM simultaneously. We fully implemented ODSE and have conducted extensive experiments to assess the performance of our proposed schemes in a real cloud environment.

Keywords: Searchable encryption · Write-Only ORAM
Multi-server PIR · Privacy-preserving clouds

1 Introduction

Data outsourcing allows a client to store their data on the cloud to reduce data management and maintenance costs. Despite its merits, cloud services come with severe privacy issues. The client may encrypt their data with standard encryption to protect their privacy. However, these techniques also prevent the client from

© IFIP International Federation for Information Processing 2018
Published by Springer International Publishing AG, part of Springer Nature 2018. All Rights Reserved
F. Kerschbaum and S. Paraboschi (Eds.): DBSec 2018, LNCS 10980, pp. 113–130, 2018.
https://doi.org/10.1007/978-3-319-95729-6_8

performing basic operations (e.g., search/update) over the outsourced encrypted data. This significantly degrades the benefits of cloud services. In the following, we first outline the current state-of-the-art techniques and their limitations and then, present our methods towards addressing these challenges.

1.1 State-of-the-Art and Limitations

Information Leakage in DSSE. The concept of searchable symmetric encryption (SSE) was first proposed by Song et al. [24]. This construction can only search on static encrypted data. Curtmola et al. [11] introduced single-keyword-searched SSE with formal security definition, followed by refinements with extended capabilities such as ranked query [27], multi-keyword search [26] or their combinations [7]. Dynamic Searchable Symmetric Encryption (DSSE) was introduced by Kamara et al. [17], which offers both search and update on encrypted files $\mathcal{F}$ via an encrypted index $\mathbf{I}$ representing keyword-file relationships. Many DSSE schemes have been proposed, each offering various performance, functionality and security trade-offs [4] (e.g., [6,9,17,20,29,31]).

It is known that all standard DSSE schemes leak significant information, which are vulnerable to statistical inference analysis [8,16,18,30]. There are two sources of information leakages in DSSE: (i) leakages through search and update on encrypted index $\mathbf{I}$, (ii) leakages due to access of encrypted files $\mathcal{F}$. Specifically, since the search and update tokens are deterministic, all DSSE schemes leak access patterns on both $\mathbf{I}$ and $\mathcal{F}$. Furthermore, most of them also leak the content of updated files during the update (i.e., forward-privacy) and historical updates (add/delete) on the keyword during the search on $\mathbf{I}$ (i.e., backward-privacy). By exploiting these leakages, recent studies have shown that, sensitive information about encrypted queries and files can be recovered [8,18]. Zhang et al. [30] has presented file-injection attacks that can determine which keywords have been searched, especially in forward-insecure DSSE schemes. Although some DSSE schemes with improved security (e.g., forward and backward privacy) have been proposed (e.g., [6]), they rely on extremely costly public key operations and still leak access patterns. Liu et al. [18] demonstrated an attack that can determine which keywords have been searched by observing the frequency of search queries (search patterns). Zhang et al. [30] has indicated that, *future research on DSSE should focus on sealing information leakages rather than accepting them by default*. Unless these leakages are prevented, a trustworthy deployment of DSSE for privacy-critical applications may remain extremely difficult.

Performance Hurdles of the Existing Approaches to Reduce Information Leakages in DSSE. Several attempts (e.g., [5,15]) are either highly costly or unable to completely seal all leakages in DSSE access patterns. Generic Oblivious Random Access Machine (ORAM) [25][1] can hide access patterns, and therefore, it can prevent most of the information leakages in DSSE.

---

[1] By generic ORAM, we mean oblivious techniques that can hide operation type (whether it is read or write), as opposed to PIR or Write-Only ORAM.

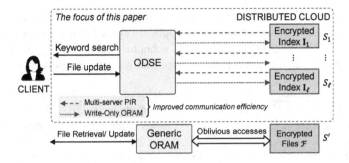

Fig. 1. Our research objective and high-level approach.

Garg et al. [12] proposed TWORAM scheme, which optimizes the round-trip communication under $\mathcal{O}(1)$ client storage when using ORAM to hide *file access patterns*[2] in DSSE. Despite its merits, prior studies (e.g., [9,21]) stated that generic ORAM (e.g., [25]) is still costly to be used in DSSE due to its logarithmic communication overhead. Although several ORAMs with $\mathcal{O}(1)$ bandwidth complexity have been introduced recently, they are still very costly due to the use of Homomorphic Encryption (HE). The performance of such schemes has been shown to be worse than $\mathcal{O}(\log N)$-bandwidth ORAMs [2].

1.2 Our Research Objective and Contributions

It is imperative to seal information leakages from accessing encrypted files $\mathcal{F}$ and encrypted index $\mathbf{I}$. Since the size of individual files in $\mathcal{F}$ might be arbitrarily large and each search/update query might involve a different number of files, to the best of our knowledge, generic ORAM seems to be the only option for oblivious access on $\mathcal{F}$. *The objective of this paper is to design oblivious access techniques on $\mathbf{I}$, which are more efficient than using generic ORAM, by exploiting special properties of searchable encryption and $\mathbf{I}$ as elaborated in Fig. 1.* Particularly, we identify a suitable data structure for $\mathbf{I}$ that allows search and update to operate on separate dimensions. This property permits us to harness communication-efficient techniques such as Write-Only ORAM for update and, by exploiting distributed cloud infrastructure, multi-server PIR for search with low computation overhead. Note that the low communication and computation are important factors in practice since they directly translate into the low end-to-end delay and consequently, improve the quality of services of cloud systems. Notice that the price to pay for such low delay is the collusion vulnerability in the distributed setting, where we assume a limited number of servers that can collude with each other, which is the common adversarial model of multi-server PIR techniques (see Sects. 2 and 4).

---

[2] It differs from the objective of this paper, where we focus on hiding access patterns on the encrypted index in DSSE (see Sect. 5 for clarification).

We propose a series of Oblivious Distributed Encrypted Index $\mathbf{I}$ on the distributed cloud infrastructure with the application on DSSE, which we refer to as ODSE (Fig. 1). We present two ODSE schemes called $\mathsf{ODSE}_{\mathsf{xor}}^{\mathsf{wo}}$ and $\mathsf{ODSE}_{\mathsf{it}}^{\mathsf{wo}}$, each offering various desirable performance and security properties as follows.

- *Low end-to-end delay:* ODSE schemes achieve low end-to-end-delay, which are 3×–57×faster than the use of efficient generic ORAMs (e.g., [22,25]) (with optimization [12]) on encrypted index under real network settings (see Sect. 5).
- *Full obliviousness with Information-theoretic security:* ODSE seals information leakages due to accesses on encrypted index $\mathbf{I}$ that lead into statistical attacks such as forward/backward privacy, query types (search/update), hidden size and access patterns. $\mathsf{ODSE}_{\mathsf{xor}}^{\mathsf{wo}}$ and $\mathsf{ODSE}_{\mathsf{it}}^{\mathsf{wo}}$ offer computational and information-theoretic security for $\mathbf{I}$ and operations on it, respectively.
- *Robustness against malicious servers:* $\mathsf{ODSE}_{\mathsf{it}}^{\mathsf{wo}}$ can tolerate a certain number of malicious servers in the system.
- *Full-fledged implementation and open-sourced framework:* We fully implemented all the proposed ODSE schemes, and evaluated their performance on real-cloud infrastructure. To the best of our knowledge, we are among the first to open-source an oblivious access framework for DSSE encrypted index that can be publicly used for comparison and wide adaptation (see Sect. 5).

It is clear that the standard DSSE constructions (e.g., [9]) are much faster, but also less secure than our proposed methods in the sense of leaking more information beyond the access patterns (e.g., forward-privacy, backward-privacy) over the encrypted index. Compared with standard DSSE where access patterns are leaked by default, ODSE schemes offer higher security by sealing all these leakages at the cost of higher latency. Nevertheless, they are more efficient than using generic ORAM techniques atop the DSSE encrypted index to seal such leakages in some certain cases regarding database and query sizes. We provide the detail analysis in Sect. 5.

2   Preliminaries and Building Blocks

Notation. We denote $\mathbb{F}_p$ as a finite field where p is a prime. Operators $\|$ and $\oplus$ denote the concatenation and XOR, respectively. $(\cdot)_{\mathsf{bin}}$ denotes the binary representation. $\mathbf{u} \cdot \mathbf{v}$ denotes the inner product of two vectors $\mathbf{u}$ and $\mathbf{v}$. $x \xleftarrow{\$} \mathcal{S}$ denotes that x is randomly and uniformly selected from set $\mathcal{S}$. Given I as a row/column of a matrix, $I[i]$ denotes accessing i-th component of I. Given a matrix $\mathbf{I}$, $\mathbf{I}[*, j \ldots j']$ denotes accessing columns j to j' of $\mathbf{I}$. Let $\mathcal{E} = (\mathsf{Enc}, \mathsf{Dec}, \mathsf{Gen})$ be an IND-CPA symmetric encryption: $\kappa \leftarrow \mathcal{E}.\mathsf{Gen}(1^\theta)$ generating key with security parameter θ; $C \leftarrow \mathcal{E}.\mathsf{Enc}_\kappa(M)$ encrypting plaintext M with key κ; $M \leftarrow \mathcal{E}.\mathsf{Dec}_\kappa(C)$ decrypting ciphertext C with key κ.

$([\![\alpha]\!]_1, \ldots, [\![\alpha]\!]_\ell) \leftarrow$ SSS.CreateShare(α, t): Create ℓ shares of value α

1: $(a_1, \ldots, a_t) \xleftarrow{\$} \mathbb{F}_p$

2: **return** $([\![\alpha]\!]_1, \ldots, [\![\alpha]\!]_\ell)$, where $[\![\alpha]\!]_i \leftarrow \alpha + \sum_{u=1}^{t} a_u \cdot x_l^u$ for $1 \leq l \leq \ell$

$\alpha \leftarrow$ SSS.Recover$(\{\mathcal{A}\}, t)$: Recover the value α from its shares

1: Randomly select $t+1$ shares $\{[\![\alpha]\!]_{x_i}\}_{i=1}^{t+1}$ among $\mathcal{A}$

2: $g(x) \leftarrow$ LagrangeInterpolation$\left(\{(x_i, [\![\alpha]\!]_{x_i})\}_{i=1}^{t+1}\right)$

3: **return** α, where $\alpha \leftarrow g(0)$

Fig. 2. Shamir Secret Sharing (SSS) scheme [23].

Shamir Secret Sharing (SSS). We present (t, ℓ)-threshold Shamir Secret Sharing (SSS) scheme [23] in Fig. 2. Given a secret $\alpha \in \mathbb{F}_p$, the dealer generates a random t-degree polynomial f and evaluates $f(x_i)$ for party $\mathcal{P}_l \in \{\mathcal{P}_1, \ldots, \mathcal{P}_\ell\}$, where $x_l \in \mathbb{F}_p \setminus \{0\}$ is the deterministic identifier of $\mathcal{P}_l$. We denote the share for $\mathcal{P}_l$ as $[\![\alpha]\!]_l$. The secret can be reconstructed by combining at least $t+1$ correct shares via Lagrange interpolation. Note that the secret can be recovered from a number of incorrect shares by error correction techniques (discussed in Sect. 4). We use this property to improve the robustness of our protocol in malicious settings.

SSS is t-private so that any combinations of t shares leak no information about the secret. SSS offers homomorphic properties including addition, scalar multiplication, and *partial* multiplication. We extend the notion of share of value to indicate the share of vector: $[\![\mathbf{v}]\!]_i = ([\![v_1]\!]_l, \ldots, [\![v_n]\!]_l)$ denotes the share of vector $\mathbf{v}$ for party $\mathcal{P}_\ell$, in which $[\![v_i]\!]$ is the share of component v_i in $\mathbf{v}$.

Private Information Retrieval (PIR). PIR enables private retrieval of a data item from a (unencrypted) public database server. We recall two efficient multi-server PIR protocols: *(i) XOR-based PIR* [10] (Fig. 3) which uses XOR operations and requires each server S_l to store $\mathbf{b}_l$, a replica of database $\mathbf{b}$ containing m blocks $(b_1, \ldots, b_m)$ with the same size; *(ii) SSS -based PIR* [13] (Fig. 4), which relies on homomorphic properties of SSS, where each server stores $\mathbf{b}_l$, a replica of the database $\mathbf{b}$ containing m blocks $(b_1, \ldots, b_m)$, where $b_i \in \mathbb{F}_p$.

$b \leftarrow$ PIR$^{\mathrm{xor}}(x, \langle \mathbf{b}_1, \ldots, \mathbf{b}_\ell \rangle)$: Retrieve a data item indexed x from public database

Client: $e \leftarrow$ 0's string of length m; Set $e[x] \leftarrow 1$

1: $\rho_l \leftarrow$ random binary string of length m for $1 \leq l < \ell$; Set $\rho_\ell \leftarrow \rho_1 \oplus \ldots \rho_{\ell-1} \oplus e$

2: Send ρ_i to server S_i for $1 \leq i \leq \ell$

Server: each S_l storing $\mathbf{b}_l = (b_{l1}, \ldots, b_{lm})$ on receiving ρ_l:

3: $r_l \leftarrow \bigoplus_{j \in \mathcal{J}} b_{lj}$ where $\mathcal{J} = \{j : \rho_l[j] = 1\}$ and send r_l to client

Client: on receiving $(r_1, \ldots, r_\ell)$:

4: **return** $b \leftarrow \bigoplus_{l=1}^{\ell} r_l$

Fig. 3. XOR-based PIR [10].

$b \leftarrow \mathsf{PIR^{sss}}(x, \langle \mathbf{b}_1, \ldots, \mathbf{b}_\ell \rangle)$: Retrieve a data item indexed x from public database
Client: Let $\mathbf{e} = (e_1, \ldots, e_m)$, where $e_x \leftarrow 1$, $e_i \leftarrow 0$ for $1 \le i \ne x \le n$
1: **for** $i = 1, \ldots, m$ **do**
2:     $(\llbracket e_i \rrbracket_1, \ldots, \llbracket e_i \rrbracket_\ell) \leftarrow \mathsf{SSS.CreateShare}(e_i, t)$
3: $\llbracket \mathbf{e} \rrbracket_l \leftarrow (\llbracket e_1 \rrbracket_l, \ldots, \llbracket e_m \rrbracket_l)$ and send $\llbracket \mathbf{e} \rrbracket_l$ to server S_l for $1 \le l \le \ell$
Server: each S_l storing $\mathbf{b}_l = (b_{lm}, \ldots, b_{lm})$ on receiving $\llbracket \mathbf{e} \rrbracket_l$:
4: $\llbracket b \rrbracket_l \leftarrow \llbracket \mathbf{e} \rrbracket_l \cdot \mathbf{b}_l$ and send $\llbracket b \rrbracket_i$ to client
Client: on receiving $\llbracket b \rrbracket_1, \ldots, \llbracket b \rrbracket_\ell$:
5: **return** $b \leftarrow \mathsf{SSS.Recover}(\llbracket b \rrbracket_1, \ldots, \llbracket b \rrbracket_\ell, t)$

Fig. 4. SSS-based PIR [13].

Write-Only ORAM. ORAM allows the user to hide the access patterns when accessing their encrypted data on the cloud. In contrast to generic ORAM where both read and write operations are hidden, Blass et al. [3] proposed a Write-Only ORAM scheme, which only hides the write pattern in the context of hidden volume encryption. Intuitively, $2n$ memory slots are used to store n blocks, each assigned to a distinct slot and a position map is maintained to keep track of block's location. Given a block to be rewritten, the client reads λ slots chosen uniformly at random and writes the block to a dummy slot among λ slots. Data in all slots are encrypted to hide which slot is updated. By selecting λ sufficiently large (e.g., 80), one can achieve a negligible failure probability, which might occur when all λ slots are non-dummy. It is possible to select a small λ (e.g., 4). In this case, the client maintains a stash component S of size $\mathcal{O}(\log n)$ to temporarily store blocks that cannot be rewritten when all read slots are full.

3   The Proposed ODSE Schemes

Intuition. In DSSE, keyword search and file update on $\mathbf{I}$ are read-only and write-only operations, respectively. This property permits us to leverage specific bandwidth-efficient oblivious access techniques for each operation such as multi-server PIR (for search) and Write-Only ORAM (for update) rather than using generic ORAM. The second requirement is to identify an appropriate data structure for $\mathbf{I}$ so that the above techniques can be adapted. We found that forward index and inverted index are the ideal choices for the file update and keyword search operations, respectively as proposed in [14]. However, doing search and update on two isolated indexes can cause an inconsistency, which requires the server to perform synchronization. The synchronization operation leaks significant information [14]. To avoid this problem, it is necessary to integrate both search index and update index in an efficient manner. Fortunately, this can be achieved by leveraging a two-dimensional index (i.e., matrix), which allows keyword search and file update to be performed in two separate dimensions without creating any inconsistency at their intersection. This strategy permits us to perform computation-efficient (multi-server) PIR on one dimension, and communication-efficient (Write-Only) ORAM on the other dimension to achieve oblivious search and update, respectively, with a high efficiency.

3.1 ODSE Models and Data Structures

System Model. Our model comprises a client and ℓ servers $\boldsymbol{S} = (\mathcal{S}_1, \ldots, \mathcal{S}_\ell)$, each storing a version of the encrypted index. In our system, the encrypted files are stored on S', a separate server different from $\boldsymbol{S}$ (as in [15]), which can be obliviously accessed via a generic ORAM (e.g., [25]). In this paper, we only focus on oblivious access of the encrypted index on $\boldsymbol{S}$.

Threat Model. In our system, the client is trusted and the servers $\mathcal{S}$ are untrusted. We consider the servers to be semi-honest, meaning that they follow the protocol faithfully, but can record the protocol transcripts to learn information regarding the client's access pattern. However, our system can be easily extended to deal with malicious servers that attempt to tamper the input data to compromise the correctness and the security of the system (see Sect. 4). We allow upto $t < \ell$ (privacy parameter) servers among $\mathcal{S}$ to be colluding, meaning that they can share their own recorded protocol transcripts with each other. We present the formal security model in Sect. 4.

Data Structures. Assume that the outsourced database can store up to N distinct files and M unique keywords, our index is an incidence matrix $\mathbf{I}$, where each cell $\mathbf{I}[i,j] \in \{0,1\}$ represents the relationship between the keyword at row i and the file at column j. Each keyword and file is assigned to a unique row and column index, respectively. Each row of $\mathbf{I}$ represents the search result of a keyword while the content (unique keywords) of a file is represented by a column. Since we use Write-Only ORAM for file update, the number of columns in $\mathbf{I}$ are doubled and a stash S is used to store columns of $\mathbf{I}$ during the update. Therefore, the size of search index $\mathbf{I}$ is $M \times 2N$.

We leverage two static hash tables T_w, T_f as in [28] to keep track of the location of keywords and files in $\mathbf{I}$, respectively. They have the following structure: $T := \langle \mathsf{key}, \mathsf{value} \rangle$, where key is a keyword or file ID and $\mathsf{value} \leftarrow T[\mathsf{key}]$ is the (row/column) index of key in $\mathbf{I}$. Since there are $2N$ columns in $\mathbf{I}$ while only N files, we denote $\mathcal{D}$ as the set of dummy columns that are not assigned to a particular file.

3.2 ODSE$_{\mathsf{xor}}^{\mathsf{wo}}$: Fast ODSE

We introduce ODSE$_{\mathsf{xor}}^{\mathsf{wo}}$ that harnesses XOR-based PIR and Write-Only ORAM to achieve low search and update latency.

Setup. Let Π and Π' be random permutations on $\{1, \ldots, 2N\}$ and $\{1, \ldots, M\}$ respectively. The procedure to setup encrypted index for ODSE$_{\mathsf{xor}}^{\mathsf{wo}}$ is as follows.

$(\mathcal{I}, \sigma) \leftarrow \mathsf{ODSE}_{\mathsf{xor}}^{\mathsf{wo}}.\mathsf{Setup}(\mathcal{F})$: Create distributed encrypted index from input files $\mathcal{F}$

1. Initialize a matrix $\mathbf{I}'$ of size $M \times 2N$, Set $\mathbf{I}'[*, *] \leftarrow 0$
2. Extract unique keywords $(w_1, \ldots, w_m)$ from files $\mathcal{F} = \{f_{id_1}, \ldots, f_{id_n}\}$
3. Construct $\mathbf{I}'$ for $i = 1 \ldots, m$ and $j = 1, \ldots, n$:
   (a) $T_f[id_j] \leftarrow \Pi(j)$, $T_w[w_i] \leftarrow \Pi'(i)$, $x \leftarrow \Pi'[w_i]$ and $y \leftarrow \Pi[id_j]$
   (b) If w_i appears in f_{id_j}, set $\mathbf{I}'[x, y] \leftarrow 1$
4. Generate master key as $\kappa \leftarrow \mathsf{Gen}(1^\theta)$
5. Encrypt $\mathbf{I}'$ for $i = 1, \ldots, M$ and $j = 1 \ldots, 2N$:
   (a) $\tau_i \leftarrow \mathsf{KDF}_\kappa(i)$
   (b) $\mathbf{I}[i, j] \leftarrow \mathcal{E}.\mathsf{Enc}_{\tau_i}(\mathbf{I}'[i, j])$
6. Let $\mathcal{D}$ contain column indexes that are not assigned to any file IDs
7. Output $(\mathcal{I}, \sigma)$, where $\mathcal{I} \leftarrow \{\mathbf{I}_1, \ldots, \mathbf{I}_\ell\}$ with $\mathbf{I}_i = \mathbf{I}$ and $\sigma \leftarrow (\kappa, T_w, T_f, \mathbf{c})$

Once $\mathcal{I}$ is constructed, the client sends $\mathbf{I}_i$ to server $\mathcal{S}_i$, and keeps σ as secret.

Search. Intuitively, to search for a keyword w, the client and server execute the XOR-based PIR protocol on the row dimension of $\mathbf{I}$ to privately retrieve the row data of w. Since the row is encrypted *rather than being public as in the traditional PIR model*, the client performs decryption on the retrieved data and filter dummy column indexes to obtain the search result. The detail is as follows.

$\mathcal{R} \leftarrow \mathsf{ODSE}_{\mathsf{xor}}^{\mathsf{wo}}.\mathsf{Search}(w, \mathcal{I}, \sigma)$: Search for keyword w

1. Get row index x of the searched keyword w as $x \leftarrow T_w[w]$
2. Execute $\mathbf{I}[x, *] \leftarrow \mathsf{PIR}^{\mathsf{xor}}(x, \langle \mathbf{I}_1, \ldots, \mathbf{I}_\ell \rangle)$ protocol (Fig. 3) with ℓ servers:
   (a) Each server inputs its encrypted index $\mathbf{I}_i$, where each row of $\mathbf{I}_i$ is interpreted as an item in the database
   (b) Client inputs x, and receives $\mathbf{I}[x, *]$ from protocol's output
3. Decrypt $\mathbf{I}[x, *]$ for $j = 1, \ldots, 2N$:
   (a) $\mathbf{I}'[x, j] \leftarrow \mathcal{E}.\mathsf{Dec}_{\tau_x}(\mathbf{I}[x, j])$ where $\tau_x \leftarrow \mathsf{KDF}_\kappa(x)$
4. Output $\mathcal{R} \leftarrow id'$ in Stash S and id s.t. $T_f[id] = j$ where $\mathbf{I}[x, j] = 1$ and $j \notin \mathcal{D}$

Update: The overall strategy is to perform a Write-Only ORAM on the column of $\mathbf{I}$ to achieve oblivious file update operations as follows.

$\mathsf{ODSE}_{\mathsf{xor}}^{\mathsf{wo}}.\mathsf{Update}(f_{id}, \mathcal{I}, \sigma)$: Update file f_{id}

1. Initialize a new column as $\hat{I}[i] \leftarrow 0$, for $i = 1, \ldots, M$
2. Set $\hat{I}[x_i] \leftarrow 1$, where $x_i \leftarrow T_w[w_i]$ for each keyword w_i appearing in f_{id}
3. Add $\langle id, \hat{I} \rangle$ to Stash S, add $T_f[id]$ to dummy set $\mathcal{D}$
4. Download λ random columns of encrypted index $\mathbf{I}$ from a server:
   (a) Randomly select λ column indexes $\mathcal{J} \leftarrow \{j_1, \ldots j_\lambda\}$
   (b) Get λ columns $\{\mathbf{I}_l[*, j]\}_{j \in \mathcal{J}}$ from random server $\mathcal{S}_l$
5. Decrypt each column $\mathbf{I}_l[*, j]$ for each $j \in \mathcal{J}$ and for $i = 1, \ldots, M$:
   (a) $\tau_i \leftarrow \mathsf{KDF}_\kappa(i)$
   (b) $\mathbf{I}'[i, j] \leftarrow \mathcal{E}.\mathsf{Dec}_{\tau_i}(\mathbf{I}_l[i, j])$
6. For each dummy column $\mathbf{I}'[*, \hat{j}]$:
   (a) Pick a pair $\langle id, \hat{I} \rangle$ from stash S, and set $\mathbf{I}'[*, \hat{j}] \leftarrow \hat{I}$
   (b) Set $T_f[id] \leftarrow \hat{j}$, and remove $\hat{j}$ from dummy set $\mathcal{D}$
7. Re-encrypt λ columns as $\hat{\mathbf{I}}[i, j] \leftarrow \mathcal{E}.\mathsf{Enc}_{\tau_i}(\mathbf{I}'[i, j])$ for $i = 1 \ldots, M$ and $\forall j \in \mathcal{J}$
8. Send λ columns $\{\hat{\mathbf{I}}[*, j]\}_{j \in \mathcal{J}}$ to ℓ servers, where each server $\mathcal{S}_i$ updates its encrypted index as $\mathbf{I}_i[*, j] \leftarrow \hat{\mathbf{I}}[*, j]$, for each $j \in \mathcal{J}$

3.3 ODSE$_{it}^{wo}$: Robust and IT-Secure ODSE

Although ODSE$_{xor}^{wo}$ offers highly-efficient search and update operations, it has the following security limitations: *(i)* it can only (at most) detect but cannot recover from malicious servers, which might tamper the data to compromise the privacy and correctness of the protocol. In privacy-critical applications, it is desirable to recover from malicious servers to improve the robustness of the protocol; *(ii)* the encrypted index and update operations on it are only computationally-secure due to the IND-CPA encryption.

To address the limitations of ODSE$_{xor}^{wo}$, we introduce ODSE$_{it}^{wo}$ that offers *(i)* improved robustness against malicious servers with a partial recover capability, and *(ii)* the highest level of security (i.e., information-theoretic) for both **I** and operations on it. The main idea is to share the index with SSS, and harness SSS-based PIR to conduct private search. The robustness comes from the ability to recover the secret shared by SSS in the presence of incorrect shares (see Sect. 4).

Setup: The client first constructs an index $\mathbf{I}'$ representing keyword-file relationships as in ODSE$_{xor}^{wo}$.Setup. Instead of encrypting $\mathbf{I}'$, the client creates shares of $\mathbf{I}'$ by SSS. Since SSS operates on elements in $\mathbb{F}_p$, each row of $\mathbf{I}'$ is split into $\lfloor \log_2 p \rfloor$-bit chunks before SSS computation. So, the index $\mathbf{I}_i$ is the SSS share of $\mathbf{I}'$ for server $\mathcal{S}_i$, which is a matrix of size $M \times 2N'$, where $\mathbf{I}_i[i,j] \in \mathbb{F}_p$ and $N' = N/\lfloor \log_2 p \rfloor$. The detail is as follows.

$(\mathcal{I}, \sigma) \leftarrow$ ODSE$_{it}^{wo}$.Setup($\mathcal{F}$): Create distributed share index from input files $\mathcal{F}$
1. Construct $\mathbf{I}'$ by executing steps 1–3 in ODSE$_{xor}^{wo}$.Setup procedure
2. Create SSS of $\mathbf{I}'$ for $i = 1, \ldots, M$ and $j = 1, \ldots, 2N'$:
   (a) $\hat{\mathbf{I}}[i,j]_{bin} \leftarrow \mathbf{I}'[i, (j-1) \cdot \lfloor \log_2 p \rfloor + 1, \ldots, j \cdot \lfloor \log_2 p \rfloor]]$
   (b) $(\mathbf{I}_1[i,j], \ldots, \mathbf{I}_\ell[i,j]) \leftarrow$ SSS.CreateShare($\hat{\mathbf{I}}[i,j], t$)
3. Output $(\mathcal{I}, \sigma)$, where $\mathcal{I} \leftarrow \{\mathbf{I}_1, \ldots, \mathbf{I}_\ell\}$ and $\sigma \leftarrow (T_w, T_f, \mathcal{D})$

Similar to ODSE$_{xor}^{wo}$, the client sends $\mathbf{I}_i$ to server $\mathcal{S}_i$ and keep σ as secret.

Search. The client executes the SSS-based PIR protocol on the row dimension of encrypted index to retrieve the row of searched keyword as follows.

$\mathcal{R} \leftarrow$ ODSE$_{it}^{wo}$.Search($w, \mathcal{I}, \sigma$): Search for keyword w
1. Get row index x of the searched keyword w as $x \leftarrow T_w[w]$
2. Execute $\hat{\mathbf{I}}[x,j] \leftarrow$ PIR$^{sss}(x, \langle \mathbf{I}_1[*,j], \ldots, \mathbf{I}_\ell[*,j] \rangle)$ protocol (Fig. 4) with ℓ servers for $j = 1, \ldots, 2N'$:
   (a) Each server S_i inputs a column of its shared index $\mathbf{I}_i[*,j]$, where each cell $\mathbf{I}_i[x,j]$ is interpreted as an item in the database
   (b) Client inputs x, and receives $\hat{\mathbf{I}}[x,j]$ from protocol's output. Note that client executes SSS.Recover with privacy parameter of $2t$, instead of t (step 5 in Fig. 4) to recover $\hat{\mathbf{I}}[x,j]$ correctly.
3. Form the row as $\mathbf{I}'[x,*] \leftarrow \hat{\mathbf{I}}[x,1]_{bin} || \ldots || \hat{\mathbf{I}}[x,2N']_{bin}$
4. Output $\mathcal{R} \leftarrow id'$ in Stash S and id s.t. $T_f[id] = j$ where $\mathbf{I}[x,j] = 1$ and $j \notin \mathcal{D}$

Update: We execute Write-Only ORAM on the column dimension of the encrypted index for the file update. Recall that in $\mathsf{ODSE}_{\mathsf{xor}}^{\mathsf{wo}}$, λ random columns of the original index $\mathbf{I}'$ are read to update one column. In $\mathsf{ODSE}_{\mathsf{it}}^{\mathsf{wo}}$, each column of the index $\mathbf{I}_i$ on $\mathcal{S}_i$ contains the share of $\lfloor \log_2 p \rfloor$ successive columns of $\mathbf{I}'$. Therefore, the client reads $\lambda' = \lceil \frac{\lambda}{\lfloor \log_2 p \rfloor} \rceil$ random columns of $\mathbf{I}_i$ from $t + 1$ servers to recover λ columns of $\mathbf{I}'$ before performing update. The detail is as follows.

$\mathsf{ODSE}_{\mathsf{it}}^{\mathsf{wo}}.\mathsf{Update}(f_{id}, \mathcal{I}, \sigma)$: Update file f_{id}

1. Initialize $I'[i] \leftarrow 0$ for $i = 1 \ldots, M$
2. Set $\hat{I}[x_i] \leftarrow 1$, where $x_i \leftarrow T_w[w_i]$ for each keyword w_i appearing in f_{id}
3. Add $\langle id, \hat{I} \rangle$ to Stash S, add $T_f[id]$ to dummy set $\mathcal{D}$
4. Download λ random columns of shared index I from $t + 1$ servers:
    (a) Randomly selected λ' column indexes $\mathcal{J} \leftarrow \{j_1, \ldots j_{\lambda'}\}$
    (b) Get λ' columns $\{\mathbf{I}_l[*, j]\}_{j \in \mathcal{J}, l=1 \ldots t+1}$ from $t + 1$ servers
5. Recover λ' columns for each $j \in \mathcal{J}$ and $i = 1 \ldots, M$:
    (a) $\hat{\mathbf{I}}[i, j] \leftarrow \mathsf{SSS.Recover}(\langle \mathbf{I}_1[i, j], \ldots, \mathbf{I}_\ell[i, j] \rangle, t)$
    (b) $\mathbf{I}'[i, j \cdot \lceil \log_2 p \rceil, ..., (j + 1) \cdot \lceil \log_2 p \rceil] \leftarrow \hat{\mathbf{I}}[i, j]_{\mathsf{bin}}$
6. For each dummy column $\mathbf{I}'[*, \hat{j}]$:
    (a) Pick a pair $\langle id, \hat{I} \rangle$ from stash S, and set $\mathbf{I}'[*, \hat{j}] \leftarrow \hat{I}$
    (b) Set $T_f[id] \leftarrow \hat{j}$, and remove $\hat{j}$ from dummy set $\mathcal{D}$
7. Create SSS for λ' column for each $j \in \mathcal{J}$, and $i = 1 \ldots, M$:
    (a) $\mathbf{I}[i, j]_{\mathsf{bin}} \leftarrow \mathbf{I}'[i, j \cdot \lceil \log_2 p \rceil, \ldots, (j + 1) \cdot \lceil \log_2 p \rceil]$
    (b) $(\hat{\mathbf{I}}_1[i, j], \ldots, \hat{\mathbf{I}}_\ell[i, j]) \leftarrow \mathsf{SSS.CreateShare}(\hat{\mathbf{I}}[i, j], t)$
8. Send $\hat{\mathbf{I}}_l[*, j]$ to $\mathcal{S}_l$ for each $j \in \mathcal{J}$ and $l = 1 \ldots, \ell$. Each server $\mathcal{S}_l$ updates its share index as $\mathbf{I}_l[*, j] \leftarrow \hat{\mathbf{I}}_l[*, j]$ for each $j \in \mathcal{J}$

---

4   Security

Definition 1 (ODSE security). *Let* $\boldsymbol{op} = (\mathsf{op}_1, \ldots, \mathsf{op}_q)$ *be an operation sequence over the distributed encrypted index* $\mathcal{I}$, *where* $\mathsf{op}_i \in \{ \mathsf{Search}(w), \mathsf{Update}(f_{id}) \}$, *w is a keyword to be searched and* f_{id} *is a file with keywords to be updated. Let* $\boldsymbol{ODSE}_j(\boldsymbol{o})$ *represent the ODSE client's sequence of interactions with server* $\mathcal{S}_j$, *given an operation sequence* $\boldsymbol{o}$.

An ODSE is t-secure if $\forall \mathcal{L} \subseteq \{1, \ldots, \ell\}$ *s.t.* $|\mathcal{L}| \leq t$, *for any two operation sequences* $\boldsymbol{op}$ *and* $\boldsymbol{op}'$ *where* $|\boldsymbol{op}| = |\boldsymbol{op}'|$, *the views* $\{\boldsymbol{ODSE}_{i \in \mathcal{L}}(\boldsymbol{op})\}$ *and* $\{\boldsymbol{ODSE}_{i \in \mathcal{L}}(\boldsymbol{op}')\}$ *observed by a coalition of up to t servers are (perfectly, statistically or computationally) indistinguishable.*

Remark 1. One might observe that search and update operations in ODSE schemes are performed on rows and columns of the encrypted index, respectively. This access structure might enable the adversary to learn whether the operation is search or update, even though each operation is secure. Therefore, to achieve security as in Definition 1, where the query type should also be hidden, we can invoke both search and update protocols (one of them is the dummy operation) regardless of whether the intended action is search or update.

We argue the security of our proposed schemes as follows.

Theorem 1. *$ODSE_{xor}^{wo}$ scheme is computationally $(\ell - 1)$-secure by Definition 1.*

Proof. (Sketch) *(i) Oblivious Search:* $ODSE_{xor}^{wo}$ leverages XOR-based PIR and therefore, achieves $(\ell - 1)$-privacy for keyword search as proven in [10]. *(ii) Oblivious Update:* $ODSE_{xor}^{wo}$ employs Write-Only ORAM which achieves negligible write failure probability and therefore, it offers the statistical security without counting the encryption. The index in $ODSE_{xor}^{wo}$ is IND-CPA encrypted, which offers computational security. Therefore in general, the update access pattern of $ODSE_{xor}^{wo}$ scheme is computationally indistinguishable. $ODSE_{xor}^{wo}$ performs Write-Only ORAM with an identical procedure on ℓ servers (e.g., the indexes of accessed columns are the same in ℓ servers), and therefore, the server coalition does not affect the update privacy of $ODSE_{xor}^{wo}$. *(iii) ODSE Security:* By Remark 1, $ODSE_{xor}^{wo}$ performs both search and update regardless of the actual operation. As analyzed, search is $(\ell - 1)$-private and update pattern is computationally secure. Therefore, $ODSE_{xor}^{wo}$ achieves computational $(\ell - 1)$-security by Definition 1. □

Theorem 2. *$ODSE_{it}^{wo}$ scheme is statistically t-secure by Definition 1.*

Proof. (Sketch) *(i) Oblivious Search:* $ODSE_{it}^{wo}$ leverages an SSS-based PIR protocol and therefore, achieves t-privacy for keyword search due to the t-privacy property of SSS [13]. *(ii) Oblivious Update:* The index in $ODSE_{it}^{wo}$ is SSS-shared, which is information-theoretically secure in the presence of t colluding servers. $ODSE_{it}^{wo}$ also employs Write-Only ORAM, which offers statistical security due to negligible write failure probability. Therefore in general, the update access pattern of $ODSE_{it}^{wo}$ scheme is information-theoretically (statistically) indistinguishable in the coalition of up to t servers. *(iii) ODSE Security:* By Remark 1, $ODSE_{it}^{wo}$ performs both search and update protocols regardless of the actual operation. As analyzed above, search is t-private and update pattern is statistically t-indistinguishable. Therefore, $ODSE_{it}^{wo}$ is information-theoretically (statistically) t-secure by Definition 1. □

4.1 Malicious Input Tolerance

We have shown that ODSE schemes offer a certain level of collusion-resiliency in the honest-but-curious setting where the server follows the protocol faithfully. In some privacy-critical applications, it is necessary to achieve data integrity in the malicious environment, where the adversary can tamper the query and data to compromise the correctness and privacy of the protocol. We show that ODSE schemes can be extended to detect and be robust against malicious servers as follows. In $ODSE_{xor}^{wo}$, we can leverage Message Authentication Code (e.g., HMAC) as presented in [19], where authenticated tag for each row and each column of **I** is generated. The server will perform operations (i.e., PIR, Write-Only ORAM) on such tags as similar to encrypted index data and send the result to the client.

The client can recover/decrypt the row/column as well as its authenticated tag verify the integrity.

Since $\mathsf{ODSE}_{\mathsf{it}}^{\mathsf{wo}}$ relies on SSS as the building block, we can not only detect but also be robust against malicious server. The main idea is to leverage list decoding algorithm as in [13], given that the Lagrange interpolation in SSS.Recover algorithm does not return a consistent value. Such techniques also allow to determine precisely which server has tampered the data. We refer readers to [13] for detailed description. In general, the list decoding allows $t_m \leq t < \ell - \lceil\sqrt{\ell t}\rceil$ number of incorrect shares of $[\![\alpha]\!]^{(t)}$.

5 Experimental Evaluation

5.1 Configurations

Implementation Details. We implemented all ODSE schemes in C++. Specifically, we used `Google Sparsehash` to implement hash tables T_f and T_w. We utilized `Intel AES-NI` library to implement AES-CTR encryption/decryption in $\mathsf{ODSE}_{\mathsf{xor}}^{\mathsf{wo}}$. We leveraged `Shoup's NTL` library for pseudo-random number generator and arithmetic operations over finite field. We used `ZeroMQ` library for client-server communication. We used multi-threading technique to accelerate PIR computation at the server. Our code is publicly available at

> https://github.com/thanghoang/ODSE

Hardware and Network Settings. We used Amazon EC2 with `r4.4xlarge` instance for server(s), each equipped with 16 vCPUs Intel Xeon @ 2.3 GHz and 122 GB RAM. We used a laptop with Intel Core i5 @ 2.90 GHz and 16 GB RAM as the client. All machines ran Ubuntu 16.04. The client established a network connection with the server via WiFi. We used a real network setting, where the download and upload throughputs are 27 and 5 Mbps, respectively.

Dataset. We used subsets of the `Enron` dataset to build $\mathbf{I}$ containing from millions to billions of keyword-file pairs. The largest database in this study contain around 300,000 files with 320,000 unique keywords. Our tokenization is identical to [21] so that our keyword distribution and query pattern is similar to [21].

Instantiation of Compared Techniques. We compared ODSE with a standard DSSE scheme [9], and the use of generic ORAM atop the DSSE encrypted index. The performance of all schemes was measured under the same setting and in the average-case cost, where each query involves half of the keywords/files in the database. We configured ODSE schemes and their counterparts as follows.

- *ODSE*: We used two servers for $\mathsf{ODSE}_{\mathsf{xor}}^{\mathsf{wo}}$ and three servers for $\mathsf{ODSE}_{\mathsf{it}}^{\mathsf{wo}}$ scheme. We selected $\lambda = 4$ for $\mathsf{ODSE}_{\mathsf{xor}}^{\mathsf{wo}}$, and $\lambda' = 4$ with $\mathbb{F}_p$ where p is a 16-bit prime for $\mathsf{ODSE}_{\mathsf{it}}^{\mathsf{wo}}$. We note that selecting larger p (up to 64 bits) can reduce the PIR computation time, but also increase the bandwidth overhead. We chose a 16-bit prime field to achieve a balanced computation vs. communication overhead.

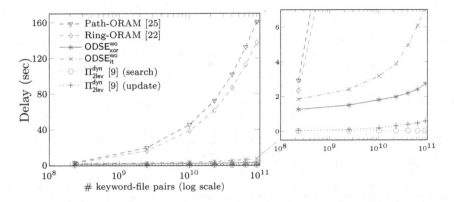

Fig. 5. Latency of ODSE schemes and their counterparts.

- *Standard DSSE*: We selected one of the most efficient DSSE schemes by Cash et al. in [9] (i.e., Π_{2lev}^{dyn} variant) to showcase the performance gap between ODSE and standard DSSE. We estimated the performance of Π_{2lev}^{dyn} using the same software/hardware environments and optimizations as ODSE (e.g., parallelization, AES-NI acceleration). Note that we did not use the Java implementation of this scheme available in Clusion library [1] for comparison due to its lack of hardware acceleration support (no AES-NI) and the difference between running environments (Java VM vs. C). Our estimation is conservative in that, we used numbers that would be better than the Clusion library.

- *Using generic ORAM atop DSSE encrypted index*: We selected *non-recursive* Path-ORAM [25] and Ring-ORAM [22], rather than recent ORAMs as ODSE counterparts since they are the most efficient generic ORAM schemes to date. Since we focus on encrypted index rather than encrypted files in DSSE, we did not explicitly compare our schemes with TWORAM [12] but instead, used one of their techniques to optimize the performance of using generic ORAM on DSSE encrypted index. Specifically, we applied the selected ORAMs on the dictionary index containing keyword-file pairs as in [21] along with the round-trip optimization as in [12]. Note that our estimates are also conservative where memory access delays were excluded, and cryptographic operations were optimized and parallelized to make a fair comparison between the considered schemes.

5.2 Overall Results

Figure 5 presents the end-to-end delays of ODSE schemes and their counterparts, where both search and update are performed in ODSE schemes to hide the actual type of operation (see Remark 1). ODSE offers a higher security than standard DSSE at the cost of a longer delay. However, ODSE schemes are 3×–57× faster than the use of generic ORAMs to hide the access patterns. Specifically, with

Table 1. Comparison of ODSE and its counterparts for oblivious access on **I**.

Scheme	Security				Delay (s)		Distributed setting[c]	
	Forward privacy	Backward privacy	Hidden access pattern	Encrypted index[a]	Search	Update	Privacy level	Improved Robustness
Standard DSSE [9]	✗	✗	✗	Computational	0.036	0.62	–	–
Path-ORAM [25]			Computational	Computational	160.6		–	–
Ring-ORAM [22]			Computational	Computational	137.4		–	–
$\mathsf{ODSE^{wo}_{xor}}$			Computational[b]	Computational	**2.8**		$\ell - 1$	✗
$\mathsf{ODSE^{wo}_{it}}$			Information theoretic	Information theoretic	**7.1**		$< \ell/2$	

This delay is for encrypted index with 300,000 files and 320,000 keywords regarding network and configuration settings in Sect. 5.1.

[a] The encrypted index in $\mathsf{ODSE^{wo}_{it}}$ is information-theoretically (IT) secure because it is SSS. Other schemes employ IND-CPA encryption so that their index is computationally secure (see Sect. 4).

[b] All ODSE schemes perform search and update protocols to hide the actual query type. In $\mathsf{ODSE^{wo}_{xor}}$, search is IT-secure due to SSS-based PIR and update is computationally secure due to IND-CPA encryption. Hence, its overall security is computational.

[c] ℓ is # servers. In $\mathsf{ODSE^{wo}_{it}}$, encrypted index and search query are SSS with the same privacy level. Generic ORAM-based solutions have a stronger adversarial model than ours since they are not vulnerable to collusion that arises in the distributed setting.

an encrypted index containing ten billions of keyword-file pairs, $\Pi^{\mathsf{dyn}}_{\mathsf{2lev}}$ cost 36 ms and 600 ms to finish a search and update operation, respectively. $\mathsf{ODSE^{wo}_{xor}}$ and $\mathsf{ODSE^{wo}_{it}}$ took 2.8 s and 7.1 s respectively, to accomplish both keyword search and file update operations, compared with 160 s by using Path-ORAM with the round-trip optimization [12]. $\mathsf{ODSE^{wo}_{xor}}$ is the most efficient in terms of search, whose delay was less than 1 s. This is due to the fact that $\mathsf{ODSE^{wo}_{xor}}$ only requires XOR operations and the size of the search query is minimal (i.e., a binary string). $\mathsf{ODSE^{wo}_{it}}$ is more robust (e.g., malicious tolerant) and more secure (e.g., unconditional security) than $\mathsf{ODSE^{wo}_{xor}}$ at the cost of higher search delay (i.e., 4 s) due to the larger search query and SSS arithmetic computations. For the file update, $\mathsf{ODSE^{wo}_{it}}$ costs 3 s, which is slightly higher than $\mathsf{ODSE^{wo}_{xor}}$ (i.e., 2.2 s) since it needs to transmit more data (4 blocks vs. 4 columns) to more servers (3 vs. 2). We further provide a comparison of ODSE schemes with their counterparts in Table 1. We dissected the total cost to investigate which factors contributed the most to the latency of ODSE schemes as follows.

5.3 Detailed Cost Analysis

Figure 6 presents the total delays of separate keyword search and file update operations, as well as their detailed costs in ODSE schemes. Note that ODSE performs both search and update (one of them is dummy) to hide the actual type of operation performed by the client.

- *Client processing:* As shown in Fig. 6, client computation contributes the least amount to the overall search delay (less than 10%) in all ODSE schemes. The client computation comprises the following operations: (1) Generate select queries (with SSS in $\mathsf{ODSE^{wo}_{it}}$ and PRF in $\mathsf{ODSE^{wo}_{xor}}$); (2) SSS recovery and IND-CPA decryption (in $\mathsf{ODSE^{wo}_{xor}}$); (3) Filter dummy columns. Note that the

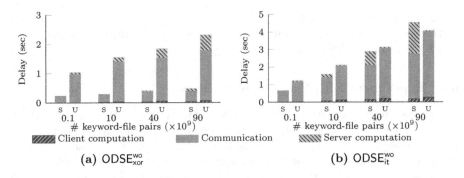

Fig. 6. Detailed search (S) and update (U) costs of ODSE schemes.

client delay of ODSE schemes can be further reduced (by at least 50%-60%) via pre-computation of some values such as row keys and select queries (only contain shares of 0 or 1). For the file update, the client performs decryption and re-encryption on λ columns (in ODSE_{xor}^{wo}), or SSS over λ' blocks (in ODSE_{it}^{wo}). Since we used crypto acceleration (i.e., Intel AES-NI) and highly optimized number theory libraries (i.e., NTL), all these computations only contributed to a small fraction of the total delay.

- *Client-server communication:* Data transmission is the dominating factor in the delay of ODSE schemes. The communication cost of ODSE_{xor}^{wo} is smaller than that of other ODSE schemes, since the size of search query and the data transmitted from servers are binary vectors. In ODSE_{it}^{wo}, the size of components in the select vector is 16 bits. The communication overhead of ODSE_{it}^{wo} can be reduced by using a smaller finite field, but at the cost of increased PIR computation on the server side.
- *Server processing:* The cost of PIR operations in ODSE_{xor}^{wo} is negligible as it uses XOR. The PIR computation of ODSE_{it}^{wo} is reasonable, as it operates on a bunch of 16-bit values. For update operations, the server-side cost is mainly due to memory accesses for column update. ODSE_{it}^{wo} is highly memory access-efficient since we organized the memory layout for column-friendly access. This layout minimizes the memory access delay not only in update but also in search, since the inner product in PIR also accesses contiguous memory blocks by this organization. In ODSE_{xor}^{wo}, we stored the matrix for row-friendly access to permit efficient XOR operations during search. However, this requires file update to access non-contiguous memory blocks. Hence, the file update in ODSE_{xor}^{wo} incurred a higher memory access delay than that of ODSE_{it}^{wo} as shown in Fig. 6.
- *Storage overhead:* The main limitation of ODSE schemes is the size of encrypted index, whose asymptotic cost is $\mathcal{O}(N \cdot M)$, where N and M are the number of files and unique keywords, respectively. Given the largest database being experimented, the size of our encrypted index is 23 GB. The client storage includes two hash tables of size $\mathcal{O}(M)$ and $\mathcal{O}(N \log N)$, the stash of size $\mathcal{O}(M \cdot \log N)$, the set of dummy column indexes of size $\mathcal{O}(N \log N)$, a counter

vector of size $\Omega(N)$ and a master key (in $\mathsf{ODSE}_{\mathsf{xor}}^{\mathsf{wo}}$ scheme). Empirically, with the same database size discussed above, the client requires approximately 22 MB in both ODSE schemes.

5.4 Experiment with Various Query Sizes

We studied the performance of our schemes and their counterparts in the context of various keyword and file numbers involved in search and update operations that we refer to as "query size". As shown in Fig. 7, ODSE schemes are more efficient than using generic ORAMs when more than 5% of keywords/files in the database are involved in the search/update operations. Since the complexity of ODSE schemes is linear to the number of keywords and files (i.e., $\mathcal{O}(M + N)$), their delay is constant and independent from the query size. The complexity of ORAM approaches is $\mathcal{O}(r \log^2(N \cdot M))$, where r is the query size. Although the bandwidth cost of ODSE schemes is asymptotically linear, their actual delay is much lower than using generic ORAM, whose cost is poly-logarithmic to the total number of keywords/files but linear to the query size. This confirms the results of Naveed et al. in [21] on the performance limitations of generic ORAM and DSSE composition, wherein we used the same dataset for our experiments.

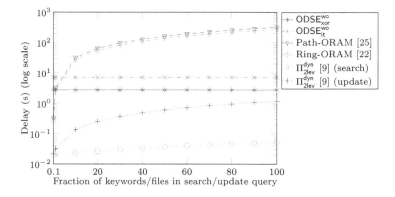

Fig. 7. Latency of ODSE schemes and their counterparts with different fraction of keywords/files involved in a search/update operation.

6   Conclusion

We proposed a new set of Oblivious Distributed DSSE schemes called ODSE, which achieve full obliviousness, hidden size pattern, and low end-to-end delay simultaneously. Specifically, $\mathsf{ODSE}_{\mathsf{xor}}^{\mathsf{wo}}$ achieves the lowest end-to-end delay with the smallest communication overhead among all of its counterparts with the highest resiliency against colluding servers. $\mathsf{ODSE}_{\mathsf{it}}^{\mathsf{wo}}$ achieves the highest level of privacy with information-theoretic security for access patterns and the encrypted index, along with the robustness against malicious servers. Our experiments demonstrated that ODSE schemes are one order of magnitude faster than the most efficient ORAM techniques over DSSE encrypted index. We have released the full implementation of our ODSE schemes for public use and wide adaptation.

References

1. The clusion library. https://github.com/encryptedsystems/Clusion/
2. Abraham, I., Fletcher, C.W., Nayak, K., Pinkas, B., Ren, L.: Asymptotically tight bounds for composing ORAM with PIR. In: Fehr, S. (ed.) PKC 2017. LNCS, vol. 10174, pp. 91–120. Springer, Heidelberg (2017). https://doi.org/10.1007/978-3-662-54365-8_5
3. Blass, E.-O., Mayberry, T., Noubir, G., Onarlioglu, K.: Toward robust hidden volumes using write-only oblivious ram. In: Proceedings of the 2014 ACM CCS, pp. 203–214. ACM (2014)
4. Bösch, C., Hartel, P., Jonker, W., Peter, A.: A survey of provably secure searchable encryption. ACM Comput. Surv. (CSUR) **47**(2), 18 (2015)
5. Bosch, C., Peter, A., Leenders, B., Lim, H.W., Tang, Q., Wang, H., Hartel, P., Jonker, W.: Distributed searchable symmetric encryption. In: 12th International Conference on Privacy, Security and Trust (PST), pp. 330–337. IEEE (2014)
6. Bost, R., Minaud, B., Ohrimenko, O.: Forward and backward private searchable encryption from constrained cryptographic primitives. Technical report, IACR Cryptology ePrint Archive 2017 (2017)
7. Cao, N., Wang, C., Li, M., Ren, K., Lou, W.: Privacy-preserving multi-keyword ranked search over encrypted cloud data. IEEE Trans. Parallel Distrib. Syst. **25**(1), 222–233 (2014)
8. Cash, D., Grubbs, P., Perry, J., Ristenpart, T.: Leakage-abuse attacks against searchable encryption. In: Proceedings of the 22nd ACM CCS, pp. 668–679 (2015)
9. Cash, D., Jaeger, J., Jarecki, S., Jutla, C.S., Krawczyk, H., Rosu, M.-C., Steiner, M.: Dynamic searchable encryption in very-large databases: data structures and implementation. IACR Cryptology ePrint Archive 2014:853 (2014)
10. Chor, B., Kushilevitz, E., Goldreich, O., Sudan, M.: Private information retrieval. J. ACM (JACM) (1998)
11. Curtmola, R., Garay, J., Kamara, S., Ostrovsky, R.: Searchable symmetric encryption: improved definitions and efficient constructions. In: Proceedings of the 13th ACM CCS, pp. 79–88. ACM (2006)
12. Garg, S., Mohassel, P., Papamanthou, C.: TWORAM: round-optimal oblivious RAM with applications to searchable encryption. IACR Cryptology ePrint Archive 2015:1010 (2015)
13. Goldberg, I.: Improving the robustness of private information retrieval. In: IEEE Symposium on Security and Privacy, pp. 131–148. IEEE (2007)
14. Hahn, F., Kerschbaum, F.: Searchable encryption with secure and efficient updates. In: Proceedings of the 2014 ACM SIGSAC Conference on Computer and Communications Security, pp. 310–320. ACM (2014)
15. Hoang, T., Yavuz, A., Guajardo, J.: Practical and secure dynamic searchable encryption via oblivious access on distributed data structure. In: Proceedings of the 32nd Annual Computer Security Applications Conference (ACSAC). ACM (2016)
16. Islam, M.S., Kuzu, M., Kantarcioglu, M.: Access pattern disclosure on searchable encryption: Ramification, attack and mitigation. In: NDSS (2012)

17. Kamara, S., Papamanthou, C., Roeder, T.: Dynamic searchable symmetric encryption. In: Proceedings of the 2012 ACM Conference on Computer and Communications Security, pp. 965–976. ACM (2012)
18. Liu, C., Zhu, L., Wang, M., Tan, Y.-A.: Search pattern leakage in searchable encryption: attacks and new construction. Inf. Sci. **265**, 176–188 (2014)
19. Moataz, T., Blass, E.-O., Mayberry, T.: CHf-ORAM: a constant communication ORAM without homomorphic encryption. Technical report, Cryptology ePrint Archive, Report 2015/1116 (2015)
20. Moataz, T., Ray, I., Ray, I., Shikfa, A., Cuppens, F., Cuppens, N.: Substring search over encrypted data. J. Comput. Secur., 1–30 (2018, preprint)
21. Naveed, M.: The fallacy of composition of oblivious ram and searchable encryption. Cryptology ePrint Archive, Report 2015/668 (2015)
22. Ren, L., Fletcher, C.W., Kwon, A., Stefanov, E., Shi, E., van Dijk, M., Devadas, S.: Ring ORAM: closing the gap between small and large client storage oblivious RAM. IACR Cryptology ePrint Archive (2014)
23. Shamir, A.: How to share a secret. Commun. ACM **22**, 612–613 (1979)
24. Song, D.X., Wagner, D., Perrig, A.: Practical techniques for searches on encrypted data. In: Proceedings of the 2000 IEEE Symposium on Security and Privacy, pp. 44–55. IEEE Computer Society (2000)
25. Stefanov, E., Van Dijk, M., Shi, E., Fletcher, C., Ren, L., Yu, X., Devadas, S.: Path ORAM: an extremely simple oblivious RAM protocol. In: Proceedings of the 2013 ACM CCS, pp. 299–310. ACM (2013)
26. Sun, W., Wang, B., Cao, N., Li, M., Lou, W., Hou, Y.T., Li, H.: Privacy-preserving multi-keyword text search in the cloud supporting similarity-based ranking. In: ACM SIGSAC AsiaCCS, pp. 71–82. ACM (2013)
27. Wang, C., Cao, N., Li, J., Ren, K., Lou, W.: Secure ranked keyword search over encrypted cloud data. In: IEEE 30th International Conference on Distributed Computing Systems, pp. 253–262. IEEE (2010)
28. Yavuz, A.A., Guajardo, J.: Dynamic searchable symmetric encryption with minimal leakage and efficient updates on commodity hardware. In: Dunkelman, O., Keliher, L. (eds.) SAC 2015. LNCS, vol. 9566, pp. 241–259. Springer, Cham (2016). https://doi.org/10.1007/978-3-319-31301-6_15
29. Zhang, R., Xue, R., Yu, T., Liu, L.: Dynamic and efficient private keyword search over inverted index-based encrypted data. ACM Trans. Internet Technol. (TOIT) **16**(3), 21 (2016)
30. Zhang, Y., Katz, J., Papamanthou, C.: All your queries are belong to us: the power of file-injection attacks on searchable encryption. In: 25th USENIX Security Symposium (USENIX Security 2016), pp. 707–720 (2016)
31. Zhou, F., Li, Y., Liu, A.X., Lin, M., Xu, Z.: Integrity preserving multi-keyword searchable encryption for cloud computing. In: Chen, L., Han, J. (eds.) ProvSec 2016. LNCS, vol. 10005, pp. 153–172. Springer, Cham (2016). https://doi.org/10.1007/978-3-319-47422-9_9

Privacy-Preserving Planarity Testing
of Distributed Graphs

Guy Barshap and Tamir Tassa[⊠]

The Open University, Ra'anana, Israel
barshag@post.bgu.ac.il, tamirta@openu.ac.il

Abstract. We study the problem of privacy-preserving planarity testing of distributed graphs. The setting involves several parties that hold
private graphs on the same set of vertices, and an external mediator that
helps with performing the computations. Their goal is to test whether
the union of their private graphs is planar, but in doing so each party
wishes to deny from his peers any information on his own private edge
set beyond what is implied by the final output of the computation. We
present a privacy-preserving protocol for that purpose which is based
on the Hanani-Tutte Theorem. That theorem enables translating the
planarity question into the question of whether a specific system of linear equations over the field $\mathbf{F}_2$ is solvable. Our protocol uses a diverse
cryptographic toolkit which includes techniques such as homomorphic
encryption, oblivious Gaussian elimination, and private set intersection.
This is the first time that a solution to this problem is presented.

Keywords: Secure multiparty computation
Privacy-preserving distributed computations
Distributed graphs · Graph planarity

1 Introduction

A planar graph $G = (V, E)$ is a graph that can be properly embedded in the
two-dimensional plane $\mathbf{R}^2$ in the following sense: there exists a bijection φ from
the vertex set V to $\mathbf{R}^2$ and a representation of each edge $e = (u, v) \in E$ as a
continuous simple curve in $\mathbf{R}^2$ with $\varphi(u)$ and $\varphi(v)$ as its end points, such that
no two curves intersect apart possibly at their end points.

Planar graphs constitute an attractive family of graphs, both in theory and
in practice. In many applications where graph structures arise, it is needed to
test the planarity of those graphs. A classical example is in the area of integrated circuit (IC) design. An IC consists of electronic modules and the wiring
interconnections between them. It can be represented by a graph in which the
vertices are the modules and the edges are the wires. An IC can be printed on
the surface of a chip iff the graph is planar, because wires must not cross each
other. Another setting in which planarity is a natural notion is in road maps.

© IFIP International Federation for Information Processing 2018
Published by Springer International Publishing AG, part of Springer Nature 2018. All Rights Reserved
F. Kerschbaum and S. Paraboschi (Eds.): DBSec 2018, LNCS 10980, pp. 131–147, 2018.
https://doi.org/10.1007/978-3-319-95729-6_9

A set of cities and interconnecting roads can be thought of as a graph; the graph vertices are the cities while the edges are connecting roads. Such a map can be constructed with non-crossing roads (in order to avoid constructing bridges or obstructing the traffic flow by stop lights) iff the corresponding graph is planar. Apart from the above motivating examples, there are cases in which the planarity of a graph can be exploited in order to simplify and expedite the solution of some computational problems. Examples include sub-graph isomorphism [1], maximal clique [2], and maximum cut [3].

In this study we consider a distributed version of the planarity testing problem. In that problem there are several parties, $P_1, \ldots, P_d$, each one holding a private graph on the same set of vertices; namely, P_i has a graph $G_i = (V, E_i)$ where V is publicly known and shared by all, while E_i is private, $1 \leq i \leq d$. They wish to determine whether the union graph $G = (V, E)$, where $E = \bigcup_{i=1}^{d} E_i$, is planar or not. As the edge sets E_i, $1 \leq i \leq d$, are private, the planarity testing should be carried out in a privacy-preserving manner. Namely, after the conclusion of the computational procedure P_i must not learn anything on E_j, $j \neq i$, beyond what is implied by G_i and the planarity of G. For example, two (or more) companies may wish to check the possibility of printing the ICs which implement their products on the same chip. They prefer not to disclose to each other their own IC design, before they are verified that they could collaborate in that manner. The algorithmic solutions which we propose herein for privacy-preserving planarity testing could be used in that application scenario.

The strict notion of perfect privacy-preservation is sometimes relaxed by allowing some leakage of information, if such a relaxation enables a more efficient computation and if the leakage of information is characterized (in order to decide, in any given application setting, whether the gain in efficiency justifies the reduction in privacy-preservation). There are many examples of studies that relax perfect privacy in order to allow practical solutions, from various domains such as distributed association rule mining [4,5], anonymization of distributed datasets [6–8], collaborative filtering [9,10], distributed graph mining [11], and distributed constraint optimization problems [12–14].

Well known characterizations for planar graphs were proposed by both Wagner [15] and Kuratowski [16]. For example, the Wagner's characterization states that a graph is planar iff it does not have K_5 (the complete graph over 5 vertices) or $K_{3,3}$ (the complete bipartite graph over 3 vertices in each part) as a minor (see Fig. 1). Namely, K_5 or $K_{3,3}$ cannot be obtained from G by a sequence of these operations: contracting edges, deleting edges, and deleting isolated vertices. However, directly applying either Wagner's characterization, or the closely-related Kuratowski's characterization, in order to test the planarity of a given graph, yields exponential-time algorithms [17].

Optimal linear time planarity testing algorithms were proposed in [18,19]. These algorithms are iterative and use a DFS-subroutine [17]. Alas, those features of these algorithms turn out to be significant obstacles when trying to devise corresponding privacy-preserving variants of these algorithms. Thus, none

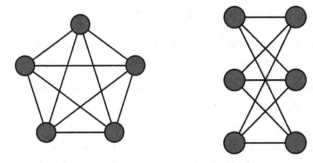

Fig. 1. The minors that cannot appear in a planar graph—K_5 and $K_{3,3}$.

of the above-mentioned approaches seem to be adequate in order to base on them an efficient privacy-preserving planarity testing protocol.

In this study we propose a privacy-preserving protocol for planarity testing of distributed graphs, which is based on the Hanani-Tutte Theorem [20]. Our protocol is based on the mediated model that was presented in [21]. In that model, there exists an external mediator T to which the parties may export some computations, but the mediator should not learn information on the private inputs of the parties or the final output. We assume that all interacting parties $(P_1, \ldots, P_d$ and $T)$ are semi-honest. Namely, they follow the protocol correctly, and do not form coalitions, but they try to extract from their view in the protocol information on the private inputs of other parties. (All privacy-related studies that we mentioned earlier also make similar assumptions.)

Due to page limitation and for the sake of clarity, we focus here on the case $d = 2$. The extension to any d is deferred to the full journal version of this study.

The outline of this work is as follows. In Sect. 2 we provide the relevant background on planarity testing, while in Sect. 3 we describe the main cryptographic toolkit that we use in our solution. We overview our solution and the two main stages of which it consists in Sect. 4. The subsequent Sects. 5 and 6 include the detailed description and analysis of each of the two stages in our solution. Finally, we conclude in Sect. 7.

2   Planarity Testing Using the Hanani-Tutte Theorem

In this section we state the Hanani-Tutte Theorem and then use it in order to translate the planarity question of a graph to the solvability of a system of linear equations over $\mathbf{F}_2$. To that end, we introduce the following definitions and notations:

- If $e \in E$ we let $a(e)$ and $b(e)$ denote the two vertices that e connects.
- A drawing D of a graph $G = (V, E)$ is an embedding of G in $\mathbf{R}^2$. Namely, it is a mapping $\varphi : V \to \mathbf{R}^2$ together with a representation of each edge $e \in E$ as a continuous simple curve that connects $\varphi(a(e))$ and $\varphi(b(e))$.

- Two edges $e, f \in E$ are called independent if $\{a(e), b(e)\} \cap \{a(f), b(f)\} = \emptyset$.
- The set of all pairs of independent edges in E is denoted E_2^{ind}.
- For a given drawing D of G and $\{e, f\} \in E_2^{ind}$, $parity_D(e, f)$ is the parity of the number of crossings between the curves representing e and f in D.

Theorem [Hanani-Tutte]. *A graph G is planar iff it has a drawing D in which* $parity_D(e, f) = 0$ *for all* $\{e, f\} \in E_2^{ind}$.

Let D be a drawing of G, $e \in E$, and $v \in V \setminus \{a(e), b(e)\}$. An (e, v)-move consists of taking a small section of the curve that represents e in D and deforming it in a narrow tunnel to make it pass over v, while not passing over any other vertex. The effect of an (e, v)-move in a drawing D is that $parity_D(e, f)$ changes for all edges f that are adjacent to v, but it remains unchanged for all other edges f (see Fig. 2).

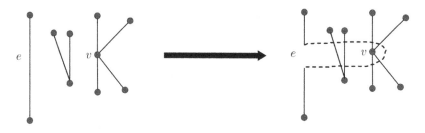

Fig. 2. An (e, v)-move. As a result, $parity_D(e, f)$ changes only for the four edges adjacent to v (from 0 to 1). For all other edges f, $parity_D(e, f)$ remains unchanged (0).

A remarkable corollary of this theorem is a planarity testing algorithm. It starts with an arbitrary drawing D of the input graph G, preferably a drawing in which $parity_D(e, f)$ can be computed efficiently for every pair of independent edges in G. Then, the algorithm tries to find another drawing D', by making a series of (e, v) moves, in which $parity_{D'}(e, f) = 0$ for all $\{e, f\} \in E_2^{ind}$. If it succeeds, then the graph is planar, otherwise it is not (see [20, Lemma 3.3]).

The existence of D' can be determined by considering the following system of linear equations. Define for each $e \in E$ and $v \in V \setminus \{a(e), b(e)\}$ a Boolean variable $x_{e,v}$; that variable equals 1 iff the transition from D to D' includes an (e, v)-move. It follows that for any pair of independent edges $\{e, f\} \in E_2^{ind}$,

$$parity_{D'}(e, f) = parity_D(e, f) + x_{e,a(f)} + x_{e,b(f)} + x_{f,a(e)} + x_{f,b(e)} \quad \text{in } \mathbf{F}_2.$$

Hence, given the drawing D, there exists a drawing D' in which $parity_{D'}(e, f) = 0$ for all $\{e, f\} \in E_2^{ind}$ iff there exists a solution to the following system of linear equations over $\mathbf{F}_2$:

$$parity_D(e, f) + x_{e,a(f)} + x_{e,b(f)} + x_{f,a(e)} + x_{f,b(e)} = 0 \quad \{e, f\} \in E_2^{ind}. \quad (1)$$

That is the Hanani-Tutte (HT hereinafter) system for the graph $G = (V, E)$ (with respect to the drawing D). It consists of $|E_2^{ind}|$ equations (one for each pair of independent edges) in $|E| \cdot (|V| - 2)$ unknowns ($x_{e,v}$ for all $e \in E$ and $v \in V \setminus \{a(e), b(e)\}$). The graph G is planar iff that system is solvable.

3   Cryptographic Toolkit

In this section we provide a birdseye view of the cryptographic primitives and procedures that we shall be using later on.

3.1   Homomorphic Encryption

An encryption function $\mathcal{F}$ is called (additively) *homomorphic* if the domain of plaintexts is a commutative additive group, the domain of ciphertexts is a commutative multiplicative group, and for every two plaintexts, m_1 and m_2, $\mathcal{F}(m_1 + m_2) = \mathcal{F}(m_1) \cdot \mathcal{F}(m_2)$. When the encryption function is randomized (in the sense that $\mathcal{F}(m)$ depends on m as well as on a random string) then $\mathcal{F}$ is called *probabilistic*. Homomorphic encryption functions allow performing arithmetic computations in the ciphertext domain. The property of being probabilistic is essential for getting semantic security.

There are many well known ciphers that are probabilistic and additively homomorphic. A basic example of such a cipher over $\mathbf{F}_2$, which we use in our protocol, is the Goldwasser-Micali cipher [22].

3.2   Deciding the Solvability of an Encrypted Linear System

Nissim and Weinreb [23] presented a method for obliviously deciding whether an encrypted system of linear equations is solvable or not. They considered a setting that involves two parties – T and P. T holds an encrypted matrix $\mathcal{F}(M)$, where M is a matrix of dimensions $k_a \times k_b$, and an encrypted vector $\mathcal{F}(\mathbf{b})$, where $\mathbf{b}$ is a column vector of dimension k_a. Both M and $\mathbf{b}$ are over the field $\mathbf{F} = \mathbf{F}_2$, while $\mathcal{F}$ is an additively homomorphic encryption over that field, for which P holds the private decryption key. Their protocol is Monte Carlo in the sense that its output may be wrong. Specifically, at the conclusion of the protocol T gets $\mathcal{F}(\beta)$ for some bit β. If the system $M\mathbf{x} = \mathbf{b}$ is not solvable then β will always be zero. Otherwise, if the system is solvable, then $\beta = 1$ with probability at least c for some positive constant c. Hence, by performing several independent runs of the protocol, it is possible to decide the solvability of the system with an error probability sufficiently small.

4   Overview of the Proposed Planarity Testing Protocol

Our planarity testing protocol has two stages. The first one consists of a preliminary check of the size of the unified edge set E. It is outlined in Sect. 4.1, and detailed in Sect. 5. The second stage includes the main protocol, in which the HT system of equations for the unified graph is constructed obliviously, and then its solvability is tested in a privacy-preserving manner. We provide a birdseye view of that stage in Sect. 4.2, and dive into its details in Sect. 6.

4.1 Testing the Number of Edges in the Unified Graph

Let $V = \{v_1, \ldots, v_n\}$ denote the vertex set in the unified graph $G = (V, E)$. A well-known result (see e.g. [17]) states that G is planar only if

$$|E| = |E_1 \cup E_2| \leq 3n - 6. \tag{2}$$

Hence, in the first stage, the three parties, P_1, P_2 and T, engage in a secure protocol for checking whether inequality (2) holds or not. If it does not, they know that the unified graph G is not planar. If it does hold, they proceed to the second stage in the verification (Sect. 4.2).

Running this stage is optional. On one hand, it leaks to the interacting parties information on $|E|$ beyond the required output about the planarity of G (specifically, whether inequality (2) holds or not). On the other hand, it may enable the parties to detect non-planarity without running the costly computation of the second stage. Hence, if in the relevant application scenario the information regarding whether inequality (2) holds or not is deemed benign, it is recommended to run this stage.

4.2 A Privacy-Preserving Implementation of the Hanani-Tutte Planarity Test

The three parties P_1, P_2 and T construct the HT system of linear equations, Eq. (1), for the unified graph G. Towards that end, they begin by constructing the system of linear equations for the complete graph on V, denoted K_V (i.e., K_V is the graph on V that has all $\binom{n}{2}$ edges):

$$x_{e,a(f)} + x_{e,b(f)} + x_{f,a(e)} + x_{f,b(e)} = parity_D(e, f) \qquad \{e, f\} \in K_2^{ind}; \tag{3}$$

here, K_2^{ind} is the set of all pairs of independent edges in K_V. The number of equations in that system is

$$N_{K_V} := |K_2^{ind}| = \frac{1}{2} \cdot \binom{n}{2} \cdot \binom{n-2}{2}. \tag{4}$$

This step can be constructed publicly with no privacy risks, since the vertex set V is known to all, and K_V is the complete graph on V. The main effort is in letting the mediator T extract from the large system in Eq. (3) the subset of equations in Eq. (1). To protect the unified graph data from T, he will get only an encrypted version of the subset of linear equations corresponding to G. The last part of the protocol is dedicated to determining whether that system has a solution or not. The main difficulty here lies in the fact that no party actually sees the relevant system of equations: only T holds that system, but he holds an encryption of that system, where the corresponding decryption key is known only to P_1.

To allow this approach, we must start with some drawing of K_V, which, in turn, induces also a drawing of G. We consider the following embedding of V in $\mathbf{R}^2$. If $V = \{v_1, \ldots, v_n\}$, then v_j is mapped into the point

$$v_j \mapsto \varphi(v_j) := (\cos(2\pi j/n), \sin(2\pi j/n)), \quad 1 \le j \le n. \tag{5}$$

Namely, the vertices $v_1, \ldots, v_n$ are mapped to equi-distant points on the unit circle, in a counter-clockwise order according to their index. The edge $e_{i,j} = (v_i, v_j)$ is then represented by the straight line segment between $\varphi(v_i)$ and $\varphi(v_j)$. Figure 3 illustrates that basic drawing for a graph over $n = 6$ vertices.

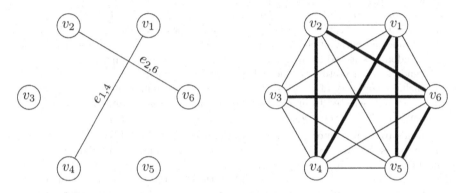

Fig. 3. Left: illustration of the embedding of $n = 6$ vertices, together with two connecting edges. Right: the corresponding drawing of K_V and of $G = (V, E)$ with $E = \{e_{1,4}, e_{1,5}, e_{2,4}, e_{2,6}, e_{3,6}, e_{5,6}\}$ (the six edges in E are marked by thicker lines).

Let us denote the above drawing of K_V (and the corresponding drawing of G, which is a sub-graph of K_V) by D. Consider now an arbitrary pair of independent edges $e_{i,j}$ and $e_{k,\ell}$; we may assume, without loss of generality, that $i < j$, $k < \ell$, and $i < k$. Then it is easy to see that $parity_D(e_{i,j}, e_{k,\ell}) = 1$ iff $i < k < j < \ell$.

The corresponding HT system (3) can be constructed publicly, by each of P_1, P_2 and T, for this drawing D of the complete graph K_V. As stated earlier, the main problem will be to identify, among those N_{K_V} equations, the $|E_2^{ind}|$ equations that relate to pairs of edges e and f that are both in E. Then, the graph $G = (V, E)$ is planar iff that sub-system of $|E_2^{ind}|$ equations has a solution. In Sect. 6 we provide the details of that computation.

5   First Stage: Testing the Size of the Unified Edge Set

Let $V_2 := \{(v_i, v_j) : 1 \le i < j \le n\}$ denote the set of all possible $\binom{n}{2}$ edges in G. Since $E = E_1 \cup E_2$, we infer that $E^c = E_1^c \cap E_2^c$, where for any subset $A \subseteq V_2$,

$A^c := V_2 \setminus A$ denotes its complement within V_2. Hence, by Eq. (2), the unified graph $G = (V, E)$ is planar only if

$$|E^c| = |E_1^c \cap E_2^c| \geq \binom{n}{2} - (3n - 6). \tag{6}$$

In order to verify the latter inequality it is possible to invoke any of the multitude of protocols for private set intersection. The first such protocol was proposed in [24], and is based on the Diffie-Hellman protocol [25]. Protocol 1, which we present below, is based on the private set intersection protocol of [24].

Protocol 1. Testing the size of the unified edge set

1: P_1 and P_2 select a large multiplicative group $\mathbf{Z}_p^*$ (p is prime) and a hash function H whose range can be embedded in $\mathbf{Z}_p^*$.
2: P_h selects a secret and random exponent $1 < \alpha_h < p - 1$, $h = 1, 2$.
3: P_1 sends to P_2 a vector $\mathbf{x}_1$ of length $\binom{n}{2}$ where, for each edge $(v_i, v_j) \in E_1^c$, $i < j$, $\mathbf{x}_1$ includes an entry of the form $H(i, j)^{\alpha_1}$, while the remaining $\binom{n}{2} - |E_1^c|$ entries are randomly selected from $\mathbf{Z}_p^*$. The order of $\mathbf{x}_1$'s entries is random.
4: P_2 sends to P_1 a vector $\mathbf{x}_2$ of length $\binom{n}{2}$ where, for each edge $(v_i, v_j) \in E_2^c$, $i < j$, $\mathbf{x}_2$ includes an entry of the form $H(i, j)^{\alpha_2}$, while the remaining $\binom{n}{2} - |E_2^c|$ entries are randomly selected from $\mathbf{Z}_p^*$. The order of $\mathbf{x}_2$'s entries is random.
5: P_1 sends to T the vector $\mathbf{y}_2$, where $\mathbf{y}_2(i) = \mathbf{x}_2(i)^{\alpha_1}$, $1 \leq i \leq \binom{n}{2}$.
6: P_2 sends to T the vector $\mathbf{y}_1$, where $\mathbf{y}_1(i) = \mathbf{x}_1(i)^{\alpha_2}$, $1 \leq i \leq \binom{n}{2}$.
7: T compares the two received vectors and finds out the number z of matching entries in them.
8: If $z < \binom{n}{2} - (3n - 6)$, T notifies P_1 and P_2 that the union graph is not planar.

As a result of Steps 1–6, which are self-explanatory, T receives two vectors, $\mathbf{y}_1$ and $\mathbf{y}_2$, each of which is of length $\binom{n}{2}$. The vector $\mathbf{y}_h$, $h = 1, 2$, includes the hash of all edges in E_h^c, raised to the exponent $\alpha_1 \alpha_2$, while the remaining $\binom{n}{2} - |E_h^c|$ entries are random elements in $\mathbf{Z}_p^*$. The number z of matching entries in those two vectors (Step 7) satisfies $z \geq |E^c|$, while with very high probability $z = |E^c|$. Indeed, if $(v_i, v_j) \in E_1^c \cap E_2^c$ then both vectors $\mathbf{y}_1$ and $\mathbf{y}_2$ will include an entry that equals $H(i, j)^{\alpha_1 \alpha_2}$; hence, those two entries will be identified by T in Step 7 as matching entries and, consequently, T will increment the counter z by 1. However, we note that T may wrongly increment the counter z due to random false matchings. False matchings can occur if there are collisions in H, namely, if there exist two pairs (i, j) and (i', j') such that $H(i, j) = H(i', j')$, or if P_1 and P_2 selected in Steps 3 and 4 random entries ξ_1 and ξ_2, respectively, so that $\xi_2^{\alpha_1} = \xi_1^{\alpha_2}$. By selecting a secure hash function with a sufficiently large range, the probability of such false matchings is negligible.

The security of Protocol 1 follows from the hardness of the Discrete Log problem. The protocol entails $O(n^2)$ hash function evaluations and exponentiations (for P_1 and P_2) and $O(n^2 \log n)$ comparisons for T. The protocol has only two rounds of communication in which $O(n^2 \log p)$ bits are transmitted.

Protocol 1 reveals to T the size of E. If P_1 and P_2 wish to prevent T from learning that information, they may modify Protocol 1 towards hiding that information. They can choose an integer $K > 0$ and then select at random an integer $k \in [0, K]$. Next, they will select $2K - k$ random and distinct elements from $\mathbf{Z}_p^*$: $a_i, 1 \leq i \leq k$, and $b_{h,i}, 1 \leq i \leq K-k, h = 1, 2$. Then, P_1 will add to $\mathbf{y}_2$ additional K entries, at random locations, with the values $a_1, \ldots, a_k, b_{1,i}, \ldots, b_{1,K-k}$, while P_2 will add to $\mathbf{y}_1$ additional K entries, at random locations, with the values $a_1, \ldots, a_k, b_{2,i}, \ldots, b_{2,K-k}$. Given those modifications, T will recover in Step 7 a value z that equals $|E^c| + k$ (with high probability).

Hence, the inequality that needs to be verified now is whether $z < \binom{n}{2} - (3n - 6) + k$. In the latter inequality, T knows the left hand side (z) while P_1 knows the right hand side, and the two parties need to verify the inequality without disclosing to each other information on the compared values beyond the information of whether the inequality holds or not. This is an instance of the celebrated Yao's millionaires' problem [26]. By invoking any of the many available protocols for solving that problem (e.g. [27]), the two parties may find out securely whether $|E^c| < \binom{n}{2} - (3n - 6)$.

Such a modification of Protocol 1 prevents T from getting $|E|$. Higher values of K will imply higher levels of obfuscation, but at the same time also higher communication and computational costs. As implied by [28, Lemma 4], if $K > \binom{n}{2}$ then the probability of T not learning anything on $|E|$ from z is exactly $1 - \binom{n}{2}/(K + 1)$; in all other cases (namely, in probability $\binom{n}{2}/(K + 1)$), T will learn either a lower or an upper bound on $|E|$.

6   Second Stage: Private Planarity Testing

Protocol 2 decides the planarity of the union graph G in a privacy-preserving manner. It begins with P_1 generating a key pair in a probabilistic additively homomorphic cipher, $\mathcal{F}$, over $\mathbf{F}_2$.

Next, the three parties execute a sub-protocol, called CONSTRUCTHTSYS-TEM (Step 2). The purpose of that sub-protocol is to construct the HT system for the union graph G, Eq. (1), in an oblivious manner. At the end of that sub-protocol T will hold an (entry-wise) $\mathcal{F}$-encryption of the coefficient matrix of that system. (We note that T will actually get an "inflated" version of that system, in the following sense: instead of an encryption of the HT system for G, Eq. (1), he will hold an encryption of the larger HT system for the complete graph K_V, Eq. (3), where all equations that relate to pairs of edges that are not in E_2^{ind} are zeroed.)

Then (Step 3), P_1 and T execute a sub-protocol, called DECIDESOLVABILITY, which decides the solvability of the encrypted system that was constructed in the previous step. T holds the encryption of the coefficient matrix and the right hand side vector for that system, while P_1 holds the relevant decryption key. The sub-protocol DECIDESOLVABILITY decides the solvability of the system in a privacy-preserving manner, that is – without decrypting the system. The Boolean flag that DECIDESOLVABILITY returns indicates the solvability of the system. If it is **true** then the system is solvable and, consequently, the union graph G is planar. Otherwise, if it is **false**, then, with high probability (which may be tuned as desired), the system is not solvable and, hence, the union graph G is not planar.

In the next sub-sections (Sects. 6.1 and 6.2) we discuss the implementation of the two main steps in Protocol 2.

Protocol 2. Privacy preserving HT planarity testing

1: P_1 generates a key pair in a probabilistic additively homomorphic cipher, $\mathcal{F}$, over $\mathbf{F}_2$. P_1 notifies P_2 and T of the public encryption key in $\mathcal{F}$.
2: P_1, P_2 and T execute CONSTRUCTHTSYSTEM. At its conclusion, T holds an $\mathcal{F}$-encryption of the HT system for the union graph, $(\mathbf{r}_{e,f} : \{e, f\} \in K_2^{ind})$.
3: P_1 and T execute DECIDESOLVABILITY$(\mathbf{r}_{e,f} : \{e, f\} \in K_2^{ind})$.
4: **if** DECIDESOLVABILITY returns **true then**
5:    Output "The union graph is planar".
6: **else**
7:    Output "The union graph is non-planar".
8: **end if**

6.1 Constructing an $\mathcal{F}$-Encryption of the HT System

Here we discuss the sub-protocol CONSTRUCTHTSYSTEM, which is implemented in Protocol 3. Before starting to do so, we take a look at the HT systems for G and for the complete graph K_V. The HT system for the complete graph K_V, with respect to the drawing D described in Sect. 4.2, is given in Eq. (3). All parties can construct that system, since K_V is a public graph. The HT system for G, Eq. (1), which determines the planarity of $G = (V, E)$, is a sub-system (subset of equations) of (3). That sub-system includes only the equations relating to pairs $\{e, f\} \in E_2^{ind} \subset K_2^{ind}$ (namely, pairs of independent edges $\{e, f\}$ where both e and f are in E).

Let $V_2 := \{e_{i,j} = (v_i, v_j) : 1 \leq i < j \leq n\}$ denote the edge set in the full graph K_V (consisting of all possible pairs of vertices from V). The set K_2^{ind} consists of all pairs of independent edges in K_V. Its size is N_{K_V} (Eq. (4)), and it consists of all pairs of edges $\{e = (v_i, v_j), f = (v_k, v_\ell)\}$ where all four indices i, j, k, ℓ are distinct (as the two edges are independent), and $i < j$, $k < \ell$, and $i < k$. Our protocol, CONSTRUCTHTSYSTEM, assumes that the set K_2^{ind} is ordered. We assume hereinafter that it is ordered lexicographically by the 4-tuple (i, j, k, ℓ).

For each edge $e \in V_2$ and $h \in \{1, 2\}$, let α_e^h be the Boolean variable denoting whether $e \in E_h$ or not. Then, $e \in E$ iff $\alpha_e^1 \vee \alpha_e^2 = 1$. Consequently, the equation that corresponds to the pair of independent edges $\{e, f\} \in K_2^{ind}$ appears in the HT system for G, Eq. (1), iff

$$\chi_{e,f} := (\alpha_e^1 \vee \alpha_e^2) \wedge (\alpha_f^1 \vee \alpha_f^2) = 1. \tag{7}$$

In the first part of CONSTRUCTHTSYSTEM (Steps 1–2), T gets the $\mathcal{F}$-encryption of $\chi_{e,f}$ for all $\{e,f\} \in K_2^{ind}$, where $\chi_{e,f}$ is the Boolean flag indicating whether $\{e,f\} \in E_2^{ind}$ (Eq. (7)), and $\mathcal{F}$ is the cipher that P_1 selected in Step 1 of Protocol 2. Towards that end, we observe that

$$\chi_{e,f} := (\alpha_e^1 \vee \alpha_e^2) \wedge (\alpha_f^1 \vee \alpha_f^2) = (\alpha_e^1 + \alpha_e^2 - \alpha_e^1 \cdot \alpha_e^2) \cdot (\alpha_f^1 + \alpha_f^2 - \alpha_f^1 \cdot \alpha_f^2). \quad (8)$$

Hence, by opening the brackets on the right hand side of Eq. (8) and then applying $\mathcal{F}$ on both sides of that equation, we get, using the homomorphism of $\mathcal{F}$ and simple algebra, that $\mathcal{F}(\chi_{e,f}) = A \cdot B^{-1}$, where

$$A = \alpha^{\alpha_f^2} \cdot \beta^{\alpha_e^2} \cdot \gamma^{1+\alpha_e^2 \cdot \alpha_f^2} \cdot \mathcal{F}(\alpha_e^2 \cdot \alpha_f^2), \quad B = (\alpha \cdot \beta)^{\alpha_e^2 \cdot \alpha_f^2} \cdot \gamma^{\alpha_e^2 + \alpha_f^2}, \quad (9)$$

and

$$\alpha := \mathcal{F}(\alpha_e^1), \ \beta := \mathcal{F}(\alpha_f^1), \ \gamma := \mathcal{F}(\alpha_e^1 \cdot \alpha_f^1). \quad (10)$$

In view of the above derivations, P_1 sends to P_2 the three values α, β, and γ, for each of the N_{K_V} pairs $\{e,f\} \in K_2^{ind}$, where the triplets (α,β,γ) are ordered by the lexicographical order over K_2^{ind} (Step 1). P_2 can then use Eq. (9) in order to compute A and B, for each such pair. Note that all powers of α, β and γ in Eq. (9) are determined by Boolean variables owned by P_2, while $\mathcal{F}(\alpha_e^2 \cdot \alpha_f^2)$ can be computed by P_2 since he has the public encryption key of $\mathcal{F}$. P_2 then sends to T a vector of length N_{K_V}, in which each entry includes the value $\mathcal{F}(\chi_{e,f}) = A \cdot B^{-1}$ for the relevant pair $\{e,f\} \in K_2^{ind}$ (Step 2).

Protocol 3. CONSTRUCTHTSYSTEM: Constructing an encryption of the HT system

---

1: P_1 sends to P_2 the vector $((\alpha,\beta,\gamma) : \{e,f\} \in K_2^{ind})$ (see Eq. (10)).
2: P_2 sends to T the vector $\mathbf{u} := (\mathcal{F}(\chi_{e,f}) : \{e,f\} \in K_2^{ind})$.
3: **for all** $\{e,f\} \in K_2^{ind}$, where $e = e_{i,j}$, $f = e_{k,\ell}$, $i < j$, $k < \ell$ and $i < k$ **do**
4:    T allocates a vector $\mathbf{r}_{e,f}$ of dimension $N+1$ where $N := \binom{n}{2} \cdot (n-2)$.
5:    T creates a bijection $\Phi : [N] \to \{(g,v) : g \in V_2, v \in V \setminus \{a(g), b(g)\}\}$.
6:    **for** $i \in [N]$ **do**
7:      $(g,v) \leftarrow \Phi(i)$.
8:      **if** $(g = e$ and $v \in \{a(f), b(f)\})$ or $(g = f$ and $v \in \{a(e), b(e)\})$ **then**
9:        $\mathbf{r}_{e,f}(i) \leftarrow \mathcal{F}(\chi_{e,f})$
10:     **else**
11:       $\mathbf{r}_{e,f}(i) \leftarrow \mathcal{F}(0)$
12:     **end if**
13:    **end for**
14:    **if** $i < k < j < \ell$ **then**
15:      $\mathbf{r}_{e,f}(N+1) \leftarrow \mathcal{F}(\chi_{e,f})$
16:    **else**
17:      $\mathbf{r}_{e,f}(N+1) \leftarrow \mathcal{F}(0)$
18:    **end if**
19: **end for**

The goal of the main loop in Steps 3–19 is to let T construct an entry-wise $\mathcal{F}$-encryption of the HT system for G, Eq. (1). That system has $|E_2^{ind}|$ equations over $|E| \cdot (n-2)$ unknowns. It is a sub-system of the full system for K_V, Eq. (3), which has N_{K_V} equations over $N := \binom{n}{2} \cdot (n-2)$ unknowns. The encrypted system that T constructs in the loop in Steps 3–19 will be of the same dimensions as the larger system for the full graph, but all rows in it that are not relevant for G will be zeroed. T will remain oblivious to the rows in the full system that he zeroes in this process. We proceed to explain how this is done.

Consider the augmented matrix that describes the HT system for K_V, Eq. (3). It has N_{K_V} rows, one for each pair $\{e, f\} \in K_2^{ind}$. Each row, $\mathbf{r}_{e,f}$, is a Boolean vector of length $N + 1$, where $N = \binom{n}{2} \cdot (n-2)$, since it includes the coefficient of each unknown variable (and there are N such variables, one for each coupling of an edge and a non-adjacent vertex) plus the right hand side ($parity_D(e, f)$). In the linear equation corresponding to the pair $\{e, f\}$, the coefficients of all variables are zero, except for four of those variables (see Eq. (3)). Hence, in the inner loop in Steps 6–13, T goes over the first N entries of $\mathbf{r}_{e,f}$; in each of the four entries that should equal 1, T places the value $\mathcal{F}(\chi_{e,f})$ (those are values that T got from P_2 in Step 2), while in all the remaining ones he places the value $\mathcal{F}(0)$ (those are encryptions that T can compute on his own since he has the public encryption key of $\mathcal{F}$). In the last position in $\mathbf{r}_{e,f}$, corresponding to the right hand side of the equation for the pair $\{e, f\}$, T places the value $\mathcal{F}(\chi_{e,f})$ in case the two edges intersect in the basic drawing D, while otherwise he places the value $\mathcal{F}(0)$ (Steps 14–18). As a result, if $\chi_{e,f} = 0$, T constructs an encryption of the all-zero equation; but if $\chi_{e,f} = 1$, T constructs an encryption of the equation for the pair $\{e, f\}$, as in Eq. (3). In summary, T gets a system of N_{K_V} encrypted equations: $|E_2^{ind}|$ of those equations are an $\mathcal{F}$-encryption of the system (1), while the remaining ones are $\mathcal{F}$-encryptions of the trivial equation (the equation in which all coefficients and right hand side are zero).

6.2 Determining the Solvability of an Encrypted Linear System

The sub-protocol DECIDESOLVABILITY (Protocol 4) decides the solvability of a system of N_{K_V} linear equations over $N = \binom{n}{2} \cdot (n-2)$ unknowns. Let M denote the $N_{K_V} \times N$ matrix of coefficients of that system, and $\mathbf{b}$ denote the right hand side vector (an N_{K_V}-dimensional column vector). The two parties that run the sub-protocol are P_1 and T. P_1 holds the decryption key in $\mathcal{F}$ (see Step 1 in Protocol 2) – a probabilistic additively homomorphic cipher over $\mathbf{F}_2$; T, on the other hand, holds $\mathcal{F}(M)$ and $\mathcal{F}(\mathbf{b})$. DECIDESOLVABILITY determines whether the system $M\mathbf{x} = \mathbf{b}$ has a solution or not. It does so in a privacy-preserving manner, i.e., without revealing to neither of the two parties information on the underlying matrix M and right hand side $\mathbf{b}$.

To do so, the two parties execute the protocol due to Nissim and Weinreb [23] that we outlined in Sect. 3.2, which enables them to obliviously decide whether an encrypted system of linear equations is solvable or not. We refer to this protocol below by the name SOLVABILITYLINEARSYSTEM.

The output of Protocol SOLVABILITYLINEARSYSTEM is $\mathcal{F}(\beta)$, where β is a bit that indicates the existence of a vector $\mathbf{x}$ for which $M\mathbf{x} = \mathbf{b}$.

We recall that the basic protocol due to Nissim and Weinreb is a true-biased Monte Carlo protocol. Namely, a **true** answer (i.e., the system is solvable) is always correct, while a **false** answer may be wrong. We assume herein that the procedure SOLVABILITYLINEARSYSTEM which is invoked in Step 1 of Protocol 4 executes the basic protocol due to Nissim and Weinreb a sufficient number of times so that the probability of a false answer to be incorrect is reduced to below some given desired threshold.

Sub-protocol 4. DECIDESOLVABILITY

1: T and P_1 run Protocol SOLVABILITYLINEARSYSTEM with inputs $\mathcal{F}(M)$ and $\mathcal{F}(\mathbf{b})$. The output $\mathcal{F}(\beta)$ goes to T.
2: T sends to P_1 the value $\mathcal{F}(\beta)$.
3: P_1 decrypts and recovers β.
4: **if** $\beta = 1$ **then**
5:     return **true**
6: **else**
7:     return **false**
8: **end if**

6.3   Privacy Analysis

The potential leakages of information to any party is due to messages that he receives from other parties. We proceed to discuss the security of each of the steps in Protocol 2 that involves exchange of messages.

In Step 1 of Protocol 3 (which is invoked by Protocol 2), P_2 receives from P_1 information relating to E_1. Specifically, for each pair of independent edges in K_V, P_2 receives the values $\alpha := \mathcal{F}(\alpha_e^1)$, $\beta := \mathcal{F}(\alpha_f^1)$, and $\gamma := \mathcal{F}(\alpha_e^1 \cdot \alpha_f^1)$. However, as that information is encrypted by $\mathcal{F}$, P_2 cannot extract information on E_1, assuming that the chosen cipher $\mathcal{F}$ is semantically secure (as is the case with the Goldwasser-Micali cipher [22] which we propose to utilize here). Similarly for Step 2 of Protocol 3 in which T receives information on E; as it is encrypted by $\mathcal{F}$, it is protected from T.

Finally, the security of Protocol 4 follows from the security of SOLVABILITY-LINEARSYSTEM that was established in [23].

6.4   Computational and Communication Costs

We begin by assessing the computational and communication costs of the first two steps in Protocol 3. The computational cost of Protocol 3 for P_1 is $2\binom{n}{2}$ encryptions (for computing α and β for all edges in K_V), and, in addition, N_{K_V} (Eq. (4)) encryptions, for computing γ for all pairs of edges in K_2^{ind} (Step 1). The computational cost of Protocol 3 for P_2 is dominated by the need to perform N_{K_V} encryptions ($\mathcal{F}(\alpha_e^2 \cdot \alpha_f^2)$) in order to compute A for all pairs of edges in

K_2^{ind}. The remaining operations for computing A and B (see Eq. (9)) in Step 2 are only multiplications (note that all exponents in Eq. (9) are 0, 1, or 2). The communication cost of Steps 1–2 in Protocol 3 is $O(N_{K_V})$ bits.

The computational costs for T due to Protocol 3 are negligible, as it has to perform no new encryptions, other than computing $\mathcal{F}(0)$ once. We note that the value $\mathcal{F}(0)$ appears in many entries in the encrypted HT linear system of equations. However, the procedure SOLVABILITYLINEARSYSTEM, which is executed in the next stage, is designed so that there is no need for T to generate here independent encryptions $\mathcal{F}(0)$ for each such entry.

The main computational bottleneck is Protocol 4. Indeed, as the underlying matrix has $k_a = N_{K_V} = O(n^4)$ rows and $k_b = \binom{n}{2} \cdot (n-2) = O(n^3)$ columns, the computational cost of running an oblivious Gaussian elimination on it is of order $O(k_a \cdot k_b^2) = O(n^{10})$. Such a computational cost severely limits the applicability of our protocol to very small graphs.

The main problem with Protocol 2 is that it runs the oblivious Gaussian elimination over an encrypted matrix that has N_{K_V} rows. We recall that the actual system, Eq. (1), has only $|E_2^{ind}|$ equations. Since $|E| \leq 3n - 6$, as verified in the first stage, then $|E_2^{ind}| = O(n^2)$. Hence, one goal is to reduce the number of rows in the encrypted HT system from $N_{K_V} = O(n^4)$ to the exact number of relevant equations $|E_2^{ind}| = O(n^2)$. Moreover, the number of columns in Eq. (1) is $|E| \cdot (n-2) \leq (3n-6) \cdot (n-2) = O(n^2)$. Hence, another goal is to reduce the number of columns (unknowns) from $O(n^3)$ to $O(n^2)$. If we achieve both goals then the cost of the oblivious Gaussian elimination would reduce to $O(n^6)$. While this time complexity still limits the scalability of the protocol, it allows its execution on graphs with several hundreds of vertices. Such time complexity renders our protocol viable for application settings such as the two motivating examples that were considered in the introduction (IC design and road networks).

6.5 Reducing the Size of the HT System

In the master thesis [29] on which this study is based, we present a variant of Protocol 2 that achieves the above mentioned goals of reducing the number of rows and number of columns in the HT system. Due to space limitations, we only outline the main ideas of that variant herein, and leave the detailed description and analysis to the full version of this study.

The main difference from Protocol 2 is that P_1 generates the encryption of the HT system for the full graph K_V, Eq. (3), and sends it to T. Then, T extracts from that large system the sub-system for G, Eq. (1). Specifically, P_1 performs a similar computation to the one that T does in Steps 3–19 of Protocol 3, where the only difference is that in Steps 9 and 15 P_1 inserts the value $\mathcal{F}(1)$ (and not $\mathcal{F}(\chi_{e,f})$ as done in Protocol 3) in the relevant entries. Before sending the encrypted matrix to T, P_1 applies on its rows and columns random permutations, which are selected jointly by P_1 and P_2 and are kept secret from T.

Recall that the matrix has $k_a = N_{K_V} = O(n^4)$ rows and $k_b+1 = \binom{n}{2} \cdot (n-2) + 1 = O(n^3)$ columns. By examining the structure of the matrix, see Eq. (3), each of the k_a rows has either four or five 1-entries, while the remaining entries are 0.

Hence, in the encrypted matrix that P_1 sends to T, there will be $O(n^4)$ entries that equal $\mathcal{F}(1)$ and $O(n^7)$ entries that equal $\mathcal{F}(0)$. P_1 cannot re-use encryptions, since it is necessary to prevent T from distinguishing between 0 and 1 entries. It is possible to generate those $O(n^7)$ encrypted entries by performing only $O(n^{3.5})$ encryptions and relying on the homomorphic property of $\mathcal{F}$ (which implies that $\mathcal{F}(0) \cdot \mathcal{F}(0) = \mathcal{F}(0)$ and $\mathcal{F}(0) \cdot \mathcal{F}(1) = \mathcal{F}(1)$).

In order to enable T to detect which rows in the encrypted matrix need to be discarded (since they relate to pairs of edges in $K_2^{ind} \setminus E_2^{ind}$), T generates a key pair in a probabilistic additively homomorphic cipher, $\mathcal{E}$, over $\mathbf{F}_2$. Then, P_1 and P_2 perform the computation in Steps 1–2 of Protocol 3 with $\mathcal{E}$ instead of $\mathcal{F}$. Hence, P_2 sends to T the vector $\mathbf{u} := (\mathcal{E}(\chi_{e,f}) : \{e, f\} \in K_2^{ind})$, where the entries are permuted in accord to the selected order of rows in the encrypted matrix that P_1 had sent earlier to T. Subsequently, T computes $\mathbf{v} := \mathcal{E}^{-1}(\mathbf{u})$ and then he removes from the matrix all rows that correspond to 0-entries in $\mathbf{v}$. A similar procedure can be used to enable T to remove columns that are irrelevant for the HT system for G. After performing those two reductions, T gets an encryption of the system in Eq. (1). That is the system on which the procedure DECIDESOLVABILITY is applied.

Such a variant of Protocol 2 has a computational cost of $O(n^6)$. It has larger communication costs than Protocol 2, as P_1 needs to transfer to T $O(n^7)$ bits. In addition, it enables T to infer $|E|$ (as the final number of columns equals $|E| \cdot (n-2)$). If the latter value is deemed sensitive, P_1 and P_2 can obfuscate it by sending to T information that will result in keeping unnecessary columns, i.e., columns relating to variables $x_{e,v}$ where $e \notin E$. Such course of action will increase the computational cost, but will prevent T from inferring $|E|$.

7   Conclusions

We introduced the problem of privacy-preserving planarity testing of distributed graphs. We presented a protocol that solves this problem. Our protocol, based on the Hanani–Tutte Theorem, protects the private edge sets of each of the parties, under the assumption that the parties are semi-honest and do not collude.

In the full version of this study [29] we present an extension of our protocol to any number of parties; we present in detail and analyze the more efficient variant of Protocol 2, which we outlined in Sect. 6.5; and we show how our protocol can be used in order to reduce the complexity of various privacy-preserving graph computations, such as testing 3-colorability or testing outer-planarity.

This study raises the following problems for future research:

(a) Improving scalability, either by devising more efficient ways to test the solvability of the HT system, or by designing a privacy-preserving version of another planarity testing algorithm.

(b) Devising privacy-preserving protocols for solving graph problems, which are known to have an efficient solution in cases where the underlying graph is planar, e.g. the sub-graph isomorphism problem, or the maximal clique problem.

(c) Enhancing the resiliency of the protocol to coalitions, and to stronger adversarial models (i.e., malicious parties).

References

1. Eppstein, D.: Subgraph isomorphism in planar graphs and related problems. J. Graph Algorithms Appl. **3**(3), 1–27 (1999)
2. Papadimitriou, C.H., Yannakakis, M.: The clique problem for planar graphs. Inf. Process. Lett. **13**(4/5), 131–133 (1981)
3. Hadlock, F.: Finding a maximum cut of a planar graph in polynomial time. SIAM J. Comput. **4**(3), 221–225 (1975)
4. Kantarcioglu, M., Clifton, C.: Privacy-preserving distributed mining of association rules on horizontally partitioned data. IEEE Trans. Knowl. Data Eng. **16**, 1026–1037 (2004)
5. Tassa, T.: Secure mining of association rules in horizontally distributed databases. Trans. Knowl. Data Eng. **26**, 970–983 (2014)
6. Jiang, W., Clifton, C.: A secure distributed framework for achieving k-anonymity. VLDB J. **15**, 316–333 (2006)
7. Tassa, T., Gudes, E.: Secure distributed computation of anonymized views of shared databases. Trans. Database Syst. **37** (2012). Article 11
8. Tassa, T., Cohen, D.: Anonymization of centralized and distributed social networks by sequential clustering. Trans. Knowl. Data Eng. **25**, 311–324 (2013)
9. Jeckmans, A., Tang, Q., Hartel, P.: Privacy-preserving collaborative filtering based on horizontally partitioned dataset. In: CTS, pp. 439–446 (2012)
10. Shmueli, E., Tassa, T.: Secure multi-party protocols for item-based collaborative filtering. In: RecSys, pp. 89–97 (2017)
11. Asharov, G., Bonchi, F., García-Soriano, D., Tassa, T.: Secure centrality computation over multiple networks. In: WWW, pp. 957–966 (2017)
12. Grinshpoun, T., Tassa, T.: A privacy-preserving algorithm for distributed constraint optimization. In: AAMAS, pp. 909–916 (2014)
13. Léauté, T., Faltings, B.: Protecting privacy through distributed computation in multi-agent decision making. J. Artif. Intell. Res. **47**, 649–695 (2013)
14. Tassa, T., Grinshpoun, T., Zivan, R.: Privacy preserving implementation of the max-sum algorithm and its variants. J. Artif. Intell. Res. **59**, 311–349 (2017)
15. Wagner, K.: Über eine eigenschaft der ebenen komplexe. Math. Ann. **114**, 570–590 (1937)
16. Kuratowski, K.: Sur le problème des courbes gauches en topologie. Fundamenta Mathematicae **15**, 271–283 (1930)
17. Patrignani, M.: Handbook on Graph Drawing and Visualization, pp. 1–42. CRC Press, Boca Raton (2013)
18. Hopcroft, J.E., Tarjan, R.E.: Efficient planarity testing. J. ACM **21**(4), 549–568 (1974)
19. Boyer, J.M., Myrvold, W.J.: On the cutting edge: simplified o(n) planarity by edge addition. J. Graph Algorithms Appl. **8**(2), 241–273 (2004)

20. Schaefer, M.: Toward a theory of planarity: Hanani-Tutte and planarity variants. J. Graph Algorithms Appl. **17**(4), 367–440 (2013)
21. Alwen, J., Shelat, A., Visconti, I.: Collusion-free protocols in the mediated model. In: Wagner, D. (ed.) CRYPTO 2008. LNCS, vol. 5157, pp. 497–514. Springer, Heidelberg (2008). https://doi.org/10.1007/978-3-540-85174-5_28
22. Goldwasser, S., Micali, S.: Probabilistic encryption and how to play mental poker keeping secret all partial information. In: STOC, pp. 365–377 (1982)
23. Nissim, K., Weinreb, E.: Communication efficient secure linear algebra. In: Halevi, S., Rabin, T. (eds.) TCC 2006. LNCS, vol. 3876, pp. 522–541. Springer, Heidelberg (2006). https://doi.org/10.1007/11681878_27
24. Meadows, C.A.: A more efficient cryptographic matchmaking protocol for use in the absence of a continuously available third party. In: IEEE Symposium on Security and Privacy, pp. 134–137 (1986)
25. Diffie, W., Hellman, M.E.: New directions in cryptography. IEEE Trans. Inf. Theory **22**(6), 644–654 (1976)
26. Yao, A.C.: Protocols for secure computations (extended abstract). In: FOCS, pp. 160–164 (1982)
27. Lin, H.-Y., Tzeng, W.-G.: An efficient solution to the millionaires' problem based on homomorphic encryption. In: Ioannidis, J., Keromytis, A., Yung, M. (eds.) ACNS 2005. LNCS, vol. 3531, pp. 456–466. Springer, Heidelberg (2005). https://doi.org/10.1007/11496137_31
28. Grinshpoun, T., Tassa, T.: P-syncbb: a privacy preserving branch and bound DCOP algorithm. J. Artif. Intell. Res. **57**, 621–660 (2016)
29. Barshap, G.: Privacy-preserving planarity testing of distributed graphs. Master thesis, Department of Mathematics and Computer Science, The Open University of Israel (2018)

Image Pixelization
with Differential Privacy

Liyue Fan[(⊠)]

University at Albany, SUNY, Albany, NY 12222, USA
liyuefan@albany.edu

Abstract. Ubiquitous surveillance cameras and personal devices have given rise to the vast generation of image data. While sharing the image data can benefit various applications, including intelligent transportation systems and social science research, those images may capture sensitive individual information, such as license plates, identities, etc. Existing image privacy preservation techniques adopt deterministic obfuscation, e.g., pixelization, which can lead to re-identification with well-trained neural networks. In this study, we propose sharing pixelized images with rigorous privacy guarantees. We extend the standard differential privacy notion to image data, which protects individuals, objects, or their features. Empirical evaluation with real-world datasets demonstrates the utility and efficiency of our method; despite its simplicity, our method is shown to effectively reduce the success rate of re-identification attacks.

Keywords: Image privacy · Differential privacy

1 Introduction

There is a massive amount of image data captured by personal and commercial cameras nowadays. Every second 835 photos are uploaded on Instagram [1]. Over 18,000 traffic cameras spanning more than 200 cities in US are reported on TrafficLand [2]. Sharing image data widely would benefit various research communities. For instance, traffic images can be shared with third-party researchers to study vehicle behaviors toward intelligent transportation systems [3]; images uploaded on social media can be utilized by computer vision researchers to test their algorithms for social relation recognition [4] and early screening of mental illnesses [5]. However, publishing the aforementioned image data would raise *privacy concerns*. In fact, traffic cameras can capture the vehicle license plate; and personal images may capture objects or text that may indicate religious belief, health, habits, and location [6].

A number of studies proposed cryptography-based solutions for image sharing [7,8], retrieval [9,10], and feature extraction [11,12] using untrusted service providers. While those solutions secure the image data with encryption,

© IFIP International Federation for Information Processing 2018
Published by Springer International Publishing AG, part of Springer Nature 2018. All Rights Reserved
F. Kerschbaum and S. Paraboschi (Eds.): DBSec 2018, LNCS 10980, pp. 148–162, 2018.
https://doi.org/10.1007/978-3-319-95729-6_10

they exhibit a few drawbacks which make them inapplicable in our setting. Firstly, crypto-based image sharing explicitly trusts the data recipients, i.e., does not account for malicious recipients, and usually requires a secure channel to exchange secrets/keys. It can be challenging in both efficiency and security for sharing data with a wide range of recipients. Secondly, the features computed by the untrusted server also need to be protected, such as shape positions and scale-invariant feature transform (SIFT), as those features often disclose sensitive information. Existing studies resort to more expensive cryptographic tools, such as homomorphic encryption and garbled circuit [11], or multiple independent servers [12], which potentially limit the feasibility of extracting complex features and enabling time-critical applications.

The sanitization of private content in image data has been studied in computer vision. Standard image obfuscation techniques, such as pixelization and blurring, are used by most privacy enhancing approaches to obscure the regions-of-interest (ROIs), including faces and texts. However, recent studies have shown that pixelization [13], blurring [13], and the P3 system [7] are not effective in privacy preservation. Given sufficient training data and the obfuscation technique, various models can be built to associate the obfuscated images to the ground truth, which can be used to decode redacted documents [13], and to re-identify faces and handwritten digits [14]. Therefore, we are in need of image obfuscation methods that can provide rigorous privacy guarantees.

The *goal* of this study is to ensure a rigorous privacy notion, *differential privacy* [15], for image data sharing. By definition, the adversary cannot effectively distinguish between secrets by observing the output of a differentially private mechanism, thus privacy is protected. To our best knowledge, our study is the first attempt of providing differential privacy guarantees for multimedia data publication. The specific contributions of the paper are as follows:

(1) To extend the standard differential privacy notion to image data, we propose the m-neighborhood notion, which allows for the protection of any sensitive information represented by up to m pixels.

(2) Given the high sensitivity of direct image publication, we propose a pixelization-based method with grid cells of $b \times b$ pixels, to achieve a utility-privacy trade off. We show that it provides differential privacy guarantees.

(3) We empirically evaluate the utility and efficiency of the differentially private pixelization with real-world image datasets with different resolutions. Two utility metrics are adopted to measure the absolute error and the perceptual quality, respectively. We show that our private method can yield similar output to the non-private pixelization.

(4) We simulate the re-identification attacks via deep learning and the results show that the differentially private pixelization significantly reduces the re-identification risk, even with low privacy requirements, i.e., $\epsilon \geq 0.1$ and $m = 16$.

The rest of the paper is organized as follows: Sect. 2 reviews recent and related literature; Sects. 3 and 4 provide the preliminaries and technical details of the differentially private pixelization; Sect. 5 presents the empirical evaluation; Sect. 6 concludes the paper and states future directions.

2   Related Work

Image Privacy Classification. Several studies (e.g., [6, 16, 17]) utilized image content features to predict the privacy settings for image sharing on online social networks (OSN). In particular, those studies explored classification models to predict whether an image is *private* or *public*: *private* images or ROIs should not be shared publicly or with OSN providers so as to stop the flow of information. While those studies show promise to understand the sensitivity of image data, the selected features often lack interpretability, e.g., after PCA projection or deep neural network features. Moreover, the classification models may not be perfectly accurate and images classified as *private* will not be shared with the public, preventing further utilization.

Image Obfuscation. Two popular image obfuscation techniques are *pixelization* (also referred to as mosaicing) and *blurring*. Pixelization [13] can be achieved by superposing a rectangular grid over the original image and averaging the color values of the pixels within each grid cell. On the other hand, blurring, i.e., Gaussian blur, removes details from an image by convolving the 2D Gaussian distribution function with the image. YouTube provides its own face blur implementation [18] for video uploads. McPherson et al. [14] studied pixelization and YouTube face blur and concluded the obfuscated images using those methods can be re-identified. In addition, a secure image sharing method named P3 [7] was also studied in [14] which encrypts the significant Discrete Cosine Transform (DCT) coefficients of the image. As YouTube face blur and P3 are not available/applicable in our study, we will focus on the pixelization technique and design a quantifiable privacy model for obfuscating image data.

Differential Privacy. Differential privacy [15] has become the state-of-the-art privacy paradigm for sanitizing statistical databases. While it provides rigorous privacy guarantees for each individual data record in the database, it is challenging to apply the standard differential privacy notion to non-aggregated data. Several variants of the privacy notion have been proposed. For instance, event-level privacy [19] aims to protect the presence of individual events in one person's data when releasing aggregated data. Local privacy [20] enables answering aggregate queries without a trusted data curator. Geo-indistinguishability [21] was proposed to release anonymized locations in a trajectory by sampling according to geo-distance in a randomized fashion. Although briefly mentioned in [22], there have not been any studies on ensuring differential privacy for image data. The goal of our work is to study the feasibility of differential privacy in image data sanitization by proposing an extended privacy model and an efficient mechanism to achieve it.

3   Preliminaries

Setting. We consider the problem setting where a data owner wishes to share one or more images with a wide range of untrusted recipients, e.g., researchers or the greater public. The data owner must sanitize the image data prior to its publication, in order to protect the privacy of individuals or objects captured in the images.

Image Data. In the paper we focus on *grayscale* images: an input image I is regarded as an $M \times N$ matrix with integer values between 0 and 255 (0 is black and 255 is white). $I(x,y)$ denotes the "pixel" value at position (x,y) in the matrix. We note that the proposed privacy model and algorithm can be extended to RGB (red-green-blue) and HSV (hue-saturation-value) representations by considering each channel separately. We assume the sensitivity of each image is *independent* of other images to sanitize. Therefore we defer the extension of our study to inter-dependent images, such as a sequence of video frames, to future work in Sect. 6.

Pixelization. The pixelization technique renders the source image using larger blocks. It is achieved by partitioning the image using a two-dimensional grid, and the average pixel value is released for each grid cell. Similar to [13], we adopt a "square" grid where the pixel width is equal to the pixel height in the grid cells, i.e., each grid cell contains $b \times b$ pixels. In general, a smaller b value yields better approximation and visual quality, as is shown in Fig. 1.

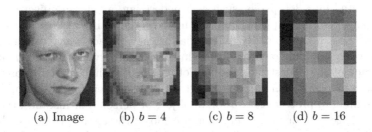

(a) Image   (b) $b = 4$ (c) $b = 8$ (d) $b = 16$

Fig. 1. A sample AT&T [23] image and its pixelization with different b values

Standard Differential Privacy. The widely adopted Differential Privacy [15] definition operates in statistical databases.

Definition 1 [ϵ-Differential Privacy]. A randomized mechanism $\mathcal{A}$ gives ϵ-differential privacy if for any neighboring databases D_1 and D_2 differing on at most one record, and for any possible output $\widetilde{D} \in Range(\mathcal{A})$,

$$Pr[\mathcal{A}(D_1) = \widetilde{D}] \le e^{\epsilon} \times Pr[\mathcal{A}(D_2) = \widetilde{D}] \tag{1}$$

where the probability is taken over the randomness of $\mathcal{A}$.

The parameter ϵ specifies the degree of privacy offered by $\mathcal{A}$, i.e., a smaller ϵ implies stronger privacy and vice versa. It has been shown [15] that ϵ-differential privacy can be achieved with *the Laplace mechanism*, by adding i.i.d. noise $\tilde{N}$ to a function f, i.e., $\tilde{f}(D) = f(D) + \tilde{N}$. Specifically, $\tilde{N}$ is drawn from a Laplace distribution with 0 mean and $\frac{\Delta f}{\epsilon}$ scale, and Δf denotes the *global sensitivity* [15], which captures the maximum difference of f between any neighboring databases. In this study, we extend the above definition to images, e.g., I_1 and I_2, and define *neighboring* images in the next section.

4   Differentially Private Pixelization

In this section we first propose the notion of neighborhood for image data, and then describe an effective privacy-preserving image publication algorithm.

Privacy Model. The concept of "neighboring images" is the key to the differential privacy notion, which should clearly define the private content under the protection of differential privacy. In this paper, we propose the following notion of image neighborhood.

Definition 2. [m-Neighborhood] Two images I_1 and I_2 are neighboring images if they have the same dimension and they differ by at most m pixels.

Allowing up to m pixels to differ enables us to protect the *presence* or absence of any object, text, or person, represented by those pixels in an image. For instance, each red rectangle in Fig. 2a illustrates sensitive information which can be represented by $\sim$360 pixels, such as a pedestrian, a van, an object on grass, and a signage. One example neighboring image is shown in Fig. 2b, differing only at the left-most pedestrian. By differential privacy, an adversary cannot distinguish between any pair of neighboring images by observing the output image. The privacy of the pedestrian, and any other sensitive information represented by at most m pixels, can thus be protected. The m-Neighborhood notion can also be applied to protect *features* of an object or person. For instance, the rectangle in Fig. 2c contains $\sim$120 pixels and encloses the area of the eyes which is reportedly the optimal feature for a range of face recognition tasks [24].

When adopting the above definition, the data owner can choose an appropriate m value in order to customize the level of privacy protection, i.e., achieving indistinguishability in a smaller or larger range of neighboring images. We assume that removing those pixels is sufficient to protect the privacy of the underlying information, by definition of differential privacy [15].

Another advantage of our proposed privacy model is that it does not require annotated or detected sensitive regions-of-interest (ROIs). But rather, we sanitize the given image[1] to protect any ROIs of size m. A straight-forward application of differential privacy is to apply Laplace perturbation to each pixel.

---

[1] The *given* image could be an entire image as in Fig. 2a, or part of an image, e.g., only face as in Fig. 2c.

(a) PETS [25]   (b) Example neighbor image   (c) AT&T [23]

Fig. 2. Sample images and an example neighboring image (Color figure online)

As up to m pixels can change and each pixel can change by at most 255, the global sensitivity of direct image perturbation is very high, i.e., $\Delta I = 255\,m$, leading to high perturbation noise. Therefore, we propose differentially private *pixelization*, which achieves differential privacy while reducing the amount of perturbation noise added to the image.

Differentially Private Pixelization (Pix). In a nutshell, our algorithm first performs pixelization on an input image, and applies Laplace perturbation to the pixelized image. Specifically, let c_k denote the k-th grid cell over an $M \times N$ image. As shown in Fig. 3, there are $\lceil \frac{M}{b} \rceil \lceil \frac{N}{b} \rceil$ cells in total. Let $K = \lceil \frac{M}{b} \rceil \lceil \frac{N}{b} \rceil$. The pixelization of an image I can be denoted as a vector of length K, i.e.,

$$P_b(I) = \{\frac{1}{b^2} \sum_{(x,y)\in c_1} I(x,y), \frac{1}{b^2} \sum_{(x,y)\in c_2} I(x,y), \dots, \frac{1}{b^2} \sum_{(x,y)\in c_K} I(x,y)\}.$$

The global sensitivity of P_b is thus $\Delta P_b = \max_{I_1,I_2} |P_b(I_1) - P_b(I_2)| = \frac{255m}{b^2}$, as the difference between any two pixels is at most 255 and up to m pixels can differ between any neighboring images I_1 and I_2.

Let $\widetilde{N} = \{\widetilde{N}_1, \widetilde{N}_2, \dots, \widetilde{N}_K\}$ and each $\widetilde{N}_k$ ($k \in \{1,\dots,K\}$) is randomly drawn from a Laplace distribution with mean 0 and scale $\frac{255m}{b^2\epsilon}$. The following theorem states the privacy guarantee of the $\widetilde{P}_b$ algorithm, where $\widetilde{P}_b(I) = P_b(I) + \widetilde{N}$, $\forall I$.

c_1	c_2	...	$c_{\lceil\frac{N}{b}\rceil}$
			$c_{2\lceil\frac{N}{b}\rceil}$
...			
...			...
...			$c_{\lceil\frac{M}{b}\rceil\lceil\frac{N}{b}\rceil}$

Fig. 3. $b \times b$ grid cells over an $M \times N$ matrix

Theorem 1. *Algorithm $\widetilde{P}_b$ satisfies ϵ-differential privacy.*

Proof. Since the $\Delta P_b = \frac{255m}{b^2}$, by definition [15] applying the Laplace mechanism to P_b achieves differential privacy.

Note that each pixel in $\widetilde{P}_b(I)$ is truncated to the range of $[0, 255]$. This postprocessing of $\widetilde{P}_b$ does not affect its privacy guarantee.

5 Experiments

Below we present the empirical evaluation of differentially private pixelization.

Datasets: We considered the Multiple Object Tracking Benchmark [25], which contains video frame sequences widely used in the MOT community. Among those, two datasets adopted in this study are: *PETS* dataset, i.e., PETS09-S2L1, showing walking pedestrians on a university campus with 795 images and 768 × 576 resolution; and *Venice* dataset, i.e., Venice-2, showing walking pedestrians around a large square with 600 images and 1920 × 1080 resolution. Both datasets were converted to grayscale. In addition, we adopted two datasets used in the re-identification attacks via deep learning [14]: *AT&T* [23] database of faces which contains 400 grayscale images of 40 individuals with 92 × 112 resolution; and *MNIST* [26] which contains 60,000 grayscale images of handwritten digits with 28 × 28 resolution.

Setup: We prototyped our method in Python, running on 2.3 GHz i5 Intel Core with 16 GB memory. The parameters take default values in Table 1, unless specified otherwise. The *utility* of our method can be measured by the standard Mean Square Error (MSE), which is defined between the input image and the sanitized image. We also adopted a widely used perceptual quality measure named Structural Similarity (SSIM) [27], which considers the perceived similarity in structural information in addition to luminance and contrast. One example of SSIM's advantage over MSE, is that an image derived by subtracting a certain value from every pixel in the input image would exhibit high structural similarity to the input at a significant absolute error. Due to this consideration, both utility measures were evaluated. In each experiment, we reported the average result among all the images in each dataset.

Table 1. Default parameter setting

Parameter	Description	Default value
ϵ	Privacy parameter	0.5
m	Number of different pixels allowed	16
b	Grid cell length	16

5.1 Impact of b

We first varied the grid cell length b to empirically evaluate its impact on the utility of the sanitized image. Note that in addition to our differential private method Pix, we included the non-private pixelization method, i.e., Pix_np, which is parameterized with the same b value, as a reference for utility. Figures 5 and 6 present the utility results measured by MSE and SSIM, respectively.

As can be seen, by increasing b, the non-private baseline yields a higher MSE and a lower SSIM in each dataset, as a result of the coarser approximation by pixelization. SSIM drops significantly from $b = 2$ to $b = 6$. On the other hand, our private method generates higher utility images when b increases, approaching the utility of the non-private baseline. This is due to a lower Laplace perturbation error, the magnitude of which is governed by $\frac{255m}{b^2}$. As shown in Fig. 4, our private method outputs an image closely

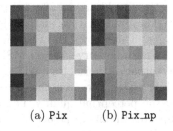

(a) Pix   (b) Pix_np

Fig. 4. Pixelization output - AT&T - $b = 16$, $m = 16$, $\epsilon = 0.5$

resembles the non-private pixelization, except for a few grid cells. Note that in Fig. 5d Pix shows an increasing trend in MSE for $2 \leq b \leq 12$. The reason is that *MNIST* depicts white (255) digits on a black (0) background, and when b is small the large Laplace noise does not significantly affect those extreme pixel values.

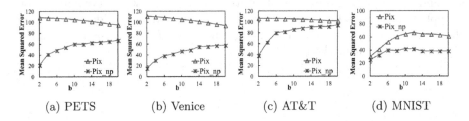

(a) PETS   (b) Venice   (c) AT&T   (d) MNIST

Fig. 5. MSE vs. varying b

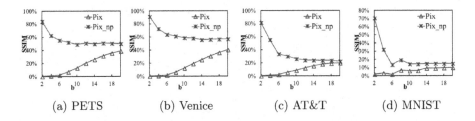

(a) PETS   (b) Venice   (c) AT&T   (d) MNIST

Fig. 6. SSIM vs. varying b

5.2   Impact of m

In the following experiment, we varied m, the number of pixels allowed to change between any pair of neighboring images, characterizing the indistinguishability requirements of the differentially private method. Intuitively, a larger m value ensures indistinguishability on a wider range of images, hence stronger privacy. The utility results are depicted in Figs. 7 and 8. Note that the non-private method

`Pix_np` should not be affected by the variation of m values. As m increases, the utility of our private method `Pix` drops, as the Laplace perturbation noise is larger. This shows the tradeoff between utility and privacy. For the *MNIST* dataset, we observe a lower MSE when $m > 32$ in Fig. 7d. The increased Laplace perturbation noise "helped" with sharing images are composed of black and white pixels. However, the increased privacy requirement has a clearer manifest on the perceptual quality, i.e., a steady decreasing trend in Fig. 10d, as SSIM captures the image structural information in addition to pixel values.

To further illustrate the utility of the differentially private pixelization, sample images generated under the default parameter setting are provided in Table 4. As can be seen, for images of larger size, e.g., the *PETS* and *Venice* datasets, setting $b = 16$ and $m = 16$ would allow the viewer to recognize the street scene and the number of pedestrians in the sanitized images. For smaller sized images, e.g., the *AT&T* and *MNIST* datasets, the pixelization grid size $b = 16$ yields a very coarse approximation, and with $m = 16$ the private perturbation mechanism inflicts a higher visual quality loss, due to smaller image sizes. Therefore, m can be adjusted by the user of our private method depending on the input image size and the privacy requirement. However, we note that when any obfuscation is applied to faces and digits, the goal is usually to reduce the identifiability of the resulting image; the example *AT&T* and *MNIST* images show promising visual results of our method.

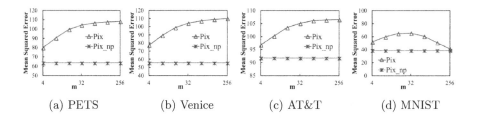

(a) PETS   (b) Venice   (c) AT&T   (d) MNIST

Fig. 7. MSE vs. varying m

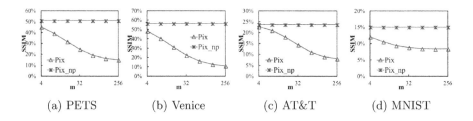

(a) PETS   (b) Venice   (c) AT&T   (d) MNIST

Fig. 8. SSIM vs. varying m

5.3   Impact of ε

We also studied the impact on utility by varying the privacy parameter ε. Intuitively, lower ε value ensures stronger privacy, and yields lower utility. As can be seen in Figs. 9 and 10, our private method Pix shows a lower MSE and a higher SSIM when increasing ε. An expected exception is observed for *MNIST* dataset in Fig. 9d, where smaller ε values, e.g., 0.1, can benefit sharing extreme pixel values. Again, the SSIM measure is shown to be more robust than MSE, exhibiting a consistently increasing trend when ε increases in Fig. 10d.

5.4   Runtime

Another important performance index is the efficiency of the proposed method. To this end, we summarized the average runtime to process one image in each dataset in Table 2. As can be seen, our private method is very efficient, taking only 66 ms to sanitize a 1920×1080 image. In every dataset, the process time per pixel is around 10^{-5} ms.

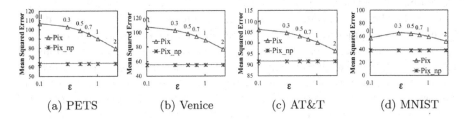

Fig. 9. MSE vs. varying ε

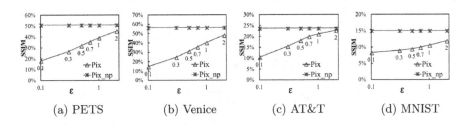

Fig. 10. SSIM vs. varying ε

5.5   Mitigation of CNN Attacks

While differential privacy provides a rigorous indistinguishability guarantee, we conducted a study similar to [14] in order to understand whether the differentially private pixelization can mitigate intelligent re-identification attacks. For this study, we partitioned the 10 images for each individual in the *AT&T* dataset

(40 individuals in total) by randomly selecting 8 images for training and using the remaining 2 for testing, as in [14]. The *MNIST* dataset is pre-partitioned with 50,000 for training and 10,000 for testing. Assume the adversary has access to the training set obfuscated by a given method, as well as the label of each training image, i.e., individual identity (1–40) and digits (0–9). The goal of the re-identification attack is to breach the privacy of the testing set, i.e., predicting the label for each testing image produced by the same obfuscation method. In this study, we compared our differentially private pixelization with a random guessing baseline and the non-private pixelization method, i.e., mosaicing. Random guessing method predicts the label of a testing image by randomly picking a label, without considering the training set. Our method was applied with the default parameter values, i.e., $b = 16$ and $m = 16$, when varying ϵ. We generated the training set and testing set for each ϵ value.

A convolutional neural network (CNN) was trained for each dataset with the suggested architecture [14]. We reported the classification results[2] of our differentially private method in Table 3. The results for "Mosaicing" were taken from the original study [14]. As can be seen, with the same grid cell length $b = 16$, our differentially private method significantly reduces the attack success rate compared to the non-private method. For the *AT&T* dataset, recall that with $\epsilon = 0.5$ the differentially private pixelization yields similar output to that of the non-private method as illustrated in Fig. 4. But the re-identification risk is lowered by more than 52%, from 96.25% to 43.75%, thanks to the randomized mechanism. As for the *MNIST* dataset, our private method also significantly reduces the success rate of the attack. Dominated by black and white pixels and at a lower resolution, the re-identification risk of *MNIST* images is less sensitive to the privacy parameter ϵ. It is worth mentioning that when $\epsilon = 0.1$, our private method is very hard to breach, and the risk is close to that of random guessing.

Table 2. Runtime of differentially private pixelization

Dataset	Dimension	Time per image (in ms)
PETS	768×576	11.95
Venice	1920×1080	66.14
AT&T	92×112	0.32
MNIST	28×28	0.05

Table 3. Accuracy (in %) of CNN re-identification attacks

Dataset	Random guess	Mosaicing [14]	DP Pixelization ($b = 16$)			
	–	16×16	$\epsilon = 0.1$	0.3	0.5	1
AT&T Top 1	2.50	96.25	3.75	18.75	43.75	77.50
MNIST Top 1	10.00	52.13	16.41	20.41	21.51	22.95

---

[2] Top 1: the label predicted most likely was evaluated.

Table 4. First row lists sample images in each dataset and second row is the corresponding differentially private pixelization, under the default parameter setting. Note that when obfuscation is applied to faces in *AT&T* and digits in *MNIST*, the desired outcome is to reduce identifiability.

PETS (768 x 576):

Venice (1920 x 1080):

AT&T (92 x 112):

MNIST (28 x 28):

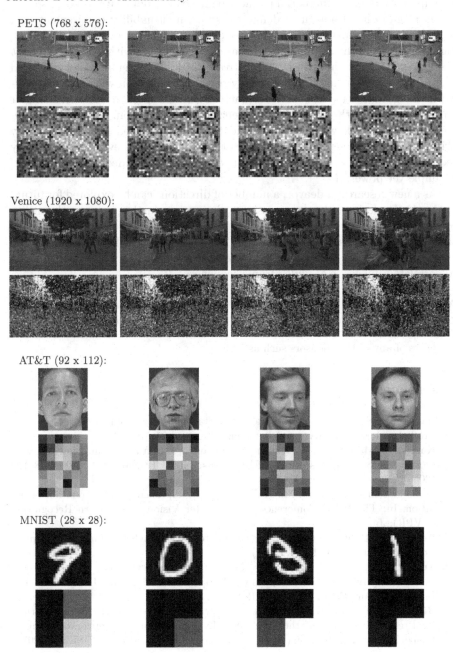

6 Conclusion and Discussion

We have presented a private image pixelization method, which was the first attempt at extending differential privacy to image data publication. We proposed the m-neighborhood notion to define the indistinguishability requirement, i.e., roughly the same output for any images differing at up to m pixels. Given the high sensitivity of direct image perturbation, pixelization with grid cells of $b \times b$ pixels was adopted to achieve a utility-privacy trade off. We empirically evaluated the utility and efficiency of differentially private pixelization with multiple real-world image datasets, and showed that our private method can yield similar output to that of the non-private pixelization. In addition, an intelligent re-identification attack was simulated and the results showed that differentially private pixelization significantly reduces the attack success even at low privacy requirements, i.e., $\epsilon \geq 0.1$ and $m = 16$. Therefore, we concluded that our method is simple yet powerful.

As a new research endeavor, a number of directions can be explored for future work: (1) the design of post-processing techniques to further improve the utility of the differentially private method, e.g., removing sharp differences; (2) the study of application-specific utility such as crowd and vehicle counting; (3) the evaluation of human users on the perceived privacy and utility; (4) the extension to correlated images, e.g., video frame sequences.

Acknowledgments. This research has been funded by NSF grant CRII-1755884 and a UAlbany FRAP-A Award. Any opinions, findings, and conclusions or recommendations expressed in this material are those of the authors and do not necessarily reflect the views of any of the sponsors such as NSF.

References

1. InternetLiveStats. http://www.internetlivestats.com. Accessed 21 Mar 2018
2. TrafficLand. http://www.trafficland.com. Accessed 21 Mar 2018
3. Kamijo, S., Matsushita, Y., Ikeuchi, K., Sakauchi, M.: Traffic monitoring and accident detection at intersections. IEEE Trans. Intell. Transp. Syst. **1**(2), 108–118 (2000)
4. Sun, Q., Schiele, B., Fritz, M.: A domain based approach to social relation recognition. In: The IEEE Conference on Computer Vision and Pattern Recognition (CVPR), July 2017
5. Reece, A.G., Danforth, C.M.: Instagram photos reveal predictive markers of depression. EPJ Data Sci. **6**(1), 15 (2017)
6. Yu, J., Zhang, B., Kuang, Z., Lin, D., Fan, J.: iPrivacy: image privacy protection by identifying sensitive objects via deep multi-task learning. IEEE Trans. Inf. Forensics Secur. **12**(5), 1005–1016 (2017)
7. Ra, M.R., Govindan, R., Ortega, A.: P3: toward privacy-preserving photo sharing. In: Presented as Part of the 10th USENIX Symposium on Networked Systems Design and Implementation (NSDI 13), Lombard, IL, pp. 515–528. USENIX (2013)

8. He, J., Liu, B., Kong, D., Bao, X., Wang, N., Jin, H., Kesidis, G.: Puppies: transformation-supported personalized privacy preserving partial image sharing. In: 2016 46th Annual IEEE/IFIP International Conference on Dependable Systems and Networks (DSN), pp. 359–370, June 2016

9. Zhang, L., Jung, T., Liu, C., Ding, X., Li, X.Y., Liu, Y.: Pop: privacy-preserving outsourced photo sharing and searching for mobile devices. In: 2015 IEEE 35th International Conference on Distributed Computing Systems, pp. 308–317, June 2015

10. Xia, Z., Wang, X., Zhang, L., Qin, Z., Sun, X., Ren, K.: A privacy-preserving and copy-deterrence content-based image retrieval scheme in cloud computing. IEEE Trans. Inf. Forensics Secur. 11(11), 2594–2608 (2016)

11. Wang, S., Nassar, M., Atallah, M., Malluhi, Q.: Secure and private outsourcing of shape-based feature extraction. In: Qing, S., Zhou, J., Liu, D. (eds.) ICICS 2013. LNCS, vol. 8233, pp. 90–99. Springer, Cham (2013). https://doi.org/10.1007/978-3-319-02726-5_7

12. Wang, Q., Hu, S., Ren, K., Wang, J., Wang, Z., Du, M.: Catch me in the dark: effective privacy-preserving outsourcing of feature extractions over image data. In: IEEE INFOCOM 2016 - The 35th Annual IEEE International Conference on Computer Communications, pp. 1–9, April 2016

13. Hill, S., Zhou, Z., Saul, L., Shacham, H.: On the (in) effectiveness of mosaicing and blurring as tools for document redaction. Proc. Priv. Enhancing Technol. 2016(4), 403–417 (2016)

14. McPherson, R., Shokri, R., Shmatikov, V.: Defeating image obfuscation with deep learning. CoRR abs/1609.00408 (2016)

15. Dwork, C., McSherry, F., Nissim, K., Smith, A.: Calibrating noise to sensitivity in private data analysis. In: Halevi, S., Rabin, T. (eds.) TCC 2006. LNCS, vol. 3876, pp. 265–284. Springer, Heidelberg (2006). https://doi.org/10.1007/11681878_14

16. Squicciarini, A.C., Caragea, C., Balakavi, R.: Analyzing images' privacy for the modern web. In: Proceedings of the 25th ACM Conference on Hypertext and Social Media, HT 2014, pp. 136–147. ACM, New York (2014)

17. Spyromitros-Xioufis, E., Papadopoulos, S., Popescu, A., Kompatsiaris, Y.: Personalized privacy-aware image classification. In: Proceedings of the 2016 ACM on International Conference on Multimedia Retrieval, ICMR 2016, pp. 71–78. ACM, New York (2016)

18. Stevens, R., Pudney, I.: Blur select faces with the updated blur faces tool, August 2017. Accessed 21 Aug 2017

19. Dwork, C., Naor, M., Pitassi, T., Rothblum, G.N.: Differential privacy under continual observation. In: Proceedings of the Forty-Second ACM Symposium on Theory of Computing, pp. 715–724. ACM (2010)

20. Duchi, J.C., Jordan, M.I., Wainwright, M.J.: Local privacy and statistical minimax rates. In: 2013 IEEE 54th Annual Symposium on Foundations of Computer Science, pp. 429–438, October 2013

21. Andrés, M.E., Bordenabe, N.E., Chatzikokolakis, K., Palamidessi, C.: Geo-indistinguishability: differential privacy for location-based systems. In: Proceedings of the 2013 ACM SIGSAC Conference on Computer and Communications Security, CCS 2013, pp. 901–914. ACM, New York (2013)

22. Jana, S., Narayanan, A., Shmatikov, V.: A scanner darkly: protecting user privacy from perceptual applications. In: 2013 IEEE Symposium on Security and Privacy, pp. 349–363, May 2013

23. Samaria, F.S., Harter, A.C.: Parameterisation of a stochastic model for human face identification. In: Proceedings of 1994 IEEE Workshop on Applications of Computer Vision, pp. 138–142, December 1994

24. Peterson, M.F., Eckstein, M.P.: Looking just below the eyes is optimal across face recognition tasks. Proc. Natl. Acad. Sci. **109**(48), E3314–E3323 (2012)

25. Leal-Taixé, L., Milan, A., Reid, I., Roth, S., Schindler, K.: Motchallenge 2015: towards a benchmark for multi-target tracking. arXiv preprint arXiv:1504.01942 (2015)

26. LeCun, Y., Bottou, L., Bengio, Y., Haffner, P.: Gradient-based learning applied to document recognition. Proc. IEEE **86**(11), 2278–2324 (1998)

27. Wang, Z., Bovik, A.C., Sheikh, H.R., Simoncelli, E.P.: Image quality assessment: from error visibility to structural similarity. IEEE Trans. Image Process. **13**(4), 600–612 (2004)

Integrity and User Interaction

Data Integrity Verification
in Column-Oriented NoSQL Databases

Grisha Weintraub[1](✉) and Ehud Gudes[2](✉)

[1] Department of Mathematics and Computer Science,
The Open University, Raanana, Israel
grisha.weintraub@gmail.com
[2] Department of Computer Science,
Ben-Gurion University of the Negev, Beer-Sheva, Israel
ehud@cs.bgu.ac.il

Abstract. Data integrity in cloud databases is a topic that has received a much of attention from the research community. However, existing solutions mainly focus on the cloud providers that store data in relational databases, whereas nowadays many cloud providers store data in non-relational databases as well. In this paper, we focus on the particular family of non-relational databases—column-oriented stores, and present a protocol that will allow cloud users to verify the integrity of their data that resides on cloud databases of this type. We like our solution to be easily integrated with the existing real-world systems and therefore assume that we cannot modify the cloud; our protocol is implemented solely on the client side. We have implemented a prototype of our solution, that uses Cloud BigTable as a cloud database, and have evaluated its performance and correctness.

Keywords: Data integrity · Database outsourcing · NoSQL

1 Introduction

For a long time, relational database management systems (RDBMS) have been the only solution for persistent data storage. However, with the phenomenal growth of data, this conventional way of storing has become problematic. To manage the exponentially growing data volumes, the largest information technology companies, such as Google and Amazon, have developed alternative solutions that store data in what have become to be known as NoSQL databases [1,2]. Some of the NoSQL features are flexible schema, horizontal scaling, and relaxed consistency. Rather than store data in heavily structured tables, NoSQL systems prefer simpler data schema such as key-value pairs or collections of documents. They store and replicate data in distributed systems, commonly across datacenters, thereby achieving scalability and high availability. NoSQL databases are usually classified into three groups, according to their data model: key-value

© IFIP International Federation for Information Processing 2018
Published by Springer International Publishing AG, part of Springer Nature 2018. All Rights Reserved
F. Kerschbaum and S. Paraboschi (Eds.): DBSec 2018, LNCS 10980, pp. 165–181, 2018.
https://doi.org/10.1007/978-3-319-95729-6_11

stores, document-based stores, and column-oriented stores. The latter group was inspired by BigTable [3] - a distributed storage system developed by Google that is designed to manage very large amounts of structured data.

In column-oriented stores data is organized in tables, which consist of row keys and column keys. Column keys are grouped into sets called column families. Column-oriented stores can be used either as internal database systems (just like BigTable inside Google) or as cloud databases - cloud services that provide users with access to data without the need for managing hardware or software. However, storing data in a cloud introduces several security concerns. In particular, since cloud users do not physically possess their data, data integrity may be at risk. Cloud providers (or some malicious entity) can change users' data, omit some of the data from query results or return a version of the data which is not the latest. In other words, data *correctness*, *completeness* and *freshness* might be compromised.

Data integrity in outsourced relational databases has been studied for several years [7–15]. Nevertheless, existing solutions are inappropriate for column-oriented NoSQL databases for the following reasons:

1. Data volumes in NoSQL are expected to be much higher than in RDBMS.
2. Data model of column-oriented systems significantly differs from relational model (e.g. a single row in column-oriented database may contain millions of columns).
3. The query model in NoSQL is much simpler than in RDBMS (e.g. joins are usually not supported).

These differences between RDBMS and NoSQL introduce both challenges and opportunities. On the one hand, data integrity assurance in NoSQL systems requires more sophisticated solutions due to its unusual data model. On the other hand, extremely simple query model of NoSQL may allow us to design much simpler and efficient protocols for data integrity verification. The goal of this paper is to demonstrate that data integrity of column-oriented NoSQL databases in the cloud can be verified better (in terms of efficiency and applicability) than it was proposed in previous work. Our main contributions are as follows:

– Development of a novel probabilistic method that allows users to verify data integrity of the data that resides in cloud column-oriented stores and its analysis.
– A demonstration of the feasibility of our method by a prototype implementation and its experimental evaluation.

The rest of the paper is structured as follows: Sect. 2 provides background information and overviews related work. Section 3 presents our method for data integrity verification in column-oriented stores. Security analysis of our approach is presented in Sect. 4. Section 5 introduces our proof-of-concept implementation and provides an experimental evaluation thereof. Section 6 presents our conclusions.

2   Background and Related Work

As mentioned earlier, the main goal of this paper is to propose a novel method that provides *data integrity* assurance for *column-oriented* NoSQL databases in the *cloud*. In this section, the relevant background is provided. In particular, an overview of column-oriented NoSQL systems is presented in Sect. 2.1, the cloud model is described in Sect. 2.2 and possible data integrity attacks are discussed in Sect. 2.3. Section 2.4 reviews related work.

2.1   Column-Oriented Stores

Column-oriented stores, also called wide column stores, extensible record stores, and column-oriented NoSQL databases are storage systems that were built after Google's BigTable [3]. A thorough review of BigTable is given in [4], below is a brief summary.

BigTable is a distributed storage system. Data in BigTable is organized in tables consisting of rows. Rows are composed of cells identified by a combination of a row key and a column key. Column key consists of a mandatory column family and an optional column qualifier. Table 1 provides an example of a typical table in BigTable:

- User ID – is a row key.
- Personal Data and Financial Data – are column families.
- Name, Phone, Email, City and Card – are column qualifiers.
- Bob – is a value located in a cell ("1457", "Personal Data: Name")

Table 1. Sample "Users" table in column-orientes store

User ID	Personal data	Financial data
1457	Phone = "781455", Name = "Bob"	Card = "9875"
1885	Email = "john@g.com", Name = "John"	
2501	Phone = "781526", City = "NY", Email = "k@zzz.com", Name = "Alice"	Card = "6652"
3456	Name = "Carol", City = "Paris"	Card = "6663"

Supported data operations are:

- *get* – returns values from individual rows.
- *scan* – iterates over multiple rows.
- *put* – inserts a value into a specified table's cell.
- *delete* – deletes a whole row or a specified cell inside a particular row.

2.2   System Model and Assumptions

Database-as-a-service paradigm (DBaaS), firstly introduced more than a decade ago [5], has become a prevalent service of today's cloud providers. Microsoft's Azure SQL Database, Amazon's DynamoDB and Google's Cloud BigTable are just a few examples. We assume that there are 3 entities in the DBaaS model (Fig. 1):

- *Data owner (DO)* – uploads the data to the cloud.
- *Cloud provider (CP)* – stores and provides access to the data.
- *Clients* – retrieve the data from the cloud.

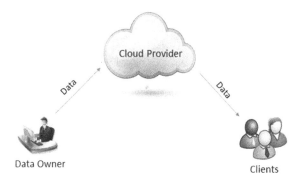

Fig. 1. DBaaS model

There is only one instance of DO and CP in our model, whereas the number of clients is not limited. The data uploaded to the cloud is stored in a column-oriented NoSQL database and all data operations (the DO's writes and clients' reads) are performed according to the column-oriented data model, described in the previous section. Our system model is both write and read intensive. The DO uploads data to the cloud by bulk loading (the rows in a bulk are not necessarily consecutive). We assume that the DO writes only append new rows to the database; existing rows are not updated. We are interested in a highly applicable solution and therefore we assume that no server changes can be performed on the cloud side.

Some of the use cases that may suit our system model are:

- *Historical financial data*—a stock exchange uploads historical stock prices to the cloud for public use.
- *Open science data*—a scientific organization uploads results of the scientific activities to the cloud for anyone to analyze and reuse.
- *Server metrics*—various server metrics (e.g. CPU, memory and network usage) are periodically uploaded to the cloud for further monitoring and analysis.

2.3   Integrity and Attack Model

We assume that the CP is trusted neither by the DO nor by the clients and that it can behave maliciously in any possible way to break data integrity. For example, the CP (or somebody that had penetrated the CP machine) may modify values of particular table cells, add or delete new rows or column families, or return partial (or empty) results to the clients' queries. We focus on data integrity protection in the following two dimensions:

1. *Correctness* – Data received by the clients was originally uploaded to the cloud by the DO and has not been modified maliciously or mistakenly in the cloud side.
2. *Completeness* – The CP returns to the clients *all* the data that matches the query. In other words, no data is omitted from the result.

Freshness is another important dimension of data integrity, meaning that the clients get the most current version of the data that was uploaded to the cloud. However, since in our system model there are no updates, freshness is not an issue.

2.4   Related Work

Existing solutions can be mainly categorized into three types. The first type is based on the Merkle Hash Tree (MHT), the second is based on digital signatures (DS), and the third uses a probabilistic approach. In the following sections, we review each of these approaches and describe their limitations pertaining to our system model.

2.5   MHT-based Approach

MHT [6] is a binary tree, where each leaf is a hash of a data block, and each internal node is a hash of the concatenation of its two children. Devanbu et al. in [7] introduce a method that uses MHT as Authenticated Data Structure (ADS) to provide data integrity assurance in the DBaaS model. The general idea is to build an MHT for every database table such that MHT leaves are hashes of table's records ordered by a search key. To reduce the I/O operations cost in both client and server sides, instead of using binary trees, trees of higher fanout (MB-Trees) can be used [8]. Different MHT-based techniques to provide efficient integrity assurance for join and aggregate queries are presented in [9,10] respectively. One of the difficulties in adopting the MHT-based approaches in practice is that RDBMS modification is required for managing ADS on the cloud side. Wei et al. in [11] propose to serialize ADS into RDBMS thereby providing integrity assurance without RDBMS modification.

   All of the MHT-based approaches discussed so far assume that the outsourced database is RDBMS. Among other things, it implies that the data is organized in accordance with the relational model and the CP stores the database and the

ADS's on a single node. These assumptions are not valid for column-oriented stores and hence another solution is required.

iBigTable [16] is a BigTable [3] enhancement that utilizes an MHT to provide scalable data integrity assurance in column-oriented NoSQL databases. It uses Merkle B+ tree – the combination of MHT and B+ tree as an ADS. iBigTable overcomes the limitations of the MHT-based approaches for RDBMS mentioned above. However, it requires modifications of core components of BigTable and hence cannot be applied directly to existing BigTable implementations. Moreover, since iBigTable relies on BigTable internal architecture it cannot be applied to column-oriented stores that have different infrastructure (e.g. Cassandra).

2.6 DS-Based Approach

A natural and intuitive approach to provide data integrity in RDBMS is to use the digital signatures scheme (e.g. RSA [17]) in the following way:

- An additional column containing a hash of concatenated record values signed by the DO's private key is added to every table.
- Clients verify record integrity by using the DO's public key.

To reduce the communication cost between client and server and the computation cost on the client side, *signature aggregation* technique [12] can be used to combine multiple record signatures into a single one. To guarantee completeness, rather than sign individual records, the DO signs consecutive pairs of records [13].

Signature based technique for RDBMS uses row-level granularity of integrity – every single row is signed by the DO and hence the smallest unit of the data retrieval is a whole row. Whereas row-level granularity is a natural decision for relational databases, it does not fit column-oriented stores design, where rows may contain millions of column values.

2.7 Probabilistic Approach

Probabilistic approaches provide only *probabilistic* integrity assurance, but do not require DBMS modifications and have better performance than MHT-based and DS-based approaches. In this approach, a number of additional records is uploaded to the cloud along with the original records. The more additional records are being uploaded, the higher is the probability to detect data integrity attack. All data is encrypted on a client side so the CP cannot distinguish between the original and the additional records. These additional records may be completely *fake* as was proposed in [14] or original records encrypted with a different (secondary) secret key as was proposed in the *dual encryption* scheme of [15].

Applying probabilistic approach to column-oriented stores raises difficulties similar to those of the signature-based approach. In addition to the granularity of a signature, granularity of additional data should be chosen according to the column-oriented data model. Another limitation is that in probabilistic approach the whole database must be encrypted.

2.8   Summary

In this section we have shown that as of today there is no practical solution for data integrity assurance in column-oriented NoSQL databases; RDBMS approaches cannot be applied directly and the only column stores approach (iBigTable) proposes a customized solution. In the next section, we will introduce our novel approach for data integrity protection in column-oriented NoSQL databases that overcomes the limitations of existing approaches presented above. Some initial ideas of our approach were outlined in [27], but were limited to key-value stores only.

3   Our Approach

Inspired by the existing probabilistic approaches for RDBMS [14,15], we propose a novel method that provides probabilistic data integrity assurance in column-oriented NoSQL databases without DBMS modification. In our solution, we also eliminate the main limitation of the existing probabilistic approaches – a requirement that the whole database must be encrypted. Below we describe our protection techniques for correctness and completeness verification.

3.1   Preliminaries

In this section we present the basic notions and concepts necessary for the implementation and analysis of our approach.

Hash function: We use collision-resistant hash function that has a property that it is computationally hard to find two inputs that hash to the same output. SHA-256 and SHA-512 [20] are examples of such functions. Hash operation on value x is denoted by $H(x)$.

Secret keys: We assume that the DO and the clients share two secret keys—one for data encryption and another one for data authenticity.

Data authentication: To verify data authenticity we use message authentication codes (MAC's). The DO signs its data according to the MAC scheme (e.g. HMAC [24]) and stores the MAC value in the cloud along with the signed data. Then, based on the MAC value and the received data, clients can verify data authenticity.

Data encryption: Sensitive data that is stored in the cloud is encrypted by the DO and then decrypted by the clients by using symmetric encryption (e.g. AES [23]).

Bloom filter: Bloom filters [18] are randomized data structures that are used to test whether an element is a member of a set. To reduce storage and network overhead Bloom filters can be compressed [19].

The notation we use is presented in Table 2.

Table 2. Notation

Symbol	Description
$\parallel$	String concatenation
D	A database
r	A database row
cf	A column family
N_{cf}^r	Number of column families in row r
r_{key}	Row key of the row r
BF_{cf}	Bloom filter containing all the columns of the family cf
p	Number of rows linked to each DB row

3.2   Correctness

We have to provide correctness assurance to the following types of client queries:

1. Get row by row key.
2. Get column family by row key and family name.
3. Get column(s) by row key, column family and column name(s).

In order to support these queries, we use the MAC scheme in the following way: When the DO inserts a new row, it calculates hash values for all of the column families and stores them in a special "I-META" column family. After that it calculates the *row hash* (hash of the concatenation of all of the column family hashes), calculates the MAC of the row hash, and stores it under the special "Row-Mac" column in "I-META" family. Then the correctness of queries is verified as follows.

Verification of Queries of Type 1. Correctness of the queries of type (1) is simply based on the computation and verification of the row MAC.

Verification of Queries of Type 2. Queries of type (2) are verified as follows:

1. Client receives the requested column family and computes its hash value.
2. Client computes the row hash from the column family hash (step 1) and all other column families' hashes from "I-META" family.
3. Client computes and verifies the row MAC.

Verification of Queries of Type 3. There is no trivial solution for queries of type (3). One possible approach would be to transform queries of type (3) into queries of type (2) by omitting column names, and then, after correctness verification for all columns, filter out all the columns but the requested ones. Another way would be to sign each column separately. However, since the number of columns in column stores may be very large, both these approaches are inevitably going to produce an enormous overhead.

In our approach, for queries of type (3) we use Bloom filters. For each column family the DO computes a Bloom filter that contains all column values of this family and stores it as a column in "I-META" family. To verify data correctness of the particular column values, clients retrieve the corresponding Bloom filter and use it to check the existence of the received values. If one of the values does not exist in the Bloom filter, the client can be completely sure that data integrity was compromised. If all the values exist, the client has a certain level of confidence (a detailed analysis is provided in Sect. 4) that the data was not tampered in the cloud side.

A malicious CP may modify the Bloom filters on the cloud side. To avoid that, we compute hash values for all of the Bloom filters and insert them into the row hash along with the column family hashes. We also add to the row hash the row key, so the CP will not be able to return unrelated data values.

Hence, the formal definitions of the row hash is as follows:

Definition 1. *Row hash*

$$H(r) = H(r_{key}||H(cf_1)||H(BF_{cf_1})||H(cf_2)||H(BF_{cf_2})...H(cf_{N_{cf}^r})||H(BF_{cf_{N_{cf}^r}}))$$

If we would apply the scheme above to the Table 1 it would look as in Table 3. The row hash of the row 1457 would be computed as follows:
H(Row-Key || Personal-Data-Hash || Financial-Data-Hash || Personal-Data-Bloom-Hash || Financial-Data-Bloom-Hash) = H(1457 || 2873992 || 1976503 || 8703341 || 5848258).

Table 3. Correctness scheme example for data from Table 1

User ID	Personal data	Financial data	I-META
1457	Phone = "781455", Name = "Bob"	Card = "9875"	Personal-Data-Hash = "2873992"
			Financial-Data-Hash = "1976503"
			Personal-Data-Bloom-Value = "0010010"
			Financial-Data-Bloom-Value = "1000000"
			Personal-Data-Bloom-Hash = "8703341"
			Financial-Data-Bloom-Hash = "5848258"
			Row-Mac = "A73Djd@83393k"

Note that our solution does not require DBMS modification but only slight schema changes (an addition of the I-META column family).

3.3 Completeness

Rows Linking. The intuition behind the *rows linking* is that every row *knows* some information about the data stored in some other rows. For example, if we would apply rows linking to the sample data from Table 1, it might look as in Table 4. Row 1457 knows that row 1885 has columns "Email" and "Name" and row 3456 has columns "Name", "City" and "Card". Row 1885 knows what columns exist in rows 2501 and 3456, etc. The formal definition of rows linking is as follows:

Definition 2. *Rows Linking*

$\forall \; x,y \in D$, *x is linked to y* $\iff$ *x contains y's row key and all its column names*

The DO is responsible for the linking between the rows when uploading the data to the cloud. This *linking data* then encrypted and stored under "I-META" column family. Afterwards, the clients can rely on linking data to verify the result completeness. For example, consider a query "get all users with id between 1000 and 2000" on Table 1 with linking data from Table 4 and the result that contains only row with id 1457. By checking linking data of the row 1457, the client knows that row 1885 should be a part of the result and thus detects the attack. Here too, the addition of linking data does not require any DBMS modification, only an addition of the new column.

Table 4. Rows linking example for data from Table 1

Row key	Linking data
1457	1885:email, name; 3456:name, city, card
1885	2501:phone, email, city, name, card; 3456:name, city, card
2501	1457:phone, name, card; 1885:email, name
3456	1457:phone, name, card; 2501:phone, email, city, name, card

To increase the probability of assurance that all inserted rows are present we use the crowdsourced verification technique.

Crowdsourced Verification. In crowdsourcing (CS) systems [21] users collaborate to achieve a goal that is beneficial to the whole community. The collaboration may be explicit (e.g. Wikipedia and Linux projects) or implicit as in ESP game [22] where users label images as a side effect of playing the game. In our approach we build CS system where users implicitly collaborate to achieve a mutual goal – database integrity assurance. It works as illustrated in Fig. 2:

1. A client sends a query to the CP.
2. The CP sends the query result along with the linking data back to the client.
3. The client builds *verification queries* based on the received linking data and sends them to the CP.

4. The CP sends the result of the verification queries back to the client.
5. The client verifies that the result of the verification queries matches the linking data.

Verification queries (step 3) are built such that the CP cannot distinguish between them and the regular client queries (step 1). Thanks to that, CP's malicious behavior with the client queries will inevitably cause malicious behavior with the verification queries as well and thus will be detected. Note that there is no dependency between the client query (step 1) and the verification queries (step 3) and hence steps 3–5 can be executed asynchronously (i.e. without hurting reads latency).

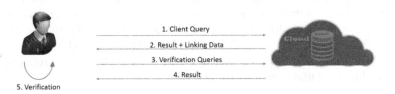

5. Verification

Fig. 2. Crowdsourced verification

To ensure that all types of queries are covered (without performing all types of queries each time) we build verification queries according to the original query type. So if the original query was of type 1, in order to build verification query we use only row keys from the linking data. For queries of type 2 and 3 we use column families and column names respectively.

4 Security Analysis

4.1 Correctness

In Sect. 3.2 above we presented our technique for data correctness verification. We considered three different types of queries that might be executed by the clients. Verification of the queries of type (1) and (2) is based on provably secure primitives—MAC scheme and collision resistant hash function, and hence provides 100% data correctness assurance.

Correctness verification of the queries of type (3) is based on Bloom filters and hence provides probabilistic correctness assurance. The DO calculates a Bloom filter for each column family cf as follows:

$$\forall c \in cf, c.name || c.value \text{ is inserted as a value to } BF_{cf}$$

Clients verify the correctness of the retrieved columns by testing their existence in the corresponding Bloom filter. If a particular column is not present in the Bloom filter, they know for sure that its value was changed. In the opposite direction, since the probability of a false positive for an element not in the Bloom filter is:

$$(1 - (1 - \frac{1}{m})^{kn})^k$$

where k is the number of the used hash functions, m is a Bloom filter size and n is a number of elements in a Bloom filter [19], if it does exist they know that the value is correct with the following probability:

$$1 - (1 - (1 - \frac{1}{m})^{kN_{col}^{cf}})^k$$

where N_{col}^{cf} is a number of columns in a column family.

Parameters m and k are chosen by the DO according to the desired level of the correctness assurance, and storage and computation time constraints. For example, for column family containing $1,000$ columns, $m = 8,192$ and $k = 5$, the client knows with the probability of 98% that the retrieved column value is correct. With a doubled Bloom filter size (i.e. $m = 16,384$) the probability to detect modified column increases to 99.8%.

4.2   Completeness

Our approach for completeness verification is based on two techniques: rows linking and crowdsourced verification, described in Sect. 3.3. Simply put, rows linking means that existence of every database row is known to p other rows and crowdsourced verification means that, in addition to their regular queries, clients perform verification queries to verify that rows whose existence is known to other rows do actually exist.

Assuming a uniform distribution of both deleted rows (denoted by d) and range of queries (denoted by q), the probability that after a single query the client will not be able to detect that at least one of the d rows was deleted from the database with $|D|$ rows (or omitted from the result) is:

$$\frac{|D| - pd}{|D|}$$

Hence, the probability of detecting an attack after q queries is:

$$1 - (\frac{|D| - pd}{|D|})^q$$

Figure 6 shows the probability to detect an attack as a function of a number of queries performed by the clients with $|D| = 1,000,000$, $p = 4$ and $d \in \{1, 5, 10, 20\}$. It can be seen that even with p as small as 4, after a relatively small number of queries (production systems receive tens of thousands of queries per second [25]) and deleted rows, the chance of the CP to escape from being caught is very low. It looks like the addition of verification queries should slow client queries, however as it is shown in the next section, since these queries are run asynchronously, they do not hurt reads latency. Some overhead in terms of CPU, I/O, and other resources on both client and server sides is still expected, but since this overhead does not affect user experience, it seems to be a reasonable price for the achieved data integrity protection.

5   Implementation and Experimental Results

For experimental evaluation, we have implemented a prototype of our solution. As a cloud column-oriented store we use Cloud BigTable – Google's NoSQL Big Data database service based on BigTable [3]. To evaluate our solution, we use Yahoo! Cloud Serving Benchmark (YCSB) framework [26]. YCSB is a framework for benchmarking database systems. The only thing which needs to be done to benchmark a database with YCSB is to implement a database interface layer. This will allow a framework client to perform operations like "read row" or "insert row" without having to understand the specific API of the database.

We use YCSB in the following way (see Fig. 3 below):

- YCSB framework already has BigTable client implementation.
- We implemented our version of BigTable client (BigTable-I) based on the techniques presented in Sect. 3. Our implementation is available online [28].
- For performance analysis, we executed different workloads on both clients (BigTable and BigTable-I) and compared their execution time.
- For correctness analysis, we used our client to upload data to the cloud. Then we deleted random rows from the database and performed random read queries until the deletion of the rows was detected.

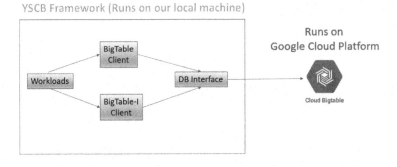

Fig. 3. Experimental evaluation with YCSB framework

5.1   Setup

For our experiments, we created Cloud BigTable cluster with 3 nodes. We configured "zone" to be "europe-west1-b" and storage type to be "HDD". For all workloads, we used random rows of 1 KB size (10 columns, 100 bytes each, plus key).

5.2   Performance Analysis

We used the following types of workloads:

- Workload A (Inserts only): Predefined number of rows are inserted into the database.
- Workload B (Reads only): Predefined number of rows are retrieved from the database.

We executed each workload three times for each client with $1,000$, $3,000$ and $5,000$ operations and with parameter p (parameter of the linking factor) set to 4 (runs with the different p values are presented in Sect. 5.3 below). The results below represent the average value of these three executions.

Workload A (Inserts Only). The cost of Bigtable-I insert operation is dominated by two encryption and one hash operations (MAC calculation and encryption of linking data). Experimental results of workload A (Fig. 4) show that this overhead increases insert execution time by 5% in average for the client.

Workload B (Reads Only). The cost of BigTable-I read operations is similar to the cost of inserts (MAC calculation and linking data decryption) with an additional cost of p verification queries. Since in our implementation we perform verification queries asynchronously, they do not impact read execution time. According to the workload B results (Fig. 5), our protocol increases read execution time by 5% in average for the client.

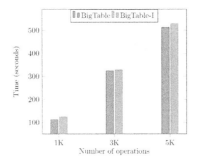

Fig. 4. Workload A results

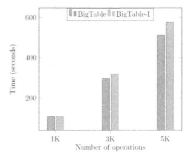

Fig. 5. Workload B results

5.3   Correctness Analysis

To demonstrate that our approach works as expected, we uploaded $10,000$ rows to the cloud via BigTable-I client. Then we deleted random rows from the cloud database (up to 20 rows) and ran "random reads" workload until the deletion of rows was detected. We performed this experiment with different values of parameter p - 4, 6 and 8. For each value of p and the number of deleted rows, we ran "random reads" workload 3 times. The results presented in Fig. 7 represent the average value of these three executions. Our experimental results support our security analysis (Sect. 4.2) – even after a relatively small number of queries and deleted rows the attack detection is inevitable. Only for the rare case of very few deletions, many queries are required.

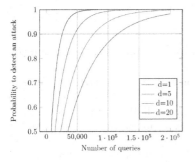
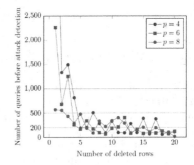

Fig. 6. Completeness verification analysis

Fig. 7. Correctness analysis results

6   Conclusions and Future Directions

In this paper, we present our novel method for data integrity assurance in cloud column-oriented stores. Our method provides both data correctness and data completeness guarantees. To verify data correctness of rows and column families we use a MAC scheme similar to the DS-based approach [12], while columns correctness is verified probabilistically by using Bloom Filters [18]. Our method for data completeness verification is inspired by crowdsourcing systems [21] - users collaborate to achieve a mutual goal - database integrity assurance. To the best of our knowledge, our work is the first work that utilizes Bloom Filters and crowdsourcing model for data correctness and data completeness verification, respectively.

The main advantage of our method over existing approaches is its high applicability - it can be applied to existing systems without modifying the server-side. We demonstrate its applicability through a proof-of-concept implementation. While using cloud column-oriented NoSQL database (Cloud BigTable) as a black-box, we have implemented our protocol solely on the client side and conducted experimental evaluation thereof. The experimental results show that our scheme imposes a reasonable overhead (around 5% in average) while it can detect an attack after a relatively small number of client queries (in most cases less than 2% of the database is queried before the attack is detected).

The challenge of data integrity in cloud databases is far from being solved. There are many different types of databases that may be addressed (e.g. document-oriented, graph databases, time-series databases). Different system models may be considered (e.g. multi-data-owner model, multi-cloud model, support for updates and freshness guarantees). For future work, we plan to address some of these challenges by using techniques developed in this work and by investigating other techniques as well.

References

1. Leavitt, N.: Will NoSQL databases live up to their promise? Computer **43**(2), 12–14 (2010)
2. Cattell, R.: Scalable SQL and NoSQL data stores. ACM SIGMOD Rec. **39**(4), 12–27 (2011)
3. Chang, F., Dean, J., Ghemawat, S., Hsieh, W.C., Wallach, D.A., Burrows, M., Gruber, R.E.: Bigtable: a distributed storage system for structured data. ACM Trans. Comput. Syst. (TOCS) **26**(2), 4 (2008)
4. Weintraub, G.: Dynamo and BigTable - review and comparison. In: Proceedings of the 28th Convention of the Electrical & Electronics Engineers in Israel, pp. 1–5. IEEE (2014)
5. Hacigms, H., Iyer, B., Mehrotra, S.: Providing database as a service. In: Proceedings of the 18th International Conference on Data Engineering, pp. 29–38. IEEE (2002)
6. Merkle, R.C.: A certified digital signature. In: Brassard, G. (ed.) CRYPTO 1989. LNCS, vol. 435, pp. 218–238. Springer, New York (1990). https://doi.org/10.1007/0-387-34805-0_21
7. Devanbu, P., Gertz, M., Martel, C., Stubblebine, S.G.: Authentic data publication over the internet. J. Comput. Secur. **11**(3), 291–314 (2003)
8. Li, F., Hadjieleftheriou, M., Kollios, G., Reyzin, L.: Dynamic authenticated index structures for outsourced databases. In: Proceedings of the 2006 ACM SIGMOD International Conference on Management of Data, pp. 121–132. ACM (2006)
9. Yang, Y., Papadias, D., Papadopoulos, S., Kalnis, P.: Authenticated join processing in outsourced databases. In: Proceedings of the 2009 ACM SIGMOD International Conference on Management of Data, pp. 5–18. ACM (2009)
10. Li, F., Hadjieleftheriou, M., Kollios, G., Reyzin, L.: Authenticated index structures for aggregation queries. ACM Trans. Inf. Syst. Secur. (TISSEC) **13**(4), 32 (2010)
11. Wei, W., Yu, T.: Integrity assurance for outsourced databases without dbms modification. In: Atluri, V., Pernul, G. (eds.) DBSec 2014. LNCS, vol. 8566, pp. 1–16. Springer, Heidelberg (2014). https://doi.org/10.1007/978-3-662-43936-4_1
12. Mykletun, E., Narasimha, M., Tsudik, G.: Authentication and integrity in outsourced databases. ACM Trans. Storage (TOS) **2**(2), 107–138 (2006)
13. Narasimha, M., Tsudik, G.: DSAC: integrity for outsourced databases with signature aggregation and chaining. In: Proceedings of the 14th ACM International Conference on Information and Knowledge Management, pp. 235–236. ACM (2005)
14. Xie, M., Wang, H., Yin, J., Meng, X.: Integrity auditing of outsourced data. In: Proceedings of the 33rd International Conference on Very Large Data Bases, pp. 782–793. VLDB Endowment (2007)

15. Wang, H., Yin, J., Perng, C.S., Yu, P.S.: Dual encryption for query integrity assurance. In: Proceedings of the 17th ACM Conference on Information and Knowledge Management, pp. 863–872. ACM (2008)
16. Wei, W., Yu, T., Xue, R.: iBigTable: practical data integrity for bigtable in public cloud. In: Proceedings of the Third ACM Conference on Data and Application Security and Privacy, pp. 341–352. ACM (2013)
17. Rivest, R.L., Shamir, A., Adleman, L.: A method for obtaining digital signatures and public-key cryptosystems. Commun. ACM **21**(2), 120–126 (1978)
18. Bloom, B.H.: Space/time trade-offs in hash coding with allowable errors. Commun. ACM **13**(7), 422–426 (1970)
19. Mitzenmacher, M.: Compressed bloom filters. IEEE/ACM Trans. Network. (TON) **10**(5), 604–612 (2002)
20. Secure Hash Standard: FIPS Publication 180–2. National Institute of Standards and Technology (NIST) (2002)
21. Doan, A., Ramakrishnan, R., Halevy, A.Y.: Crowdsourcing systems on the world-wide web. Commun. ACM **54**(4), 86–96 (2011)
22. Von Ahn, L., Dabbish, L.: Labeling images with a computer game. In: Proceedings of the SIGCHI Conference on Human Factors in Computing Systems, pp. 319–326. ACM (2004)
23. Pub, NIST FIPS: 197: Advanced encryption standard (AES). Federal Information Processing Standards Publication 197, 441-0311 (2001)
24. Krawczyk, H., Canetti, R., Bellare, M.: HMAC: Keyed-hashing for message authentication (1997)
25. Atikoglu, B., Xu, Y., Frachtenberg, E., Jiang, S., Paleczny, M.: Workload analysis of a large-scale key-value store. ACM SIGMETRICS Perform. Eval. Rev. **40**(1), 53–64 (2012)
26. Cooper, B.F., Silberstein, A., Tam, E., Ramakrishnan, R., Sears, R.: Benchmarking cloud serving systems with YCSB. In: Proceedings of the 1st ACM Symposium on Cloud Computing, pp. 143–154. ACM, June 2010
27. Weintraub, G., Gudes, E.: Crowdsourced data integrity verification for key-value stores in the cloud. In: Proceedings of the 17th IEEE/ACM International Symposium on Cluster, Cloud and Grid Computing, pp. 498–503. IEEE Press (2017)
28. BigTable-I-Client. https://github.com/grishaw/ycsb-bigtablei-binding

A Novel Hybrid Password Authentication Scheme Based on Text and Image

Ian Mackie$^{(\boxtimes)}$ and Merve Yıldırım

Department of Informatics, University of Sussex, Brighton, UK
i.mackie@sussex.ac.uk

Abstract. Considering the popularity and wide deployment of text passwords, we predict that they will be used as a prevalent authentication mechanism for many years to come. Thus, we have carried out studies on mechanisms to enhance text passwords. These studies suggest that password space and memorability should be improved, with an additional mechanism based on images. The combination of text and images increases resistance to some password attacks, such as brute force and observing attacks. We propose a hybrid authentication scheme integrating text and recognition-based graphical passwords. This authentication scheme can reduce the phishing attacks because if users are deceived to share their key passwords, there is still a chance to save the complete password as attackers do not know the users' image preferences. In addition to the security aspect, the proposed authentication scheme increases memorability as it does not require users to remember long and complex passwords. Thus, with the proposed scheme users will be able to create strong passwords without sacrificing usability. The hybrid scheme also offers an enjoyable sign-in/log-in experience to users.

Keywords: Passwords · Authentication
Recognition based graphical passwords

1 Introduction

User authentication is one of the most important parts of the security of information systems. The most common approach for authenticating human users is text passwords. Evidence shows that users generally choose weak passwords so that they can remember them easily [1,21]. This increases the possibility of the passwords being cracked. When users are requested to create long and complex passwords, they resort to coping strategies such as writing passwords down or reusing them [4]. Therefore, text-based passwords suffer from a whole variety of drawbacks such as vulnerabilities to dictionary attacks, brute force attacks and social engineering.

Graphical passwords are considered a good replacement for textual passwords. The fact that humans can recognize and remember images easier than

© IFIP International Federation for Information Processing 2018
Published by Springer International Publishing AG, part of Springer Nature 2018. All Rights Reserved
F. Kerschbaum and S. Paraboschi (Eds.): DBSec 2018, LNCS 10980, pp. 182–197, 2018.
https://doi.org/10.1007/978-3-319-95729-6_12

text can be a solution to the memorability problem [16]. However, they are more vulnerable to shoulder surfing attacks as compared to textual passwords. Also, the graphical password authentication is relatively expensive to implement which prevents it becoming widespread. To overcome the weaknesses of text and graphical passwords, this paper introduces a hybrid authentication scheme which is a combined approach of text and graphical passwords.

2 Background and Related Work

Many hybrid authentication schemes have been proposed in recent years to overcome the drawbacks of knowledge based authentication schemes. While some researchers integrated different types of graphical passwords [10], others combined graphical passwords with text passwords [12,14,17]. These researchers proposed solutions to shoulder surfing attacks to strengthen the graphical password schemes. Rao and Yalamanchili [14] proposed two authentication schemes using graphical passwords called Pair Pass Char (PPC) and Tricolor Pair Pass Char (TPPC). Both these schemes support two modes of input: keyboard entry and mouse clicks. The first mode is the text mode and the other one is the graphical mode. Rao and Yalamanchili carried out an experiment with 20 graduate students and found that the average login times increase as the password length increases in both schemes. The study also showed that the login times for TPPC scheme is higher, and rules for this scheme are more difficult to be applied. The PPC scheme provides passwords similar to that offered by conventional password systems, and it is greatly enhanced in the TPPC scheme as it uses the same character set in three colours. The login times increase where the password space is enhanced in these proposed schemes, and thus usability is sacrificed for security.

Zhao and Li [23] proposed S3PAS which is a scalable shoulder-surfing resistant password authentication scheme. S3PAS is designed for client/server environments. It integrates both graphical and textual password schemes and aims to provide resistance to shoulder surfing, hidden camera and spyware attacks. In this scheme two kinds of password are generated: original passwords and session passwords. Users create original passwords when they create their accounts and input different session passwords in every login process to protect their original passwords. There are some drawbacks in this system similar to other text based graphical password schemes. S3PAS schemes include complicated and longer login processes.

In another study, two authentication techniques based on text and colours are proposed [17]. These techniques are called pair-based authentication scheme and hybrid textual authentication scheme which are suitable for Personal Digital Assistants (PDAs). Both techniques use a grid for session passwords generation. The researchers claim that these schemes are resistant to shoulder-surfing, dictionary and brute force attacks. However, they did not conduct a detailed user study to evaluate the security of the schemes. They only measured the registration and login times of the passwords created with these schemes by 10 participants. Since these schemes are completely new to the users and there is not a proper security and usability analysis of them, these proposed techniques should be verified extensively for security usability and effectiveness in the future. Similarly, there is not any user study conducted to test the security and usability of another text-based shoulder surfing resistant graphical scheme proposed by Chen et al. [5].

Zhang et al. [22] also proposed a hybrid password scheme based on shape and text. The proposed scheme uses shapes of strokes as origin passwords and allows users to login with text passwords via traditional input devices. Although the researchers claim that the scheme is resistant to shoulder surfing, hidden camera and brute force attacks and that it has variants to strengthens the security level through changing login interface of the system, the scheme still has some security and usability drawbacks. It is not familiar to users so they may adopt simple and weak strokes. This increases the chance of attackers to obtain the passwords. Also, the password creating step is vulnerable to attacks since users have to tell the system the original shapes and strokes. Moreover, the login process of this scheme is longer than other graphical schemes. For these reasons, more advanced authentication system should be proposed to improve this method.

In a recent study, a comprehensive survey on shoulder surfing resistant text based graphical password schemes is conducted [12]. This study explained the existing security problems, possible solutions and limitations of some of these schemes. These studies primarily focused on the existing shoulder surfing attacks in text based graphical password approach. However, a guessing attack is also a potential problem for graphical password schemes because of the predictability of user-chosen graphical passwords [18,20].

3   The Novel Authentication Scheme

All the aforementioned schemes have discrete text and graphical password creation steps which considerably increase the registration and login times. Compared to these schemes, the novel hybrid authentication scheme introduced in this research shortens password creation and login times as it has an integrated registration phase. Unlike other schemes, in the proposed scheme, images are used as cues to help users to complete their complex text passwords instead of creating a second password. Thus, the proposed scheme improves recall rate without sacrificing the security against attackers. Moreover, the results of the previous studies showed that users have an adoptability problem with these schemes as they are unfamiliar to users. However, the proposed scheme substantially preserves the login experiences of users who are accustomed to traditional textual passwords. As far as is known, the proposed scheme is the first scheme in the literature associating the letters of the chosen text passwords with the images by using the Tip of the Tongue (TOT) phenomenon. This feature significantly increases the memorability of the passwords.

In the hybrid authentication method we propose, text passwords are strengthened by using images as an assistant tool for users to memorize complex character sets. Theoretically, it is a text password scheme integrating user chosen and system generated characters. However, users are allowed to choose images from image portfolios to enter the system generated characters associated with the images. In this approach, users continue to use text passwords, but strong and memorable ones. They do not have to remember complex passwords at first or write them down; with the help of the images they will be able to memorize them naturally.

The proposed scheme has many advantages in terms of security and usability. It allows users to create and memorize cryptographically strong passwords easily. It eliminates the risk of passwords being hacked by dictionary attacks. It also secures the passwords against shoulder surfing attacks. It is a user-friendly authentication scheme.

The next sections describe the proposed scheme in detail considering its design and security and usability aspects.

3.1   System Design

To test the proposed authentication scheme, a web application which also works on mobile phones has been designed and implemented. This application uses ASP as the server side programming, JavaScript as the client side programming, and an SQL database is used to store the data.

The user authentication process in the designed scheme has two main steps: a registration phase and a login phase. The registration phase consists of creating key passwords and image selection. The reasons behind key design decisions and how they relate to security and usability considerations are explained at every stage of the registration and login phases in the following sections. The flowcharts of the registration and login phases are illustrated in Fig. 1.

Registration Phase. In the first step of the registration phase, users are asked to enter their username or email address in the username field. Then they are asked to create a key text password called key characters. The only restriction about the key password is that the first four characters should be upper- or lower-case characters. The reason why the minimum length of key password is set to four characters is that every user can remember it easily.

After creating the key password, the image selection process begins. This is an integrated process of retyping the key password and choosing the images. While users retype their key passwords in the "password" field, an associated image portfolio appears each time they type a particular letter. For each typed letter, there is a related image portfolio consisting of 20 images. This relation comes from the idea of choosing images of objects, famous people, activities or known figures which their names initials is the typed letter. It means, for example, when users type "a", as a character in their key passwords, an image portfolio appears including images whose names are starting with "a" (the images of alpha, apple, Albert Einstein etc.). Then users select the images from the image portfolio. Users have to select an image from each set of images. This selection will be performed so as users type the characters under the images into the password

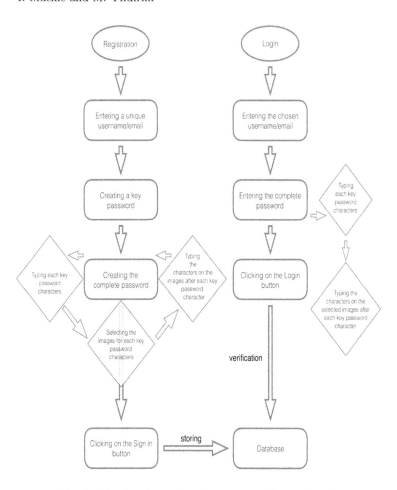

Fig. 1. The flowchart of registration and login phases.

field but not click on the image. There are a set of two random characters under each image combining one alphanumerical character and one digit or letter. Briefly, users will enter these two-characters after each character of their key password. To make it easy for users to recognize which characters they should enter, the password field is designed to include small and large squares. The small squares coloured in green is to enter each character of key passwords, and the larger squares coloured in red is to enter the characters under the images. This helps users not to be confused of the order of the characters. In this study, users are expected to choose four images in total which are associated to four letters in their key password, considering the memorability issues. Therefore, there are four small green squares for the first four alphabetical characters of the key password. Also, there are four larger red squares for the two sets of characters placed under the images. The last large square is to enter the rest of the key password's characters.

The number of images in each portfolio is set for the first test of the scheme. The theoretical password space calculated in this way have satisfying results to provide high security.

This progress allows users to create a complex password mixing their key passwords and the random characters associated with the selected images. The characters under each image change for different users. The registration phase of the scheme is illustrated in the Fig. 2(a–e) step by step with the example username, user-1, and the password, abcd123.

As seen in the figures, the password abcd123 which is created as the key password by the user whose username is user-1 turned into a complex password ah*b-pcJ:d&x123 including upper case, lower case, number and special keyboard characters at the end of the experiment. The user chose the images of Abraham Lincoln, bag, cake and yellow dress and entered the characters under those images. The user does not have to remember the complex, 15 characters long password as remembering the key password and the four images will suffice. Even if users create four character password composed of only lower case characters, it will turn into a complex password including different type of characters when the password creation process ends.

The proposed scheme has a help feature which visualize the password creation instructions for users step by step. When the creation of a mixed password is completed, the sign up button becomes active to so that users can complete the registration process. All the details including username and complete passwords entered in the registration phase are stored into the database which will be used during the login phase for verification.

Login Phase. In the login phase users are asked to enter their user name/email and their passwords (mixed password). Users will be able to see the images like in the registration phase but the order of images within the set will be random at every login time. After a while as users continue to login the system, they will be able to memorize their complex passwords so they might not need to look at the images. The system has a feature which allows users to hide pictures whenever they want; this decreases the susceptibility shoulder surfing attacks. In case they have difficulties to recall the part of their passwords, they can view the images by simply ticking the "invisible pictures" box. The screen-shot of the login phase of the authentication scheme is shown in Fig. 3.

In the login phase, while supplying the username/email and password information, independent of whether or not they match those defined during password creation, the image portfolios will continue to appear based on the typed character. Users must correctly enter the characters under all images pre-chosen for their accounts in each round of password verification. If any information is wrong, the user will be shown a "access denied" message at the end of the login phase. Seeing an image portfolio including no familiar image allows legitimate users to immediately realize that they entered a different character from key passwords characters and gives them chance to fix it. However, this prevents an attacker from knowing that the characters tried are invalid.

(a) Entering the username and the key password (key characters).

(b) Entering the first character of the key password and characters under the selected image from the portfolio.

(c) Entering the second character of the key password and characters under the selected image from the portfolio.

(d) Entering the third character of the key password and characters under the selected image from the portfolio.

(e) Entering the fourth character of the key password, characters under the selected image from the portfolio and rest of the characters of the key password.

Fig. 2. (a–e) User registration phase of the proposed scheme.

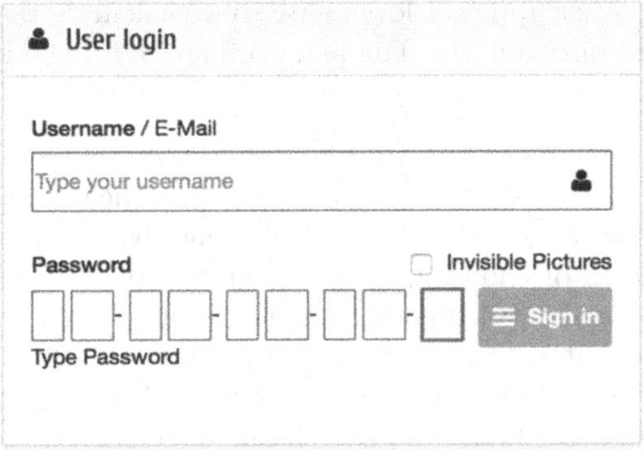

Fig. 3. User login phase of the proposed scheme.

After the successful entries of both username/email and password, the users are allowed to access their accounts.

3.2 Security and Usability Analysis

The following sections presents the security and usability analysis of the proposed scheme. The password space of the scheme is formulated and its resistance to attacks is discussed under the security analysis. Password creation, login time and memorability of the passwords created with the scheme are discussed under the usability analysis.

Security Analysis. A new password scheme should allow users to create passwords which are strong enough against guessing, brute-force and observation attacks. The quality of a password authentication scheme depends on how it is effective to limit attempts to guess users' passwords either by people who know them or a computer-based cracking program trying the possible passwords [10,11]. Password strength is determined by measuring the password space which is the maximum possible number of passwords generated by the system. The password space of the novel authentication scheme is formulated in the following section.

Password Space. The strength of the proposed scheme can be evaluated by measuring both the entropy of the user chosen key-text password and the graphical password parts. Assume that the password space of the key password created by the users in our scheme is P_1, the length of the key password is l and n is the numbers of the characters in an alphabet from which the key passwords characters are randomly selected such as an alphabet including English upper and lower letters, digits and non-alphanumeric characters. The key password which is l characters long has an entropy of $l \cdot \log_2 n$ bits. In our scheme, however, this should be somewhat lower than this since at least four letters of the key password must be either upper or lower case so we calculate the password space of the key password in two parts. The password space for the key password is:

$$P_1 = (l - 4) \cdot \log_2 n_1 \cdot 4 \cdot \log_2 n_2$$

To find the total password space, we also calculate the entropy of image based passwords. Let P_2 be the password space of image based passwords, and c be the number of rounds of choosing images from the related portfolios which is 4 in our case since at least 4 different images should be chosen from different portfolios. Assume that n is the numbers of images in each portfolio, and k is the number of images selected from each portfolio. The entropy of a randomly selected images and accordingly the two-character sets is:

$$P_2 = c \cdot \log_2 \frac{n!}{(n - k)!}$$

The password space of the proposed scheme is: $P = P_1 \times P_2$. Choosing different parameters, for example increasing the values of k, n or c can increase security, but also decreases usability. We believe that remembering a key password and four images from different portfolios consisting of twenty images will not be a burden for users' memory, but it can increase the resistance to dictionary attacks by increasing password space in practice. Text passwords used in practice are generally far from randomly and independently selected. Most of the user passwords consist of only lowercase or digits which significantly decreases the entropy. For example, a randomly generated 8-character password consisting of digits (0–9), lowercase (a–z), and uppercase (A–Z) has $8 \cdot \log_2 62 = 47.6$ bits of entropy if all characters were selected randomly and independently. However, in practice they have far less bits than this [19]. Considering the realistic scenario, the added security from image selection parts of the proposed scheme becomes more significant. The integrated scheme significantly decreases the possibility of successful dictionary attacks.

Resistance to Attacks. As stated above, the proposed authentication scheme decreases the chance of attackers to obtain passwords via brute-force and dictionary attacks. The scheme has an integrated step of creating complex passwords based on text and images, which increases the numbers of possible passwords generated by the system, the password space.

While selecting the images and entering the associated characters, the input is given through keyboard rather than clicking on the images to prevent other people to observe the password over the user's shoulder. Allowing users to use mouse to enter the input maybe would make the system more adaptable but also more susceptible to shoulder surfing attacks. It supports client-server environment and its main advantage is the resistance to brute force and shoulder surfing attacks. However, the handicap of the scheme is that people who look over the user's shoulder can find out the previous character of the key password when they see the image portfolio. They of course, will not know the preferred image as users do not click on the images but this is still a risk for part of the password. This might be prevented by not placing images of objects, foods or famous people whose names' initials is same in a portfolio, but we prefer to evaluate its efficiency on memorizing images.

Usability Analysis. The idea of associating the images with the letters in the key passwords to increase the memorability of the final complex passwords come from the phenomenon called *Tip of the Tongue (TOT)*. The phenomenon refers to failing to retrieve a word from memory or partial recall but feeling that the retrieval is imminent [2,9]. It reveals that lexical access occurs in several stages. People who experience this phenomenon can often recall some features of the target word mostly *the first letter*, or its syllabic stress and words similar in sound or meaning [3,15]. The first letters of words are also important for coding words. For this purpose, phonetic alphabets are produced including code words which are assigned to each letter [7]. Users can code the words by assigning them to the letters in their key password to recall later. Associating the typed letters with images will help users to recall both the images and key characters.

Furthermore, to increase the memorability, the images in each portfolio are chosen from different categories including famous people, objects, sport activities, known art figures, animals, foods and places to be used in the authentication scheme similar to the Story scheme [8]. This allows users to have many options in which they can select the most appropriate one to themselves as well as the most probable one remember.

To evaluate the effectiveness of the scheme an empirical study was conducted with users. The next section presents the details of this study.

4   Methodology

An empirical study was conducted with the students at the University of Sussex in order to evaluate the security and usability of the proposed hybrid authentication scheme. In addition to the security and usability aspects, the study is also used to evaluate the user satisfaction of the proposed scheme. To perform this study, an ethical approval was sought and obtained from the University of Sussex.

4.1   The Design and Apparatus

A web application was developed to test the security, usability and user satisfaction of the designed authentication scheme. The application also works on mobile phones enabling users to create strong passwords. The apparatus used in this study included a password register/login page of the designed authentication scheme; a questionnaire for the participants; and consent forms to read and accept for the participants.

First, the participants were asked to create an account using the scheme and login afterwards. The participants were shown a register/login page to enter their username and create a password. Once the participants had registered the application, they were given a questionnaire to fill out. The questionnaire included 6 questions related to users' experiences and satisfaction with the scheme. The average time to complete the study including registration and filling the questionnaire was approximately 10–15 min.

4.2   The Procedure

At the beginning of the empirical study, the participants were assigned a unique ID number. The participants were given information about the study and asked to read and accept the consent form. Once they had accepted the consent form, they were able to register the application. For those participants who were interested in getting more information about the study researcher's contact information were provided in the consent form. After the participants registered the application successfully, they were asked to fill the questionnaire. Participants were asked to login to the websites after a week and a month to find out whether they recall their passwords.

4.3   The Measurements

There are several measurements involved in the empirical study: the password strength, cracking time, creation and login time, memorability and user satisfaction. To measure the security of the new authentication scheme, created passwords were analysed using the "Password Meter" [13] and "How Secure is my Password?" [6] tools. While the "Password Meter" measured the strength of the passwords created with the scheme, "How Secure is my Password?" measured the password cracking times.

The other elements measured in this empirical study were the password creation and login times. The researcher measured these while participants were testing the authentication scheme. To measure the memorability, participants were contacted approximately after a week and a month, and asked to login the system again to understand whether they remember or not their passwords. User satisfaction were measured based on questionnaire responses of the participants to evaluate the authentication scheme.

52 students studying in the University of Sussex were recruited to participate in this empirical study. There were 29 females and 23 male participants. Undergraduate students as well as postgraduate students participated in the study: 33 of the participants were undergraduate students, 19 of them were postgraduate students. Usability and security evaluation of the scheme based on the analysis of the collected data is presented in the following sections.

5 Results

Here we give the results and an analysis of the empirical study.

5.1 The Password Analysis

Password Strength. To evaluate the strength of the passwords created with the proposed authentication scheme, an empirical study was conducted with 52 participants. All the passwords created with the scheme were between 12 to 16 characters in length. Since eight characters come from the selected images provided by the scheme inherently, the length of user-chosen key passwords were 6 characters long on average. The "Password Meter" is used as a tool to measure the password strength. All participants created passwords with this scheme, and all of them were strong passwords according to the measurement results. The passwords created by the participants were scored out of 100 and the least score was 81, whereas the mean password strength was $M = 96.50(SD = 5.96)$. However, this tool alone is not sufficient to determine the resistance of a password to cracking. The user-generated passwords should be strong enough to password guessing attacks. The next section discusses the password cracking times of the passwords created with the proposed scheme by the participants.

Password Creation and Login Time. The password creation time and login time of the participants were measured by the researcher during the experiment. Table 1 summarizes the time it takes to create a password and to login in seconds. It took about one or two minutes on average to create a password or to login for participants.

Memorability. Passwords created with the proposed authentication scheme were remembered correctly most of the time. Although there was a slight decrease from a weeks duration to a month, still 75% of 52 participants remembered their passwords correctly, and successfully logged in to the system. Table 2 shows the login success rates after a week and a month period.

Table 1. Password creation and login times in the empirical study.

	Password creation time	Login time
Proposed authentication scheme	$M = 94.08$ $(SD = 19.93)$	$M = 57.40$ $(SD = 15.73)$

Table 2. Login success rates in the empirical study.

	Login success rates (after a week)	Login success rates (after a month)
Proposed authentication scheme	90.38% (47/52)	75% (39/52)

5.2   The Results Based on the Survey Responses

User Satisfaction. Participants were asked about their experiences on the use of the novel authentication scheme to create an account. 92% of the participants liked the method of password creation with the scheme. 94% of them considered that it was fun to use, and similarly, 90% of the participants considered that the scheme was easy to use (see Fig. 4).

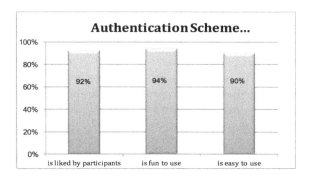

Fig. 4. Participants' opinion with regard to the use of the proposed scheme.

When it comes to the beliefs of participants in the method used by the proposed authentication scheme, results showed that most participants agreed that this method created stronger passwords than other commonly used methods (89%). However, agreement was less on creating more memorable passwords with this method, though still more than half of the participants (58%) agreed that this method would create more memorable passwords. Figure 5 illustrates the participants' perception of the proposed schemes ability to allow users to create strong and memorable passwords. However, results of the experiments showed that the actual memorability rates were higher than participants expected.

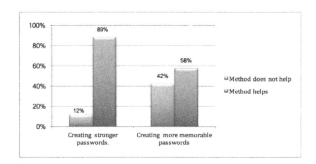

Fig. 5. Users perception of the proposed scheme's ability to produce strong and memorable passwords.

In addition to the users' thoughts of the efficiency of the new authentication scheme on creating strong and memorable passwords, they were also asked whether they will prefer to use the scheme or not. Only 5 out of 52 participants (9.6%) reported that they would not prefer to use the scheme neither for important passwords nor for others. On the other hand, 30 participants (32.7%) reported they would use the novel scheme for important passwords and 17 participants (57.7%) would use it for all passwords. The empirical study gave results that show the proposed authentication scheme provides usability and security, as well as high user satisfaction rates.

6   Discussion

Traditional text passwords alone are vulnerable to brute-force and dictionary attacks as users choose weak and predictable passwords in favour of memorability. On the other hand, graphical passwords alone are subject to shoulder surfing attacks. They also introduce usability issues by making password creation process longer for users. For these reasons, a hybrid authentication scheme integrating text and recognition-based graphical passwords is proposed in this paper. The design of the proposed scheme differs from other combined schemes since it offers an integrated registration phase rather than two or three different steps. It largely preserves the sign-in and log-in experiences of users who are accustomed to use text passwords. The proposed scheme does not suggest a discrete graphical password creation step, instead it uses the images as cues to help users to create complex text passwords and memorize them easily. This also provides a usable authentication method by decreasing the steps of password verification. The proposed hybrid authentication method is implemented and an empirical study is conducted to evaluate its effectiveness on producing strong and memorable passwords.

Users authenticate themselves in a similar way as they do with conventional text-passwords, without increasing the registration time unreasonably. The small difference with the registration and login time can be tolerated whereas the additional security is added to the scheme over the usual text password authentication. In the empirical study, the participants used the authentication scheme to login only twice in a month. When this scheme is used for real systems, the login times are likely to decrease as the frequency of logging into the system will be higher. As time goes by, users will also be able to memorize their passwords and will not need to resort to images to enter the characters.

The resulting scheme is easy to use, and it helps users to create memorable as well as strong passwords which are resistant to dictionary attacks. Since the images in the registration phase are randomly placed in the portfolio every time, they include different characters for different users, and they are chosen by entering the characters under them through keyboard but not clicking on them provide a resistance to shoulder surfing attacks. It also provides a large password space by combining the text and images to create passwords. This reduces the possibility of cracking the passwords for third parties. The results of the study showed that password cracking times are significant so as to eliminate brute-force and dictionary attacks.

With regards to improving the proposed hybrid password authentication, an immediate endeavour that can be carried out is to investigate whether the relation between the typed character with the first letters of the names of objects, famous people, activities etc. in images affects the security. These relations have been inspired by the Tip of the Tongue phenomenon in the hope of increasing the memorability of passwords. In the conducted user study, the majority of the participants indeed remembered correctly their passwords but yet it is difficult to say if this is caused by the association between the key passwords characters and image portfolios. While expecting to increase usability, it might reduce the security by increasing the chance of shoulder surfing attacks. This is the dilemma of proposed scheme that need to be clarified so further investigations will be useful to find out the impact of associating typed characters with images on password security and memorability. This is an interesting research question as the challenge of balancing security and usability remains. It is also worthwhile making slight modifications on the scheme in order to increase usability. For example, the characters placed under the images can be changed each time even for the same user which means creating a one-time password each time. The security and usability evaluation of such scheme might yield interesting results.

References

1. Adams, A., Sasse, M.A.: Users are not the enemy. Commun. ACM **42**(12), 40–46 (1999). https://doi.org/10.1145/322796.322806
2. Brown, A.: A review of the tip-of-the-tongue experience. Psychol. Bull. **109**(2), 204–223 (1991)
3. Brown, R., McNeill, D.: The tip of the tongue phenomenon. J. Verbal Learn. Verbal Behav. **5**(4), 325–337 (1966)
4. Burnett, M., Kleiman, D. (eds.): Perfect Passwords. Syngress Publishing Inc., Rockland (2006)
5. Chen, Y.L., Ku, W.C., Yeh, Y.C., Liao, D.M.: A simple text-based shoulder surfing resistant graphical password scheme. In: IEEE 2nd International Symposium on Next-Generation Electronics. pp. 161–164. IEEE, February 2013. https://doi.org/10.1109/ISNE.2013.6512317
6. Collider, S.: How secure is my password? (2016). https://howsecureismypassword.net. Accessed 14 Jan 2017
7. Crystal, D.: Dictionary of Linguistics and Phonetics, vol. 30. Wiley, New York (2011)
8. Davis, D., Monrose, F., Reiter, M.: On user choice in graphical password schemes. In: Proceedings of The 13th USENIX Security Symposium, pp. 151–164. USENIX Association, San Diego (2004)
9. Encyclopedia.com: Tip-of-the-tongue phenomenon - dictionary definition of tip-of-the-tongue phenomenon. http://www.encyclopedia.com/psychology/encyclopedias-almanacstranscripts-and-maps/tip-tongue-phenomenon. Accessed 9 Nov 2016
10. Haque, M., Imam, B.: A new graphical password: combination of recall & recognition based approach. Int. J. Comput. Electric. Autom. Control Inf. Eng. **8**(2), 320–324 (2014)

11. Haque, M., Imam, B., Ahmad, N.: 2-round hybrid password scheme. Int. J. Comput. Eng. Technol. (IJCET) **3**(2), 579–587 (2012)
12. Mokal, P., Devikar, R.: A survey on shoulder surfing resistant text based graphical password schemes. Int. J. Sci. Res. (IJSR) **3**(4), 747–750 (2014)
13. Passwordmeter.com. (n.d.): Password strength checker (2017). http://www.passwordmeter.com. Accessed 5 Jan 2017
14. Rao, K., Yalamanchili, A.: Novel shoulder-surfing resistant authentication schemes using text-graphical passwords. Int. J. Inf. Netw. Secur. **1**(3), 163–170 (2012)
15. Schwartz, B., Metcalfe, J.: Tip-of-the-tongue (TOT) states: retrieval, behaviour, and experience. Memory Cognit. **39**(5), 737–749 (2011)
16. Shepard, R.: Recognition memory for words, sentences and pictures. J. Verbal Learn. Verbal Behav. **6**, 156–163 (1967)
17. Sreelatha, M., Shashi, M., Anirudh, M., Ahamer, M., Manoj Kumar, V.: Authentication schemes for session passwords using color and images. Int. J. Netw. Secur. Appl. **3**(3), 111–119 (2011)
18. Van Oorschot, P., Thorpe, J.: Exploiting predictability in click-based graphical passwords. J. Comput. Secur. **19**(4), 669–702 (2011)
19. van Oorschot, P.C., Wan, T.: TwoStep: an authentication method combining text and graphical passwords. In: Babin, G., Kropf, P., Weiss, M. (eds.) MCETECH 2009. LNBIP, vol. 26, pp. 233–239. Springer, Heidelberg (2009). https://doi.org/10.1007/978-3-642-01187-0_19
20. Vorster, J., van Heerden, R.: A study of perceptions of graphical passwords (2015). https://www.researchgate.net/publication/283712970_A_Study_of_Perceptions_of_Graphical_Passwords. Accessed 2 June 2016
21. Yan, J., Blackwell, A., Anderson, R., Grant, A.: Password memorability and security: empirical results. IEEE Priv. Secur. **2**(5), 25–31 (2004)
22. Zhang, Y., Monrose, F., Reiter, M.K.: The security of modern password expiration: an algorithmic framework and empirical analysis. In: Proceedings of the 17th ACM Conference on Computer and Communications Security, pp. 176–186 (2010)
23. Zhao, H., Li, X.: S3PAS: a scalable shoulder-surfing resistant textual-graphical password authentication scheme. In: 21st International Conference on Advanced Information Networking and Applications Workshops, AINAW 2007, vol. 2, pp. 467–472, May 2007. https://doi.org/10.1109/AINAW.2007.317

"It's Shocking!": Analysing the Impact and Reactions to the A3: Android Apps Behaviour Analyser

Majid Hatamian[1]([✉]), Agnieszka Kitkowska[2], Jana Korunovska[3], and Sabrina Kirrane[3]

[1] Chair of Mobile Business and Multilateral Security, Goethe University Frankfurt, Frankfurt am Main, Germany
majid.hatamian.h@ieee.org
[2] Karlstad University, Karlstad, Sweden
agnieszka.kitkowska@kau.se
[3] Vienna University of Business and Economics, Vienna, Austria
{jana.korunovska,sabrina.kirrane}@wu.ac.at

Abstract. The lack of privacy awareness in smartphone ecosystems prevents users from being able to compare apps in terms of privacy and from making informed privacy decisions. In this paper we analysed smartphone users' privacy perceptions and concerns based on a novel privacy enhancing tool called *Android Apps Behaviour Analyser (A3)*. The *A3* tool enables user to behaviourally analyse the privacy aspects of their installed apps and notifies about potential privacy invasive activities. To examine the capabilities of *A3* we designed a user study. We captured and contrasted privacy concern and perception of 52 participants, before and after using our tool. The results showed that *A3* enables users to easily detect their smartphone app's privacy violation activities. Further, we found that there is a significant difference between users' privacy concern and expectation before and after using *A3* and the majority of them were surprised to learn how often their installed apps access personal resources. Overall, we observed that the *A3* tool was capable to influence the participants' attitude towards protecting their privacy.

Keywords: Smartphone ecosystems · Android · Privacy
Permission · Privacy concern · Privacy behaviour

The authors would like to thank: A. K. Lieberknecht, C. Stern, H. Chen and Y. Obreshkov that partially contributed in the data collection task. This research work has received funding from the H2020 Marie Skłodowska-Curie EU project "Privacy&Us" under the grant agreement No. 675730.

F. Kerschbaum and S. Paraboschi (Eds.): DBSec 2018, LNCS 10980, pp. 198–215, 2018.
https://doi.org/10.1007/978-3-319-95729-6_13

1   Introduction

In the last decade, the privacy of data users/owners has become a growing concern due to the massive increase in personal information utilised in smartphone apps [1], social networks [2], outsourced search applications [3,4], etc.

Smartphone apps are designed with consideration for the demands and constraints of the smartphones and to take advantage of any specialised capabilities that they have. The smartphone apps market is rapidly growing. In 2017, the total number of iOS and Android apps available on their marketplace were 2.2 and 3.5 millions, respectively [5]. Furthermore, the number of mobile app downloads has grown to 197 billion worldwide in 2017, which is almost 50 billion more than 2016 [6]. Such enormous number of apps available and the high number of downloads resulted in increased dependency on apps. In 2017, eMarketer released a study showing the average amount of time people spent using apps is two hours, 25 minutes per day [7]. The Techcrunch's report showed that on average, smartphone owners used nine apps per day and 30 apps per month. Accordingly, it was argued that smartphone users rely heavily on apps [8]. For instance, Marketing Land [9] reported that the smartphone users spent 86% of their internet usage time using apps. As a result, the landscape of smartphone use today is very much app-focused. All of these factors make smartphones an attractive target for privacy invasion.

Each app can request a certain number of permissions which allows it to gain access to the device resources such as contacts, location, storage, camera, etc. In older Android versions (prior to version 6.0), users had to grant permissions requested by each app at the install time and they were not able to restrict those permissions later. However, with the release of Android 6.0, the users were given control, and they are able to restrict the requested permissions even at runtime. Although this feature enables users to better preserve their privacy, prior studies have shown that few users are aware of it, hence permissions are often ignored even though they might appear irrelevant to the real functionality of the app [10]. This is due to the fact that many users do not understand the technical and sometimes ambiguous definitions of permissions [11]. Additionally, most of them value the use of the apps more than their personal information, despite the fact that the apps collect large amounts of personal information, for various purposes ranging from functionality to empower their ads mechanisms [12,13].

The invasive nature of smartphone apps, harvesting personal data has been demonstrated in many studies. The Wall Street Journal reported a study in which 101 popular smartphone apps were examined for personal information gathering activities. Their results showed that more than half of the apps exhibited at least one risky behaviour, such as location tracking, transmission of a smartphone's unique device ID number, or the gathering of other personal information [14]. A report by Appthority showed that 95% of the top 200 free apps and 80% of the top paid apps for Apple and Android phones did the same [15]. Chia et al. [16] studied risk signaling concerning the privacy intrusiveness of Android apps in two repositories. Their results showed that the number of dangerous permissions an app requested was positively correlated with its popularity. Therefore, the fact that an app is popular does not imply that it respects users' privacy.

This paper presents the results of interviews and surveys of 52 participants who used our privacy enhancing tool called *Android Apps Behaviour Analyser (A3)* that is solely designed and implemented for Android devices. In this study, we examine, compare and contrast smartphone users' concern and expectation, by leveraging a user study as a reference point for understanding smartphone-specific concerns and perceptions. This study is aimed to (1) propose a privacy enhancing tool for smartphone users to support them for informed privacy decision-making, (2) test our hypothesis that smartphone users are willing to take action and change their privacy attitude once they realise how their personal resources are treated by their installed apps, and (3) provide data over the understanding of users' privacy concern and expectation in using smartphone apps.

The rest of the paper is organised as follows: Sect. 2 reviews the existing works in the literature related to the privacy concern and expectation analysis of smartphone users. Section 3 describes the main concepts associated to the *Android Apps Behaviour Analyser (A3)* as a novel privacy enhancing tool for Android users. Section 4 presents the research steps and design decisions taken in the implemented user study to analyse the impact of *A3* on the users' privacy concern and expectation and the obtained results are then presented in Sect. 5. Finally, we conclude the paper and point the future directions of research in Sect. 6

2   Related Work

Kelley et al. [17] tried to identify possible causes and incentives for users to willingly share their location with advertisers. The results showed that users were highly concerned about their personal data. Almost 80% (19 out of 24) of the people questioned expressed the highest level of concern towards an unsolicited transfer of personal data gathered about them by a company on a corporate level (e.g. to other companies, institutions, governments, etc.). The authors concluded that the users are least concerned when they share information about being at certain pre-selected locations. The study suggested that this could be attributed, in part to the fact, that users may like being informed regarding certain promotion activities or other similar events related to the places specified (e.g. coupons for favourite restaurants). Differently, Chin et al. [18] studied overall privacy and security expectations of the users in choosing apps. They first surveyed 60 smartphone users to measure their willingness to perform certain tasks using their smartphones to test the hypothesis that people currently avoid using their phones due to privacy and security concerns. Second, they investigated why and how the users trust a certain app. The results showed that users are more concerned and conservative about privacy on their smartphones than their laptops. The authors also identified the threats which scare smartphone users of using smartphones (e.g. malicious apps, data loss, etc.). Based on these results, they suggested some recommendations to ameliorate privacy and security confidence of users to increase trust in choosing apps. A different user-centric study was published by Felt et al. [12]. They presented a risk ranking of sensitive smartphone resources by user concerns. A successive open-end enquiry among a group of 42 participants gathered personal descriptions and ratings of a subset of evaluated risks which disclosed that the lowest-ranked risks are seen as disturbances, the highest-ranked risks however represent serious issues. They found that warnings in Android and iOS do not satisfy users' concerns. They concluded that future permission systems should consider user concerns when deciding which permissions are protected with warnings.

Lin et al. [10] investigated privacy expectations of smartphone users. The main goal of the authors was to figure out when an app violates users' expectations. Having considering this and by arguing that if a user's mental model aligns with what the app actually does, the authors claimed there would be fewer privacy issues since the user is adequately informed of the actual app's behaviour. This brought them to the point of allowing users to see the most common mis-expectations about an app by revising users' mental model. For this reason, they suggested the use of both crowdsourcing users' mental models and profiling mobile apps using log analysis tools. Amini [19] employed crowdsourcing as part of a procedure to analyse mobile apps privacy expectation. Participants were asked to rate their expectation and comfort feeling according to the access of sensitive information related to the identified tasks. Thus, by considering the context of apps as well as privacy invasive behaviour, an assessment of the desirability of this information leakage can be depicted. Continuing this work, Amini et al. [20] envision the tool *AppScanner*, consisting of different sub-modules, to be able to evaluate mobile apps privacy on a large scale. Enhancing the work presented before, crowdsourcing still presents a main component for gathering user's expectation related to the privacy behaviour of apps. The analysis of the past research lead to the following research questions:

RQ-1: What are people's privacy expectations of mobile apps?
RQ-2: Do people have correct mental models of mobile apps resource access behaviour?
RQ-3: Are privacy concerns and trust correlated with people's expectations?

In [21], the authors studied the compliance of accessing permissions by installed apps with regard to the users' expectation. To this end, they modified the Android OS to log whenever an installed app accessed a permission-protected resource and then gave modified smartphones to 36 participants who used them as their primary phones for one week. Afterwards, they showed various instances over the past week where apps had accessed certain types of data and asked whether those instances were expected, and whether they would have wanted to deny access. The results showed that 80% of the participants would have preferred to prevent at least one permission request, and overall, they stated a desire to block over a third of all requests. This is an important work that revealed the discrepancy between users' expectation and actual app behaviour. One of the most relevant outcomes from their work is identification of the need of transparency with regard to which app accesses which resources and at what frequency. A study from 2017 by Crager et al. [22] considered a different type of threat for users' privacy that comes from smartphones' sensors and other wearables. One specific threat that they presented was from an advertising software developer kit (SDK), that used the smartphone's microphone to listen the near-ultrasonic sounds placed in the TV, radio and Web ads, which could be eventually used to infer the user's preferences. The results showed that users were only aware of the location tracking, and had not been considering the other three, namely Device-Fingerprinting, Keystroke-Monitoring and Acoustic Eavesdropping. As expected, users learning about the threats were immediately concerned about their privacy. The authors concluded that more efforts should be put into educating trivial (not experienced) users about the possible threats, but acknowledged the fact that the users would generally avoid using an app or a device if its security system affects usability.

Having included related work from 2011 to 2017, we conclude that although people are concerned, they are not in fact, fully aware how their data is being treated and how this affects their privacy. The part we shall be more concerned about is that the users, even after being alerted, tend not to change their behaviour (attitude) and instead try to rationalise using privacy-violating apps and willingly ignoring or accepting the possible risks. This behaviour, was coined in the literature as *privacy paradox* meaning that people's attitude toward privacy does not align with their actual behaviour [23,24]. This phenomenon is frequently assigned to psychological biases and heuristics that accompanies decision-making process. In the digital context the *privacy paradox* could be diminished by the reduction of information asymmetry. Currently, the end-users are not provided with a sufficient and understandable information about the data collection processes, unlike the service providers who have all the information about their data collection practice. Due to the lack of information, users are trapped in the *bounded rationality*, where the rational maximisation of benefits is restricted due to the limits of cognitive abilities [25].

Unlike the mentioned studies, we aim to increase the smartphone users awareness of privacy. By proposing a transparency tool called *Android Apps Behaviour Analyser (A3)* we analyse the behaviour of installed apps on the user's smartphone to identify privacy deviated activities. Out tool does not rely on the existing reviewed techniques for log analysis that require modification the OS (or root access). Additionally, we perform a user study to examine the users' privacy concern and expectation after revealing how much and to which level their personal information is accessed with/without their awareness. Hence, our remaining research questions are:

RQ-4: Is A3 tool capable of increasing mobile privacy awareness and altering privacy concerns?

RQ-5: What are people's reactions for the A3 tool and to the information it provides?

3   Technical Implementation: The A3 Tool

This section elaborates on the technical implementation followed in this paper to develop the *A3* tool including its respective components. Fig. 1 shows a high level architecture of *A3*. As it can be seen, *A3* has several components. In principle, the log reader component is responsible to read device's logs, and accordingly, produce the raw data. These data are then sent to the data mining component which aims to analyse the apps' privacy behaviour. The results obtained from the data mining component are then sent to the user for further evaluation and decision.

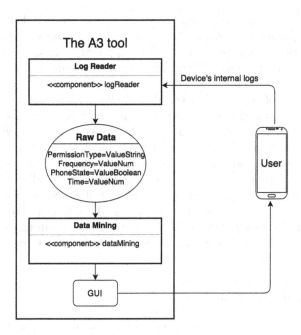

Fig. 1. A high level overview of the *A3* tool.

3.1   Log Reader Component

Throughout the implementation phase, we consistently target three main goals. Firstly, *A3* must work without any need for root access to the OS. Secondly, there must not be any modification to the core of the OS. Lastly, it should be capable of being installed on the recent versions of Android. We implemented the log reader based on AppOps which is a privacy manager tool and introduced in Android 4.3. However, Google decided to make it hidden in later versions of Android and it is currently inaccessible, unless the device is rooted [26]. To the best of our knowledge, root access is only necessary to access the AppOps management system, e.g. to tell the system to deny access to one of the operations that is controlled by AppOps. We found that to view the AppOps logs, there is no need to root the device, and they are accessible to any app with debugging privileges [27,28]. Generally, in order to collect the logs, a timer is sent to the `PermissionUsageLogger` service periodically. When it is received, the logger queries the AppOps service that is already running on the phone for a list of apps that have used any of the operations we are interested in tracking. We then check through that list and for any app that has used an operation more recently than we have checked, we store the time at which that operation was used in our own internal log. These timestamps can then be counted to get a usage count.

3.2   Data Mining Component

This component is supposed to behaviourally analyse the installed apps by getting help from the results obtained from the log reader component. This is done according to a rule-based approach which is supposed to increase the functionality and flexibility of our data mining component. Consequently, we have defined a set of privacy deviated behaviour detection rules that are aimed to analyse the privacy behaviour of the users' installed apps. We initially defined a set of sensitive permissions (introduced by Android[1]) and we mainly analyse the accesses to these resources. For example, consider the device's screen is off and it is in the horizontal orientation (and the user does not talk on the phone, meaning that the `AUDIO` permission is not being used). In such situation, we assume that the user does not use the phone (e.g. the phone lies on the desk) and if one of the sensitive resources is accessed by a given installed app, we record this and report to the user about the detail of the access (date, time and reason together with a short explanation). Therefore, the users can transparently manage their resource accesses (due to space limitations, we refrained from explaining all the defined rules).

3.3   Graphical User Interface

The *A3* tool informs users of the potential misuses of their personal data. For this reason, we emphasize *how* the privacy indicators are shown to the user. Therefore, the Graphical User Interface (GUI) plays a crucial role in *A3*. The GUI offers the following functionality:

App selection. In order to follow the principle of data minimisation [29], the users are given this option to choose the apps that they are interested to analyse their privacy behaviour, meaning that the users can freely choose which app(s) should be scanned (Fig. 2(a)).

Scan intervals. We have given users the ability to decide about the desired scan intervals, meaning that they can determine the watchdog intervals at which the sensitive resources are scanned for any potential privacy invasive activity (Fig. 2(b)).

---

[1] https://developer.android.com/guide/topics/permissions/requesting.html.

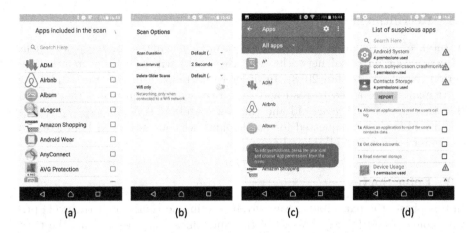

Fig. 2. *A3* user interface (a) app selection (b) scan intervals (c) permission restriction, and (d) behaviour analysis.

Permission restriction. As Google has initiated a new permission manager system in Android 6.0 and later versions, we have embedded a direct access to this permission manager system to revoke/grant permissions for any app (Fig. 2(c)).

Behaviour analysis. The users are able to check which personal resources (permissions) have been accessed by their installed apps. They can also observe the time and frequency of accesses. Accordingly, a synopsis of apps and resources accessed including the corresponding timestamps are communicated to the user. This also entailed to translate the technical terms of permissions defined by Android (e.g. `PHONE_STATE`, `COARSE_LOCATION`, etc.) to understandable definitions for the ordinary users (Fig. 2(d)).

4 The Design of the User Study

The user study comprises four main phases, including, recruitment, enter survey, a one week apps' behaviour analysis, and exit survey. In order to link enter and exit surveys, we supplied participants with an anonymous personal code. We asked participants about their privacy concerns, attitudes and expectations of the personal information that their smartphone would collect and transfer before and after using *A3*. The results gathered from this user study provide us with a sound foundation to compare the users expectations with actual results obtained from *A3*. This helps and supports users to judge to which extent their expectations match what the apps are doing in the reality. In the following, each phase is described in detail.

4.1   Recruitment

In total, 52 participants were recruited through placing an online recruitment advertisement on social networks (e.g. Facebook) within a three month time period (Nov 2017 to Jan 2018). In order to participate in the user study, the participants were asked to read and sign a consent form in which they stated that they are over 18 years old and they own Android smartphones. To reduce potential biases, we requested for participants without advanced knowledge in computer science and IT related areas.

4.2   Enter Survey

In this phase, the participants were given certain questions about their: (1) privacy concern and (2) expectation of the smartphone apps behaviour. We tried to reuse the questions from [10,18,30,31] and adapted them to our application domain. The majority of the survey used Likert [32] like item scales to measure the privacy concern and expectation of the participants in the area of smartphones. The scores ranged from one extreme attitude (not at all concerned) to another (extremely concerned). In the first set of questions, we collected data on participant demographics, privacy concern and expectation. In the demographics section, we asked participants to provide information on their demographic background, such as their age and gender. We then investigated participants' privacy concern when using a smartphone app in different scenarios such as when the information they shared was considered sensitive in general, or when an app accessed information that did not seem as relevant. Lastly, we collected data on participants' expectation of what information they believed had been accessed by different kinds of apps.

4.3   Apps Privacy Behaviour: A One Week Analysis

After the successful completion of the enter survey, the participants gave us the permission to install $A3$ on their smartphones and they agreed to keep it running for one week. In order to make sure whether this one week time period is representative enough, we purchased ten Android smartphones and we installed the $A3$ tool on them. We then let $A3$ to run in the background for two weeks while it was scanning each individual phone (during this period, we never interacted with the devices, ensuring that they have sufficient battery level). We found that after almost one week, it is possible to observe a significant number of permission (resource) accesses by installed apps which would give us an indicator/understanding about the apps' behaviour. That is why we decided to choose the one week time slot. During the one-week interval, participants launched $A3$ on their smartphones and performed their usual daily activities with their phones while the tool was scanning all the resource accesses by their installed apps. It is worth to mention that we did not collect any personal information and all the scan results remained on the users' phones (the analysis results were not transmitted to external parties, servers, etc.).

4.4 Exit Survey

At the end of the week, the participants returned to our lab. They were presented with the results of the analysis of their installed apps' behaviour and completed the exit survey. We asked the participants to go through the results of the scans to see how their personal resources have been treated by their installed apps during the one week period. The questions in the exit survey examined how participants' expectation changed as a result of using *A3*, e.g. whether they changed their privacy attitude, do they have the intention/willingness to change their behaviour, what do they think about *A3*, whether its results are informative, annoying, expected, etc. Finally, each participant was compensated by a €15 Amazon voucher.

5 Results

5.1 General Exploration over the Data

Among 52 study participants, the majority (48.1%) were between 25–34 years old. The sample was almost equally distributed among two genders, females (42.3%) and males (57.7%). Most of the respondents held higher education, either bachelor's (57.7%) or master's degree and higher (26.6%). The detailed demographics are presented in Table 1.

Table 1. Participants demographics.

Demographic	Group	N	%
Age	18–24	16	30.8
	25–34	25	48.1
	35–44	7	13.5
	45 or older	4	7.7
Gender	Female	22	42.3
	Male	30	57.7
Education	High school	4	7.7
	Some college	4	7.7
	Bachelors degree	30	57.7
	Masters degree or higher	14	26.9
IT experience	Not at all	21	40.4
	Trivial	20	38.5
	Moderate	9	17.3
	A lot	2	3.8

Only three (5.7%) participants admitted that they read privacy policy before installing the new smartphone app, while 17 (32.7%) said they never read it, 23 (44.2%) said they read it rarely, and nine (17.3%) sometimes. The majority of respondents expressed their lack of knowledge about privacy in general ($N = 31$, 59.6%). Most of them were certain ($N = 23$, 32.7%) or not sure ($N = 16$, 30.8%) whether they have a basic knowledge about technical terms of privacy and security.

The participants admitted that they prefer social media and convenience to privacy and security. 16 (30.8%) said it is very true and 16 (30.8%) said rather true. Additionally, 33 (63.5%) participants confessed that they actively use social media.

Regardless, most participants stated that they feel motivated, and spend considerable time trying to protect their online privacy ($N = 32$, 61.5%). 29 (55.8%) respondents did not feel confident that somebody could track or monitor their online activities, and 15 (28.8%) were not sure how they feel about it.

5.2   User Expectation

In the enter survey we asked participants about their expectations of apps behaviour (**RQ-1**). First, we wanted to know how likely they think the app which they did not create an account for, will have access to sensitive information (i.e. location, contacts, etc.). The majority of participants said that it is not likely ($N = 22$, 42.3%) or only slightly likely ($N = 12$, 23.1%). The small percentage of respondents thought it is moderately ($N = 10$, 19.2%), or very and extremely likely ($N = 8$, 15.3%). Additionally, we asked to what extent the respondents agree with the following statement *Smartphone apps are only accessing resources and permissions which are related to their functionality (e.g. navigation apps need to have access to your location etc.)*. In total 20 participants strongly or somewhat agreed with the statement (38.4%), and 13 (25%) were neutral about it.

We wanted to examine whether participants would like to know more about the data collection and processing of smartphone apps. First, we asked if they would like to know what personal information is accessed by apps installed on their smartphones. The majority of participants strongly agreed ($N = 36$, 69.2%) or somewhat agreed ($N = 10$, 19.2%) with such statement. Additionally, we asked whether they would like to know how their personal information is used by apps installed on their phones. Once again, the participants even strongly agreed ($N = 39$, 75%) or somewhat agreed ($N = 9$, 17.3%) that they wish to know it.

5.3   App Resource Access Behaviour

We were interested to identify whether participants have the correct mental model for the frequency of access to the phone resources of certain app types (**RQ-2**). Therefore, in the enter survey we asked participants whether they have a social network, messaging and navigation app installed (most common sensible app categories to ordinary users), and if so, how many times such app is accessing their phone's location, storage, contacts, accounts, phone number, audio, calendar, camera and SMS/MMS. To see whether the assumptions were close to reality, in the exit survey we asked respondents to provide the access information from the *A3* tool, collected over the week.

In general, respondents underestimated the frequency of resource access by different apps. Among the respondents who had social network app on their phones ($N = 34$), 48.1% underestimated the location access, 59.6% storage, 30.8% contacts while 38.8% overestimated camera access. Similarly, the owners of messaging apps ($N = 46$) underestimated the numbers of access to location ($N = 20$, 30.8%), storage ($N = 43$, 88.5%), contacts ($N = 34$, 65.4%), accounts ($N = 33$, 63.5%), audio ($N = 28$, 53.8%), camera ($N = 21$, 40.4%). Lastly, the respondents highly underestimated the navigation apps resource access, such as location ($N = 41$, 78.7%) and storage ($N = 44$, 84.6%). We found that the real frequencies of apps accessing various resources vary, and where really high, some of them reaching over 40000 times per day.

5.4 Privacy Concern Aspects in Smartphone Apps

General Privacy Concerns and Trust. We developed a Likert scale [32] to investigate privacy concerns and online trust. We checked the reliability, and Cronbach α was .848 for the five *trust* items, and .754 for the five *privacy concerns* items. The Cronbach alpha is a reliability test that should be applied to check whether the scale is consistent, and whether it measures the desired attitude. It is based on the calculation of the average value of the reliability coefficients of all available items when divided into two half-tests [33].

We applied Spearman test for correlations to investigate whether there are relationships between privacy concerns, trust and expectations (**RQ-3**). The Spearman correlation was used because the data did not meet the assumptions of parametric tests. Spearman correlation is used on the ranked data, and it measures the strength of the relationship between two variables [34]. We found significant correlations between *trust* and the role of an app reputation when deciding upon personal information disclosure ($r_s = .35$, $p < .05$). There was a positive correlation between *trust* and a belief that an app accesses only resources related to its functionality ($r_s = .49$, $p < .001$). Additionally, we found a negative correlation between *trust* and refusal of providing personal data to smartphone apps ($r_s = -.41$, $p < .05$), apps' access to sensitive information ($r_s = -.30$, $p < .05$) and the restrictions of applications' permissions ($r_s = -.40$, $p < .05$).

Further, we found a significant correlation between *privacy concerns* and willingness to uninstall the app, if it violates users' privacy ($r_s = .38$, $p < .05$). Lastly, there was a correlation between concerns and fear about the safety of information ($r_s = .30$, $p < .05$).

We used Spearman test for correlations to examine whether people with higher levels of *privacy concerns* rank higher the importance of clear information about app's access to different types of personal information (when deciding on app's download or usage). We identified positive correlations between privacy concerns and importance of information about access to the phone's location, storage, contacts, accounts, audio, and camera (Table 2).

Table 2. Spearman correlations: privacy concerns and importance of clear information about the apps access to different types of personal information.

Information type	Correlation	Sig. (2-tailed)
Location	.494	.000
Storage	.335	.015
Contacts	.362	.008
Accounts	.522	.000
Audio	.386	.005
Camera	.508	.000

Privacy Issues in Smartphone Apps. One of the research goals was to investigate whether the *A3* tool is capable of increasing smartphone users' privacy awareness (**RQ-4**). To examine this we used repetitive measures, pre- and post questionnaires asking participants about their privacy concerns in the context of smart-phone apps. We applied Wilcoxon test to measure whether the participants' level of privacy concern changed after using *A3*. We used Wilcoxon test because we it is suitable for ordinal, ranked data. This test enables a direct comparison in related design studies, between participant's scores in two conditions [35].

The test indicated that in the exit survey, participants scored significantly higher on concerns about personal data being leaked or transferred to third parties ($Z = -5.106, p < .001$). Similarly their concerns were significantly higher about data falsification ($Z = -4.088, p < .001$), online bullying and flaming ($Z = -3.7006, p < .001$), receiving spam emails ($Z = -5.056, p < .001$), and receiving behavioural adds ($Z = -4.080, p < .001$). Further, after a week of using *A3* participants were more worried about government surveillance ($Z = -4.375, p < .001$) and about apps accessing irrelevant information ($Z = 5.442, p < .001$). However, there was no significant difference in before and after scores regarding the level of concern about their credit card being used by others.

5.5   Reaction to the Transparency Tool

Overall, we were interested in how the participants react to the A3 tool, and to the information it has provided (**RQ-5**). After using the *A3* tool for a week, the majority of respondents were surprised to learn how often apps access their personal resources ($N = 46$, 88.5%). The respondents found information provided by *A3* shocking ($N = 40$, 76.9%) but informative ($N = 36$, 69.3%). The participants realised that some apps access permissions that are not related to their functionality ($N = 49$, 94.3%), and they were shocked about it

($N = 46$, 88.4%). In regards of privacy intentions and concerns, participants expressed the willingness to restrict apps permissions in the future ($N = 46$, 88.5%), as well as uninstalling some of the apps that they find privacy invasive ($N = 40$, 86.9%). The majority ($N = 46$, 88.5%) found themselves more worried about privacy than before using *A3*, and they intend to report privacy invasive behaviours ($N = 32$, 61.6%), e.g. in the form of user comment on the Google Play Store to increase the privacy awareness of other users. Similarly, they expressed a willingness to read privacy policies before installing the app ($N = 36$, 69.3%). Lastly, the respondents admitted they would like to have tool like *A3* earlier ($N = 47$, 90.4%) and if possible wish to use it to monitor their smartphone apps behaviour ($N = 43$, 82.7%).

5.6 Additional Findings

Privacy Sensitivity Degree of Different Smartphone Resources. We asked respondents about the sensitivity of different types of information, on a scale from *Not at all sensitive* to *Extremely sensitive*. The participants perceived as extremely sensitive storage information (photos & videos)($N = 20$, 38.5%), audio ($N = 15$, 28.5%), camera ($N = 17$, 32.7%). They perceived as a not at all sensitive calendar information ($N = 16$, 30.8%) and SMS/MMS ($N = 13$, 25%). The other information types were scored as moderately (accounts on your phone, phone number) or slightly (location, contacts) sensitive.

The Spearman correlation tests identified significant positive correlations between the information sensitivity and privacy concerns. There was a weak correlation between concerns and sensitivity of location and accounts. Additionally, sensitive information about the storage, audio and calendar was correlated with concerns. Further, we found that there is a significant negative correlation between trust and sensitivity level of contacts, calendar and SMS/MMS information. The results of correlation analysis are presented in Table 3.

Table 3. Spearman correlations: privacy concerns and trust with information sensitivity.

	Sensitive information	Correlation	Sig.(2-tailed)
Privacy Concerns	Location	.286	.040
	Storage	.417	.002
	Accounts	.277	.047
	Audio	.326	.018
	Calendar	.327	.018
Trust	Contacts	−.277	.047
	Calendar	−.346	.012
	SMS/MMS	−.276	.047

5.7   Discussion

Our findings confirm that *A3* is able to affect the way by which people are concerned about their privacy. Although the majority of the participants (65.4%) said it is not likely or slightly likely that an app which they did not create an account for, will have an access to sensitive resources, the participants realised it is incorrect. They reported a higher number of apps that were not being used by them during the one week analysis, but still they were accessing users' personal resources in a very aggressive manner (without any user interaction, e.g. account creation, etc.). Further, 38.4% of the participants believed that smartphone apps only access resources relevant to their functionality (e.g. a weather forecasting app requires access to location). However, we discovered that some apps (e.g. health & fitness, navigation, etc.) that do not need to excessively request or access privacy sensitive information, are doing so without users' knowledge.

Overall, the information provided by *A3* raised the participants' privacy awareness after a trial period. This indicates that the reduction of information asymmetry by providing users with information about the apps resource access, may help to overcome or at least reduce the *privacy paradox*. However, this requires further investigation in different experimental settings enabling examination of causal relationship between the attitude and behaviour prior and after using the *A3* tool. Additionally, our results demonstrated that users have an inaccurate mental model of apps' resource access behaviour, and they mostly underestimated the frequency of permission accesses by their installed apps. However, the participants expressed willingness to change their attitude and behavior after using the tool. This willingness to change suggests that the tool such as *A3* could adjust users mental models, raising privacy awareness and enabling informed privacy decision-making.

5.8   Limitations

The scope of this paper comprises Android OS. Regardless of the choice of the research area, currently the *A3* tool cannot be applied to other smartphone platforms (e.g. iOS). Another limitation is the low number of participants (52 people) due to the complexity of the study. This happened due to several reasons. Firstly, *A3* is solely executable on Android devices, correspondingly, we missed lots of participants who showed interest but they were not technically qualified to participate in the study (e.g. iOS users). Secondly, since *A3* is not publicly available on the Google Play Store, several interested people expressed that they do not feel comfortable to install an app from unknown sources on their phones. Further, we tried our best to keep the study safe from any biases (e.g. to not focus on privacy experts). Unfortunately, in such studies, it is challenging to have a diverse type of participants which would further enhance the validity of our analysis.

6 Conclusion

In this paper, we studied the smartphone users' privacy awareness by conducting a user study based on an implemented privacy enhancing tool (*A3*). We examined the applicability of such tool with the real users and investigated the users' reaction to *A3*. Thus, we performed a user study comprising of 52 participants and we analysed their privacy concern and expectation before and after using the *A3* tool. The results clearly showed that users' privacy concern and expectation changed after using *A3*. We identified that users' privacy awareness increased due to the implication of *A3*. Moreover, we observed that users mostly have poor knowledge of how their installed apps treat their personal sensitive resources. Additionally, we found that there is a gap between what smartphone users perceive about privacy and what is happening in the reality by their installed apps. Study participants were shocked once they understood how their apps are accessing their resources without their knowledge, especially when accessing resources that are not necessary for the appropriate functionality of an app. As a result, we believe that the smartphone users need such privacy enhancing tool to better protect their privacy and to make informed privacy decisions. Although the results showed the changed perceptions of privacy issues that might be due to the use of *A3*, for the future work we plan to implement an explanatory study investigating the role of *A3* tool in the causal relationship of privacy attitude-behaviour change. This will enable us to contrast the control group with the experimental group for a more confident comparative analysis.

References

1. Gilbert, P., Chun, B.G., Cox, L., Jung, J.: Automating privacy testing of smartphone applications. Technical report CS-2011-02, Duke University (2011)
2. Raad, E., Chbeir, R.: Privacy in online social networks. In: Chbeir, R., Bouna, B.A. (eds.) Security and Privacy Preserving in Social Networks. LNSN, pp. 3–45. Springer, Vienna (2013). https://doi.org/10.1007/978-3-7091-0894-9_1
3. Razeghi, B., Voloshynovskiy, S.: Privacy-preserving outsourced media search using secure sparse ternary codes. In: Proceedings of IEEE International Conference on Acoustics, Speech and Signal Processing (ICASSP), Calgary, Canada, pp. 1–5 (2018)
4. Razeghi, B., Voloshynovskiy, S., Kostadinov, D., Taran, O.: Privacy preserving identification using sparse approximation with ambiguization. In: Proceedings of IEEE International Workshop on Information Forensics and Security (WIFS), Rennes, France, pp. 1–6 (2017)
5. Number of apps available in leading app stores. https://www.statista.com/statistics/276623/number-of-apps-available-in-leading-app-stores/. Accessed 5 Apr 2018
6. Number of mobile app downloads worldwide in 2016, 2017 and 2021. https://www.statista.com/statistics/271644/worldwide-free-and-paid-mobile-app-store-downloads/. Accessed 5 April 2018
7. eMarketer unveils new estimates for mobile app usage. https://www.emarketer.com/Article/eMarketer-Unveils-New-Estimates-Mobile-App-Usage/1015611. Accessed 5 Apr 2018

8. Report: Smartphone owners are using 9 apps per day, 30 per month. https://techcrunch.com/2017/05/04/report-smartphone-owners-are-using-9-apps-per-day-30-per-month/. Accessed 5 Apr 2018
9. More time on Internet through smartphones than PCs. https://marketingland.com/nielsen-time-accessing-internet-smartphones-pcs-73683. Accessed 5 Apr 2018
10. Lin, J., Amini, S., Hong, J.I., Sadeh, N., Lindqvist, J., Zhang, J.: Expectation and purpose: understanding users' mental models of mobile app privacy through crowdsourcing. In: Proceedings of ACM Conference on Ubiquitous Computing (UbiComp 2012), Pittsburgh, Pennsylvania, USA, pp. 501–510 (2012)
11. Felt, A.P., Ha, E., Egelman, S., Haney, A., Chin, E., Wagner, D.: Android permissions: user attention, comprehension, and behavior. In: Proceedings of the 8th ACM Symposium on Usable Privacy and Security (SOUPS 2012), pp. 1–3, New York, NY, USA (2012)
12. Felt, A.P., Egelman, S., Wagner, D.: I've got 99 problems, but vibration ain't one: a survey of smartphone users' concerns. In: Proceedings of the 2nd ACM Workshop on Security and Privacy in Smartphones and Mobile Devices (SPSM 2012), pp. 33–44, New York, NY, USA (2012)
13. Solove, D.J.: Nothing to Hide: The False Tradeoff between Privacy and Security. Yale University Press, London (2011)
14. Your apps are watching you. https://www.wsj.com/articles/SB10001424052748704694004576020083703574602. Accessed 5 Apr 2018
15. Appthority exposes security and privacy risk behind top 400 mobile apps. https://www.appthority.com/company/press/press-releases/appthority-exposes-security-and-privacy-risks-behind-top-400-mobile-apps/. Accessed 5 Apr 2018
16. Chia, P.H., Yamamoto, Y., Asokan, N.: Is this app safe? A large scale study on application permissions and risk signals. In: Proceedings of the 21st International Conference on World Wide Web, pp. 311–320, Lyon, France (2012)
17. Kelley, P.G., Benisch, M., Cranor, L.F., Sadeh, N.: When are users comfortable sharing locations with advertisers? In: Proceedings of the SIGCHI Conference on Human Factors in Computing Systems, pp. 2449–2452, Vancouver, BC, Canada (2011)
18. Chin, E., Felt, A.P., Sekar, V., Wagner, D.: Measuring user confidence in smartphone security and privacy. In: Proceedings of the 8th Symposium on Usable Privacy and Security, Washington, D.C., USA, Article No. 1 (2012)
19. Amini, S.: Analyzing mobile app privacy using computation and crowdsourcing. In: Proceedings of the ACM Conference on Ubiquitous Computing, Ph.D. dissertation (2014)
20. Amini, S., Lin, J., Hong, J.I., Lindqvist, J., Zhang, J.: Mobile application evaluation using automation and crowdsourcing. In: Proceedings of the Workshop on Privacy Enhancing Tools (2013)
21. Wijesekera, P., Baokar, A., Hosseini, A., Egelman, S., Wagner, D., Beznosov, K.: Android permissions remystified: a field study on contextual integrity. In: Proceedings of the 24th USENIX Security Symposium, pp. 499–514, Washington, D.C., USA (2015)
22. Crager, K., Maiti, A., Jadliwala, M., He, J.: Information leakage through mobile motion sensors: user awareness and concerns. In: Proceedings of the 2nd European Workshop on Usable Security, pp. 1–15, Paris, France (2017)
23. Brown, B.: Studying the Internet experience, HP Laboratories Technical report HPL (2001). http://shiftleft.com/mirrors/www.hpl.hp.com/techreports/2001/HPL-2001-49.pdf

24. Norberg, P.A., Horne, D.R., Horne, D.A.: The privacy paradox: personal information disclosure intentions versus behaviors. J. Consum. Aff. **41**(1), 100–126 (2007)
25. Acquisti, A., Taylor, C.R., Wagman, L.: The economics of privacy. J. Econ. Lit. **54**(2), 442–492 (2016)
26. Google removes vital privacy feature from Android, claiming its release was accidental. https://www.eff.org/deeplinks/2013/12/google-removes-vital-privacy-features-android-shortly-after-adding-them/. Accessed 17 July 2016
27. Hatamian, M., Serna-Olvera, J.: Beacon alarming: informed decision-making supporter and privacy risk analyser in Smartphone applications. In: Proceedings of the IEEE International Conference on Consumer Electronics (ICCE), pp. 468–471, Las Vegas, NV, USA (2017)
28. Hatamian, M., Serna, J., Rannenberg, K., Igler, B.: FAIR: fuzzy alarming index rule for privacy analysis in smartphone apps. In: Lopez, J., Fischer-Hübner, S., Lambrinoudakis, C. (eds.) TrustBus 2017. LNCS, vol. 10442, pp. 3–18. Springer, Cham (2017). https://doi.org/10.1007/978-3-319-64483-7_1
29. Article 5 of Regulation (EU) 2016/679 of the European Parliament and of the Council of 27 April 2016 on the protection of natural persons with regard to the processing of personal data and on the free movement of such data, and repealing Directive 95/46/EC (General Data Protection Regulation), Official Journal of the European Union, vol. 59 (2016)
30. Aldhafferi, N., Watson, C., Sajeev, A.S.M.: Personal information privacy settings of online social networks and their suitability for mobile internet devices. Int. J. Secur. Priv. Trust Manag. **2**(2), 1–17 (2013)
31. Rao, A., Schaub, F., Sadeh, N., Acquisti, A., Kang, R.: Expecting the unexpected: understanding mismatched privacy expectations online. In: Proceedings of the 12th Symposium on Usable Privacy and Security (SOUPS), pp. 77–96, Denver, CO, USA (2016)
32. Likert, R.: A technique for the measurement of attitudes. Arch. Psychol. **22**, 5–55 (1932)
33. Gliem, J.A., Gliem, R.R.: Calculating, interpreting, and reporting Cronbach's alpha reliability coefficient for likert-type scales. In: Proceedings of Midwest Research to Practice Conference in Adult, Continuing, and Community Education, Columbus, Ohio, USA, pp. 82–88 (2003)
34. Field, A., Miles, J., Field, Z.: Discovering Statistics Using SPSS. Sage Publications Ltd., Thousand Oaks (2013)
35. Greene, J., D'Oliveira, M.: Learning to Use Statistical Tests in Psychology. Open University Press, Milton Keynes (2005)

Security Analysis and Private Evaluation

FlowConSEAL: Automatic Flow Consistency Analysis of SEAndroid and SELinux Policies

B. S. Radhika[1(✉)], N. V. Narendra Kumar[2], and R. K. Shyamasundar[1]

[1] Indian Institute of Technology Bombay, Mumbai, India
radhikabs184@gmail.com, shyamasundar@gmail.com
[2] Institute for Development and Research in Banking Technology, Hyderabad, India
naren.nelabhotla@gmail.com

Abstract. SELinux/SEAndroid policies used in practice contain tens of thousands of access rules making it hard to analyse them. In this paper, we present an algorithm for reasoning about the consistency of a given policy by analysing the *information flows* implied by it. For this purpose, we model SELinux policy rules using the Readers-Writers Flow Model (RWFM). Using this model, our method identifies all possible indirect flows due to a given policy that could lead to inconsistency. One of the main features of the method is that it not only identifies inconsistencies in the policy but also traces the rules that lead to inconsistency. To distinguish between benign and vulnerable indirect flows, we further categorise the indirect rules that directly contradict `neverallow` rules in the policy and hence have a high potential for information leak. We further rank the rules and domains based on the number of policy violations they cause. We have also implemented a tool FlowConSEAL based on the above method and have applied it on various SELinux/SEAndroid policies for providing a succinct feedback to the user.

1 Introduction

In this digital era, protecting data from intentional and unintentional misuse has become a major concern. Security of Operating System (OS) plays a vital role in data protection and privacy. With Linux kernel forming the core of a wide range of computing devices ranging from mobile phones to supercomputers, its security is of paramount importance. Over the years, several efforts have been made to enhance the security of Linux, SELinux [1] being a prominent example.

Traditionally, Linux supports Discretionary Access Controls (DAC) where access decisions are taken based on the user identity and the permission bits of the object. It is well known that DAC alone is not powerful enough to effectively protect the system because of its inherent weaknesses.

We thank Asokan N, Elena R and Filippo B for their invaluable insights on SEAndroid policy analysis and for sharing SEAndroid policies in early stages of the work.

© IFIP International Federation for Information Processing 2018
Published by Springer International Publishing AG, part of Springer Nature 2018. All Rights Reserved
F. Kerschbaum and S. Paraboschi (Eds.): DBSec 2018, LNCS 10980, pp. 219–231, 2018.
https://doi.org/10.1007/978-3-319-95729-6_14

SELinux introduced Mandatory Access Controls (MAC) to overcome DAC's drawbacks and enhance security through fine-grained access control. It does so by labeling every entity in the system such as files, sockets, processes etc., and specifying a policy to control accesses based on the labels of subjects and objects involved in actions. In addition to providing better protection against unauthorized accesses, SELinux also helps in confining the attack in case of a breach. From Android 4.3 onward SELinux is also being used in Android (referred to as SEAndroid) to provide better application sandboxing and fine-grained access control[1].

In SELinux systems, a well-written policy is the key to protecting the system resources against security threats. However, as these policies get larger and complex, assuring the consistency of all the rules and information flows allowed by them becomes difficult. Currently, the tools [2] used for writing and analysing these policies are not sufficient for detecting information leaks in them. In this paper, we describe a method to analyse information flows implied by a given SELinux policy, and verify their consistency with respect to the accesses in the given policy. The main contributions of the paper are:

1 Automatically analysing consistency of SELinux policies via implied information flows (IF), enabling the policy writers in preventing IF leaks.
2 Identifying and producing evidence for indirect IFs which violate **neverallow** rules specified by the policy.
3 Identifying security critical rules and domains.
4 Implementation of the tool FlowConSEAL to demonstrate the effectiveness of our approach by applying it on various real-life policies.

In the rest of the paper, background is provided in Sect. 2, followed by the need for IF analysis of SELinux policies in Sect. 3. Our approach and experimental analysis are given in Sect. 4 and Sect. 5 respectively. Discussion on related work is presented in Sect. 6. Conclusions are presented in Sect. 7.

2   Background

2.1   SELinux

SELinux is a MAC system implemented using Linux Security Module (LSM) framework [3]. LSM modules work on top of Linux's built-in DAC and enhance its security. In an SELinux system, every subject (active entities like processes) and object (passive entities like files,sockets etc.) is assigned a label which consists of four fields corresponding to SELinux user, role, type and an optional level and it is denoted as `user:role:type[: level]`. The third field `type` represents the logical grouping to which the entity belongs (`type` of a subject is commonly referred as a domain). Although SELinux supports policies based on both `type`

---

[1] As SELinux and SEAndroid policies have the same syntax, our approach is applicable to both families.

field (Type Enforcement policy) and `level` field (MLS, MCS policies), Type Enforcement (TE) policies are the most commonly used in practice. The analysis presented in this paper is focused on SELinux TE policies.

TE policy supports several types of rules. In this paper we are concerned with two predominant rules - `allow` and `neverallow`. Every time a subject attempts to perform an action on an object, a request is sent to the SELinux module. Access decision is taken based on the subject and object's label. By default, every access is denied. `allow` rules are used to explicitly grant access permission. Unlike `allow`, the `neverallow` rules are used at policy compilation time to ensure that there are no corresponding `allow` rules. The general syntax of these rules is `rule source target:class permissions` where `rule` represents the rule name, `source` represents the `type` of the subject requesting the access, `target` represents the `type` of the object which is being accessed, `class` represents the category of the object (such as file, socket etc.) and `permissions` denote actions associated with the object class.

2.2   Readers-Writers Flow Model (RWFM)

In a MAC system, we can ensure information flow security by employing a suitable formal information flow model and ensuring that the MAC policy conforms to the model. In this paper, we use RWFM [4] model to capture the information flows in a given SELinux policy. RWFM is a powerful lattice-based information flow model based on Dennings model [5]. It can be used to provide both confidentiality and integrity. It supports dynamic labeling and declassification. Also, it can capture several well-known models like BLP [6], Biba [7] etc. Its labeling and access rules are described below.

Labeling: Let S and O be the set of subjects and objects in the system respectively. An RWFM label, also called as RW Class is defined as a triplet (s, R, W), where $s \in S$ denotes the owner of the information in the class, $R \in 2^S$ denotes the set of subjects which can read the objects of the class, and $W \in 2^S$ denotes the set of subjects which can write or which have influenced the class.

Access Rules: Let $owner(x), R(x)$ and $W(x)$ be the functions mapping $S \cup O$ to the *owner*, *readers* and *writers* components of the label respectively. Under the above labeling model, access rules of RWFM are specified as follows:

- A subject s is allowed to read an object o if $owner(s) \in R(o)$ and $R(o) \supseteq R(s)$ and $W(o) \subseteq W(s)$
- A subject s is allowed to write an object o if $owner(s) \in W(o)$ and $R(s) \supseteq R(o)$ and $W(s) \subseteq W(o)$

3   Consistency Problem of SELinux Policies

In this section, we explain the indirect and contradictory rules and the associated security concern. Consider the following set of rules **R**:

```
1 neverallow mozilla_t security_t:file write;
2 allow mozilla_t user_home_t:file write;
3 allow sysadm_sudo_t user_home_t:file read;
4 allow sysadm_sudo_t security_t:file write;
```

The second rule in **R** permits `mozilla_t` to write to `user_home_t:file`. The third rule allows `sysadm_sudo_t` to read from `user_home_t:file`, and the last rule allows `sysadm_sudo_t` to write to `security_t:file`. When actions permitted by the last three rules are performed in that sequence, `mozilla_t` can write some data into `user_home_t` file, and `sysadm_sudo_t` can then read this content and write it into a `security_t` file. As a result, `mozilla_t` can indirectly write to a `security_t` file which the policy writer intended to prevent using Rule 1.

SELinux enforcement of the policy fails to prevent such accesses because it only controls individual accesses, and does not take the information flows caused by these actions into account. Whenever a subject performs an action on an object, the action results in an information flow between them. The direction of such flow depends on the nature of the action. In case of a read, information flows from the object to the subject, whereas in case of a write, flow is from the subject to the object. When multiple actions are performed, the resulting information flow may lead to unintended accesses.

The main objective of this paper is to identify all potential indirect accesses caused by chaining legal accesses of a policy. However, not all of them necessarily lead to a security breach. We focus only on the set of indirect accesses which have corresponding `neverallow` rules in the policy similar to the indirect access resulted due to rules 2–4 in **R** which contradicts rule 1. Such rules allow the accesses explicitly denied by the policy writers and hence are obviously a security concern and need to be further analysed. We call such rules as contradictory rules and study their impact on security. Our analysis provides useful feedback to policy writers which can be used to better understand the impact of their rules and develop flow secure policies.

4   SELinux Policy Analysis: Our Approach

Our approach has five main steps that are described in detail below:

Step 1: Canonicalization of rules
 In practice, a rule may contain sets of domains, types, object classes and permissions. In such cases, a single rule corresponds to multiple accesses, one for each (domain, type, class, permission) combination in the rule. To understand the effect of each individual access on the information flow, it is necessary to consider each such combination as a separate rule. So we canonicalize rules such that each resulting rule corresponds to a single access. It will help us extract

precise information such as the rules responsible for an indirect flow, number of indirect rules caused by each domain and so on. Further, to clearly differentiate between objects of same type but different object classes, we use both type and class to uniquely identify such combinations. In the rest of the paper we use the term "object type" to refer to this combination unless specified otherwise. We define a function *canonicalize()* which takes a policy as input and returns the set of corresponding canonicalized rules.

Consider the following simplified policy P consisting of set of domains $D = \{d1, d2\}$, set of object types $T = \{t1, t2\}$, and permissions r and w which correspond to read and write operations respectively.

Policy Rules in P

```
1 allow d1 t1 {r, w}
2 allow d2 t2 {r, w}
3 allow d1 t2 {w}
```

Canonicalized Rules of P

```
1 allow d1 t1 r
2 allow d1 t1 w
3 allow d2 t2 r
4 allow d2 t2 w
5 allow d1 t2 w
```

Step 2: Extraction of labels of object types

In our analysis, we consider information flows between domains and object types in terms of RWFM rules. For this, we first need to assign RWFM labels to the domains and object types. Since we are working at the granularity of domain/object types, we ignore the owner field of the RWFM label. Thus the labels are of the form (R, W), where R stands for readers and W for writers/influencers.

For extracting readers and writers of any object type, we need to find the set of domains which have read and write permissions for that object type respectively. We do this by iterating over all the `allow` rules in the policy. For each `allow` rule of the form `allow d t r`, we add d to $R(t)$ and for `allow d t w`, we add d to $W(t)$. This procedure is described in Algorithm 1.

At present, we focus only on read and write permissions in the policy since they are the high bandwidth channels. Other permissions can be mapped into either read or write depending on whether they cause outward or inward information flow. Our implementation is generic and can use such mappings to consider any permission of interest.

On applying Step 2 on the set of rules obtained from Step 1, $t1$'s label will be $(\{d1\}, \{d1\})$ and $t2$'s label will be $(\{d2\}, \{d1, d2\})$.

Algorithm 1. LabelObjectTypes	**Algorithm 2.** LabelDomains
Data: Canonicalized policy rules **Result:** Labels (L_{ot}) of all the object types in the policy	**Data:** Canonicalized policy rules and L_{ot} **Result:** Labels (L_d) of all the domains in the policy

foreach $t \in T$ **do**
   | $R(t) = W(t) = \{\}$
 end
	foreach $d \in D$ **do**
	   | $R(d) = W(d) = D$
	 end
	 foreach $t \in T$ **do**

foreach *rule* "allow d t perm" **do**
   if *perm* $= r$ **then**
     | $R(t) = R(t) \cup d$
   else if *perm* $= w$ **then**
     | $W(t) = W(t) \cup d$
   end
 end
	foreach $d \in R(t)$ **do**
	     | $R(d) = R(d) \cap R(t)$
	   end
	   foreach $d \in W(t)$ **do**
	     | $W(d) = W(d) \cap W(t)$
	   end
	 end

Step 3: Extraction of labels of domains

Once the labels of object types are obtained, we use them to derive labels for domains in the policy. Algorithm 2 describes this procedure. Here we start with the universal set of domains for reader and writer sets. For each object type t which contains d in its reader set, we update the $R(d)$ as the intersection of $R(t)$ and $R(d)$. Since read operation causes information flow from object to subject, as per RWFM rule, the label of the domain (subject) should dominate the label of the type (object). For this, $R(d) \subseteq R(t)$ should hold. Hence we update $R(d)$ as $R(d) \cap R(t)$. Similarly, when a domain d is in writer set of an object type t, we update $W(d)$ as $W(d) \cap W(t)$. On applying this algorithm on the sample policy, label of $d1$ will be $(\{d1\}, \{d1\})$ and label of $d2$ will be $(\{d2\}\{d1, d2\})$.

Step 4: Identification of indirect accesses

Once we have the labels for all the object types and domains in the policy, we apply the following RWFM access checks on each `allow` rule in the policy:

$$d \in R(t) \Rightarrow (R(t) \supseteq R(d)) \wedge (W(t) \subseteq W(d)) \tag{1}$$

$$d \in W(t) \Rightarrow (R(d) \supseteq R(t)) \wedge (W(d) \subseteq W(t)) \tag{2}$$

These checks help us verify whether the information flows caused due to the accesses respect the permissions specified in the policy. Algorithm 3 describes the procedure used for the checks.

Algorithm 3. AccessRuleChecks

Data: Canonicalized policy rules, labels of object types (L_{ot}), and labels of all domains (L_d)
Result: Set of rules corresponding to indirect flow
IndirectRulesSet = {}
foreach *rule "allow d t perm"* **do**
    if *perm = r AND $W(t) \not\subseteq W(d)$* **then**
        foreach *d1 $\in (W(t) - W(d))$* **do**
            foreach *t1 which has $d \in W(t1)$* **do**
                | IndirectRulesSet = IndirectRulesSet ∪ {allow d1 t1 w }
            end
        end
    else if *perm = w AND $R(d) \not\supseteq R(t)$* **then**
        foreach *d1 $\in (R(t) - R(d))$* **do**
            foreach *t1 which has $d \in R(t1)$* **do**
                | IndirectRulesSet = IndirectRulesSet ∪ {allow d1 t1 r }
            end
        end
    end
end

With the label derivation methods described in Step 2 and 3, we can say that the conditions $R(t) \supseteq R(d)$ in (1) and $W(d) \subseteq W(t)$ in (2) will always be satisfied. Hence, we check only the remaining conditions. Failure to satisfy these conditions imply the presence of indirect flows. i.e if the condition $W(t) \subseteq W(d)$ fails in (1), then all the domains in $(W(t) - W(d))$ can indirectly write to all the types that d can write. Similarly, if $(R(d) \supseteq R(t))$ in the above condition fails, that means that all the domains in $(R(t) - R(d))$ can read everything that d can read. We construct `allow` rules corresponding to these indirect accesses and store them in IndirectRulesSet. Applying these checks to our sample policy will show that the check fails at rule 5. Here $R(d1) \not\supseteq R(t2)$. Hence $d2$ can read $t1$ even though there is no rule granting this permission.

The steps described above can detect only one level of indirection i.e indirect flows via a single pair of subject and object. However, there can be multiple levels of indirect flows. For example, if we add rules `allow d3 t3 {r, w}` and `allow d2 t3 {w}` to our example policy, it would lead to a two level indirection. To find multi-level indirect flows, we first need to add the first level indirect rules identified i.e rules in IndirectRuleSet to our policy rules and repeat Step 2 to Step 4. We do this until there are no more indirect flows caused by the rule set. Algorithm 4 describes this procedure.

Algorithm 4. SELinuxPolicyConsistencyCheck

Data: SELinux policy P
Result: Set of all possible indirect allows
consistent = False
RuleSet = Canonicalize(P)
while *not consistent* **do**
    L_{ot} = LabelObjectTypes(RuleSet)
    L_d = LabelDomains(RuleSet, L_{ot})
    IndirectRuleSet = AccessRuleChecks(RuleSet, L_{ot}, L_d)
    if *IndirectRuleSet is ∅* **then**
    | consistent = True
    else
    | RuleSet = RuleSet ∪ IndirectRuleSet
    end
end

For each rule in the RuleSet, along with the rule components, we store the iteration number in which the rule was generated (*Iteration*), set of rules causing the rule (*Cause*), and whether the rule is contradiction or not (*Contradiction*).

Step 5: Extraction of crucial information
In this step we extract the following information by using the data collected in the previous step:

Analysing Individual Rules: Here we try to understand the impact of each policy rule on flow security. We count the number of contradictions caused by each rule in the policy. Higher the number for a rule, larger is its potential to cause harm.

Analysing Domains: Here we study each domain in the policy and count the contradictions caused by them. The domains are then ranked based on this count. This information helps the system developers to understand the priorities that should be given while developing the processes in those domains.

Analysing Indirect Accesses: As seen in the earlier sections, a one-level indirection between a subject-object pair is caused by chaining of 3 accesses. For each such indirection, we store the rule corresponding to the second access as the causing rule. This helps in generating the complete sequence of rules causing a particular indirection. We can use this procedure recursively to determine a complete sequence of original policy rules causing any multi-level indirection.

Remarks: Given a general access matrix model [8] along with the assertion that a certain subject s can acquire a right 'x' on object o, it is of interest[2] to generate a command/rule sequence that could lead to the new state from the original state of the access matrix. From the given access rules, FlowConSEAL generates the new *rights* acquired by processes along with the sequence of rules required for realizing that *right*.

5   Experimental Analysis and Illustration

We have implemented FlowConSEAL using Python 2.7. Our implementation and experiments are performed on Ubuntu 16.10 running on a virtual machine configured with 64GB RAM. We demonstrate the effectiveness of FlowConSEAL on two policies, the Reference policy (`refpolicy- 2.20170805`)[3] which is the base policy used by all the Linux distributions for developing their SELinux policies and the SEAndroid policy provided as part of the Android Open Source Project (AOSP) tree in Android 7[4].

5.1   Analysis of Policies by FlowConSEAL

Here we provide a brief[5] analysis of the above two polices obtained through FlowConSEAL as depicted in Table 1.

Number of Types, Object Classes and Permissions: SELinux doesn't have any predefined types whereas object classes and associated permissions are predefined. Policy writers define types based on the resources and services they want to confine and the overall security goals. Larger number of types help specifying fine-grained rules. But with increase in types, associated rules also increase drastically and the policy management becomes difficult. As general purpose Linux systems provide comparatively large number of services and resources, naturally, SELinux Reference policy contains larger number of types, object classes and permissions than Android's AOSP policy.

Number of Canonicalized `allow` and `neverallow` Rules: Our tool parses the policy only once and stores the canonicalized `allow` and `neverallow` rules separately. All further processing is done on these rules. Hence performance of the tool depends on the number of `allow` and `neverallow` rules.

Number of Iterations: Number of iterations required to generate all possible indirect rules indicates the levels of indirect flows present in the policy. AOSP policy conforms to RWFM check in its second iteration i.e., it contains only single level of indirection. However, note that the Reference policy contains two levels of indirection.

---

[2] Note that it is a specific problem instance rather than the 'safety problem'.

[3] https://github.com/TresysTechnology/refpolicy.

[4] https://android.googlesource.com/platform/manifest/.

[5] A full extended report on FlowConSEAL is available at http://isrdc.iitb.ac.in/ reports/isrdc-tr-2018-rks-rbs-selinux-static.pdf.

Table 1. Experimental analysis

	Reference policy	AOSP policy
Policy size	3.3 MB	521.6 KB
Number of types	1276	612
Number of object classes	127	63
Number of permissions	447	286
Number of canonicalized allow rules	10374	24418
Number of canonicalized neverallow rules	22893	2369117
Number of iterations	2	1
Number of indirect rules generated	232189	244466
Number of contradictions	1545	11529
% of indirect allows that are contradictions	0.665	4.715
% of neverallows that are contradictions	6.75	0.486
Execution time	41 min	3 min

Number of Indirect and Contradictory Rules: The tool identifies all possible indirect information flows. As we can see in the table for both the policies, these rules are in hundreds of thousands in number. In order to avoid false positives and reduce these rules to a manageable subset, we consider only the contradictory rules. Larger the number of contradictions, weaker is the security of the policy. From the table, the Reference policy has lower number of contradictions even though it has large number of indirect flows.

Percentage of Indirect Allows that are Contradictions: This factor indicates the extent to which indirect rules can be exploited to cause policy violations. Theoretically, for perfect security, this number should be zero. The Reference policy with only 0.665% of its indirect allows causing contradiction, prove to be much more stronger against policy violations using indirect allows.

Percentage of neverallows that are Contradictions: This factor indicates the extent of potential policy violations. Larger the percentage, weaker is the security. From the table, we can notice that in case of the AOSP policy only 0.486% of neverallows can be violated using the indirect rules. Hence comparatively, this is a well written policy with respect to information flow.

Execution Time: From the table, we can see that the execution time especially that for the Reference policy is considerably high. However, considering the large size of the policy and the size of the meta data being generated (10 GB in case of the Reference policy), and the fact that this analysis is performed only once, we can say the tool is quite useful.

Number of Contradictory Rules Generated by each Rule: This is useful for understanding the impact of each rule on the flow security. Tables 2 and 3 show the top 3 allow rules along with the number contradictions that they cause (Ctd_r Count) in the Reference and AOSP policy respectively.

Domain Ranking: Here the number of contradictions caused by each domain is counted. Using this, we can get the domains which have high potential to be exploited to gain an unauthorized access. Therefore subjects in these domains need to be designed and implemented carefully. From our experiments, we noticed that high ranking domains are mostly system processes and daemons which are trusted by the system. However, considering the large number of policy violations that we have observed, it is important that these contradictions are carefully analysed, and the processes running in these domains are thoroughly verified to be safe against any attacks leading to those contradictions.

Table 2. Ctd_r count (Reference Policy)

Allow rule in the RuleSet	Ctd_r Count
systemd_tmpfiles_t device_t:lnk_file write	468
udev_t device_t:lnk_file write	468
getty_t devlog_t:sock_file read	146

Table 3. Ctd_r count (AOSP Policy)

Allow rule in the RuleSet	Ctd_r Count
init cgroup:dir read	5166
init urandom_device:chr_file read	5166
system_server cgroup:dir read	927

6   Related Work

Preventing unauthorized information flows (IF) is crucial for ensuring security. Uzun et al. [9] propose a method for preventing unauthorized IF in access matrix model based DAC systems. They identify one-step transitive flows and eliminate them by revoking necessary permissions; FlowConSEAL not only identifies multi-level indirections, but also provides a sequence of rules that lead to each indirect flow.

Over the years, several tools have been developed to understand and analyse SELinux policies [2]. SETools [10] is one of the commonly used collection of tools. It provides several tools for searching rules, comparison of policies and, IF analysis which is limited to listing all the flows between domains specified by the user. Unlike FlowConSEAL, it does not support verification of flows against a security model or checking if the indirect flows are contradicting any neverallow rules. PAL [11] is a logic programming tool that supports SELinux policies by first translating them into a logic program. The user needs to construct appropriate queries to analyse the policy. Thus, the onus is on the user to come up with properties as queries which is not an easy task. In comparison, FlowCon-SEAL yields the possible indirect flows, contradictions etc., without any user intervention.

Gokyo [12] analyses integrity of the "Example policy" using manually specified high integrity types as Trusted Computing Base (TCB). The tool considers only one level indirections between TCB types and non-TCB types, and checks for conflicts between the integrity goal and the policy rules. Similarly, SCIATool [13] also analyses integrity conflicts between TCB and non-TCB entities using Colored Petri-nets.

Several visualization-based SELinux policy analysis tools [14–16] have been developed to help policy writers to better understand the policies. Gove [14] presents a tool for understanding and comparing SELinux/SEAndroid policies by creating graph representations. SPTrack [16] helps visualize SELinux policies as well as its attack logs to track IF. SEGrapher [15] generates cluster-based focus-graphs of policies based on clustering.

Several tools have been developed specifically for SEAndroid policy analysis. [17] analyses SEAndroid policies from Android 5.0 devices from a number of OEMs and identify patterns of common problems. SELint [18] is an extensible tool built to help policy writers in writing secure SEAndroid policies. It's built-in plug-ins mainly focus on making a policy more compact and readable and identify potentially dangerous rules by assigning a risk score to each rule. The risk score of a rule is computed based on the risk level and trust level of the rule components whose values are policy-dependent and need to be manually configured by the policy writers. A semi-automated tool to identify potential SEAndroid policy misconfigurations is presented in [19]. EASEAndroid [20] analyses SEAndroid policies using large-scale semi-supervised learning.

To sum up, FlowConSEAL provides a succinct analysis of SELinux policies and enables the user to decide on benign and vulnerable indirect flows. One distinct characteristic of FlowConSEAL is that it works like a "pushbutton" tool unlike others that need user supplied abstraction of queries/properties.

7   Conclusions

In this paper, we have presented an efficient method and a tool FlowConSEAL to analyze information flows in SELinux/SEAndroid policies. Our method verifies the consistency of the policies in terms of indirect flows and helps in identifying potential vulnerabilities. Furthermore, we also rank the policy rules and domains based on their potential to misuse information. The tool enables the policy writers to understand the security loopholes in the policy and handle them appropriately to protect systems against flawed and malicious applications. The experimental results demonstrate the effectiveness of the method. One of the distinct advantage of using RWFM model is its capability to capture all the influencers succinctly.

References

1. Loscocco, P., Smalley, S.: Integrating flexible support for security policies into the linux operating system. In: USENIX Annual Technical Conference, pp. 29–42 (2001)
2. Eaman, A., Sistany, B., Felty, A.: Review of existing analysis tools for SELinux security policies: challenges and a proposed solution. In: Aïmeur, E., Ruhi, U., Weiss, M. (eds.) MCETECH 2017. LNBIP, vol. 289, pp. 116–135. Springer, Cham (2017). https://doi.org/10.1007/978-3-319-59041-7_7
3. Wright, C., Cowan, C., Smalley, S., Morris, J., Kroah-Hartman, G.: Linux security modules: general security support for the linux kernel. In: USENIX, pp. 17–31 (2002)
4. Kumar, N.V.N., Shyamasundar, R.K.: A complete generative label model for lattice-based access control models. In: Cimatti, A., Sirjani, M. (eds.) SEFM 2017. LNCS, vol. 10469, pp. 35–53. Springer, Cham (2017). https://doi.org/10.1007/978-3-319-66197-1_3
5. Denning, D.E.: A lattice model of secure information flow. CACM **19**(5), 236–243 (1976)
6. Bell, D.E., LaPadula, L.J.: Secure computer systems: Mathematical foundations. Technical report MTR-2547-VOL-1, MITRE CORP BEDFORD MA (1973)
7. Biba, K.J.: Integrity considerations for secure computer systems. Technical report MTR-3153-REV-1, MITRE CORP BEDFORD MA (1977)
8. Harrison, M.A., Ruzzo, W.L., Ullman, J.D.: Protection in operating systems. Commun. ACM **19**(8), 461–471 (1976)
9. Uzun, E., Parlato, G., Atluri, V., Ferrara, A.L., Vaidya, J., Sural, S., Lorenzi, D.: Preventing unauthorized data flows. In: Livraga, G., Zhu, S. (eds.) DBSec 2017. LNCS, vol. 10359, pp. 41–62. Springer, Cham (2017). https://doi.org/10.1007/978-3-319-61176-1_3
10. TresysTechnology: Setools: Policy analysis tools for SELinux. https://github.com/TresysTechnology/setools Accessed Nov 2017
11. Sarna-Starosta, B., Stoller, S.D.: Policy analysis for security-enhanced linux. In: WITS Proceedings, pp. 1–12 (2004)
12. Jaeger, T., Sailer, R., Zhang, X.: Analyzing integrity protection in the SElinux example policy. In: USENIX Security Symposium-Volume 12, p. 5 (2003)
13. Zhai, G., Guo, T., Huang, J.: SCIATool: a tool for analyzing SElinux policies based on access control spaces, information flows and CPNs. In: Yung, M., Zhu, L., Yang, Y. (eds.) INTRUST 2014. LNCS, vol. 9473, pp. 294–309. Springer, Cham (2015). https://doi.org/10.1007/978-3-319-27998-5_19
14. Gove, R.: V3SPA: a visual analysis, exploration, and diffing tool for selinux and seandroid security policies. In: IEEE VizSec, pp. 1–8 (2016)
15. Marouf, S., Shehab, M.: SEGrapher: Visualization-based SELinux Policy Analysis. In: Symposium on Configuration Analytics and Automation, SafeConfig (2011)
16. Clemente, P., Kaba, B., Rouzaud-Cornabas, J., Alexandre, M., Aujay, G.: SPTrack: visual analysis of information flows within SELinux policies and attack logs. In: Huang, R., Ghorbani, A.A., Pasi, G., Yamaguchi, T., Yen, N.Y., Jin, B. (eds.) AMT 2012. LNCS, vol. 7669, pp. 596–605. Springer, Heidelberg (2012). https://doi.org/10.1007/978-3-642-35236-2_60
17. Reshetova, E., Bonazzi, F., Nyman, T., Borgaonkar, R., Asokan, N.: Characterizing SEAndroid policies in the wild. In: ICISSP, pp. 482–489 (2016)

18. Reshetova, E., Bonazzi, F., Asokan, N.: Selint: an SEandroid policy analysis tool. In: ICISSP, pp. 47–58 (2017)
19. Chen, H., Li, N., Enck, W., Aafer, Y., Zhang, X.: Analysis of SEAndroid policies: combining MAC and DAC in Android. In: ACM ACSAC, pp. 553–565 (2017)
20. Wang, R., Enck, W., Reeves, D.S., Zhang, X., Ning, P., Xu, D., Zhou, W., Azab, A.M.: EASEAndroid: automatic policy analysis and refinement for security enhanced android via large-scale semi-supervised learning. In: USENIX Security Symposium, pp. 351–366 (2015)

On Understanding Permission Usage Contextuality in Android Apps

Md Zakir Hossen and Mohammad Mannan[✉]

Concordia Institute of Information Systems Engineering, Concordia University,
Montreal, Canada
{m_osssen,mmannan}@ciise.concordia.ca

Abstract. In the runtime permission model, the context in which a permission is requested/used the first time may change later without the user's knowledge. Our goal is to understand how permissions are *requested* and *used* in different contexts in the runtime permission model, and compare them to identify potential inconsistencies. We present ContextDroid, a static analysis tool to identify the contexts of permission request/use, and analyze 6,790 apps (chosen from an initial set of 10062 apps from the Google Play Store). Our preliminary results show that apps often use permissions in dissimilar contexts: 15% of the apps use the permissions in contexts where users are not prompted and may be unaware; 46% of the apps use the permissions in multiple contexts while only 20% of the apps request permissions in multiple contexts. We hope our study will attract more research into non-contextual usage (and possible abuse) of permissions in the runtime model, and may spur further work in the design of finer-grained permission control.

Keywords: Android · Smartphone · Permission model · App analysis

1 Introduction

The runtime permission model enables context-based control of resources. The new model was introduced in Android 6.0 to facilitate user decision by providing situational context (e.g., current state of the app representing the purpose of resource access) when the permissions are requested for the first time. However, an app can trick a user to grant a permission in a valid context, and then use it in malicious/unexpected contexts without the user's consent/knowledge. For example, accessing GPS when the user attempts to find the current location in a map is a valid context, but accessing GPS when the app is in the background may be unwanted. Indeed, such contextual differences defy user expectations [10,13,14]. In contrast to the contextual analysis of resource access in the old install-time permission model [7,8,15], such studies in the runtime model are limited. Wijesekera *et al.* [13] modify an older version of Android to analyze contextual integrity of Android apps and conclude that users mostly rely on the

© IFIP International Federation for Information Processing 2018
Published by Springer International Publishing AG, part of Springer Nature 2018. All Rights Reserved
F. Kerschbaum and S. Paraboschi (Eds.): DBSec 2018, LNCS 10980, pp. 232–242, 2018.
https://doi.org/10.1007/978-3-319-95729-6_15

surrounding context in which a permission is requested to grant/deny a permission [14]. In this work, we focus on regular apps that are developed/adapted for the runtime permission model and perform the first study to understand the contextual use of resources in the runtime permission model using 6,790 regular apps.

We develop ContextDroid, a static analysis tool that extracts the *context* when a permission is requested and used in an app using an app-wide call graph. We define a context based on the active User Interface (UI) component that is requesting the permission (and using it, if granted). To differentiate between user activities and identify contexts, we leverage five Android components (`Activity`, `Fragment`, `Service`, `AsyncTask` and `Broadcast Receiver`), representing different types of UI and functionality. There are several challenges in statically extracting contextual information from Android apps, e.g., handling obfuscation introduced by widely-used ProGuard [1] and similar tools. While Android framework classes and methods are excluded from obfuscation, classes derived from support libraries that are shipped with the APK are obfuscated by ProGuard (unless configured otherwise by the developer). We must identify `Fragments` and permission related APIs that are derived from the support libraries. We use a combination of an extended call graph and sub-signature matching to identify contexts in obfuscated code.

Our evaluation reveals a large difference between permission request vs. use. Only 20% apps request permissions in multiple contexts, while 46% of the apps use the permissions in multiple contexts, indicating that apps use permissions more often than they request for and in varying contexts without the user's knowledge. Moreover, we find that apps request a permission in one context without using it and use the permission in another context without requesting the user. The context of permission use doesn't match with the context in which it is requested in 15% of the apps. Our findings suggest that apps often fail to provide situational context while requesting permissions – one of the best practices suggested by Google [3] in the runtime permission model.

Contributions. (i) We present ContextDroid that statically extracts the contexts in which the permissions are requested and the contexts in which they are used, by leveraging the call paths that lead to sensitive API calls associated with permissions. Our methodology for context identification may be useful for other studies. (ii) We analyze 6,790 (chosen from 10,062) regular Android apps to understand contextual resource usage under the runtime permission model. To the best of our knowledge, this is the first study on contextual resource usage in the runtime permission model, involving apps that target only the new model. (iii) Our tool, albeit primitive, can be used by app market maintainers to identify apps that may be violating user expectation and subject them to further analysis. We will make our tool and source code publicly available.

2   Background

In this section, we briefly describe the necessary background of the Android components and its permission model.

Android Components. `Activity`, `Service`, `Content Provider`, `Broadcast Receiver`, `Fragment`, and `AsyncTask` are some of the major components of Android. Apart from `Content Provider` that helps manage app data, other components represent various elements associated with the UI and events. All these components have their own *life-cycle* methods, and act as entry points for the components (and the corresponding app functionality).

`Activity` and `Fragment` are foreground UI components allowing users to interact with the app. An `Activity` can represent a standalone full screen UI. `Fragment`s can be considered as UI modules representing part or full screen of an `Activity`. An `Activity` can hold multiple `Fragment`s, and a `Fragment` can be reused in multiple `Activities`. Multiple `Fragment`s inside the same `Activity` represents different UI and functionality.

`Service` is a background component that runs without any UI. `Broadcast Receiver` receives updates from the OS whenever there is a change of state and can perform tasks without interacting with the UI. App developers can also implement their own `Broadcast Receivers` and broadcast an update to trigger a background task. `AsyncTask` performs minor tasks in the background and communicates results to the UI thread.

All these components have their own entry points that can be used to perform specific tasks. Background components can also be used independently outside the visible user flow. We differentiate contexts mainly by identifying whether a permission is requested/used in any of these components.

Runtime Permission Model. Android maintains a set of dangerous permissions to protect privacy sensitive resources. While individual dangerous permissions regulate access to specific actions or tasks (e.g., READ_PHONE _STATE), they are categorized/clustered into permission groups to protect specific resources (e.g., READ_SMS, WRITE_SMS are grouped into SMS). In the runtime model, dangerous permissions are requested at runtime when the app first uses them. However, instead of showing prompt for each permission, it requests for permission for the permission group.

3   Methodology

We develop ContextDroid as a static analysis tool by leveraging app-wide call graph and Android permission mappings to extract the contexts (Fig. 1). The app-wide call graph is generated by FlowDroid [4], a state of the art information flow tracking tool. We use permission mappings from Au *et al.* [5] and Backes *et al.* [6] to map API calls to associated permissions.

3.1   Context Definition

We define context based on what components the user is using when they are requested for a resource, or the resource is accessed. We determine this by identifying the five Android components (i.e., `Activity`, `Service`, `Fragment`, `Broadcast Receiver` and `AsyncTask`). As discussed in Sect. 2, these Android components represent different types of UIs and functionalities. We consider these components as the key elements representing different contexts.

We consider multiple instances of the same component type to be different in terms of context. For example, if an app uses the same permission in different `Activities`, they are considered as different contexts. If a permission is used in multiple `Fragments`, they are also considered as different contexts even if they reside inside the same `Activity`. `Activity` and `Fragment` are considered as foreground contexts as the user can directly interact with them through the UI. `Service`, `Broadcast Receiver`, and `AsyncTask` do not have their own UI, and we consider them to be background contexts. The difference in the way these components work enables us to differentiate between the active components of an app when a permission is requested or used. However, to infer what the users might consider as unexpected behavior is non-trivial, and may vary greatly depending on how they view the importance of their privacy [13]. While a finer-grained approach can be taken to further differentiate the context, we believe that our definition provides an overall view of how permissions are used in various components (contexts in our definition) by the apps.

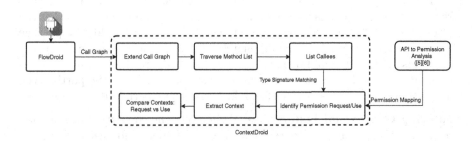

Fig. 1. Overview of ContextDroid

3.2   Identifying Contexts

We consider the following three factors while identifying the contexts in which permissions are requested and used: *Activation event* (an entry point of the call graph), *Request API* (used to show permission prompts at runtime) and *Sensitive API* (protected by dangerous permissions).

Context of Permission Use. We search each method in the call graph and identify API calls associated with permissions. We match the type signature of the APIs inside the method with APIs from the permission mappings. If we find a match, we first check whether it is a standalone method representing an *activation event*. If not, we traverse back to all the callers of that method until we find the activation events. We then extract contextual information that includes the component type (e.g., `Activity`), class name, method name and the callers of the method in which the sensitive API call is made.

We identify different instances of the same component type by using a combination of class name and component type. To handle class name obfuscation where component type cannot be identified, we recursively traverse back to the parent classes of the method and identify whether it is a child of any of the Android component classes.

Context of Permission Request. In the runtime model, apps can request permissions by using one of the Request APIs. To infer the requesting context, we identify calls to different instances of *requestPermissions()* APIs and follow a similar approach described for permission usage to identify the active component.

However, unlike the system API calls that are not obfuscated by Pro-Guard (with Google Play Services library being an exception), support library APIs that are shipped with the APK can be obfuscated in the release build (unless the developer excludes certain classes from obfuscation). The support library contains APIs that also request permissions. For example, apps can request permission by *requestPermissions()* call through the *ActivityCompat* or *ContextCompat* class from the support library. To handle such instances, we use partial type signature matching to identify the context of permission request. We first identify whether the method contains permission strings, e.g., android.permission.AUDIO. If found, we examine subsequent API calls that take the permission strings as a parameter. Specifically, we identify whether the package name of the method partially matches with a support library package (e.g., *android.support.v4.a.a* partially matches with the package name of support library version 4). If a match is found, we further compare the parameter signature of the API with request APIs from the support library. If the partial type signatures match, we consider this as an instance where permission is requested.

Analyzing Contextual Differences. We analyze the contextual information associated with permission requests and usage to understand their differences. For each permission required by the app, we find whether the permission is requested and used in multiple contexts. We compare the number of contexts identified for a permission, both in terms of when it is requested and when it is used. If the number of contexts differ, we tag it as a permission that is used in unexpected and dissimilar contexts. If the numbers match, we directly compare the contexts to determine whether they match or not.

3.3 Extended Call Graph

Identifying obfuscated `Fragments` (e.g., by ProGuard [1]) that are derived from support libraries is not straight forward. To identify `Fragment` contexts that are otherwise excluded from the call graph (e.g., due to obfuscation), we use an extended call graph in ContextDroid. We first iterate through all the methods in the call graph and identify the class in which they are declared. If the component type of the class cannot be identified, we iterate through the parent classes to determine whether they can be identified as one of the contextual elements. If the component type cannot be determined, we attempt to find whether the class is derived from the support library `Fragment`.

We start with the package name of the method and perform partial matching with the support library package and iterate through the parent classes and their package names until we find a match. Then, we extract the method list of that class. Android `Fragments` used in third party apps must override the *OnCreateView()* method. To determine whether the class is a `Fragment` component, we match the return and parameter types (i.e., sub-signature) of the listed methods with *OnCreateView()*. If the sub-signature matches, we tag it as a `Fragment` and include the methods of that class in the call graph.

4 Analysis and Results

We select apps that target the runtime permission model from AndroZoo [2]. We analyze 10062 apps and identify permission request/usage of dangerous permissions in 6790 apps. For the rest of the apps, we could not identify any instance of permission use or request, although permissions were declared in the manifest (similar to past findings, e.g., [9]). We present our contextual analysis results mainly in terms of resources (i.e., permission groups). Each resource consists of related individual permission request/usage as identified by ContextDroid.

Performance. We perform our analysis on an Intel Core i7 3.60 GHz processor with 24 GB of memory running Ubuntu 16.04. For an average app (of size around 20 MB), our analysis takes on average under a minute, including time taken by FlowDroid. Note that we first use FlowDroid to generate an app-wide call graph; this takes most of the time in our analysis (approximately 95%). We believe that ContextDroid can be integrated into app security tools (maintained by app markets) to identify permission use in unexpected contexts.

Permission Requests. We find that about 20% of the apps request at least one permission in multiple contexts. Access to Storage (35%), Location (23%), Camera (20%), Contacts (8%), and Phone (7%) are requested in multiple contexts more often compared to others. Users may see different contexts while they are requested for the same permission. Note that when a permission is given in one context, the app can use it in the other contexts without showing a prompt to the user.

Permission Usage. Permission usage in multiple contexts is more prevalent compared to permission requests. 46% of apps use at least one permission in more than one context. Location (57%) and Phone (26%) resources are used the most in multiple contexts. Comparing the number of times these two resources were requested in multiple contexts reveals that these resources are very often used in contexts where users may not see a prompt. For example, we found only 580 instances where Location access is requested in multiple contexts, while

3327 instances are found where Location is used in multiple contexts. In contrast, Storage is not as frequently used in multiple contexts (no. request: 892 vs. use: 53). Note that, this difference may be partly attributed to the relatively small number of permission mappings for Storage used in our analysis. Permissions for Location, Phone and Contacts are also often used in the background contexts, suggesting these permissions are used regardless of whether the app is being actively used or not; see Fig. 2.

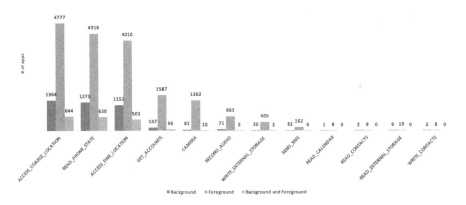

Fig. 2. The number of apps using permissions in background/foreground components, compared to the number of apps that use permissions in both types of components.

Contextual Differences. We investigate the prevalence of mismatching context between permission request and use. To make a fair comparison, we only include permissions for which we could extract both, the request context and the usage context in an app. We could identify 2722 permissions from 2012 apps with both request and usage contexts.

We find 1420 permissions being used in dissimilar contexts (i.e., the context of request for these permissions do not match the context of their use). More precisely, either these permissions are requested in contexts where they are not used at all, or the permissions are used in a context where the user may not see a request prompt. The average number of dissimilar contexts for these permissions is 2.25. In other words, if the permissions are granted in their request context, they may be used in two or more contexts without users' knowledge. Furthermore, we find 525 instances where dissimilar contexts include asking for a permission in foreground and using it in background. We acknowledge that such dissimilarity in context may be legitimate depending on the type of app. We do not attempt to justify the use of permissions in dissimilar contexts and leave it as future work.

We identify seven resources that are used in dissimilar contexts. Location, Storage, Phone and Contacts are used in varying contexts more often than the rest. While not as high, Camera and Microphone are also used in dissimilar usage contexts where the user might be unaware. Interestingly, we find seven apps that request Camera permission in foreground and uses it in a background `Service`; and two apps use Microphone in a similar fashion. Figure 3 shows the number of times various resources are accessed in dissimilar contexts.

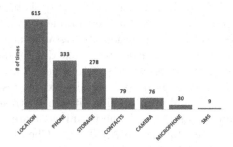

Fig. 3. The number of times different resources are accessed in dissimilar contexts.

Case Study. We take a messaging app named TextTray as an example. As a messaging app it is obvious for the app to request for the SMS resource. We found one foreground context (`Activity` component) where the permission prompt is shown. Assuming the user will grant the permission based on the context, we identify a valid use of that permission in the same context. However, we also notice a background context (in a `Service`) where messages are sent. While sending messages is the core functionality of any messaging app, such difference in the contexts can indeed be unexpected. Google later removed this app from Google Play.

5   Related Work

Several studies analyzed contextual resource usage in the install-time permission model. Yang et al. [15] define context based on environmental attributes (e.g., time of the day), to differentiate between malware and benign apps. In contrast, we define context differently, and target only regular apps. Wijesekera et al. [13] perform a user study to identify contextual differences and user reactions during permission use. They identify visibility to be an important context factor that validates resource access, and found user dissatisfaction while the context of permission usage changes subsequently. Both these studies analyze apps developed for the install-time permission model. Therefore, it is difficult to understand what context the user might see to make a decision on the permission in the runtime model. We analyze apps that are developed for the runtime model that enables us to identify the real contexts of a request prompt.

Another study by Wijesekera et al. [14] combines user privacy preference and surrounding contextual cues to predict user decisions. The key idea is to differentiate between the contexts of permission use and based on prior decisions made by the user, automatically grant or request users for a permission. While identifying the contextual differences in permission usage closely relates to this work, on both occasions [13,14], the analysis was performed on a modified version of Android protected by the old permission model with apps not designed for the runtime model. In comparison to these studies that perform dynamic analysis to extract contextual information, we use static analysis to evaluate apps that are specifically designed and adapted for the runtime permission model.

Micinski *et al.* [10] tie user interactions to resource access in the runtime model. They develop a dynamic analysis tool named AppTracer to analyze the extent to which user interactions and resource accesses are related. A corresponding user study reveals that users generally expect resource access right after interaction with a related app functionality. In contrast, we focus on the different Android components in which the permissions are requested and used along with user interactions. Similar to AppTracer, Chen *et al.* [7] propose the Permission Event Graph (PEG) model, representing the relation between resource access and event handlers. They combine static and dynamic approaches to analyze regular and malicious apps. However, their analysis is also based on the old permission model, and cannot differentiate between the context of permission request and usage.

Another line of work use the permissions listed in the manifest to generate risk signals and rank apps based on permission usage. Wang *et al.* [12] use permission request patterns to identify potentially malicious apps. Taylor *et al.* [11] develop a contextual ranking framework based on listed permissions. They propose relative ranking of apps by identifying whether an app of a specific category requests for permission(s) that are not required by other apps in the same category. However, they do not consider how the listed permissions are used by the apps. Merlo *et al.* [9] propose a risk scoring framework based on permission utilization by apps. In comparison, we identify different contexts where the permissions are actually used and compare them with contexts where users see a request prompt.

6   Conclusions and Future Work

We present the first large-scale (using 6,790 regular apps) study on the contextual differences in Android apps in the runtime permission model. Our ContextDroid static analysis tool extracts the contexts in which apps request and use dangerous permissions. Our findings suggest a significant gap between the number of times the users see a request prompt indicating the use of a permission versus the number of times it is actually used. Difference in contexts of permission request and use implies the prevalence of permission use without users knowledge, even in the runtime permission model.

Both the ContextDroid tool and our experiments can be extended in future work. ContextDroid currently cannot identify sensitive and request API calls inside methods that are not included in the call graph (e.g., due to advanced forms of obfuscation beyond ProGuard [1] and similar tools). We identify sensitive API calls based on permission mappings from prior work [5,6]. If an

API is missing in the mapping list, ContextDroid will fail to identify the usage of the associated permission. Although we identify unexpected or dissimilar contexts, some of these occurrences might indeed be legitimate/benign depending on the functionality of the app. However, usage in contexts where users may not be aware should still be a matter of concern and needs a closer look. In this work, we do not attempt to classify whether such dissimilarity in contexts imply malicious intent by the app; we also leave this as future work.

Acknowledgements. We are grateful to anonymous reviewers for their comments and suggestions. The second author is supported in part by an NSERC Discovery Grant.

References

1. Shrink your code and resources (2017). https://developer.android.com/studio/build/shrink-code.html
2. Allix, K., Bissyandé, T.F., Klein, J., Le Traon, Y.: AndroZoo: collecting millions of Android apps for the research community. In: Conference on Mining Software Repositories. ACM (2016)
3. Android: App permissions best practices (2018). https://developer.android.com/training/permissions/usage-notes
4. Arzt, S., Rasthofer, S., Fritz, C., Bodden, E., Bartel, A., Klein, J., Le Traon, Y., Octeau, D., McDaniel, P.: FlowDroid: precise context, flow, field, object-sensitive and lifecycle-aware taint analysis for Android apps. ACM Sigplan Not. (2014)
5. Au, K.W.Y., Zhou, Y.F., Huang, Z., Lie, D.: PScout: analyzing the Android permission specification. In: CCS. ACM (2012)
6. Backes, M., Bugiel, S., Derr, E., McDaniel, P.D., Octeau, D., Weisgerber, S.: On demystifying the Android application framework: re-visiting Android permission specification analysis. In: USENIX Security (2016)
7. Chen, K.Z., Johnson, N.M., D'Silva, V., Dai, S., MacNamara, K., Magrino, T.R., Wu, E.X., Rinard, M., Song, D.X.: Contextual policy enforcement in Android applications with permission event graphs. In: NDSS (2013)
8. Felt, A.P., Egelman, S., Wagner, D.: I've got 99 problems, but vibration ain't one: a survey of smartphone users' concerns. In: SPSM. ACM (2012)
9. Merlo, A., Georgiu, G.C.: RiskInDroid: machine learning-based risk analysis on android. In: De Capitani di Vimercati, S., Martinelli, F. (eds.) SEC 2017. IFIP AICT, vol. 502, pp. 538–552. Springer, Cham (2017). https://doi.org/10.1007/978-3-319-58469-0_36
10. Micinski, K., Votipka, D., Stevens, R., Kofinas, N., Mazurek, M.L., Foster, J.S.: User interactions and permission use on Android. In: CHI. ACM (2017)
11. Taylor, V.F., Martinovic, I.: SecuRank: starving permission-hungry apps using contextual permission analysis. In: SPSM. ACM (2016)
12. Wang, Y., Zheng, J., Sun, C., Mukkamala, S.: Quantitative security risk assessment of android permissions and applications. In: Wang, L., Shafiq, B. (eds.) DBSec 2013. LNCS, vol. 7964, pp. 226–241. Springer, Heidelberg (2013). https://doi.org/10.1007/978-3-642-39256-6_15
13. Wijesekera, P., Baokar, A., Hosseini, A., Egelman, S., Wagner, D., Beznosov, K.: Android permissions remystified: a field study on contextual integrity. In: USENIX Security (2015)

14. Wijesekera, P., Baokar, A., Tsai, L., Reardon, J., Egelman, S., Wagner, D., Beznosov, K.: The feasibility of dynamically granted permissions: aligning mobile privacy with user preferences. In: Security & Privacy Symposium. IEEE (2017)
15. Yang, W., Xiao, X., Andow, B., Li, S., Xie, T., Enck, W.: AppContext: differentiating malicious and benign mobile app behaviors using context. In: ICSE. IEEE (2015)

Private yet Efficient Decision Tree Evaluation

Marc Joye[1]([envelope]) and Fariborz Salehi[2]

[1] NXP Semiconductors, San Jose, CA, USA
marc.joye@nxp.com
[2] California Institute of Technology, Pasadena, CA, USA
fsalehi@caltech.edu

Abstract. Decision trees are a popular method for a variety of machine learning tasks. A typical application scenario involves a client providing a vector of features and a service provider (server) running a trained decision-tree model on the client's vector. Both inputs need to be kept private. In this work, we present efficient protocols for privately evaluating decision trees. Our design reduces the complexity of existing solutions with a more interactive setting, which improves the total number of comparisons to evaluate the decision tree. It crucially uses oblivious transfer protocols and leverages their amortized overhead. Furthermore, and of independent interest, we improve by roughly a factor of two the DGK comparison protocol.

Keywords: Data mining · Privacy · Integer comparison
Decision trees

1 Introduction

Machine learning techniques are currently widely used for many real-world applications. These applications range from spam detection [1], face and pattern recognition [21,25], to the analysis of genome sequencing and financial markets [17,22]. Unfortunately, in many cases, data mining and privacy are perceived to be at odds since the data mining algorithm requires access to the user's information in the clear. Privacy is especially relevant to applications handling sensitive data. As an example, consider the case of a medical study to diagnose a certain disease. In this scenario, medical profiles of patients are considered as highly sensitive data and their usage has to be compliant with regulations [7] such as Health Insurance Portability and Accountability Act (HIPAA).

An important class of machine learning algorithms is known as *classification* where each datapoint belongs to a certain class. The goal is to generate a model that can predict the class of a new datapoint. These models are useful in applications that provide personalized services, such as recommender systems [29], credit scoring models [35], automatic medical assessments [4], etc.

© IFIP International Federation for Information Processing 2018
Published by Springer International Publishing AG, part of Springer Nature 2018. All Rights Reserved
F. Kerschbaum and S. Paraboschi (Eds.): DBSec 2018, LNCS 10980, pp. 243–259, 2018.
https://doi.org/10.1007/978-3-319-95729-6_16

In this paper, we address the problem of *privacy-preserving* classification. We focus on commonly used classifiers: *decision trees*. Decision trees are simple classifiers that consist of a collection of decision nodes in a tree structure. A classical example is the twenty-question game where one player has in mind some object and another player tries to guess the object with no more than 20 yes-or-no questions. Decision trees are non-linear models for classification, yet they are easy to interpret since their evaluation simply corresponds to a tree traversal.

The *secure evaluation* of decision trees involves two parties. A server possesses a decision-tree model and a client wishes to evaluate the model. This is a typical setting in a cloud-based query system, where the service provider has a model which was trained by integrating the data of thousands of users and the client wants to learn the output of the model for her input data. An evaluation protocol is said to be secure, when at the conclusion of the protocol execution, the server cannot learn anything about the client's data and the client cannot learn additional information about the server's model.

The output of a decision-tree model is computed by traversing the tree, level by level. At each level, an entry of the client's input is compared against a fixed threshold and the result indicates how to traverse to the next level. The comparison at each visited node has to be performed in a secure way, otherwise there would be information leakage about the client's input and/or the server's model. At the heart of our privacy-preserving decision-tree evaluation lies an efficient protocol for the secure comparison of private values. It is worth mentioning that comparison is an essential building block for developing many other secure machine learning algorithms. These include clustering [8], support vector machines (SVM) [32], matrix factorization [26], regression [27], and neural networks [23]. Hence, the proposed comparison algorithms can improve the performance of a wide range of applications.

Related work. Privacy-preserving data mining was introduced in [2], [20], [12]. These works present different approaches to securely construct decision trees. Protocols for the private evaluation of decision trees were subsequently developed in [5] and more recently in [7], [34], [31]. In [7], Bost *et al.* express the decision tree as a polynomial whose output is the result of the classification. Their representation requires a small number of multiplications and is evaluated using a fully homomorphic encryption scheme. Wu *et al.* [34] reduce the problem of decision-tree evaluation to the oblivious transfer of a leaf node. Assuming a complete decision tree, they hide its structure to the client by applying a random permutation. They so gain an order of magnitude reduction in client computation and bandwidth. Tai *et al.* [31] replace the evaluation step in [34] via linear functions. This leads to better performance for sparse decision trees. Finally, we note that [34] and [31] also introduce extended protocols that are made secure against malicious adversaries.

In [9–11], Damgård, Geisler, and Krøigaard (DGK) present an elegant two-party protocol for comparing private values. It was later modified in [13] and [33], and adapted in [7,34]. It relies on additively homomorphic encryption.

The DGK protocol and its variants are dominated by exponentiations in the group underlying the homomorphic encryption scheme. Those are costly operations. Another drawback in the DGK protocol is the communication cost. The former issue was addressed by Veugen in [33]. The author was able to divide the computational workload by approximately a factor of two, *on average*. Unfortunately, the resulting implementation is subject to timing attacks [16].

Our contributions. We devise privacy-preserving comparison protocols that reduce by roughly a factor of two *both* the computational complexity and the necessary bandwidth. Furthermore, unlike [33], provided proper implementation the proposed protocols are made resistant against timing attacks.

Another contribution of this work is a new protocol for evaluating a decision tree model. We borrow from [34] the astute idea of hiding the indexes of the comparison nodes using a random permutation at each level of the tree. However, we reduce the number of comparisons with a more interactive setting. Doing so, we also take advantage of the amortized complexity of efficient OT protocols. The works of [34] and [31] require a comparison for every internal node. In our setting, a single comparison per level is required. For a decision tree of depth d, this amounts to a total of d comparisons. This has to be compared with the m comparisons in [31,34], where $m \gg d$ is the number of internal nodes.

Paper outline. The rest of the paper is organized as follows. The next section introduces some cryptographic tools. Sections 3 and 4 are the core of the paper. They present a new design for evaluating decision trees in a privacy-preserving fashion, making use of an enhanced comparison protocol. The security and performance are discussed in Sect. 5. Finally, Sect. 6 concludes the paper.

2 Cryptographic Tools

2.1 Additively Homomorphic Encryption

An *additively homomorphic encryption scheme* [30] consists of a tuple of four algorithms (KeyGen, Enc, Dec, AddH). On input a security parameter κ, the key generation algorithm KeyGen returns a matching pair (pk, sk) of public key and secret key. Let $\mathcal{M}$ denote the message space. The encryption algorithm Enc is a randomized algorithm that takes as input pk and a plaintext $m \in \mathcal{M}$, and returns a ciphertext c. Given a valid ciphertext c, the decryption algorithm Dec, using sk, returns the corresponding plaintext m.

For homomorphic encryption, the message space $\mathcal{M}$ is modeled as a finite ring. Additional public-key algorithm AddH operates on ciphertexts. It takes as input the encryption of two messages $m, m' \in \mathcal{M}$ and returns an encryption of $m + m'$. When the public key is clear from the context, it is customary to write an encryption of m as $[\![m]\!]$ in lieu of $\mathsf{Enc}_{pk}(m)$. We then use the 'boxplus' operator ($\boxplus$) to denote the addition of two ciphertexts. Hence, an encryption of $m + m'$ is obtained as $[\![m + m']\!] = [\![m]\!] \boxplus [\![m']\!]$. Likewise, for a known constant d, the encryption of $d \cdot m$ can be obtained from the encryption of m as

$[\![d \cdot m]\!] = d \cdot [\![m]\!]$; *i.e.*, as $\sum_{i=1}^{d}[\![m]\!] = [\![m]\!] \boxplus [\![m]\!] \cdots \boxplus [\![m]\!]$ (d times). Finally, we write $[\![m]\!] \boxminus [\![m']\!]$ for $[\![m]\!] \boxplus [\![-m']\!] = [\![m - m']\!]$.

2.2 Oblivious Transfer

Oblivious transfer (OT) [28], [14] is a two-party protocol between a chooser and a sender. On a 1-out-of-N OT, the sender has a set of N t-bit strings $\{\sigma_0, \sigma_1, \ldots, \sigma_{N-1}\}$. The chooser selects an index $j \in \{0, 1, \ldots, N-1\}$ and exactly obtains from the sender the string σ_j in an oblivious way (*i.e.*, the sender does not know the value of j). Oblivious transfer protocols can be constructed from many cryptographic assumptions. Efficient implementations are provided in [24], [3]; see also Appendix A.

3 Private Comparison of Integers

In this section, we introduce our enhanced design for the secure comparison of t-bit values based on additively homomorphic encryption. To make the presentation easier to follow, we describe it in stages. We start with a basic protocol which is not secure when some prior information is known. We then extend it to get full security regardless of the inputs.

3.1 Basic Protocol

The setting is as follows. Each party possesses a private t-bit value: Party A (Alice) has $x = \sum_{i=0}^{t-1} x_i 2^i$ while party B (Bob) has $y = \sum_{i=0}^{t-1} y_i 2^i$. The goal for parties A and B is to respectively obtain at the conclusion of the protocol bits δ_A and δ_B such that $\delta_A \oplus \delta_B = \mathbb{1}\{x \leqslant y\}$. Neither party can learn anything more about the other party's input.

We depict in Fig. 1 the protocol by describing the different steps performed by the two parties. Party B is equipped with an additively homomorphic public-key encryption scheme. We let $[\![m]\!]$ denote the encryption of a message $m \in \mathcal{M}$ under B's public key; see Sect. 2.1. The message space $\mathcal{M}$ is assumed to be a finite integral domain and to satisfy $\#\mathcal{M} \geqslant t + 1$.

Remark 1. In Step 3 (Fig. 1), note that given $[\![y_i]\!]$, A can obtain $[\![x_i \oplus y_i]\!]$ as $[\![y_i]\!]$ if $x_i = 0$, and as $[\![1]\!] \boxminus [\![y_i]\!]$ if $x_i = 1$.

To show the correctness of the protocol, it is useful to introduce some notation. For a t-bit integer $a = \sum_{i=0}^{t-1} a_i 2^i$ with $a_i \in \{0, 1\}$, we let $\bar{a}$ denote the complement of a; *i.e.*, $\bar{a} = 2^t - a - 1$. In particular, for $t = 1$, $a = a_0$ and $\bar{a} = \overline{a_0} = 1 - a_0$. With this notation, we can reformulate an observation made in [9, Sect. 3].

Proposition 1. *Let* $x = \sum_{i=0}^{t-1} x_i 2^i$ *and* $y = \sum_{i=0}^{t-1} y_i 2^i$, *with* $x_i, y_i \in \{0, 1\}$, *be two t-bit integers. Define*

$$\begin{cases} c_{-1} = \sum_{j=0}^{t-1}(x_j \oplus y_j), \\ c_i = x_i + \overline{y_i} + \sum_{j=i+1}^{t-1}(x_j \oplus y_j) & \text{for } 0 \leqslant i \leqslant t - 1. \end{cases}$$

---

1. Party B encrypts the bits of $y = \sum_{i=0}^{t-1} y_i\, 2^i$ under his public key and sends $[\![y_i]\!]$, $0 \leqslant i \leqslant t-1$, to A.

2. Party A computes the Hamming weight of x (*i.e.*, the number of nonzero bits of x). Let h denote the Hamming weight of x. There are three cases to consider:

   (a) if $h > \lfloor t/2 \rfloor$, A sets $\delta_A = 0$;

   (b) if $h < \lceil t/2 \rceil$, A sets $\delta_A = 1$;

   (c) if $h = t/2$ (this can only occur when t is even), A chooses a random value in $\{0, 1\}$ for δ_A.

3. Next, party A forms a set $\mathscr{L}$ of indexes i such that

   (a) $\mathscr{L} \supseteq \mathscr{L}'$ where $\mathscr{L}' = \{0 \leqslant i \leqslant t-1 \mid x_i = \delta_A\}$; and

   (b) $\#\mathscr{L} = \lfloor t/2 \rfloor$.

   For each $i \in \mathscr{L}$, A draws at random a non-zero element $r_i \in \mathcal{M}$ and computes

$$[\![c_i^*]\!] = r_i \cdot \left([\![1 + (1 - 2\delta_A)x_i]\!] \boxplus ((2\delta_A - 1) \cdot [\![y_i]\!]) \boxplus \left(\textstyle\sum_{j=i+1}^{t-1}[\![x_j \oplus y_j]\!]\right) \right) .$$

   Finally, she computes

$$[\![c_{-1}^*]\!] = r_{-1} \cdot \left([\![\delta_A]\!] \boxplus \textstyle\sum_{j=0}^{t-1}[\![x_j \oplus y_j]\!] \right)$$

   for a random non-zero element $r_{-1} \in \mathcal{M}$. Party A sends the $\lfloor t/2 \rfloor + 1$ ciphertexts $[\![c_i^*]\!]$ in a *random order* to B.

4. Using his private key, party B decrypts the received $[\![c_i^*]\!]$'s. If one is decrypted to zero, B sets $\delta_B = 1$. Otherwise, he sets $\delta_B = 0$.

Fig. 1. Basic comparison protocol.

Then $x < y$ if and only if there exists some unique index i with $0 \leqslant i \leqslant t-1$ such that $c_i = 0$. Moreover, $x = y$ if and only if $c_{-1} = 0$ and $c_i = 1$ for $0 \leqslant i \leqslant t-1$.

Proof. As defined, c_i is the sum of nonnegative terms. Therefore, for $0 \leqslant i \leqslant t-1$, $c_i = 0$ is equivalent to (i) $x_i = \overline{y_i} = 0$ and (ii) for $i + 1 \leqslant j \leqslant t-1$, $x_j \oplus y_j = 0$. This in turn is equivalent to (i) $x_i < y_i$ and (ii) for $i + 1 \leqslant j \leqslant t-1$, $x_j = y_j$; that is, $x < y$. To see that index i such that $c_i = 0$ is unique, suppose that $c_{i'} = 0$ for some $i' \neq i$. Without loss of generality, assume that $i' < i$. This leads to $c_{i'} = x_{i'} + \overline{y_{i'}} + \sum_{j=i'+1}^{t-1}(x_j \oplus y_j) \geqslant x_i \oplus y_i = 1$, a contradiction.

The second part of the proposition is clear. If $\sum_{j=0}^{t-1} x_j\, 2^j = \sum_{j=0}^{t-1} y_j\, 2^j$ then $c_{-1} = 0$ and $c_i = 1$ for $i \geqslant 0$.   □

By reversing the roles of x and y in Proposition 1, we get as an immediate corollary the following proposition.

Proposition 2. *Let $x = \sum_{i=0}^{t-1} x_i\, 2^i$ and $y = \sum_{i=0}^{t-1} y_i\, 2^i$, with $x_i, y_i \in \{0, 1\}$, be two t-bit integers. For $0 \leqslant i \leqslant t-1$, define*

$$c_i = y_i + \overline{x_i} + \textstyle\sum_{j=i+1}^{t-1}(y_j \oplus x_j) .$$

Then $x \leqslant y$ if and only if there exists no index i with $0 \leqslant i \leqslant t-1$ such that $c_i = 0$.

Proof. If there were such an index i, this would imply $y < x$ by Proposition 1. The absence of such an index therefore implies $y \geqslant x$. $\qquad\square$

We are now ready to show that the protocol must terminate with the correct result. Following [33], depending on the value of h (see Step 2 in Fig. 1), we distinguish three cases.

1. Suppose first that the Hamming weight of x is greater than $\lfloor t/2 \rfloor$ (and thus $\delta_A = 0$). This means that x has more ones than zeros in its binary representation. Specifically, among the t bits of x, at most $\lfloor t/2 \rfloor$ bits are equal to 0. Furthermore, for $0 \leqslant i \leqslant t - 1$, Proposition 1 shows that c_i needs only to be evaluated when $x_i = 0$ since when $x_i = 1$ we already know that the corresponding c_i cannot be zero. The case $x = y$ is taken into account using c_{-1}.
2. Now suppose that the Hamming weight of x is less than $\lceil t/2 \rceil$ (and thus $\delta_A = 1$). In this case, among the t bits of x, at most $\lfloor t/2 \rfloor$ bits are equal to 1. We can then make use of Proposition 2. With at most $\lfloor t/2 \rfloor$ tests for $c_i = 0$ (*i.e.*, when $x_i = 1$), we can decide whether $x \leqslant y$.
3. The last case is when the Hamming weight of x is $t/2$ (and thus δ_A is equiprobably equal to 0 or 1). This supposes t even. In this case, among the t bits of x, $t/2$ bits are equal to 0 and $t/2$ bits are equal to 1. Proposition 1 or Proposition 2 can be used indifferently to decide after at most $t/2 = \lfloor t/2 \rfloor$ tests for $c_i = 0$ whether $x \leqslant y$.

The above analysis shows that (i) only the indexes $i \in \mathscr{L}'$ need to be tested, and (ii) $\#\mathscr{L}' \leqslant \lfloor t/2 \rfloor$. If $\#\mathscr{L}' < \lfloor t/2 \rfloor$ then additional indexes are added to $\mathscr{L}'$ to form $\mathscr{L}$. This ensures that $\#\mathscr{L}$ is always equal to $\lfloor t/2 \rfloor$ and is aimed at preventing timing attacks. Now the correctness follows by noting that the $[\![c_i^*]\!]$'s include the encryptions of $r_i \cdot c_i$ for all $i \in \mathscr{L}'$. It is also important to see that $[\![c_{-1}^*]\!]$ is the encryption of a non-zero value when $\delta_B = 1$.

By construction, $\delta_B = 1$ if one of the $[\![c_i^*]\!]$'s decrypts to 0.

- When $\delta_A = 0$, Proposition 1 is used. A decryption to 0 means $x \leqslant y$. We therefore have $\mathbb{1}\{x \leqslant y\} = 1 = \delta_A \oplus \delta_B$, as desired.
- When $\delta_A = 1$, Proposition 2 is used and a decryption to 0 means $x \nleqslant y$. Then, $\mathbb{1}\{x \leqslant y\} = 0 = \delta_A \oplus \delta_B$, as desired.

If none of the $[\![c_i^*]\!]$'s decrypts to 0 then $\delta_B = 0$. When $\delta_A = 0$, this means $x \nleqslant y$; when $\delta_A = 1$, this means $x \leqslant y$. In both cases, we have $\mathbb{1}\{x \leqslant y\} = \delta_A \oplus \delta_B$, as desired.

3.2   Full Protocol

The basic protocol needs special care. In particular, it requires that the Hamming weight of x *a priori* has the same probability to be greater than $\lfloor t/2 \rfloor$ or less than $\lceil t/2 \rceil$. This guarantees that δ_A is uniformly distributed over $\{0, 1\}$. Indeed, if party B knows for example that the Hamming weight of x is more likely less than $\lceil t/2 \rceil$ (and thus δ_A is more likely equal to 1), a value $\delta_B = 0$ tells party B that x is more likely less than or equal to y since $\delta_A \oplus \delta_B = \mathbb{1}\{x \leqslant y\}$.

We modify our basic protocol so that it remains secure when party B has some prior knowledge on the Hamming weight of x. The resulting distribution of δ_A will always be uniform over $\{0, 1\}$, independently of the value of x. The full protocol is detailed in Fig. 2.

---

1. (a) Party B generates a random mask $\eta \in \mathbb{Z}_{2^t}$, forms $y^* = y + \eta \mod 2^t$ and $Y^* = \lfloor \frac{y+\eta}{2^t} \rfloor$, and sends y^* to A.
   (b) Likewise, party A generates a random t-bit integer $x' \in \mathbb{Z}_{2^t}$, computes $z^* = y^* + x' - x \mod 2^t$ and $Z^* = \lfloor \frac{y^* + x' - x}{2^t} \rfloor$, and sends z^* to B.
   (c) Party B removes the mask and defines the t-bit integer $y' = z^* - \eta \mod 2^t$. B also defines $Y' = \lfloor \frac{z^* - \eta}{2^t} \rfloor$.
2. Parties A and B apply the basic comparison protocol (Fig. 1) on t-bit integers x' and y'.
   Let δ'_A and δ'_B denote the respective outputs for A and B of the protocol, with $\delta'_A \oplus \delta'_B = \mathbb{1}\{x' \leqslant y'\}$.
3. Party A sets $\delta_A = \delta'_A$ if Z^* is even, and $\delta_A = \delta'_A \oplus 1$ otherwise.
4. Party B sets $\delta_B = \delta'_B$ if $(Y^* + Y')$ is even, and $\delta_B = \delta'_B \oplus 1$ otherwise.

Fig. 2. Full comparison protocol.

It is worth remarking that x' as defined in Step 1b (Fig. 2) is a *random* t-bit integer. There is therefore no way for party B to gain more information on its Hamming weight.

The correctness of the protocol is easily verified. By definition, we have $y^* = y + \eta - 2^t Y^*$, $z^* = y^* + x' - x - 2^t Z^*$, and $y' = z^* - \eta - Y' 2^t$. This leads to

$$\delta_A \oplus \delta_B = \mathbb{1}\{x \leqslant y\} = \left\lfloor \frac{y + 2^t - x}{2^t} \right\rfloor = \left\lfloor \frac{y' + 2^t - x'}{2^t} \right\rfloor + Y^* + Y' + Z^*$$

$$= (\delta'_A \oplus \delta'_B) + Y^* + Y' + Z^* .$$

Reducing the above relation modulo 2 yields $\delta_A + \delta_B \equiv \delta'_A + \delta'_B + Y^* + Y' + Z^*$ (mod 2), a solution of which is $\delta_A = \delta'_A + Z^* \mod 2$ and $\delta_B = \delta'_B + Y^* + Y' \mod 2$.

3.3 Further Settings

Encrypted comparison bit. Let δ denote the comparison bit; *i.e.*, $\delta = \mathbb{1}\{x \leqslant y\}$. In certain settings, a party wishes to produce an encryption of δ at the end of the protocol, rather than a share δ_A of δ (the other share, δ_B, being held by the other party). In this case, we can add the following step to our comparison protocols:

5. Party B encrypts δ_B using his public key and sends $[\![\delta_B]\!]$ to A. Upon receiving $[\![\delta_B]\!]$, party A computes the encryption of δ as $[\![\delta]\!] = [\![\delta_B]\!]$ if $\delta_A = 0$, and $[\![\delta]\!] = [\![1]\!] \boxminus [\![\delta_B]\!]$ otherwise.

Encrypted inputs. There exists another practical setting for the comparison of private inputs. Suppose that one party possesses $[\![x]\!]$ and $[\![y]\!]$, the encryption of two t-bit values $x = \sum_{i=0}^{t-1} x_i\, 2^i$ and $y = \sum_{i=0}^{t-1} y_i\, 2^i$. The other party possesses the corresponding decryption key. Our protocols easily generalize to cover this setting as well. An example is given in Sect. 4.2.

Other frameworks. The technique we employed is fairly generic and can be adapted to increase the efficiency of other bit-wise comparison protocols, including the protocol in [18].

4   Application: Private Evaluation of Decision Trees

Secure comparison protocols find numerous practical applications. We apply the results of the previous section to the *private* evaluation of decision trees. As the values being compared will be random, our basic protocol (Fig. 1) suffices.

4.1   Problem Setup

There are two parties involved: a client and a server. The client has a private feature vector $\boldsymbol{x} = (x_1, x_2, \ldots, x_n) \in \mathbb{Z}^n$ and the server possesses a decision tree model $\mathfrak{T} \colon \mathbb{Z}^n \to \mathbb{Z}$. At the end of protocol, the client obtains the value $z_r := \mathfrak{T}(\boldsymbol{x})$ and learns nothing else; the server learns nothing.

In a binary tree, each internal node $\nu_k^{(\ell)}$ (with $0 \leqslant k \leqslant \ell$) at level ℓ in the tree is associated with a Boolean function

$$f_k^{(\ell)}(\boldsymbol{x}) = \mathbb{1}\big\{ x_{i_k^{(\ell)}} \leqslant T_k^{(\ell)} \big\}, \tag{1}$$

where $i_k^{(\ell)}$ is an index in the feature vector $\boldsymbol{x} \in \mathbb{Z}^n$, and $T_k^{(\ell)}$ is a threshold.

The depth of the tree (*i.e.*, the longest path from the root to a leaf) is denoted by d. The number of internal nodes is denoted by m. Without loss of generality, we assume that $\mathfrak{T}$ is a *complete* binary decision tree; that is, a binary decision tree with exactly 2^ℓ nodes at each level ℓ. We note that it is easy to derive a complete binary decision tree by introducing *dummy* internal nodes and assigning an arbitrary value in $\{0, 1\}$ for the corresponding Boolean function $f_k^{(\ell)}(\boldsymbol{x})$. This is illustrated in the figure below on a decision tree of depth $d = 2$.

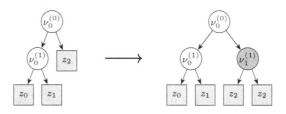

Fig. 3. Transforming a binary decision tree into a complete binary decision tree.

4.2   From Public to Private Evaluation

On input x, the evaluation of a decision tree starts at the root node. At each level ℓ, depending on the result of $f_k^{(\ell)}(x)$, either the left branch (for 0) or the right branch (for 1) is taken. The process is repeated until a leaf node is reached. The output of $\mathfrak{T}(x)$ is z_r, the value of the so-obtained leaf node.

Public evaluation. When the feature vector x and the decision tree $\mathfrak{T}$ are available in the clear, the decision tree can be evaluated by performing d comparisons. Let $\beta_\ell \in \{0, 1\}$ denote the result of the decision (0 or 1) at level ℓ, for $\ell = 0, 1, \ldots, d - 1$. It turns out that

$$\begin{cases} \beta_0 = f_0^{(0)}(x) \\ \beta_\ell = f_{(\beta_0, \ldots, \beta_{\ell-1})_2}^{(\ell)}(x) & \text{for } \ell = 1, \ldots, d - 1 \end{cases} \tag{2}$$

Consequently, the index r of the corresponding leaf node can be expressed as $r = (\beta_0, \beta_1, \ldots, \beta_{d-1})_2 = \sum_{\ell=0}^{d-1} \beta_\ell 2^{d-1-\ell}$, where $(\beta_0, \beta_1, \ldots, \beta_{d-1})_2$ represents the binary expansion of r.

Example 1. Figure 4 depicts an example of a binary decision tree with 4 levels. In this example, the index r of the output, z_r, is given by $r = (\beta_0, \beta_1, \beta_2, \beta_3)_2 = (0, 1, 0, 1)_2 = 5$.

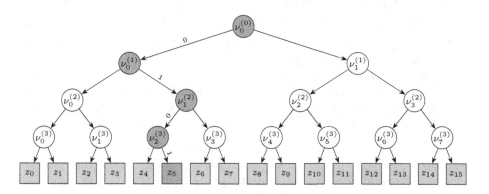

Fig. 4. Evaluation of a decision tree.

Private evaluation. In the private setting, the server knows the model $\mathfrak{T}$ (including $i_k^{(\ell)}$ and $T_k^{(\ell)}$, for $0 \leqslant \ell \leqslant d-1$) while the client knows $x = (x_1, \ldots, x_n)$.

- For $\ell = 0$, we have $\beta_0 = \mathbb{1}\{x_{i_0^{(0)}} \leqslant T_0^{(0)}\}$. However, the private comparison protocols of Sect. 3 do not directly apply because the value of $i_0^{(0)}$ is unknown to the client. This issue is resolved by providing the server with $[\![x_i]\!]$, for $1 \leqslant i \leqslant n$. Here, $[\![x_i]\!]$ denotes an encryption[1] of x_i under the public-key of

---

[1] We use triple brackets rather than double brackets to indicate that the encryption scheme may be different from the one used for the comparisons.

the client. The encryption scheme is supposed being additively homomorphic with message space $\mathcal{M}$ such that $\#\mathcal{M} \geqslant 2^{t+\kappa}$ for a certain security parameter κ. Using the techniques developed in the previous section, the client and server can now engage in a two-party protocol to secret-share the decision bit $\beta_0 = b_0 \oplus b_0'$ —where the server holds b_0 and the client holds b_0'. Details are provided in Step 2 of Fig. 6.

- For $\ell = 1, \ldots, d-1$, Eqs. (1) and (2) become $\beta_\ell = \mathbb{1}\{x_{i_{k^\star}^{(\ell)}} \leqslant T_{k^\star}^{(\ell)}\}$ with $k^\star := k^\star(\ell) = (\beta_0, \ldots, \beta_{\ell-1})_2$. In particular, for $\ell = 1$, we obtain

$$\beta_1 = \mathbb{1}\{x_{i_{k^\star}^{(1)}} \leqslant T_{k^\star}^{(1)}\} \quad \text{with } k^\star = \beta_0 = \begin{cases} b_0' & \text{if } b_0 = 0 \\ b_0' \oplus 1 & \text{otherwise} \end{cases}.$$

Specifically, if $b_0 = 0$, the server knows that the client possesses the correct result of the comparison; i.e., $b_0' = \beta_0$. If $b_0 = 1$, the server knows that the client possesses the flipped result. To maintain the consistency, the server uses a copied version $\mathfrak{T}^*$ of the initial tree. If $b_0 = 1$, the server updates $\mathfrak{T}^*$ by switching the left subtree and the right subtree at level $\ell = 1$. What is important to observe here is that $k^\star$ coincides with b_0' in $\mathfrak{T}^*$. Hence, the client can obtain $[\![x_{i_{k^\star}^{(1)}} - T_{k^\star}^{(1)} + \mu_1]\!]$ —and in turn $x_{i_{k^\star}^{(1)}} - T_{k^\star}^{(1)} + \mu_1$ after decryption— from the server, where μ_1 is a mask chosen by the server to hide the value of $x_{i_{k^\star}^{(1)}} - T_{k^\star}^{(1)}$. Next, the client and server engage in a two-party protocol to secret-share the decision bit $\beta_1 = b_1 \oplus b_1'$. To prevent the server to learn the index $k^\star$, $[\![x_{i_{k^\star}^{(1)}} - T_{k^\star}^{(1)} + \mu_1]\!]$ is obtained via oblivious transfer. Again, refer to Step 2 in Fig. 6 for details.

The same process is iterated for $\ell = 2, \ldots, d-1$. Each time $b_\ell = 1$, the server switches all subtrees of $\mathfrak{T}^*$ at level ℓ and calls $\mathfrak{T}^*$ the so-obtained tree.
- At this stage the client knows $(b_0', \ldots, b_{d-1}')_2$, which is the index of the leaf node containing the result in the permuted tree $\mathfrak{T}^*$. The client engages in a 1-out-of-2^d OT with the server and thereby learns z_r.

Example 2 (Example 1 cont'd). Suppose that the server successively obtains $b_0 = 1$, $b_1 = 0$, $b_2 = 1$, and $b_3 = 1$. For $\ell = 1, \ldots, 3$: if $b_\ell = 1$ the subtrees at level ℓ are switched. This is illustrated in Fig. 5. The bottom picture is the final permuted tree $\mathfrak{T}^*$.

Our decision-tree evaluation protocol is given in Fig. 6. The permuted tree $\mathfrak{T}^*$ is represented at level $\ell \geqslant 1$ by the string $\sigma^{(\ell)} = (b_0, \ldots, b_{\ell-1})_2$; $\mathfrak{T}^* = \mathfrak{T}$ for $\ell = 0$. Step 2d in Fig. 6 outputs shares of the decision at level ℓ. It is worth noting that a *single* execution of the comparison protocol is run per level.

Proposition 3. *With the notation of Fig. 6, for $0 \leqslant \ell \leqslant d-1$, the server and the client secret-share the decision bit at each level; i.e.,*

$$b_\ell \oplus b_\ell' = \beta_\ell = \mathbb{1}\{x_{i_{k^\star}^{(\ell)}} \leqslant T_{k^\star}^{(\ell)}\} \quad \text{where } k^\star = \sigma^{(\ell)} \oplus j \ .$$

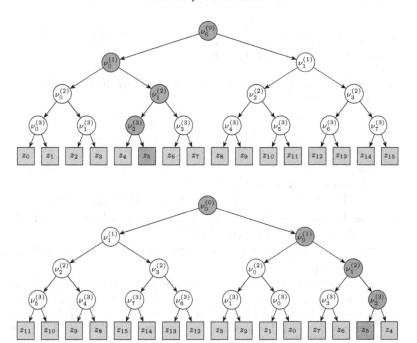

Fig. 5. Public vs. private evaluation of a decision tree.

Proof. From $m'_\ell = M'_\ell - \lfloor M'_\ell/2^t \rfloor 2^t$ and $m_\ell = \mu_\ell - \lfloor \mu_\ell/2^t \rfloor 2^t$, we can write

$$\delta_\ell \oplus \delta'_\ell = \mathbb{1}\{m'_\ell \leqslant m_\ell\} = \left\lfloor \tfrac{m_\ell + 2^t - m'_\ell}{2^t} \right\rfloor = \left\lfloor \tfrac{\mu_\ell + 2^t - M'_\ell}{2^t} \right\rfloor - \left\lfloor \tfrac{\mu_\ell}{2^t} \right\rfloor - \left\lfloor \tfrac{M'_\ell}{2^t} \right\rfloor \ .$$

Furthermore, defining $s = \sigma^{(\ell)} \oplus j$, we have $M'_\ell = M_j^{(\ell)} = x_{i_s^{(\ell)}} - T_s^{(\ell)} + \mu_\ell$. Hence, we get

$$\left\lfloor \tfrac{\mu_\ell + 2^t - M'_\ell}{2^t} \right\rfloor = \left\lfloor \tfrac{T_s^{(\ell)} - x_{i_s^{(\ell)}} + 2^t}{2^t} \right\rfloor = \mathbb{1}\{x_{i_s^{(\ell)}} \leqslant T_s^{(\ell)}\} \ .$$

Putting the two relations together, modulo 2, yields

$$\mathbb{1}\{x_{i_s^{(\ell)}} \leqslant T_s^{(\ell)}\} \equiv \delta_\ell + \delta'_\ell + \left\lfloor \tfrac{\mu_\ell}{2^t} \right\rfloor + \left\lfloor \tfrac{M'_\ell}{2^t} \right\rfloor \pmod{2} \ .$$

This concludes the proof by noting that $s = k^\star$, $b_\ell = \delta_\ell + \lfloor \mu_\ell/2^t \rfloor \pmod 2$, and $b'_\ell \equiv \delta'_\ell + \lfloor M'_\ell/2^t \rfloor \pmod 2$. □

As a result, the client learns the classification result $\mathfrak{T}(\boldsymbol{x})$ at the end of the protocol in Fig. 6.

5   Discussion

5.1   Security Considerations

The decision tree evaluation protocol presented in Fig. 6 is secure in the *semi-honest model*, a.k.a. *honest-but-curious model*. It assumes two semantically

1. The client encrypts the entries of the feature vector $\boldsymbol{x} = (x_1, x_2, \ldots, x_n)$ and sends $[\![x_i]\!]$, for $1 \leqslant i \leqslant n$, to the server.
2. For $\ell = 0, \ldots, d - 1$:
   (a) The server chooses a random $(t + \kappa)$-bit mask μ_ℓ. It also defines $m_\ell = \mu_\ell \bmod 2^t$ and
   $$\sigma^{(\ell)} = \begin{cases} 0 & \text{if } \ell = 0 \\ (b_0, \ldots, b_{\ell-1})_2 & \text{otherwise} \end{cases}.$$
   For $k = 0, \ldots, 2^\ell - 1$:
      i. The server sets $s \leftarrow k \oplus \sigma^{(\ell)}$.
      ii. The server computes[a] $[\![M_k^{(\ell)}]\!] = [\![x_{i_s^{(\ell)}} - T_s^{(\ell)} + \mu_\ell]\!]$.
   (b) The client sets $j \leftarrow (b_0', \ldots, b_{\ell-1}')_2$ and engages in a 1-out-of-2^ℓ OT with the server to obtain the value of $[\![M_j^{(\ell)}]\!]$.
   (c) The client decrypts $[\![M_j^{(\ell)}]\!]$, gets $M_j^{(\ell)}$, and defines $M_\ell' = M_j^{(\ell)}$ and $m_\ell' = M_j^{(\ell)} \bmod 2^t$.
   (d) Client and server run the basic comparison protocol (Fig. 1) on inputs m_ℓ' and m_ℓ. At the end of the protocol, they respectively obtain a bit δ_ℓ' and δ_ℓ such that $\delta_\ell \oplus \delta_\ell' = \mathbb{1}\{m_\ell' \leqslant m_\ell\}$. The server sets $b_\ell = \delta_\ell$ if $\lfloor \mu_\ell / 2^t \rfloor$ is even, and $b_\ell = \delta_\ell \oplus 1$ otherwise. The client sets $b_\ell' = \delta_\ell'$ if $\lfloor M_\ell' / 2^t \rfloor$ is even, and $b_\ell' = \delta_\ell' \oplus 1$ otherwise.
3. For $k = 0, \ldots, 2^d - 1$, the server sets $z_k^* \leftarrow z_{k \oplus \sigma^{(d)}}$ where $\sigma^{(d)} = (b_0, \ldots, b_{d-1})_2$. The client sets $j \leftarrow (b_0', \ldots, b_{d-1}')_2$ and engages in a 1-out-of-2^d OT with the server to obtain the value of z_j^*.

---

[a] For dummy nodes, the server can instead draw a random ciphertext for $[\![M_k^{(\ell)}]\!]$.

Fig. 6. Secure decision tree evaluation protocol.

secure additively homomorphic encryption schemes, $[\cdot]$ and $[\![\cdot]\!]$, and a semi-honest secure 1-out-of-N OT protocol. Informally, if the parties interact according to the protocol specification, the semi-honest model guarantees that (i) the client only learns the classification result and a bound d on the depth of the decision tree, and (ii) the server learns nothing.

The security is defined via the ideal-world/real-world simulation paradigm; see *e.g.* the excellent tutorial provided in [19, Chap. 6]. The security proof of our main construction is standard. We refer the reader to [34, Sect. 2.3] for precise security definitions and to [34, Theorem 3.2] for the proof technique.

Selecting parameter κ. Step 2a in Fig. 6 requires a random mask μ_ℓ to blind the value of $x_{i_{k \oplus \sigma^{(\ell)}}^{(\ell)}} - T_{k \oplus \sigma^{(\ell)}}^{(\ell)}$ in

$$M_k^{(\ell)} = x_{i_{k \oplus \sigma^{(\ell)}}^{(\ell)}} - T_{k \oplus \sigma^{(\ell)}}^{(\ell)} + \mu_\ell,$$

for $k = 0, \ldots, 2^\ell - 1$. In Step 2c, as the output of the 1-out-2^ℓ OT, the client obtains $M'_\ell = M_j^{(\ell)}$ for a single value $j \in [0, \ldots, 2^\ell - 1]$. This justifies that the same mask μ_ℓ can be re-used at level ℓ, for each successive value of k.

Moreover, when the message space $\mathcal{M}$ for $[\![\cdot]\!]$ is much larger than the set $\{0, 1\}^t$, since $x_{i_{k \oplus \sigma(\ell)}^{(\ell)}}$ and $T_{k \oplus \sigma(\ell)}^{(\ell)}$ are t-bit values, there is no need to draw the mask μ_ℓ in the whole range of $\mathcal{M}$. Any $(t + \kappa)$-bit value for a relatively short security length κ will generate a mask that *statistically* hides $x_{i_{k \oplus \sigma(\ell)}^{(\ell)}} - T_{k \oplus \sigma(\ell)}^{(\ell)}$.

When the message space $\mathcal{M} = \mathbb{Z}_{2^t}$ (like in [6]), μ_ℓ and M'_ℓ are defined modulo 2^t as elements in $\mathbb{Z}_{2^t}$ (and thus $\lfloor \mu_\ell / 2^t \rfloor = \lfloor M'_\ell / 2^t \rfloor = 0$). Parameter κ will be in this case set to 0.

5.2   Performance Analysis

We compare the proposed evaluation protocol with the two most recent protocols, Wu *et al.* (PETS 2016) and Tai *et al.* (ESORICS 2017), *in the semi-honest setting.*

Let $\mathfrak{T}$ be a binary decision tree of depth d with m [non-dummy] internal nodes (*i.e.*, decision nodes). Let also n be the number of entries in the feature vector; each entry being represented as a t-bit integer. Both the computation and bandwidth are analyzed. For the computation complexity, we count the number of public-key operations performed by each of the parties. For the bandwidth, we count the number of ciphertexts sent by one party to the other.

Table 1. Comparison.

	Bandwidth		Computation	
	Client	Server	Client	Server
Wu *et al.* [34]	$nt + m + 1$	$mt + m + 2^d$	$O((n + m)t + d)$	$O(mt + 2^d)$
Tai *et al.* [31]	$nt + m$	$mt + 2(m + 1)$	$O((n + m)t)$	$O(mt)$
Ours (Fig. 6)	$d(\lfloor t/2 \rfloor + 2) + n$	$dt + 2^{d+1} - 1$	$O(n + dt)$	$O(m + dt)$

In our protocol, the client first encrypts the feature vector. This requires $O(n)$ public-key operations and produces n ciphertexts. Next, in the main loop, at each level ℓ (for $0 \leqslant \ell \leqslant d - 1$), the client mainly performs two steps with the server: (1) one 1-out-of-2^ℓ OT where the client is the chooser and (2) one comparison of two t-bit integers. We assume that the OT is implemented with the Naor-Pinkas protocol (see Appendix A) and that the comparison makes use of our comparison protocol (Fig. 1). So, on the client's side, the OT requires in total for the main loop $O(d)$ public-key operations and $d - 1$ ciphertexts; the comparison requires in total $O(dt)$ public-key operations and $d(\lfloor t/2 \rfloor + 1)$ ciphertexts. The last step is a 1-out-of-2^d OT, which requires $O(1)$ public-key operation and one ciphertext. Summing up, the total complexity for the client amounts to

$O(n+dt)$ with $n+d-1+d(\lfloor t/2 \rfloor+1)+1 = d(\lfloor t/2 \rfloor+2)+n$ ciphertexts. On the server's side, the server processes in addition m encryptions (Step 2a in Fig. 6) to form $[\![M_k^{(\ell)}]\!]$ for the non-dummy nodes. This corresponds to a complexity of $O(m)$. The OT in the main loop requires in total $O(d)$ public-key operations and $2^d - 1$ ciphertexts. The comparison requires $O(dt)$ public-key operations and dt ciphertexts (we suppose here that the server plays the role of Party B; cf. Fig. 1). The last step for the final OT incurs for the server $O(1)$ public-key operation and 2^d ciphertexts. Consequently, the total complexity for the server is of $O(m+dt)$ and the needed bandwidth is of $2^d - 1 + dt + 2^d = dt + 2^{d+1} - 1$ ciphertexts.

A typical value for the precision is $t = 64$. As shown in Table 1, since $d \ll m$, the proposed protocol greatly reduces the workload on both the client's and server's sides. The bandwidth usage is also improved on the client's side with our protocol. On the server's side, the savings depend on the tree sparsity. Denser decision trees give rise to more savings; for a complete binary tree (i.e., $m = 2^d - 1$), our protocol saves $(2^d - d)t$ ciphertexts on the server's side.

5.3   Random Forests

As in [34], our main construction extend to the evaluation of *random forests*. Introduced by Ho [15], the random forest improves the quality of the classification task by combining the results of a multitude of decision trees. A random forest $\mathfrak{F}$ can be defined as an ensemble of decision trees, $\mathfrak{F} = \{\mathfrak{T}_i\}_i$. Its output is computed by taking the majority vote; i.e., $\mathfrak{F}(\boldsymbol{x}) = \mathrm{maj}\{\mathfrak{T}_i(\boldsymbol{x})\}_i$.

6   Conclusion and Future Work

In this work, we introduced an enhanced comparison protocol and several extensions thereof. As an application, combined with a novel design strategy and a number of optimizations, we developed an efficient protocol for the private evaluation of decision trees.

Future work. An interesting direction for future work is to design a privacy-preserving evaluation protocol in the multi-user setting, wherein the feature vector and/or the model are shared among multiple entities. Another interesting direction is to extend the protocol to make it secure against malicious adversaries.

A   Naor-Pinkas OT Protocol

Let $\mathbb{G} = \langle g \rangle$ be a group of order q, in which the Diffie-Hellman assumption holds. Let also a cryptographic hash function H mapping to $\{0,1\}^t$, modeled as a random oracle. The sender selects at random $K_1, \ldots, K_{N-1} \in \mathbb{G}$ and computes $y = g^x$ for some random integer $x \in \mathbb{Z}_q$. The sender's public key is

$(g, y, K_1, \ldots, K_{N-1})$ and the secret key is x. The sender pre-computes $S_i = (K_i)^x$ for $1 \leqslant i \leqslant N - 1$.

The sender's input is a set of N bit-strings $\sigma_0, \ldots, \sigma_{N-1} \in \{0, 1\}^t$. Suppose a chooser (Carol) wishes to get string σ_j for some $j \in \{0, \ldots, N - 1\}$. The amortized 1-out-of-N Naor-Pinkas OT protocol [24, §3.1] proceeds as follows.

1. The chooser draws a random integer $r \in \mathbb{Z}_q$ and computes $pk_j = g^r$. If $j \neq 0$, she sets $pk_0 = K_j/pk_j$. She sends pk_0 to the sender.
2. The sender computes $(pk_0)^x$ and then, for $1 \leqslant i \leqslant N - 1$, sets $(pk_i)^x$ as $(pk_i)^x = S_i/(pk_0)^x$. Next, he chooses a nonce R and encrypts each string σ_i as $c_i = H((pk_i)^x, R, i) \oplus \sigma_i$, for $0 \leqslant i \leqslant N - 1$. He sends $(c_0, \ldots, c_{N-1}, R)$ to the chooser.
3. The chooser recovers σ_j as $c_j \oplus H(y^r, R, j)$.

Interestingly, the protocol can be re-used multiple times. After the one-time initialization phase, each transfer only costs a single exponentiation (in $\mathbb{G}$) plus $N - 1$ multiplications for the sender. The chooser essentially computes one exponentiation per transfer.

References

1. Abu-Nimeh, S., Nappa, D., Wang, X., Nair, S.: A comparison of machine learning techniques for phishing detection. In: 2nd Annual eCrime Researchers Summit, pp. 60–69. ACM (2007). https://doi.org/10.1145/1299015.1299021
2. Agrawal, R., Shrikant, R.: Privacy-preserving data mining. ACM SIGMOD Record **29**(2), 439–450 (2000). https://doi.org/10.1145/335191.335438
3. Asharov, G., Lindell, Y., Schneider, T., Zohner, M.: More efficient oblivious transfer extensions. J. Cryptol. **30**(3), 805–858 (2017). https://doi.org/10.1007/s00145-016-9236-6
4. Azar, A.T., El-Metwally, S.M.: Decision tree classifiers for automated medical diagnosis. Neural Comput. Appl. **23**(7–8), 2387–2403 (2013). https://doi.org/10.1007/s00521-012-1196-7
5. Barni, M., et al.: Secure evaluation of private linear branching programs with medical applications. In: Backes, M., Ning, P. (eds.) ESORICS 2009. LNCS, vol. 5789, pp. 424–439. Springer, Heidelberg (2009). https://doi.org/10.1007/978-3-642-04444-1_26
6. Benhamouda, F., Herranz, J., Joye, M., Libert, B.: Efficient cryptosystems from 2^k-th power residue symbols. J. Cryptol. **30**(2), 519–549 (2017). https://doi.org/10.1007/s00145-016-9229-5
7. Bost, R., Popa, R.A., Tu, S., Goldwasser, S.: Machine learning classification over encrypted data. In: 22nd Annual Network and Distributed System Security Symposium (NDSS 2015). The Internet Society (2015). https://doi.org/10.14722/ndss.2015.23241
8. Bunn, P., Ostrovsky, R.: Secure two-party k-means clustering. In: 14th ACM Conference on Computer and Communications Security (CCS 2007), pp. 486–497. ACM (2007). https://doi.org/10.1145/1315245.1315306
9. Damgård, I., Geisler, M., Krøigaard, M.: Efficient and secure comparison for online auctions. In: Pieprzyk, J., Ghodosi, H., Dawson, E. (eds.) ACISP 2007. LNCS, vol. 4586, pp. 416–430. Springer, Heidelberg (2007). https://doi.org/10.1007/978-3-540-73458-1_30

10. Damgård, I., Geisler, M., Krøigaard, M.: Homomorphic encryption and secure comparison. Int. J. Appl. Cryptography **1**(1), 22–31 (2008). https://doi.org/10.1504/IJACT.2008.017048
11. Damgård, I., Geisler, M., Krøigaard, M.: A correction to Efficient and secure comparison for on-line auctions. Int. J. Appl. Cryptography **1**(4), 323–324 (2009). https://doi.org/10.1504/IJACT.2009.028031
12. Du, W., Zhan, Z.: Building decision tree classifier on private data. In: IEEE Workshop on Privacy, Security, and Data Mining. Conferences in Research and Practice in Information Technology, vol. 14. Australian Computer Society (2002). http://crpit.com/confpapers/CRPITV14Du.pdf
13. Erkin, Z., et al.: Privacy-preserving face recognition. In: Goldberg, I., Atallah, M.J. (eds.) PETS 2009. LNCS, vol. 5672, pp. 235–253. Springer, Heidelberg (2009). https://doi.org/10.1007/978-3-642-03168-7_14
14. Even, S., Goldreich, O., Lempel, A.: A randomized protocol for signing contracts. Commun. ACM **28**(6), 637–647 (1985). https://doi.org/10.1145/3812.3818
15. Ho, T.K.: The random subspace method for constructing decision forests. IEEE Trans. Pattern Anal. Mach. Intell. **20**(8), 832–844 (1998). https://doi.org/10.1109/34.709601
16. Kocher, P.C.: Timing attacks on implementations of Diffie-Hellman, RSA, DSS, and other systems. In: Koblitz, N. (ed.) CRYPTO 1996. LNCS, vol. 1109, pp. 104–113. Springer, Heidelberg (1996). https://doi.org/10.1007/3-540-68697-5_9
17. Libbrecht, M.W., Noble, W.S.: Machine learning applications in genetics and genomics. Nat. Rev. Genet. **16**(6), 321–332 (2015). https://doi.org/10.1038/nrg3920
18. Lin, H.-Y., Tzeng, W.-G.: An efficient solution to the millionaires' problem based on homomorphic encryption. In: Ioannidis, J., Keromytis, A., Yung, M. (eds.) ACNS 2005. LNCS, vol. 3531, pp. 456–466. Springer, Heidelberg (2005). https://doi.org/10.1007/11496137_31
19. Lindell, Y. (ed.): Tutorials on the Foundations of Cryptography. Information Security and Cryptography. Springer, Cham (2017). https://doi.org/10.1007/978-3-319-57048-8
20. Lindell, Y., Pinkas, B.: Privacy preserving data mining. J. Cryptol. **15**(3), 177–206 (2002). https://doi.org/10.1007/s00145-001-0019-2
21. Liu, C., Wechsler, H.: Gabor feature based classification using the enhanced Fisher linear discriminant model for face recognition. IEEE Trans. Image Process. **11**(4), 467–476 (2002). https://doi.org/10.1109/TIP.2002.999679
22. Min, J.H., Lee, Y.C.: Bankruptcy prediction using support vector machine with optimal choice of kernel function parameters. Expert Syst. Appl. **28**(4), 603–614 (2005). https://doi.org/10.1016/j.eswa.2004.12.008
23. Mohassel, P., Zhang, Y.: SecureML: A system for scalable privacy-preserving machine learning. In: 2017 IEEE Symposium on Security and Privacy, pp. 19–38. IEEE (2017). https://doi.org/10.1109/SP.2017.12
24. Naor, M., Pinkas, B.: Efficient oblivious transfer protocols. In: 12th Annual ACM-SIAM Symposium on Discrete Algorithms (SODA 2001), pp. 448–457. ACM/SIAM (2001). https://dl.acm.org/citation.cfm?id=365411.365502
25. Nasrabadi, N.M.: Pattern recognition and machine learning. J. Electronic Imaging **16**(4), 049901 (2007). https://doi.org/10.1117/1.2819119
26. Nikolaenko, V., Ioannidis, S., Weinsberg, U., Joye, M., Taft, N., Boneh, D.: Privacy-preserving matrix factorization. In: 20th ACM Conference on Computer and Communications Security (CCS 2013), pp. 801–812. ACM (2013). https://doi.org/10.1145/2508859.2516751

27. Nikolaenko, V., Weinsberg, U., Ioannidis, S., Joye, M., Boneh, D., Taft, N.: Privacy-preserving ridge regression on hundreds of millions of records. In: 2013 IEEE Symposium on Security and Privacy, pp. 334–348. IEEE (2013). https://doi.org/10.1109/SP.2013.30

28. Rabin, M.O.: How to exchange secrets by oblivious transfer. Technical report TR-81. Harvard University (1981). https://ia.cr/2005/187

29. Resnick, P., Varian, H.R.: Recommender systems. Commun. ACM **40**(3), 56–58 (1997). https://doi.org/10.1145/245108.245121

30. Rivest, R.L., Adleman, L., Dertouzous, M.L.: On data banks and privacy homomorphisms. In: Foundations of Secure Computation, pp. 169–179. Academic Press (1978). https://people.csail.mit.edu/rivest/RivestAdlemanDertouzos-OnDataBanksAndPrivacyHomomorphisms.pdf

31. Tai, R.K.H., Ma, J.P.K., Zhao, Y., Chow, S.S.M.: Privacy-preserving decision trees evaluation via linear functions. In: Foley, S.N., Gollmann, D., Snekkenes, E. (eds.) ESORICS 2017. LNCS, vol. 10493, pp. 494–512. Springer, Cham (2017). https://doi.org/10.1007/978-3-319-66399-9_27

32. Vaidya, J., Yu, H., Jiang, X.: Privacy-preserving SVM classification. Knowl. Inf. Syst. **14**(2), 161–178 (2008). https://doi.org/10.1007/s10115-007-0073-7

33. Veugen, T.: Improving the DGK comparison protocol. In: 2012 IEEE International Workshop on Information Forensics and Security (WIFS 2012), pp. 49–54. IEEE (2012), https://doi.org/10.1109/WIFS.2012.6412624

34. Wu, D.J., Feng, T., Naehrig, M., Lauter, K.: Privately evaluating decision trees and random forests. Proc. Priv. Enhancing Technol. 2016(4), 335–355 (2016). https://doi.org/10.1515/popets-2016-0043

35. Yap, B.W., Ong, S.H., Husain, N.H.M.: Using data mining to improve assessment of credit worthiness via credit scoring models. Expert Syst. Appl. **38**(10), 13274–13283 (2011). https://doi.org/10.1016/j.eswa.2011.04.147

Fixing Vulnerabilities

Breaking and Fixing the Security Proof of Garbled Bloom Filters

Cédric Van Rompay[(⊠)] and Melek Önen

EURECOM, Biot, France
{vanrompa,onen}@eurecom.fr

Abstract. We identify a flaw in the proof of security of Garbled Bloom Filters, a recent hash structure introduced by Dong et al. (ACM CCS 2013) that is used to design Private Set Intersection (PSI) protocols, a important family of protocols for secure cloud computing. We give counter-examples invalidating a claim that is central to the original proof and we show that variants of the GBF construction have the same issue in their security analysis. We then give a new proof of security that shows that Garbled Bloom Filters are secure nonetheless.

Keywords: Garbled bloom filter · Private set intersection
Provable security

1 Introduction

Private Set Intersection (PSI) protocols is one of the most important family of protocol for secure computation that plays a central role in cloud computing (see Sect. 1 of [4]). Garbled Bloom Filters (GBF) are a recent hash structure introduced by Dong et al. in [4] (ACM CCS 2013) that are useful in the design of PSI protocols. The idea of GBF is to combine a Bloom Filter (BF) with XOR-based secret sharing to enable efficient test membership with regard to a set while hiding the presence of elements in this set that were not searched for. The construction of Dong et al. had quite a large impact in research as it was used [3,15–17], improved [11,12] and cited [5,7,9,10,14] numerous times already.

The proof of Dong et al. can be summarized the following way: In a first part they use a property of Bloom Filters to show that some event happens with negligible probability; then in a second part they assume the absence of the previously mentioned event and invoke the security of XOR-based secret sharing to conclude the proof. This invocation of the security of XOR-based secret sharing is done in a very immediate way, neglecting the fact that the functioning of GBF, however heavily inspired by the XOR-based secret sharing scheme, is not strictly speaking an instance of this scheme. The same remarks hold for a PSI protocol suggested by Pinkas et al. in [11], based on the original GBF construction by Dong et al., for which the proof of security is very short and follows a reasoning similar to the one of Dong et al.

© IFIP International Federation for Information Processing 2018
Published by Springer International Publishing AG, part of Springer Nature 2018. All Rights Reserved
F. Kerschbaum and S. Paraboschi (Eds.): DBSec 2018, LNCS 10980, pp. 263–277, 2018.
https://doi.org/10.1007/978-3-319-95729-6_17

In this paper we show that a simple invocation of the security of XOR-based secret sharing is in fact not sufficient to show that GBFs are secure. We do so by providing a counter-example, and further a larger class of counter-examples, that invalidate the claims made in both previously mentioned proofs.

We show however that GBFs do satisfy their claimed security properties by providing a new, more rigorous proof.

1.1 Organization of the Paper

In Sect. 2 we describe Bloom Filters, Garbled Bloom Filters as introduced by Dong et al. in [4], and the original proof of Dong et al. for the security of Garbled Bloom Filters. In Sect. 3 we give a counter example (and a class of counter-examples) that invalidates the proof of Dong et al. In Sect. 4 we describe the impact of our results on other GBF constructions that were inspired by the one of Dong et al. In Sect. 5 we give a new proof of security for the GBF construction of Dong et al. Finally in Sect. 6 we compare this work with related work.

2 Preliminaries

2.1 Notations

We make use of the following usual conventions: With X a set, we denote by $x \overset{\$}{\leftarrow} X$ the fact that x is sampled uniformly from X. With i a positive number, we denote by $[i]$ the sequence $(1, 2, \ldots, i)$. A function $\mu(\cdot)$ is *negligible* if for every positive polynomial $p(\cdot)$ and all sufficiently large n, it holds that $\mu(n) \leq 1/p(n)$. Throughout the paper, λ denotes the security parameter and two probability ensembles $\mathcal{X} = \{X_\lambda\}_{\lambda \in \mathbb{N}}$ and $\mathcal{Y} = \{Y_\lambda\}_{\lambda \in \mathbb{N}}$ are said to be *computationally indistinguishable* [6, Definition 7.30] denoted $\mathcal{X} \overset{c}{\equiv} \mathcal{Y}$, if for every probabilistic polynomial-time distinguisher D there exists a negligible function μ such that:

$$\left| Pr[D(1^\lambda, x) = 1; x \overset{\$}{\leftarrow} X_\lambda] - Pr[D(1^\lambda, y) = 1; y \overset{\$}{\leftarrow} Y_\lambda] \right| \leq \mu(\lambda)$$

2.2 Bloom Filters

Bloom Filters (BFs), introduced by Bloom in [1] and further studied by Broder and Mitzenmacher in [2], are a hash structure that aims at efficiently testing membership in a set. A BF is an array B of M bits associated with k random hash functions $h_1, \ldots, h_k : \{0, 1\}^* \to [M]$. B is initialized by setting all the array values to zero and one inserts an element $x \in S$ in B by setting $B[h_i(x)]$ to 1 for all i. Finally one checks the presences of x in the set S encoded by B by testing whether $B[h_i(x)]$ is equal to 1 for all $i \in [k]$; if it is not the case then x cannot be in S, otherwise x is in S with high probability. Following [12] we use the notation h_* to denote the set of all positions corresponding to an element x or a set S:

$$h_*(x) = \{h_i(x) \; \forall i \in [k]\}$$

$$h_*(S) = \bigcup_{x \in S} h_*(x)$$

We will denote by BF_S the Bloom Filter encoding set S when there is no ambiguity about what parameters M and $(h_i)_{i \in [k]}$ where used.

The event that x appears to be encoded in B while it is actually not in S is called a *false positive*. Dong et al. [4] show that the probability for $x \notin S$ to cause a false positive is negligible in the number of hash functions k. As a consequence, setting the number of hash function as greater or equal to the security parameter (which is what Dong et al. do) results in a false positive probability negligible in the security parameter.

Broder and Mitzenmacher in [2] show that the optimal value for k, that minimizes the false positive probability for a given M and set size N, is:

$$k = \ln(2)\frac{M}{N} . \tag{1}$$

They also show that with this value of k about half of the bits are set after insertion of all the elements in S.

2.3   Garbled Bloom Filters

Garbled Bloom Filters (GBFs) were introduced by Dong et al. in [4] (ACM CCS 2013). GBF is a variant of BF that has some security properties making it suitable for the design of Private Set Intersection (PSI) protocols (see [11] for a description of PSI and a review of most recent schemes, including the one of [4]).

Like a BF, a GBF is an array of length M associated with k random hash functions $h_1, \ldots, h_k : \{0,1\}^* \to [M]$. However the components of a GBF are not bits but bit strings of length λ. One inserts x in a GBF B by ensuring that $\bigoplus_i B[h_i(x)] = x$, and checks the presence of x in B by testing the same equality.

During insertion, each share is picked uniformly at random as in a XOR secret sharing scheme, except the shares that were already set by the insertion of a previous element that are left unchanged. Components that were never wrote during insertion of the whole set are filled with random values. Algorithm 1 gives a more formal description of how a GBF is built. As with "normal" Bloom Filters, we will denote by GBF_S a GBF encoding set S when there is no ambiguity as to the parameters used.

The security property of GBFs, which will be given formally in Sect. 2.5, can be informally described as follows:

Definition 1 (Security of GBF – informal). *Let S and C be two sets; Given only $\{GBF_S[i] \; \forall i \in h_*(C)\}$ one cannot get any information about $S - C$.*

2.4   Private Set Intersection Based on GBF

We give a quick overview of how GBFs are used in the design of Private Set Intersection (PSI) protocols with one-sided output. Informally, a PSI protocol

---

Algorithm 1: An algorithm for building a GBF representing set S with parameters $M, (h_i)_{i=1...k}, \lambda$

   Algorithm: GBF.Build

Input: $S, M, (h_i)_{i=1...k}, \lambda$
Output: B
Initialize B as an empty array of length M ;
for $x \in S$ **do**
    if $\exists j \in h_*(x)$: $(B[j]$ *is empty*$)$ **then**
        for $i \in h_*(x) - \{j\}$ **do**
            if $B[i]$ *is empty* **then**
                $B[i] \xleftarrow{\$} \{0,1\}^\lambda$;
        set $B[j] \leftarrow x \oplus \bigoplus_{i \in h_*(x)-\{j\}} B[i]$;
    else
        Abort. ;
Fill any remaining empty component with fresh random values ;

---

is a protocol between two parties, each having a set, who want to compute the intersection of their respective sets without revealing more information than this intersection. In the one-sided output setting only one party, called the *receiver*, learns the intersection, while the other party, called the *sender*, learns nothing.

In the PSI protocol of Dong et al. [4], the sender holds a set S and computes GBF_S while the receiver holds a set C and computes BF_C. Both parties use the same (G)BF parameters.

The two parties then run an Oblivious Transfer (OT) protocol, that is a protocol that allows a party (called *receiver* and that matches the receiver of the PSI protocol) to retrieve a record in a database held by another party (the *sender*, who again matches the sender of the PSI protocol) without revealing to the sender which record was retrieved by the receiver and without revealing to the receiver the other records in the database.

The OT protocol is used in the PSI protocol of [4] by the receiver in order to retrieve the components of GBF_S corresponding to the "ones" in BF_C. For any element in $S \cap C$, its corresponding components were retrieved so the receiver is able to assert its presence in $S \cap C$. At the same time, the security property of GBFs guarantee that the receiver got no information about any element of $S - C$. As for the sender, the privacy properties of the OT protocol suffice to prevent him from learning anything about the set C of the receiver.

2.5   Original Proof of Security by Dong et al. [4]

The security of GBF is expressed by Theorem 4 in [4] which we reformulate in an equivalent way in Theorem 1 of this paper. This theorem requires the definition of the intersection between a GBF and a BF sharing the same parameters (see Sect. 4.2 of [4]).

Definition 2 (Intersection between a GBF and a BF). *Let* $M, (h_i)_{i=1...k}$ *and* λ *be some GBF parameters. Let* S *and* C *be two sets, and let* GBF_S *and* BF_C *be built with parameters* $M, (h_i)_{i=1...k}$ *(and* λ *for the GBF). The intersection of* GBF_S *and* BF_C, *noted* $GBF_S \cap BF_C$, *is defined as:*

$$(GBF_S \cap BF_C)[i] \leftarrow \begin{cases} GBF_S[i] & \textit{if } BF_C[i] = 1 \\ a \textit{ random value} & \textit{otherwise} \end{cases}$$

Dong et al. show that $GBF_S \cap BF_C$ is a correct GBF encoding $S \cap C$. We also define the notion of "extraction" of a GBF with a BF, which is equivalent to the notion of intersection but will make our proof in Sect. 5 simpler. We will use the notion of intersection mostly in Sect. 3 in order to stay as close as possible to the notation of Dong et al., and in Sect. 5 we will mostly use the notion of extraction. With extraction, "non-selected" components are simply dropped, or equivalently set to a special "empty" value, instead of being replaced by a random value. It should be obvious that one obtains as much information from a uniform independent random value than from a fixed value.

Definition 3 (Extraction of a GBF with a BF). *Let* $M, (h_i)_{i=1...k}$ *and* λ *be some GBF parameters. Let* S *and* C *be two sets, and let* GBF_S *and* BF_C *be built with parameters* $M, (h_i)_{i=1...k}$ *(and* λ *for the GBF). The extraction of* GBF_S *using* BF_C, *noted* $\mathsf{Extract}(BF_C, GBF_S)$, *is defined as:*

$$\mathsf{Extract}(BF_C, GBF_S)[i] \leftarrow \begin{cases} GBF_S[i] & \textit{if } BF_C[i] = 1 \\ empty & \textit{otherwise} \end{cases}$$

We now give Theorem 4 of [4] in a slightly reformulated but equivalent form:

Theorem 1 (Security of GBF (Theorem 4 of [4])). *Let* λ *and* $N \in \mathbb{N}$ *and let* $k = \lambda$ *and* $M = Nk/\ln(2)$; *let* $(h_i)_{i \in [k]}$ *be a sequence of random oracles* $\{0,1\}^* \to [M]$. *we have*

$$(S, C, GBF_S \cap BF_C) \stackrel{c}{\equiv} (S, C, GBF_{S \cap C} \cap BF_C)$$

Where S *and* C *have at most* N *elements. Equivalently with our "extraction" notation:*

$$(S, C, \mathsf{Extract}(BF_C, GBF_S)) \stackrel{c}{\equiv} (S, C, \mathsf{Extract}(BF_C, GBF_{S \cap C}))$$

The proof Dong et al. give for Theorem 1 is reproduced below, with only minor modifications to make it match our notation. Namely, what is written $GBF_{C \cap S}$, $GBF'_{C \cap S}$ and $GBF''_{C \cap S}$ in the original text is written respectively $GBF_S \cap BF_C$, $GBF_{S \cap C}$ and $(GBF_S \cap BF_C) \cap BF_{S \cap C}$ in ours. We give a quick overview of their proof: In their "case 1", they show that the probability that some element of $S - C$ has all its positions in $h_*(C)$ is negligible; then in "case 2" they argue that if no element of $S - C$ has all its elements in $h_*(C)$, the distribution of $GBF_S \cap BF_C$ is then identical to the one of $GBF_{S \cap C}$. They invoke *"the security of the XOR-based secret sharing scheme"* to argue that an element of $S - C$ of which one of the shares was re-randomized during intersection cannot leave any trace in the resulting GBF (this is the argument we will go against in Sect. 3).

(Proof of Theorem 1 as it appears in [4])
Given $GBF_S \cap BF_C$, we modify it to get $(GBF_S \cap BF_C) \cap BF_{S \cap C}$. We scan $GBF_S \cap BF_C$ from the beginning to the end and for each location i, we modify $(GBF_S \cap BF_C)[i]$ using the following procedure:

- If $(GBF_S \cap BF_C)[i]$ is a share of an element in $C \cap S$, then do nothing.
- Else if $(GBF_S \cap BF_C)[i]$ is a random string, do nothing.
- Else if $(GBF_S \cap BF_C)[i]$ is a share of an element in $S - C \cap S$, replace it with a uniformly random λ-bit string.

The result is $(GBF_S \cap BF_C) \cap BF_{S \cap C}$. Every $(GBF_S \cap BF_C)[i]$ must fall into one of these three cases, so there is no unhandled case.

Now we argue that the distribution of $(GBF_S \cap BF_C) \cap BF_{S \cap C}$ is identical to $GBF_{S \cap C}$. To see that, let's compare each location in $(GBF_S \cap BF_C) \cap BF_{S \cap C}$ and $GBF_{S \cap C}$. From Algorithm 1 and the above procedure, we can see that $(GBF_S \cap BF_C) \cap BF_{S \cap C}$ and $GBF_{S \cap C}$ contain only shares of elements in $S \cap C$ and random strings. Because $(GBF_S \cap BF_C) \cap BF_{S \cap C}$ and $GBF_{S \cap C}$ use the same set of hash functions, for each $0 \le i \le m - 1$, $((GBF_S \cap BF_C) \cap BF_{S \cap C})[i]$ is a share of an element in $C \cap S$ iff $GBF_{S \cap C}$ is a random string. The distribution of a share depends only on the element and the random strings are uniformly distributed. So the distribution of every location in $(GBF_S \cap BF_C) \cap BF_{S \cap C}$ and $GBF_{S \cap C}$ are identical therefore the distributions of $(GBF_S \cap BF_C) \cap BF_{S \cap C}$ and $GBF_{S \cap C}$ are identical.

Then we argue that the distribution of $(GBF_S \cap BF_C) \cap BF_{S \cap C}$ is identical to $GBF_S \cap BF_C$ except for a negligible probability η.

Case 1: $GBF_S \cap BF_C$ encodes at least one elements in $S - C \cap S$. In this case the distribution of $(GBF_S \cap BF_C) \cap BF_{S \cap C}$ differs from the distribution of $GBF_S \cap BF_C$. From Theorem 3, the probability of each element in $S - C \cap S$ being encoded in $GBF_S \cap BF_C$ is ϵ. Since there are $d = |S| - |C \cap S|$ elements in $S - C \cap S$, the probability of at least one element is falsely contained in $GBF_S \cap BF_C$ is:

$$\eta = [\text{skipped...}] \le 2d\epsilon$$

As we can see η is negligible if ϵ is negligible.

Case 2: $GBF_S \cap BF_C$ encodes only elements from $C \cap S$. In this case, each element of $S - C \cap S$ may leave up to $k - 1$ shares in $GBF_S \cap BF_C$. The only difference between $GBF_S \cap BF_C$ and $(GBF_S \cap BF_C) \cap BF_{S \cap C}$ is that in $(GBF_S \cap BF_C) \cap BF_{S \cap C}$, all "residues" shares of elements in $S - C \cap S$ are replaced by random strings. From the security of the XOR-based secret sharing scheme, the residue shares should be uniformly random (otherwise they leak information about the elements). Thus the procedure does not change the distribution when modifying $GBF_S \cap BF_C$ into $(GBF_S \cap BF_C) \cap BF_{S \cap C}$. So the distributions of $GBF_S \cap BF_C$ and $(GBF_S \cap BF_C) \cap BF_{S \cap C}$ are identical. The probability of this case is at least $1 - \eta$.

Since $(GBF_S \cap BF_C) \cap BF_{S \cap C} \equiv GBF_{S \cap C}$ always holds and $GBF_S \cap BF_C \equiv (GBF_S \cap BF_C) \cap BF_{S \cap C}$ in case 2, we can conclude that $Pr[GBF_S \cap BF_C \equiv GBF_{S \cap C}] \geq 1 - \eta$ thus $|Pr[D(GBF_S \cap BF_C) = 1] - Pr[D(GBF_{S \cap C}) = 1]| \leq \eta$. $\square$

3 Invalidation of the Proof in [4]

The end of the proof contains the following assertion: "$(GBF_S \cap BF_C) \cap BF_{S \cap C} \equiv GBF_{S \cap C}$ *always holds and* $GBF_S \cap BF_C \equiv (GBF_S \cap BF_C) \cap BF_{S \cap C}$ *holds in case 2*". This should result in $GBF_{S \cap C} \equiv GBF_S \cap BF_C$ in case 2. We invalidate this claim by giving a counter-example. Let the number of hash functions be $k = 3$; let x and y be two elements of $S - C$ such that $h_1(x) = h_1(y)$ and that for all $i \neq 1$, $h_i(x) \in h_*(C)$ and $h_i(y) \in h_*(C)$. This example is illustrated in Fig. 1. Note that this example can be situated in the case 2 of the proof of [4] as it does not require any element of S to have all its positions in $h_*(C)$.

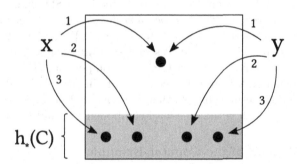

Fig. 1. Illustration of our counter-example.

We have that GBF_S must satisfy the following equations where we note $GBF_S[h_i(x)]$ as x_i (and similarly with y):

$$x_1 \oplus x_2 \oplus x_3 = x \tag{2}$$
$$y_1 \oplus y_2 \oplus y_3 = y \tag{3}$$
$$x_1 = y_1 \tag{4}$$

Combining (2), (3) and (4) gives:

$$x \oplus y = x_1 \oplus x_2 \oplus x_3 \oplus y_1 \oplus y_2 \oplus y_3$$
$$x \oplus y = x_2 \oplus x_3 \oplus y_2 \oplus y_3$$

If we re-write the latter equation without our short-hand notation, we have that GBF_S satisfies the following:

$$x \oplus y$$
$$= GBF_S[h_2(x)] \oplus GBF_S[h_3(x)] \oplus GBF_S[h_2(y)] \oplus GBF_S[h_3(y)] \quad (5)$$

Regarding $GBF_S \cap BF_C$, it does not satisfy equations (2) and (3) anymore because the component $GBF_S[h_1(x)]$ was replaced by a fresh random value during the intersection operation; but it still satisfies equation (5) as it only involves components that were not re-randomized during intersection, thanks to the fact that $h_2(x), h_3(x), h_2(y)$ and $h_3(y)$ are in $h_*(C)$.

On the other hand $GBF_{S\cap C}$, which was built without the knowledge of x and y, does not satisfy (5) (except with a very small probability). As a result a GBF where relation (5) *does not* hold is a valid outcome for the distribution of $GBF_{S\cap C}$ but not for the distribution of $GBF_{S\cap BF_C}$. Those distributions cannot be identical, and the proof given in [4] of Theorem 1 is wrong. The same counter-example can also be used to invalidate the claims that "$GBF''_{C\cap S} \equiv GBF'_{C\cap S}$" and that "$GBF_{C\cap S} \equiv GBF''_{C\cap S}$".

This is not just a typo in [4], but truly a flaw in the proof. Recall, the proof uses the fact that any $x \in S - C$ has, with overwhelming probability, one of its positions, say $h_1(x)$, out of $h_*(C)$. As a result this component is overwritten during intersection (or never retrieved in a PSI scenario). Dong et al. then invoke "the security of the XOR-based secret sharing scheme" to argue that no information can be obtained about $x_1 \oplus x_2 \oplus x_3$. But the GBF construction is not the exact same thing as a XOR secret sharing scheme, and the argument does not hold. More precisely, in a GBF the component $GBF_S[h_1(x)]$ (or x_1) may not be independent from other components in the GBF and in particular its value can be tied to the value of other components that may be in $h_*(C)$ and are thus "visible", which is the case with components y_2 and y_3 in our example.

3.1   Generalization of the Counter-Example

We give a larger class of situations where the same claims prove wrong. Let $P(S, C)$ (or just P if there is no ambiguity about the inputs) be the set of positions that appear an odd number of times in $(h_*(x) \; \forall x \in S - C)$:

$$P(S, C) = \{p \in h_*(S - C) \; : \; |\{(x, i) \in (S - C) \times [k] \; : \; h_i(x) = p\}| \bmod 2 = 1\}$$

Then GBF_S satisfies the following relation, of which (5) is a special case, and which is obtained the same way as (5) was obtained:

$$\bigoplus_{S\cap C} x = \bigoplus_{p \in P} GBF_S[p] \quad (6)$$

If moreover $P \subset h_*(C)$, none of the concerned components are re-randomized during intersection so $GBF_S \cap BF_C$ satisfies the same relation, that is:

$$\bigoplus_{S\cap C} x = \bigoplus_{p \in P} (GBF_S \cap BF_C)[p] \quad (7)$$

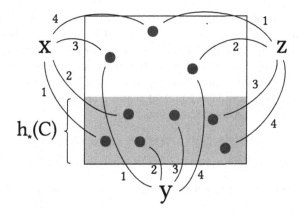

Fig. 2. An example of a more general counter-example involving 3 elements of $S - C$.

Figure 2 illustrates such a more general case with 4 hash functions and involving 3 elements x, y and z where $GBF_S \cap BF_C$ would satisfy the following relation (but $GBF_{S \cap C}$ would not):

$$x \oplus y \oplus z = x_1 \oplus x_2 \oplus y_2 \oplus y_3 \oplus z_3 \oplus z_4$$

4   Other GBF Constructions

We describe the consequences of our findings on the other GBF constructions that were inspired by the one of Dong et al., namely the ones of Pinkas et al. [11, Sect. 4.3] (USENIX Security 2014), and Rindal and Rosulek [12] (EUROCRYPT 2017).

4.1   Pinkas et al. [11]: Same Situation as Dong et al. [4]

The construction of Pinkas et al. presents many optimizations over the one of Dong et al., for instance through the use of *random OT* instead of "classical" OT, but it also has a more essential difference with the construction of Dong et al. in that the sum of the components associated to an element need not be equal to the element itself. Instead, all component values are all chosen uniformly at random and the sender sends for each element in her set a "summary value" that is the sum of the components corresponding to this element, that is:

$$\{\bigoplus_i GBF_S[h_i(s)] \quad \forall s \in S\}$$

The receiver retrieves the components corresponding to her own elements via OT and compute similar sums for these elements. Finally, the receiver compares the sums she computed with the sums she received to learn which elements are in both sets.

The reasoning used by Pinkas et al. to show the security of this construction is similar to the reasoning of Dong et al., namely, that unless there is a $s \in S$ such that $h_*(s) \subset h_*(C)$ then the view of the receiver is not just computationally indistinguishable from a simulated view, but truly independent from $S - C$.

Unfortunately the same problem appears as with the proof of Dong et al. Take for instance the example of Fig. 1: if x and y are in the sender's set S, then the receiver must have received these two values:

$$K_x = GBF_S[h_1(x)] \oplus GBF_S[h_2(x)] \oplus GBF_S[h_3(x)]$$
$$K_y = GBF_S[h_1(y)] \oplus GBF_S[h_2(y)] \oplus GBF_S[h_3(y)]$$

and because $h_1(x) = h_1(y)$ the XOR of these two received values is equal to:

$$\begin{aligned} &K_x \oplus K_y \\ &= GBF_S[h_2(x)] \oplus GBF_S[h_3(x)] \oplus GBF_S[h_2(y)] \oplus GBF_S[h_3(y)] \end{aligned} \tag{8}$$

Which only depends on values the receiver knows. The receiver is then able to detect the presence of x and y in $S - C$ by testing whether any two summary values have their sum equal to (8).

Again, and as with the GBF construction of Dong et al. [4], the construction of Pinkas et al. is actually secure since our new proof given in Sect. 5 should also apply. This means that such S and C are actually very hard to find. Nevertheless this shows that the security of the GBF construction of [11] cannot be proven simply by invoking the low probability to have $h_*(s) \subset h_*(C)$ for some $s \in S$.

4.2   Rindal and Rosulek [12]: No Apparent Issues

Rindal and Rosulek [12] present a new PSI protocol following the idea of the GBF-based PSI protocol of Pinkas et al. [11, Sect. 4.3] we presented in the previous section. They keep most of the ideas of Pinkas et al., including the use of random OT and the optimizations it enables, as well as the idea of having the sender sending summary values. However they build these summary values in a different way, which is essentially:

$$K_x = H \left(x \mid\mid \bigoplus_{i \in h_*(x)} GBF_S[i] \right)$$

where H is a secure hash function and $\mid\mid$ denotes concatenation.

Interestingly, the presence of the hash function breaks the algebraic properties of the summary values that were used in the previous section, meaning that all the counter-examples we gave so far do not apply on the construction of Rindal and Rosulek. This construction may thus be secure even against someone knowing a subset $X \subset S - C$ such that $P(X, C) \subset h_*(C)$. But more importantly, the security proof Rindal and Rosulek give for their construction [12, Sect. 5.3] differs a lot from the proofs of Dong et al. [4] and of Pinkas et al. [11], and we did not find in the paper of Rindal and Rosulek the issue we identified in [4,11].

Note however that the construction of Rindal and Rosulek and of Pinkas et al. cannot always be used as a drop-in replacement of the original construction of Dong et al. One example is a Searchable Encryption protocol [13] that uses Garbled Bloom Filters but where the receiver looks up several GBFs and must be unable to know what response (in the form of components retrieved) comes from what filter. This requires that the receiver must be able to decide on the result of a lookup ("present" or "absent") using only the components retrieved and without remembering what was the component that was being looked for. The authors modify the GBF construction of Dong et al. by having the components corresponding to an element having their sum equal to a fixed value instead of the value of the element itself:

$$\bigoplus_{i \in h_*(C)} GBF_S[i] = 0$$

Such a property could not be reached in a trivial way using the construction of Rindal and Rosulek (or even the one of Pinkas et al.) because the sending of summary values by the sender requires that the receiver knows what to compare these values with, which requires that the receiver knows what GBF the values correspond to. This shows why the study of the security proof of constructions other than the one of Rindal and Rosulek is still relevant.

5 New Proof of Security

5.1 New Case Distinction

Our proof follows the idea of the proof of Dong et al. [4]: we consider two cases, one that occurs with negligible probability and one in which the two distributions are actually identical, and this results in the two distributions being indistinguishable. What differs between our proof and the one of [4] is the case separation: as we saw, the assumption of case 2 of [4] that no element in $S - C$ has all its positions in $h_*(C)$ does not suffice to have $GBF_S \cap BF_C \equiv GBF_{S \cap C}$.

Instead, we make the following remark: it is very unlikely that there is some subset X of $S - C$ such that all the positions in $h_*(X)$ being mapped by a single element in X happens to be in $h_*(C)$. Said differently, for any subset $X \subset S - C$ there is at least one position in $h_*(X)$ that is both out of $h_*(C)$ and corresponds to a single element of X. Note that this covers the situation described in Sect. 3.1 (an thus our counter-examples in Figs. 1 and 2 too): if all the position in $h_*(S - C)$ mapped an odd number of times are in $h_*(C)$, then all the positions out of $h_*(C)$ are mapped at least 2 times. Formally we define the *mapped-once positions of X* , noted $m(X)$, and the *never-mapped positions of X* , noted $n(X)$, as follows:

Definition 4 (Mapped-once and never-mapped positions of a set). *Let* $X \subset \{0,1\}^*$; *the set of mapped-once positions of X is defined as:*

$$m(X) := \{p \in h_*(X) \ : \ \exists!(x,i) \in X \times [k] \ : \ h_i(x) = p\}$$

Similarly, the set of never-mapped positions of X is defined as:

$$\boldsymbol{n}(X) := \{p \in h_*(X) \ : \ \nexists (x,i) \in X \times [k] \ : \ h_i(x) = p\}$$

The never-mapped positions of X correspond to the zeroes in BF_X.

We then have the following:

Theorem 2. *Let $X \subset S - C$, then:*

$$P[\boldsymbol{m}(X) \subset h_*(C)] \leq negl(\lambda) \tag{9}$$

Proof: We explain why Equation (9) holds. Our explanation is in two parts: First we argue that the size of $\boldsymbol{m}(X)$ must be of size larger than k; from then the probability that all these positions are in $h_*(C)$ is lesser than the probability for one element to have all its positions in $h_*(C)$, which is already negligible (proved by Dong et al. in their "case 1"). We start by showing that $|\boldsymbol{m}(X)| \geq k$ with overwhelming probability. Consider the sequence of sets $X_1, X_2, \ldots, X$ where each set has one more element than the previous one. The number of mapped-once positions of $X_i = X_{i-1} \cup \{x\}$ for some i and some x is then the number of mapped-once positions of X_{i-1} plus the positions of x that are in $\boldsymbol{n}(X_{i-1})$ (some new mapped-once positions), minus the positions of x that are in $\boldsymbol{m}(X_{i-1})$ (positions that are not mapped-once anymore). Statistically, we thus have the following expected difference:

$$E[|\boldsymbol{m}(X_i)| - |\boldsymbol{m}(X_{i-1})|] = k\frac{\boldsymbol{n}(X_{i-1})}{M} - k\frac{\boldsymbol{m}(X_{i-1})}{M} \tag{10}$$

That is:

$$\boldsymbol{m}(X_1) = k$$
$$E[\boldsymbol{m}(X_2)] = \boldsymbol{m}(X_1) + k\frac{M-k}{M} - k\frac{k}{M}$$
$$= 2k\left(1 - \frac{k}{M}\right)$$

$$\ldots$$

Now because $|X| \leq |S - C| \leq |S| \leq N$, and due to the way GBF parameters are created (see Sect. 2.2) BF_X and *a fortiori* BF_{X_i} should have not less than half of its bits unset, so $\boldsymbol{n}(X_i) \geq M/2$ and $k\frac{\boldsymbol{n}(X_{i-1})}{M} \geq k/2$. At the same time $\boldsymbol{m}(X_{i-1})$ is always very small compared to M. It should then obvious that $|\boldsymbol{m}(X)| \geq k$. Finally as we already explained, the probability for $\boldsymbol{m}(X)$ to be a subset of $h_*(C)$ is negligible because it is less than the probability for a single element to have all its positions in $h_*(C)$, given that we already show it has a size greater than k. $\qquad \square$

5.2 New Proof of Security

We give a new proof of Theorem 1, that is, we show that:

$$(S, C, \mathsf{Extract}(BF_C, GBF_S)) \overset{c}{\equiv} (S, C, \mathsf{Extract}(BF_C, GBF_{S \cap C}))$$

We consider two cases as it is done by Dong et al. [4]: The first case is where there is a $X \subset S - C$ such that $m(X) \subset h_*(C)$. From Theorem 2, This case happens with negligible probability. The second case is thus where there is no such X, and we show that in this case the distributions are identical by showing that any outcome of one distribution is a valid outcome of the other. Let B be an outcome of the right-hand distribution, that is, the one with $GBF_{S \cap C}$; we show how to build a GBF B' that is a valid outcome of GBF_S such that $Extract(BF_C, B') = B$. We build B' the following way: We start from B which, recall, is a Garbled Bloom Filter with all its components not in domain of C being empty. We will insert each element of $S - C$ in B, keeping components that were already set untouched. Insertion happens just as in the GBF.Build algorithm. When all elements have been inserted, the remaining components are filled with random values, just as in the end of GBF.Build. If the algorithm did not halt, the resulting B' encodes every element of $S \cap C$ (from the initial values from B) and every element of $S - C$ (that we just inserted). As a result, B' is a valid GBF_S and $Extract(BF_C, B')$ is a valid outcome for $Extract(BF_C, GBF_S)$.

We now show that the algorithm does not halt. Recall, the building algorithm halts when an element that must be inserted only maps to positions that are not empty. Since we are in the case where no $X \subset S - C$ satisfies $m(X) \subset h_*(C)$, there must be a position in $h_*(S - C)$ that is not in $h_*(C)$ and which is mapped by a single element $y \in S - C$. As a result if $(S - C) - \{y\}$ was inserted without halting, then the final y can be inserted without halting as well. This reasoning can be repeated to show that $(S - C) - \{y\}$ can be inserted without halting as well, and recursively $S - C$ can be inserted entirely without halting.

Finally given an outcome B of $Extract(BF_C, GBF_S)$ one can trivially build a valid GBF B' encoding $S \cap C$ such that $Extract(BF_C, B') = B$: it suffices to fill all empty components of B with random values. As a result we have $Extract(BF_C, GBF_S) \equiv Extract(BF_C, GBF_{S \cap C})$ in our second case, and this ends the proof of Theorem 1.   □

Note that this proof would also apply to the construction of Pinkas et al. [11].

6 Related Work

Security issues in the paper of Dong et al. [4] where identified by Rindal and Rosulek [12] and by Lambæk [8], but none of these issues apply on the protocol that we study in this paper. Indeed, [4] describes two protocol: one that aims at providing security against honest-but-curious adversaries, which is the one that is being studied in this paper, and one that aims at providing security against malicious adversaries. The issues identified in [8,12] only concern the malicious-security protocol, and do not apply to the honest-but-curious-security protocol (both present the honest-but-curious-security protocol as satisfying its claimed properties).

By contrast, the issues we identify concern the security of the GBF construction. This property is invoked in the security proofs for both the honest-but-curious-security protocol and the malicious-security one, so the two protocols are affected. The issue we identify is thus different, and more general, than the ones identified in [8,12].

7   Conclusion

Garbled Bloom Filters are a hash structure which, however still recent, already had a significant impact on the design of secure protocols. We showed that the security analysis of Garbled Bloom Filter contains a subtle difficulty as the intuition that GBF security derives almost immediately from the security of XOR-based secret sharing is actually false. Nevertheless we show that all existing GBF constructions actually satisfy their claimed security property by providing a new, more rigorous proof. This should strengthen the confidence we can have in the GBF construction and promote a large use of it in the domain of secure protocol design.

Acknowledgements. We would like to thank the anonymous reviewers for valuable comments. This work was supported by the EU FP7 ERANET program under grant CHIST-ERA-2016 UPRISE-IOT.

References

1. Bloom, B.H.: Space/time trade-offs in hash coding with allowable errors. Commun. ACM **13**(7), 422–426 (1970). http://doi.acm.org/10.1145/362686.362692
2. Broder, A.Z., Mitzenmacher, M.: Survey: network applications of bloom filters: a survey. Internet Math. **1**(4), 485–509 (2003). https://doi.org/10.1080/15427951.2004.10129096
3. Dong, C., Chen, L.: A fast secure dot product protocol with application to privacy preserving association rule mining. In: Tseng, V.S., Ho, T.B., Zhou, Z.-H., Chen, A.L.P., Kao, H.-Y. (eds.) PAKDD 2014. LNCS (LNAI), vol. 8443, pp. 606–617. Springer, Cham (2014). https://doi.org/10.1007/978-3-319-06608-0_50
4. Dong, C., Chen, L., Wen, Z.: When private set intersection meets big data: an efficient and scalable protocol. In: 2013 ACM SIGSAC Conference on Computer and Communications Security, CCS 2013, Berlin, Germany, pp. 789–800, 4–8 November 2013. https://doi.org/10.1145/2508859.2516701
5. Ghosh, E., Ohrimenko, O., Papadopoulos, D., Tamassia, R., Triandopoulos, N.: Zero-knowledge accumulators and set algebra. In: Cheon, J.H., Takagi, T. (eds.) ASIACRYPT 2016. LNCS, vol. 10032, pp. 67–100. Springer, Heidelberg (2016). https://doi.org/10.1007/978-3-662-53890-6_3
6. Katz, J., Lindell, Y.: Introduction to Modern Cryptography, 2nd edn. CRC Press, Boca Raton (2014)

7. Kiss, A., Liu, J., Schneider, T., Asokan, N., Pinkas, B.: Private set intersection for unequal set sizes with mobile applications. In: IACR Cryptology ePrint Archive 2017, p. 670 (2017). http://eprint.iacr.org/2017/670

8. Lambaek, M.: Breaking and fixing private set intersection protocols. In: IACR Cryptology ePrint Archive 2016, p. 665 (2016). http://eprint.iacr.org/2016/665

9. Lentz, M., Erdélyi, V., Aditya, P., Shi, E., Druschel, P., Bhattacharjee, B.: SDDR: light-weight, secure mobile encounters. In: Proceedings of the 23rd USENIX Security Symposium, San Diego, CA, USA, pp. 925–940, 20–22 August 2014. https://www.usenix.org/conference/usenixsecurity14/technical-sessions/presentation/lentz

10. Patsakis, C., Zigomitros, A., Solanas, A.: Privacy-aware genome mining: server-assisted protocols for private set intersection and pattern matching. In: Proceedings of 28th IEEE International Symposium on Computer-Based Medical Systems, CBMS 2015, Sao Carlos, Brazil, pp. 276–279, 22–25 June 2015. https://doi.org/10.1109/CBMS.2015.70

11. Pinkas, B., Schneider, T., Zohner, M.: Faster private set intersection based on OT extension. In: Proceedings of the 23rd USENIX Security Symposium, San Diego, CA, USA, pp. 797–812, 20–22 August 2014. https://www.usenix.org/conference/usenixsecurity14/technical-sessions/presentation/pinkas

12. Rindal, P., Rosulek, M.: Improved private set intersection against malicious adversaries. In: Coron, J.-S., Nielsen, J.B. (eds.) EUROCRYPT 2017. LNCS, vol. 10210, pp. 235–259. Springer, Cham (2017). https://doi.org/10.1007/978-3-319-56620-7_9

13. Rompay, C.V., Molva, R., Önen, M.: Secure and scalable multi-user searchable encryption (2018)

14. Wang, X.S., Huang, Y., Zhao, Y., Tang, H., Wang, X., Bu, D.: Efficient genome-wide, privacy-preserving similar patient query based on private edit distance. In: Proceedings of the 22nd ACM SIGSAC Conference on Computer and Communications Security, Denver, CO, USA, pp. 492–503, 6–12 October 2015. http://doi.acm.org/10.1145/2810103.2813725

15. Wen, Z., Dong, C.: Efficient protocols for private record linkage. In: Symposium on Applied Computing, SAC 2014, Gyeongju, Republic of Korea, pp. 1688–1694, 24–28 March 2014. http://doi.acm.org/10.1145/2554850.2555001

16. Zhao, Y., Chow, S.S.M.: Are you the one to share? secret transfer with access structure. PoPETs 2017(1), 149–169 (2017). https://doi.org/10.1515/popets-2017-0010

17. Zheng, Q., Xu, S.: Verifiable delegated set intersection operations on outsourced encrypted data. In: Proceedings of 2015 IEEE International Conference on Cloud Engineering, IC2E 2015, Tempe, AZ, USA, pp. 175–184, 9–13 March 2015. https://doi.org/10.1109/IC2E.2015.38

USBlock: Blocking USB-Based Keypress Injection Attacks

Sebastian Neuner[1]([envelope]), Artemios G. Voyiatzis[1], Spiros Fotopoulos[2], Collin Mulliner[3], and Edgar R. Weippl[1]

[1] SBA Research, Vienna, Austria
{sneuner,avoyiatzis,eweippl}@sba-research.org
[2] University of Patras, Patras, Greece
spiros@physics.upatras.gr
[3] mulliner.org, New York, USA
collin@mulliner.org

Abstract. The Universal Serial Bus (USB) is becoming a prevalent attack vector. *Rubber Ducky* and *BadUSB* are two recent classes of a whole spectrum of attacks carried out using fully-automated keypress injections through innocent-looking USB devices. So far, defense mechanisms are insufficient and rely on user participation in the trust decision.

We propose USBlock, a novel approach to detect suspicious USB devices by analyzing the *temporal* characteristics of the USB packet traffic they generate, similarly to intrusion detection approaches in networked systems.

Our approach is unique in that it does not to involve at all the user in the trust decision. We describe a proof-of-concept implementation for Linux and we assess the effectiveness and efficiency of our approach to cope with temporal variations in typing habits and dynamics of legitimate users.

Keywords: Security · USB · BadUSB · Linux kernel · System security

1 Introduction

The Universal Serial Bus (USB) is by far the most widely-used connector for modern computer systems. It is used to connect a plethora of peripheral devices to computers, including keyboards, mice, cameras, printers, and storage media. Many different attack vectors abuse the pervasiveness of USB, as for example dropping USB thumb drives on parking lots for users to pick up and attach on their computers [19]. As network-based defenses steadily improve and can block efficiently the malicious network traffic reaching an organization, USB becomes an attractive entry point for penetrating an organization.

© IFIP International Federation for Information Processing 2018
Published by Springer International Publishing AG, part of Springer Nature 2018. All Rights Reserved
F. Kerschbaum and S. Paraboschi (Eds.): DBSec 2018, LNCS 10980, pp. 278–295, 2018.
https://doi.org/10.1007/978-3-319-95729-6_18

Under the hood, USB is more than a simple connector. It is a complex *communication protocol*, often implemented and offered as a firmware. Lately, there are devices on the market with the ability to update their USB firmware. This capability has been exploited as a subtle attack vector, hiding malicious functionality on an abstraction layer that modern computer antivirus cannot cope with. BadUSB[1] and Rubber Ducky[2] classes of attacks are successful demonstrations of the attack feasibility. The associated threat is rather high: at this level the device interfaces directly with device drivers that run in the most privileged level of modern consumer-grade operating systems (e.g., as ring-0 modules of the Linux kernel).

In this paper, we provide insights on how these USB-protocol-level attacks work and explore how their attack patterns can be detected at the system level. Such an approach relieves the end user from being involved in trust decisions and thus, makes the security of the system less dependent to user actions. Specifically, we make the following contributions:

– We study the behavioral characteristics of Rubber Ducky and BadUSB classes of attacks.
– We devise criteria for automating their detection.
– We design, implement, and evaluate a simple yet *very effective and extensible* system-level countermeasure based on USB packet traffic analysis to detect and defend against such attacks *without* requiring user intervention.

The rest of the paper is structured as follows: Sect. 2 provides the necessary background information for the USB protocol and related attacks and defenses. Section 3 studies the temporal characteristics of USB-based attacks and proposes a system-level defense mechanism. Section 4 describes a prototype implementation of our proposal and evaluates its efficiency in real-world settings. Finally, Sect. 5 presents our conclusions and discusses future directions of work.

2   Background

2.1   The USB Protocol

USB is the most widely-used computer peripheral connector today. USB 3.2 is its latest revision. The USB device communication is based on a tiered-star topology with one dedicated master controller. Besides the controller, a hub manages the connected USB devices. If the master controller acts as a hub too, then the hub is called the "root hub". Every USB hub uses seven bits to address connected USB devices. This leads to a limit of 127 attachable USB devices per hub.

The connection of a USB device to a hub works as follows[3]: The USB hub waits for new devices to be plugged in. Upon connection, channels for communication are created: the so-called "endpoints", acting as sources and sinks of data.

---

[1] https://srlabs.de/badusb/.

[2] https://github.com/hak5darren/USB-Rubber-Ducky.

[3] http://www.beyondlogic.org/usbnutshell/usb3.shtml.

The endpoints are logically grouped together to "interfaces" and are announced to the host via "interface descriptors".

The USB communication is realized by exchanging "USB packets" over the shared serial bus. The USB protocol defines four transfer types (Control, Isochronous, Interrupt, and Bulk) and three packet types (Token, Data, and Status).

Modern operating systems, including Microsoft Windows, Linux, and Apple Mac OS, utilize the information collected by the hub from the connected USB devices to (dynamically) load the appropriate device drivers. For each announced interface descriptor of a device, the operating system combines the device-provided device class, interface class, and vendor and product identifiers (VID and PID respectively) to decide which capabilities are provided by the device and to bind the appropriate device driver(s).

As an example, a modern USB mouse may offer the capabilities of a human interface device (HID) and those of a display (e.g., to display its sensitivity level). Or a USB headset may offer the capabilities of an audio output device and that of a constrained HID for its volume up/down and mute buttons. In such cases, the devices will have two different interfaces and each of them will get a different driver bound to it.

2.2   USB Protocol Security

The USB protocol does not dictate a form of device authentication. Rather, every USB hub *blindly trusts* any information announced by the connected device about their capabilities. We note that modern USB devices incorporate, for legitimate reasons, multiple functionalities (e.g., a mouse announcing itself also as a display device). Such functionalities are hard for a user to link together and reason for any associated risk. These combined with the wide prevalence of USB devices, render USB an attractive attack vector [1,21].

In the past, the entry barrier for realizing attacks based on the inherent weaknesses of the USB protocol was very high. It dropped significantly by the time USB firmware chips with reflashing capabilities became available on the open market[4]. On the one hand, firmware updates for consumer products are often a necessity due to shortened time-to-market and insufficient testing. The alternative would be a product recall which would cause a logistics nightmare. On the other hand, firmware updates significantly lower the resources and expertise for launching USB-based attacks.

Figure 1 depicts the principle of a USB device and endpoint setups, which occur during the Control transfer phase using Setup packets. In this example, the device announces support for two functionalities, namely a mass storage and a keyboard (HID device). The former seems like a normal behavior, assuming that the user plugged in a USB thumb drive or external disk. In this case, the user expects that the operating system (host) will load the mass storage device driver and be able to further interact with the storage device. However, we note

---

[4] https://adamcaudill.com/2014/10/02/making-badusb-work-for-you-derbycon/.

that without having knowledge of the device specifics, this announcement could also have been an attack vector.

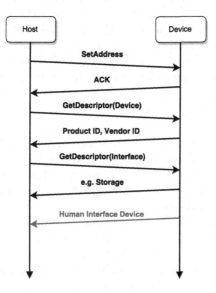

Fig. 1. USB packet sequence diagram (malicious behavior)

The latter announcement forces the host to bind a keyboard driver as well. If the announcement comes from a modified, malicious firmware, then the first step of the attack is already successful. The firmware then launches the second step of its attack. This involves sending keypresses from the (non-existent) keyboard. This "USB-based keypress injection attack" assumes that the system interaction caused by these keypresses will go unnoticed by the user and, thus, will succeed to deliver the malicious actions (e.g., download from the Internet or access from the USB storage and then execute a zero-day malware).

So far, various attacks exploiting the inherent weaknesses of the USB protocol have been proposed [13]. We review the most characteristic of them in the following paragraphs.

2.3   BadUSB and IRON-HID

The BadUSB attack enables a USB storage device to act not only as a SCSI device (mass storage), but also as an HID one. By acting as a keyboard, the data coming from the connected USB device is interpreted as keypresses. An attack can install a backdoor to the host system or "call home" over the network for example. From that point on, the attacker has total control over the infected host system.

Researchers and practitioners work both on improving BadUSB-like attacks and reducing their attack surfaces. In the so-called "IRON-HID" attack, additional programmable hardware (e.g., a Teensy board[5]) is hidden in places like keyboards and portable USB batteries [7]. By connecting a smartphone to the crafted USB battery via a crafted USB On-The-Go cable, the smartphone is switched into USB host mode. From that moment on, the smartphone is able to eavesdrop on all USB communications. IRON-HID can be used also to inject fake keypresses with the aim to brute-force the Android screen unlock PIN.

2.4 Rubber Ducky

The *Rubber Ducky* is a physical device designed by the Hak5 group[6]. The Rubber Ducky works as a normal keyboard when it comes to driver binding: it simply needs the operating system's HID driver to work. However, the Rubber Ducky delivers USB-based payloads (keypresses pre-defined by an attacker) upon being connected to the victim system.

The pre-defined keypresses are written in Ducky Script, a simple-to-use scripting language[7]. Once the payload is developed, it is compiled into a binary and placed on the microSD card of the Rubber Ducky device. Upon connecting the Rubber Ducky to a host computer, the built-in Atmel AT32UC3B1256 chip of Rubber Ducky emulates the pre-defined keypresses in the *fastest* rate the USB port can deliver and the device driver of the attacked system can handle.

2.5 BadAndroid

BadAndroid[8], like BadUSB, adds malicious functionality to an otherwise benign Android device. In contrast with BadUSB, the firmware of the Android device needs not be flashed.

A possible attack scenario using BadAndroid looks like the following: using social engineering, an attacker pretends that she needs to charge the battery of her Android smartphone and asks to plug it in to the target's laptop. While the smartphone is connected for charging, BadAndroid actually alters the routing table of the host (laptop) system without the user noticing, i.e., it changes the default network gateway of the laptop to be the IP address of the Android smartphone. From that moment on, all the network traffic of the laptop is routed via the smartphone, enabling the attacker to inspect and alter the whole bi-directional network traffic.

In a second attack scenario, BadAndroid could change the entries for the laptop's DNS servers and, therefore, redirect the laptop's traffic to servers controlled by the attacker.

---

[5] https://www.pjrc.com/teensy/.

[6] https://hak5.org.

[7] https://github.com/hak5darren/USB-Rubber-Ducky/wiki/Duckyscript.

[8] https://srlabs.de/blog/wp-content/uploads/2014/07/BadAndroid-v0.1.zip.

2.6   BadBIOS

A maliciously-crafted BIOS hidden on the USB device could be installed on the computer by emulating keypresses at boot time[9]. This BadBIOS overrides the original BIOS and becomes the default BIOS to boot from. This allows an attacker to execute commands even before the actual operating system is loaded.

The applicability of BadBIOS is demonstrated[10] for modern Smart TVs. In this case, a Smart TV is forced to produce high-frequency audio signals. These signals contain information which is then transmitted to other devices.

2.7   Other Attacks

The published literature includes USB-based attacks that exploit weaknesses beyond the ones spawned by BadUSB. The *teensy* USB development board[11] is designed to instrument and audit USB drivers, ports, and related software. This board is reprogrammable and can be used to launch attacks that are based on emulating keypresses and mouse movements.

The current version of the *USBdriveby* attack tool[12] targets Apple iOS devices. Once successful, USBdriveby alters the routing entries of the attacked system so as to redirect traffic to spoofed websites. The tool also installs a backdoor for the case the user detects the route modifications and changes them back to the legitimate ones.

2.8   Defenses Against USB-Based Attacks

There have been proposals in the literature for defending against USB-based attacks, especially after the Stuxnet malware, which spread via infected USB drives and penetrated air-gapped systems [6,10]. A first attempt towards more organizational security of USB device security is described in [22]. There, a trust management scheme, namely TMSUI, is proposed. TMSUI protects an ICS by allowing the connection of USB storage devices *only* on certain protected terminals and *only* for a specific amount of time.

ProvUSB is an architecture for fine-grained provenance collection and tracking on smart USB devices [17]. ProvUSB aims at environments where the use of pre-approved-only USB drives can be controlled and enforced.

UScramBle is a proposal for protecting against eavesdropping attacks that are feasible due to the broadcast nature of (pre-USB 3.0) hub-to-device communication [12]. It can be used to defend against reverse engineering of legitimate devices.

---

[9] https://srlabs.de/wp-content/uploads/2014/11/SRLabs-BadUSB-Pacsec-v2.pdf.
[10] https://nakedsecurity.sophos.com/2015/11/16/badbios-is-back-this-time-on-your-tv/.
[11] https://www.pjrc.com/teensy/.
[12] http://samy.pl/usbdriveby/.

A line of defense against BadUSB-like attacks incorporates the user into the trust decision. One example is USBWall [9]. USBWall uses a Beagle Board[13] in order to enumerate USB devices on behalf of the operating system. As soon as the enumeration is carried out, the user is asked to decide whether the USB device must be removed from the system or is safe for further use. USBCheckIn is a hardware-based approach, where the user is forced to actively interact with the HID using guided patterns so as to authorize its use [5].

The "G DATA USB Keyboard Guard" software[14] is another system that relies on the users' decision whether a USB device is malicious or benign. There, when a new HID device is connected to the protected computer, the software asks the user to decide if the device interface(s) are to be trusted or not. Once a decision is made, the device (in fact, the combination of product and vendor identifiers) is either whitelisted or blacklisted so as to avoid asking again in the future. If an attacker flashes a malicious device to present with a previously whitelisted combination of product and vendor identifiers (e.g., a legitimate keyboard), then their attack will go unnoticed.

GoodUSB is a similar approach described in [16]. GoodUSB includes a Linux kernel module that maps USB devices to specific whitelisted drivers. Upon connection of a new USB device, GoodUSB involves the user to decide if it should allow or deny the new device. If the user marks the device as malicious, the control is transferred to a virtualized USB honeypot running on QEMU-KVM. This allows to monitor and profile the activity of the USB device for further analysis.

USBFILTER is a packet-level filter (firewall) for USB communications developed for the Linux kernel space [18]. The user defines access rules in USBTables, the userland component of USBFILTER and the kernel-space component checks each USB packet received for match with one of the rules and decides to either forward or drop it. By design, USBFILTER supports only per-packet processing. Given the simplicity of the supported rules, attackers can evade the rules by adjusting their behavior accordingly; overall USBFILTER is a *deterministic* solution that detects already known attacks and does not have any anomaly detection capabilities [13].

Cinch is an approach similar in principles to USBFILTER [2]. However, Cinch isolates all USB devices from the host and passes communication through a virtual machine acting as a gateway that enforces the access policies.

SandUSB offers a GUI for the users to mark a newly plugged-in device as malicious or benign [11]. Should the users consider the device being malicious, they can either blacklist it or redirect it to a USB sandbox for further analysis.

---

[13] https://beagleboard.org.
[14] https://www.gdatasoftware.com/en-usb-keyboard-guard.

3   A Novel Approach for Detection of USB-Based Keypress Injection Attacks

We consider a keypress injection attack as the most severe USB-based threat to system security. This is because a carefully-crafted attack, launched through innocent-looking keypresses, leverages the powerful resources and flexibility of the host system so as to take over the full control of the system itself.

The proposed defenses against keypress injection attacks until now have in common that they rely at some point on user decisions. The user insights in such low-level system trust decisions is not an optimal solution. This is especially true when such interactions break their mental model for the primary task at hand, so as to cope with a secondary one [3,4].

In the following, we explore how we can detect and defend against USB-based keypress injection attacks by performing USB packet traffic analysis at the system level, *without* involving the user in the decision loop. Our aim is to simplify attack detection and offer neutralization upon connection of a malicious USB device that acts as a keyboard. This includes fast detection and no user involvement in the security decision.

3.1   Threat Model

We assume an enterprise environment where computers are equipped with USB ports and the users are free to plug in and unplug USB devices for their day-to-day work duties (e.g., mass storage devices, headsets, and web cameras for teleconferences).

We further assume that the attackers succeed in connecting a crafted device with a malicious USB firmware to one or more of these computers. This can be achieved by the attackers themselves, if they have physical access to the targeted computer, inside or outside the premises of the enterprise. Or, by handing in a malicious device to legitimate users and exploit their curiosity (e.g., drop a USB thumb drive in their postal mailbox) or apply a social engineering attack vector (e.g., "can you please print the file from my USB thumb drive?").

We do not consider attack vectors such as USB storage media loaded with malware (e.g., exploit the "autorun" feature). Mitigations for such attacks are already offered by commercial antivirus products [14]. We also do not consider attacks that exploit (unknown) vulnerabilities of the USB device drivers of the host operating system triggered by malformed USB packets [8]. Rather, we assume that all USB packets are well-formed and valid according to the USB protocol.

3.2   Patterns of Keypress Injection Attacks

The first step for developing appropriate defenses is to get a better understanding of the keypress injection attack patterns. Towards this direction, we experimented with two USB device types that their firmware can be updated and for which appropriate reflashing tools are available. The first one was a Rubber Ducky device. The second one was a Toshiba USB 3.0 USB drive.

In the case of Rubber Ducky, it sufficed to compile a new firmware, which contained an attack payload, by using the provided compiler and then copy the firmware on its SD card.

The case of the benign Toshiba USB drive required some additional steps. First, the original firmware of the device was dumped, then the attack payload was integrated in the firmware, and finally the firmware was written back to the chip. This was not an error-free process. Our first attempts ended up with unusable (bricked) devices and unreliable functionality of the controller chip resulting in unstable behavior.

We also prepared a desktop computer that acted as the host for the attacks. We used the Wireshark network protocol analyzer[15] to monitor the USB connections and collect the related USB packet traces for further analysis.

As an attack demonstration scenario, we opted to use the automatic launch of a text editor in the Linux operating system, including some text filling. Once connected, the malicious devices registered themselves as keyboards and sent the necessary keypresses. The sequence of events was as follows:

1. An artificial delay of 500 ms.
2. Send the ALT key followed by the F2 key in order to prepare an application launch.
3. An artificial delay of 500 ms.
4. Send a string of characters for launching a text editor (e.g., gEdit or mousepad), followed by the ENTER key.
5. An artificial delay of 500 ms.
6. Send one paragraph of text comprising 515 characters from the Bacon Ipsum (http://baconipsum.com/) text.

Albeit not malicious in nature, the attach scenario above serves as a baseline for building weaponized attacks, such as opening a terminal, disabling any running antivirus service, and running a wget command to download malicious code to the attacked system. The artificial delays are necessary to provide the operating system with enough time to successfully respond to issued commands, e.g., opening the text editor. The attack script sends 526 keypresses in total.

We ran each attack (BadUSB and Rubber Ducky) ten times and collected in total 20 Wireshark traces. We analyzed these traces and focused on the timing patterns of the KEY_DOWN events that are sent when a key on a keyboard is pressed.

Figure 2 depicts the distribution of the distance between each of the 5,260 recorded events (i.e., the interarrival time of the keypresses) for each of the ten repetitions of each attack in box-and-whisker diagrams. There are only a couple of outliers for each trace (Capture ID), which are at about 1.35 s (in the case of BadUSB) and 1.00 s (in the case of Rubber Ducky). The median value in both cases is about 6 ms and almost all values are concentrated in a narrow band around this value, as depicted in Fig. 2a and b.

---

[15] https://wireshark.org/.

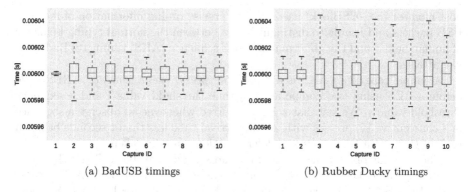

(a) BadUSB timings   (b) Rubber Ducky timings

Fig. 2. Interarrival times of KEY_DOWN events in collected traces (outliers excluded for the sake of clarity)

This was a stable behavior in all traces and for both attacks; Rubber Ducky exhibits a greater variability, but still within the narrow band. We ran repeated experiments with all the payloads made available by the Rubber Ducky authors[16]. There were in total more than 70 different payloads at the time of writing. The analysis of the traces revealed that *all* of the payloads produced the keypresses with no delay, i.e., the USB-based keypress injection attacks try to conclude their malicious actions as fast as possible.

From an attack point of view, it is a rational choice to inject keypresses as fast as possible: for an attack to be successful, all the events of the script must execute without being interrupted by any user-initiated typing activity. Since the attacked system has two keyboards now, it is possible that the user continues their typing activity. In this case, typing will intermix with the (fake) keypresses of the attack script and, thus, neutralize the latter by accident (and possibly frustrate the user with the extra characters). The less the time in between the (fake) keypresses, the more the probability of a successfully-launched attack. This is a key observation for the design of our defense.

3.3   Keystroke Dynamics

Research in *keystroke dynamics* (or *keystroke-based biometrics*) suggests that human typing patterns exhibit variations and these "typing dynamics" can be strong enough to be used for authentication or identification purposes [15]. Also, human beings cannot perform better than 80 ms between their keypressess [20]. In contrast, our analysis reveals that BadUSB-like attacks inject keypresses at an almost stable rate of 6 ms. These two rates differ by an order of magnitude.

3.4   USBlock: Blocking Malicious USB Packet Traffic

USBlock is a defense we devised that exploits the temporal gap between human and BadUSB-like attack typing dynamics. The design assumption is that a USB

---

[16] https://github.com/hak5darren/USB-Rubber-Ducky/wiki/Payloads.

host monitor (i.e., USBlock) has access to precise timing information of received USB packets and is able to distinguish *fast* between the normal typing behavior of human beings and the abnormal keypress sequence (AKS) timings of BadUSB-like attacks.

A simple case of an AKS is a *"rapid (keypress) event sequence"* (RES). We define a RES using two components, a time threshold value t and a sequence threshold value s. We say that a RES occurred whenever we observe a sequence of s consecutive keypresses with an interarrival time less than t seconds between each of them. If a RES occurs, a defense action must be taken.

The selection of the exact values for t and s is a design choice. The t-threshold can be any value $0.006 < t < 0.08$, i.e., anything between the 6 ms median value of the BadUSB-like attacks and the lower limit of 0.08 s for humans. A t close to the lower bound of 0.006 makes USBlock *more prone* to false negatives, thus, risking a successful attack going unnoticed. Yet, it reduces the probability of false positives, as humans cannot type that fast. In contrast, a t close to the upper bound 0.08 makes USBlock *more prone* to false positives, thus, risking user complaints on legitimate usage scenarios. Our analysis of the collected attack and human-typing traces (cf. Sect. 4) suggests that a $t = 0.02$ is a sufficient threshold for the current generation of BadUSB-like attacks.

An $s = 1$ makes USBlock *blindly aggressive* (many false positives), penalizing even in a single occurrence of a keypress under the timing threshold. In contrast, a large s (e.g., over 100) allows USBlock to make *confident decisions* on the presence of an AKS. However, one must account two additional points. First, if the decision algorithm does not react in real-time, it risks to allow an attack to have occurred already by the time a (correct) decision is made. This is unacceptable from a security point of view. Second, the length of the attack vector, i.e., the number of keypresses injected to realize the attack, might be lower than s (e.g., only 20 or 30 keypresses compared to an $s = 100$). In this case, USBlock will fail to detect the attack altogether, as there are not enough "malicious" keypresses present to react on.

Our analysis of the available traces suggests that a short $s = 3$ offers the clear advantage that a keypress injection attack is detected and prevented just after the very first few fast keypresses are sent. The attack traces *contained not a single case* where two or more outlier values came in pairs or bursts. Furthermore, to the best of our knowledge, no attack vector can be realized with only three keypresses. Hence, $s = 3$ is an excellent choice.

The capabilities of USBlock are better demonstrated with an example of a defense realization against current generation of Ducky Script malicious payloads. A USB monitor runs as a piece of software on the host system and measures the interarrival times of keypresses sent by each connected USB device for a RES, using the t and s parameters. When a RES is detected, the USB monitor instructs the USB hub to switch off the power of the USB port for some (e.g., ten) seconds (configurable). It also instructs the operating system to unload (unbound) the respective device driver. This in effect blocks access to the suspicious device. We highlight that *no additional* piece of hardware is needed for performing these actions. The disconnection approach ensures that no user involvement is required in restoring the connectivity of other USB devices that are possibly attached to the specific USB port where the attack occurred.

One may argue that the design opts for a rather aggressive reaction to suspicious events. We believe that our two-step disablement approach accommodates this. It is better for users to notice an occasional interruption of their normal flow (in case the events are indeed produced that fast by human beings) rather than risking an infection by a malicious device. If the interruptions become too frequent, it is an indication of an attack in progress (e.g., a USB drive trying to relaunch the attack). In this case, it would be better for the IT support personnel to inspect the offending system.

3.5 USBlock Defenses Against Advanced Attacks

USBlock with RES defends currently against *all known* malicious Ducky Script payloads. The approach of USBlock is generic enough and allows to realize and integrate new defenses against new attacks. As the cat-and-mouse game between attackers and defenders might evolve for BadUSB-like attacks, RES can be replaced by a more complex AKS detection logic. Such logic will push attackers to adjust keypress injection rates to mimic human behavior. This task will be more and more difficult to both realize in the constrained environment of USB firmware and to match specific user typing patterns. At the moment, this is not deemed necessary and would incur additional and unnecessary processing overhead.

We note that USBlock with RES cannot be defeated by malicious firmware that delays the launch of the payload (i.e., the start of the attack), once the fake device is plugged. USBlock is continuously monitoring for keypress events. Hence, when a RES occurs, USBlock will detect it, no matter how long ago the fake device was plugged.

One may argue that a malicious Ducky Script can introduce delays between keypresses to avoid detection. However, the constant interarrival time of the keypresses is an easily-detectable AKS pattern. Should a Ducky Script can generate random delays between keypresses, these must occur as a human typing pattern, sparse in time. At this rate, they will become intermixed with the normal typing activity of the user (and thus, neutralized) or they will become noticeable by the user, as the attacks do not happen "in the blink of an eye" anymore (e.g., the cursor is moved or the focus of the working window is lost). Should the user is incapable or unwilling of noticing the additional typing activity on their monitor, we must resort on enterprise network security defenses that might be able to detect the malicious activity of the attacked system, once infected.

Clearly, analyzing the typed *command strings* (from humans or scripts) and reasoning about their (possibly) malicious *intentions* is beyond the scope of USBlock. Such fine-grained keypress analysis will probably not be acceptable by the users, as it severely violates their privacy creating an Orwellian feeling of constant monitoring.

One may argue that a malicious USB firmware can monitor the status of the operating system and launch the payload during periods of user inactivity (e.g., when there is no typing activity for a long time). We are not aware of such capabilities for Ducky Scripts and, to the best of our knowledge, such information cannot be requested by the USB firmware from the operating system over USB packets. Even if such capabilities exist in first place, USBlock is on the side of the operating system. Thus, it can also access such information and integrate them into its decision logic to block malicious USB traffic. We further note that such an attack cannot be launched at all if the screen is locked (e.g., due to inactivity or a precautious measure by the user when plugging an untrusted device).

3.6   Limitations of USBlock

While USBlock defends successfully against keypress injection attacks, it does not come free of limitations. USBlock lies and relies on information at the level of the operating system. As such, it cannot defend against attacks launched at the BIOS level, as is the case of BadBIOS discussed in Sect. 2.

Hardware keys, like Yubico YubiKey[17], are a popular means of two-factor authentication. Such devices identify themselves to the operating system as keyboards and "type" one-time passwords and other sensitive information on behalf of their owner. Hence, USBlock will interpret the YubiKey rapid keypresses as an attack. To overcome this, USBlock implements internally the following check for YubiKey devices: if a connected USB device reports a (VID, PID) of Yubico, the RES logic is disabled for this device. Rather, USBlock monitors the USB device traffic to ensure that the USB packet payload comprise exclusively "MODHEX" characters[18]. This is an improved approach over (VID, PID) whitelisting [16], as anyone can fake the reported (VID, PID). As discussed earlier in Sect. 2, these are inherent limitations of the USB protocol itself rather than of USBlock. The host system must blindly trust the information provided by peripheral devices without any authentication support.

4   Proof-of-Concept Implementation and Evaluation

We now describe a proof-of-concept implementation of the designed system and its evaluation in realistic environments. The evaluation comprises two parts: the first part relates to the long-term stability of the prototype and to evaluating the effect of the temporal variations in typing habits; the second part explores the typing dynamics of different users.

---

[17] https://www.yubico.com/products/yubikey-hardware/.

[18] The modified hexadecimal characters are {b, c, d, e, f, g, h, i, j, k, l, n, r, t, u, v}, cf. https://www.yubico.com/support/knowledge-base/categories/articles/one-time-password-otp/.

4.1   Proof-of-Concept Implementation

We realized a proof-of-concept implementation for the Linux operating system comprising two parts. The first part is a Linux loadable kernel module (for kernel version 4.2) that monitors for the keypresses. Being in the kernel, this part is as close as possible to the raw information about keypresses received from the USB device and enriches them with very precise timings. The kernel module then forwards the enriched information to the second part residing in userland. The communication between the two parts occurs over a `netlink` socket that is registered in both the kernel space and userland. This is an approach similar to the one of [18]. However, the latter does not support timestamps and multi-packet processing, which are necessary for our aims.

The second part is a Python script. This part implements the rapid event sequence (RES) detection logic and is responsible for unbinding the offending USB driver from the kernel. This effectively disconnects the device interface from the system. If the driver of the device is automatically re-bound (as part of an ongoing attack), then, as an additional protective measure, the driver for the corresponding USB hub on which the device is connected is also unbound for ten seconds. This effectively removes all the devices connected on this hub. The unbind/re-bind procedure is repeated until a user action is initiated or a system administrator takes over. We note that the USB packet processing, from kernel capture to RES detection (via the Python script) and reaction, requires on average about 0.3 ms per packet. Hence, it takes 1 ms to detect an $s = 3$ RES. This is more than enough processing time, given that the median interarrival time for BadUSB-like keypress injections is about 6 ms.

4.2   Evaluation of Temporal Variations

We evaluated the effect of temporal variations in typing as follows. We installed the prototype in one of the authors' computers, a notebook running Ubuntu 15.10. The notebook was used on a day-to-day basis with a USB-connected keyboard for a period of three months. The aim was twofold: on the one hand, to evaluate the stability of the prototype and to discover any problems that it might cause; on the other hand, to study the user's typing behavior in the course of a long period that involved a multitude of typing activities including code development, debugging, system administration tasks, scientific paper writing, preparation of talks and presentations, shell scripting, email typing, and web browsing.

We instrumented the kernel module `usbmon` [23] to collect and log the USB events and act as a middleware between the kernel and our offline analysis tools. In userland, the `TShark` part of the Wireshark bundle was used to "listen" to USB events sent by `usbmon`. A Python script was used to generate `pcap`-formatted files containing all the USB-related events. A second Python script was then used to process the files and store the collected information into a database for later analysis.

Overall, we did not experience any kind of stability problems while operating the prototype and the additional monitoring infrastructure. Neither we experienced any kind of measurable performance degradation. It did not cause any side effects (at least that we became aware of). Thus, the temporal variations in typing did not affect the operation of the prototype.

We collected in total timing information for more than 466,000 keypresses over more than 60 working days. Less than 1% of them were below the $t = 0.02$ s threshold, while the vast majority ranked quite higher. The median value of interarrival times was 0.10 s, while the average time was 0.21 s.

There was *no single case* of three or more consecutive keypresses with an interarrival time below the defined threshold. Thus, it was never the case that the prototype unbound the USB keyboard device driver, i.e., we experienced *no false positives*.

4.3   Evaluation of Typing Dynamics

The second phase of the evaluation was a study on the effect of the typing dynamics. We designed a small-scale user study so as to collect evidence about typing patterns and compare them against the behavior of the Rubber Ducky and BadUSB attacks as well as published literature for typing dynamics.

We developed a research prototype system comprising a headless Raspberry Pi Model 2B running Ubuntu server 15.10, a USB keyboard, and a battery pack for autonomous operation. Similarly to the previous evaluation, we used a kernel module to collect the keypress timing information and send them to a userland application. The latter collected and aggregated the information prior to storing them into a database for later processing.

We recruited 33 volunteers from our organization for this experiment. We visited each participant at their desk and asked them to type a short text in the comfort of their desk using our research prototype system. We offered the participants the option to either plug in their keyboard or use the keyboard of our prototype. All but one participants opted to use our keyboard, as it felt more convenient for them not to unplug their keyboard, or because they were using laptops and docking stations.

We asked the participants to type the same, randomly-selected paragraph of the Bacon Ipsum text comprising 71 characters. Figure 3 depicts the distribution of the distance between each of the 71 recorded events (i.e., the keypresses interarrival time) produced by each participant in box-and-whisker diagrams. The diagrams indicate that each participant exhibited different typing patterns. Almost all diagrams contain a large number of outliers towards larger numbers. Delays of one or even three seconds between keypresses are noticed. The overall median value was 0.20 s and the average time reached 0.30 s. Despite the per-participant differences, there was *not a single case* where our research prototype detected erroneously a RES, i.e., once more, there were *zero false positives*.

Our typing dynamics analysis results are in alignment with published literature [15]. Hence and for the sake of research efficiency and economy, we opted not to expand the study to more participants.

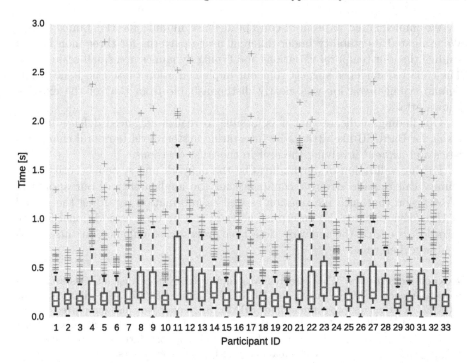

Fig. 3. Temporal variations in the typing dynamics experiment.

The second part of the evaluation confirmed that typing dynamics are quite stable among users, despite some unavoidable differentiations. More importantly, even in short texts, the human typing dynamics are clearly above the detection threshold we have defined and clearly distinguishable from that of the Rubber Ducky and BadUSB attacks (cf. Figs. 2 and 3). Thus, such information can serve as a heuristic for detecting and defending against the attacks.

5   Conclusions and Future Work

BadUSB-like attacks are a realistic threat. Yet, system-level defenses cannot be realized in the form of malware analysis tools for USB firmware. USB device whitelisting can offer some protection in specific usage scenarios, but its usability is hindered when scaling in enterprise-level networks. Proposed defenses in the literature mandate the user involvement in the trust decisions. This is a suboptimal, error-prone design choice.

In this paper, we studied the *temporal* characteristics of BadUSB-like attacks. We proposed USBlock to block malicious USB packet traffic. Our proposal is extensible and can integrate additional features for coping with future, advanced attacks. Residing on the side of the operating system, USBlock has an advantage over a malicious USB firmware payload executing on a peripheral device and interacting with the main system.

We implemented a proof-of-concept defense module for the Linux kernel. We evaluated its stability under different usage patterns for three months and studied the user temporal variations and typing dynamics in a small-scale study. The collected evidence suggest that our implementation caused no issues while human typing behavior was clearly distinguishable from that of the existing known attacks.

Our findings indicate that it is feasible to realize advanced defense mechanisms for BadUSB-like attacks by integrating system-level temporal characteristics and *without* involving the user in the trust decisions.

Further validation of our findings by the network and system security community can provide stronger confidence for the applicability of our approach. We envision that such information as well as information regarding the spread of USB devices across an enterprise network can be used as additional feature in order to enrich the malware detection process and enhance our arsenal in fighting cybercrime.

Acknowledgements. This research was supported by the Austrian Research Promotion Agency (FFG) through the BRIDGE 1 grant P846070 (SpeedFor) and the COMET K1-Centres programme line (SBA2). S. Neuner was also supported by the Austrian Marshall Plan Foundation through a Marshall Plan Scholarship. We thank Prof. E. Kirda and W. Robertson for their valuable support during the early stages of this research as well as the participants in the typing experiments.

References

1. Anderson, B., Anderson, B.: Seven Deadliest USB Attacks. Syngress, Maryland Heights (2010)
2. Angel, S., Wahby, R.S., Howald, M., Leners, J.B., Spilo, M., Sun, Z., Blumberg, A.J., Walfish, M.: Defending against malicious peripherals with Cinch. In: USENIX Security Symposium (2016)
3. Dingledine, R., Mathewson, N.: Anonymity loves company: usability and the network effect. In: Workshop on the Economics of Information Security (WEIS) (2006)
4. Fidas, C., Voyiatzis, A., Avouris, N.: When security meets usability: a user-centric approach on a crossroads priority problem. In: 14th Panhellenic Conference on Informatics (PCI 2010), Tripoli, Greece, 10–12 September 2010 (2010)
5. Griscioli, F., Pizzonia, M., Sacchetti, M.: USBCheckIn: preventing BadUSB attacks by forcing human-device interaction. In: 2016 14th Annual Conference on Privacy, Security and Trust (PST), pp. 493–496. IEEE (2016)
6. Guri, M., Kachlon, A., Hasson, O., Kedma, G., Mirsky, Y., Elovici, Y.: GSMem: data exfiltration from air-gapped computers over GSM frequencies. In: 24th USENIX Security Symposium (USENIX Security 2015), pp. 849–864 (2015)
7. Han, S., Shin, W., Kang, J., Park, J.H., Kim, H., Park, E., Ryou, J.C.: IRON-HID: create your own bad USB (white paper). In: HITBSecConf 2016 - Amsterdam. The 7th Annual HITB Security Conference in the Netherlands (2016)
8. Johnson, P., Bratus, S., Smith, S.: Protecting against malicious bits on the wire: automatically generating a USB protocol parser for a production kernel. In: Proceedings of the 33rd Annual Computer Security Applications Conference, Orlando, FL, USA, 4–8 December 2017, pp. 528–541. ACM (2017)

9. Kang, M.: USBWall: a novel security mechanism to protect against maliciously reprogrammed USB devices. Master's thesis, University of Kansas (2015)
10. Langner, R.: Stuxnet: dissecting a cyberwarfare weapon. Secur. Priv. IEEE **9**(3), 49–51 (2011)
11. Loe, E.L., Hsiao, H.C., Kim, T.H.J., Lee, S.C., Cheng, S.M.: SandUSB: an installation-free sandbox for USB peripherals. In: 2016 IEEE 3rd World Forum on Internet of Things (WF-IoT), pp. 621–626. IEEE (2016)
12. Neugschwandtner, M., Beitler, A., Kurmus, A.: A transparent defense against USB eavesdropping attacks. In: Proceedings of the 9th European Workshop on System Security, EuroSec 2016, pp. 6:1–6:6. ACM (2016)
13. Nissim, N., Yahalom, R., Elovici, Y.: USB-based attacks. Comput. Secur. **70**(Supplement C), 675–688 (2017)
14. Pham, D.V., Syed, A., Halgamuge, M.N.: Universal serial bus based software attacks and protection solutions. Digit. Invest. **7**(3), 172–184 (2011)
15. Teh, P.S., Teoh, A.B.J., Yue, S.: A survey of keystroke dynamics biometrics. Sci. World J. **2013**, 24 (2013)
16. Tian, D.J., Bates, A., Butler, K.: Defending against malicious USB firmware with GoodUSB. In: Proceedings of the 31st Annual Computer Security Applications Conference, pp. 261–270. ACM (2015)
17. Tian, D.J., Bates, A., Butler, K.R., Rangaswami, R.: ProvUSB: block-level provenance-based data protection for USB storage devices. In: Proceedings of the 2016 ACM SIGSAC Conference on Computer and Communications Security (CCS 2016), New York, NY, USA, pp. 242–253. ACM (2016)
18. Tian, D.J., Scaife, N., Bates, A., Butler, K., Traynor, P.: Making USB great again with USBFILTER. In: 25th USENIX Security Symposium (USENIX Security 2016), Austin, TX, pp. 415–430. USENIX Association (2016)
19. Tischer, M., Durumeric, Z., Foster, S., Duan, S., Mori, A., Bursztein, E., Bailey, M.: Users really do plug in USB drives they find. In: 2016 IEEE Symposium on Security and Privacy (SP). IEEE (2016)
20. Umphress, D., Williams, G.: Identity verification through keyboard characteristics. Int. J. Man Mach. Stud. **23**(3), 263–273 (1985)
21. Wang, Z., Stavrou, A.: Exploiting smart-phone USB connectivity for fun and profit. In: Proceedings of the 26th Annual Computer Security Applications Conference, pp. 357–366. ACM (2010)
22. Yang, B., Qin, Y., Zhang, Y., Wang, W., Feng, D.: TMSUI: a trust management scheme of USB storage devices for industrial control systems. In: Qing, S., Okamoto, E., Kim, K., Liu, D. (eds.) ICICS 2015. LNCS, vol. 9543, pp. 152–168. Springer, Cham (2016). https://doi.org/10.1007/978-3-319-29814-6_13
23. Zaitcev, P.: The usbmon: USB monitoring framework. In: Linux Symposium, p. 291 (2005)

Networked Systems

Virtually Isolated Network: A Hybrid Network to Achieve High Level Security

Jia Xu[1](✉) and Jianying Zhou[2]

[1] Singtel, Singapore, Singapore
jia.xu@singtel.com
[2] Singapore University of Technology and Design, Singapore, Singapore
jianying_zhou@sutd.edu.sg

Abstract. This paper proposes a hybrid network system (called as "Virtually Isolated Network") that combines an existing low bandwidth isolated network and the Internet, to implement a low cost overlay network with high bandwidth and high level security (precisely, information-theoretic security), without sacrificing security of the existing isolated network. Our approach consists of two main ideas: (1) Connect an isolated network and the Internet in a proper way using 4 physical unidirectional links (also known as "Data Diode" or "Air Gap"), so that the isolated network remains physically isolated; (2) Hide a small part of ciphertext from adversary by exploiting the property of isolated network and using a secret sharing approach.

Keywords: Isolated network · Hybrid network
Unidirectional network link · Encryption · Secret sharing
Information dispersal algorithm · Information-theoretic security

1 Introduction

Many existing critical industry systems (e.g. power generation plants, nuclear plants, chemical plants, subway/metro transportation system, etc.) leverage their physical and cyber security on closed or isolated system. They prevent unauthorized entrance using high walls and security guards. Their network systems

---

The first author is supported by the National Research Foundation, Prime Minister's Office, Singapore under its Corporate Laboratory@University Scheme, National University of Singapore, and Singapore Telecommunications Ltd. The second author is supported by the National Research Foundation (NRF), Prime Minister's Office, Singapore, under its National Cybersecurity R&D Programme (Award No. NRF2014NCR-NCR001-31) and administered by the National Cybersecurity R&D Directorate. Part of this work was done when the first author worked in Institute for Infocomm Research, Singapore.

© IFIP International Federation for Information Processing 2018
Published by Springer International Publishing AG, part of Springer Nature 2018. All Rights Reserved
F. Kerschbaum and S. Paraboschi (Eds.): DBSec 2018, LNCS 10980, pp. 299–311, 2018.
https://doi.org/10.1007/978-3-319-95729-6_19

are physically disconnected from the Internet, making remote attacks via the Internet impossible. If the strict physical security protection is always enforced properly, for example, no one is allowed to setup new wired or wireless communication from the closed system to outside, USB port is disabled, then only a very low (or ideally zero) bandwidth of convert channel between the isolated network and the Internet is possible to escape from detection by existing cyber and physical security solutions.

We found that some legacy isolated industry control systems have very small bandwidth in their backbone isolated network, due to historical reason. For example, some metro system has relative large LAN speed in each metro station, but the backbone network connecting each station with the centralized control server has only 2 Mbps bandwidth. Such limited backbone network bandwidth is becoming the bottleneck of the whole isolated industry network, since more new services are introduced with time, e.g. CCTV real time video. It will require a huge investment and take a lot of time to upgrade the physical cable network: In a modern city, laying a new fiber path for a long distance is very challenging and may introduce significant side effect to urban transportation system. Therefore, there is an urgent demand to boost the bandwidth of existing legacy isolated network at low cost.

In this paper, we will propose a hybrid network architecture, by connecting an existing isolated network and the Internet in a smart way such that the isolated network remains isolated from the Internet, without sacrificing the security level of the existing isolated network. Meanwhile, we will propose a new encryption method using "encrypt-then-secret-sharing" approach, split the ciphertext into two parts and transmit separately via two communication channels of the hybrid network. Essentially, our novel encryption method can achieve unconditional security, assuming the adversary cannot monitor or eavesdrop the two communication channels simultaneously. Eventually, we are able to boost the bandwidth of legacy isolated network by about 60 times at a very low cost. Our main contributions include

- We design a *unidirectional* hybrid network architecture to connect isolated network and Internet, in a way that the isolated network remains physically isolated. Such unidirectional network is very useful to constantly transmit sensor data from field sensors to a data collection server in an isolated network. Our solution can significantly increase the bandwidth of legacy isolated network at low cost.
- We design a novel data protection method by combining encryption and secret-sharing. By hiding partial ciphertext from adversary, our new method can achieve unconditional security.

The rest of this paper is organized as below: Sect. 2 will discuss the related works. Section 3 will describe the hybrid network architecture and protocol. Section 4 will propose our novel encryption method. Section 5 will show our experiment result. Section 6 will conclude the paper.

2   Related Works

Symmetric encryption scheme (e.g. AES, Blowfish[1], and Triple DES[2].) could be the most widely adopted cryptographic primitive to protect data confidentiality, especially for large volume of data. AES [2] is a typical example of symmetric encryption scheme, and has been widely adopted in industry due to its security and efficiency for more than one decade.

In additional to encryption techniques, another well-known cryptographic primitive that can be used to protect data confidentiality is "secret-sharing" scheme invented by Shamir [10]. Compared to encryption scheme (e.g. AES [2]) which can only achieve conditional security, secret-sharing scheme may achieve unconditional security (also known as information-theoretic security), assuming the adversary cannot collect sufficient number of shares.

Despite its strong security, Shamir's secret sharing scheme has significant drawbacks when protecting data confidentiality: (1) for (t, n)-secret sharing scheme, the storage overhead is as large as $(n-1)$ times of size of the secret (i.e. the plaintext to be protected); (2) the reconstruction [7] (or decoding) process is not as efficient as DES or AES.

Rabin [8] proposed "information dispersal algorithm" with zero storage overhead, such that the sum of sizes of all shares is equal to the size of secret message size. His solution is conceptually simple: Let row vector $m = (m_0, m_1, \ldots, m_n)$ be the secret message. Choose an invertible n by n matrix $\mathbf{T}$ with inverse matrix $\mathbf{T}^{-1}$. By multiplying row vector m with matrix $\mathbf{T}$, we obtain the n shares $c = (c_0, c_1, \ldots, c_{n-1}) = m \times \mathbf{T}$. Accordingly, the original secret message m can be recovered by matrix multiplication $m = c \times \mathbf{T}^{-1}$. Recently, Resch and Plank [9] coined the term "All or Nothing" (AONT, for short) for information dispersal algorithm. Othman and Mokdad [1] proposed to protect communication confidentiality by sending each share of message in distinct network path from the same sender to the same receiver (Fig. 1).

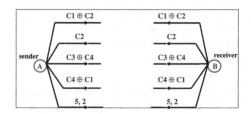

Fig. 1. Enhancing data security in Ad Hoc networks based on multipath routing

In the example shown in the above figure, the message is divided into 4 equal-length parts C_1, C_2, C_3 and C_4, and each part is delivered via a distinct

---

[1] https://www.schneier.com/academic/blowfish/.

[2] http://csrc.nist.gov/publications/nistpubs/800-67-Rev1/SP-800-67-Rev1.pdf.

network path from the sender to the receiver. Readers can easily figure out how to recover all of 4 parts $C_1 \ldots C_4$ on the receiver side, if all transmissions are free of errors.

Alternatively, Krawczyk [5] attempted to make each share shortened, by dividing ciphertext of the long secret message into n pieces, and then apply Shamir's secret sharing scheme over the encryption key. Thus, the storage overhead is linear in short encryption key size and is a fraction of secret message size.

It is also worthy to pointing out, in network coding techniques (e.g. [3,4,6,11]), data streams could be merged or divided in any intermedia communication node. Unlike this work, their purpose is to improve the network throughput, efficiency and scalability, as well as resilience to attacks and eavesdropping.

3 Network Architecture

We will construct a unidirectional *Virtually Isolated Network* (VIN for short). If bidirectional communication is required, then two sets of VIN can be combined to achieve bidirectional communication, at the cost that security level of the existing isolated network will be downgraded from physical isolation to software isolation.

3.1 Network Hardware Components

The network hardware components of virtually isolated network are described as below, and summarized in Table 1. Their interconnection is illustrated in Fig. 2.

- **Sender:** The Sender device will encrypt incoming data stream and split it into two output streams with possibly unequal sizes. The smaller output stream will be sent to Repeater 1 via a unidirectional physical network link (a.k.a data diode or air gap), and the larger output stream will be sent to Repeater 3 via another unidirectional physical network link, too. Ideally, the Sender device is recommended to be designed as a minimum single feature hardware/software system, more precisely, a customized FPGA chip running a customized driver, since unnecessary hardware or software components may potentially introduce more vulnerabilities.
- **Receiver:** The Receiver device will receive two input streams via unidirectional network link from Repeater 2 and Repeater 4, merge them together and decrypt them. Like the Sender device, ideally, the Receiver device will also be designed as a minimum single feature hardware/software system, more precisely, a customized FPGA chip running a customized driver.
- **Repeater** 1,2,3,4: Repeater 1 (3, respectively) will receive data stream via unidirectional network link from Sender, and relay the data stream to Repeater 2 (4, respectively) via *bidirectional* isolated network (Internet, respectively). These Repeater devices will run generic hardware/software system with customized configuration. Except availability protection, no special security protection is required.

– (Existing) **Isolated Network:** A network which is physically disconnected with the Internet. Without loss of generality, we assume this is a TCP/IP network in this work.
– (Existing) **Internet:** The global system of interconnected computer networks that use the Internet protocol suite (TCP/IP) to link billions of devices worldwide[3].

Computation Hardware and Software Specification

– The computation hardware in Sender/Receiver device could be a customized single feature FPGA, which has only TCP/IP network stack, encryption and error correcting code functionality. Software in Sender/Receiver is a minimum driver, and no full OS (like Linux, Windows, etc.) is required.
– The computation hardware and software in Repeater devices could be standard commercial products. Repeaters should have storage as buffer. We will develop our own software to convert between the UDP data stream (on unidirectional network link side) and TCP data stream (on bidirectional network link side).

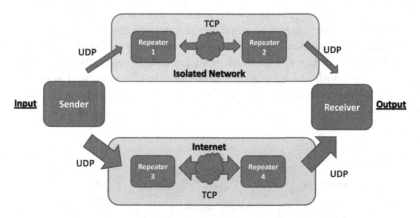

Fig. 2. Network architecture diagram of virtually isolated network (Color figure online)

All of Sender, Receiver and Repeater devices are well protected against physical attack or unauthorized access. Digital protection mechanism of privacy and integrity of communication data lies in both Sender and Receiver devices. Even if all Repeater devices are compromised, the privacy and integrity of the communication data should not be affected, although availability of communication data could be jeopardized.

---

[3] Source: https://en.wikipedia.org/wiki/Internet.

Table 1. Hardware components of virtually isolated network

Device	Hardware	Software	Network input	Network output	Security risk	Protection
Sender	FPGA (A.E., ECC, TCP/IP)	Driver	Bidirectional	2 unidirectional	Confidentiality and integrity	Crypto, minimum system, frequent key refresh, physical protection
Receiver	FPGA (A.E., ECC, TCP/IP), buffer storage	Driver	2 unidirectional	Bidirectional	Confidentiality and integrity	Crypto, minimum system, frequent key refresh, Physical Protection
Repeater 1, 3	Generic (TCP/IP), buffer storage	Generic OS	1 unidirectional	Bidirectional	Availability	Physical protection, multi-path routing
Repeater 2, 4	Generic (TCP/IP)	Generic OS	Bidirectional	1 unidirectional	Availability	Physical protection, multi-path routing

Note: A.E. refers to Authenticated Encryption. ECC refers to Error Correcting Code.

We will construct a new cryptographic algorithm for Sender and Receiver devices, which can split a data stream into two streams in a secure manner. We will design a minimum hardware/software system for Sender and Receiver devices, instead of adopting a generic hardware/software system for Sender and Receiver devices, since a generic system is much more complex and consists of a lot of features and functionalities, which are not required by the virtually isolated network and could potentially bring more vulnerabilities to the entire system. To ensure availability of the constructed virtually isolated network, we will guard Repeater devices with strong physical protection mechanism, and adopt multi-path routing with redundant data packets between Repeaters in Internet, as showed in Fig. 3.

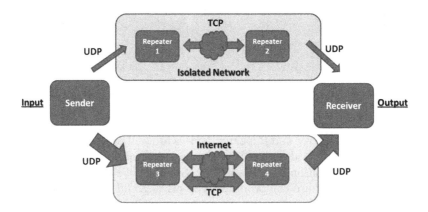

Fig. 3. Multi-path routing between Repeater 3 and 4

3.2   Network Communication

Network Protocol. The Sender or Receiver communicates with Repeater (1–4) using UDP protocol, and Repeater 1 (3, respectively) and Repeater 2 (4, respectively) communicate using TCP protocol, as illustrated in Fig. 2.

The transmission reliability of bidirectional link relies on standard TCP ACK-and-Resend mechanism. Furthermore, multiple-path delivery[4] (as illustrated in Fig. 3) of redundant data packet can increase availability against denial of service attack. The underlying UDP protocol by itself is not reliable against data loss. The transmission reliability of unidirectional link relies on the following factors:

- Highly reliable unidirectional communication link, therefore order is preserved, although UDP protocol is used (e.g. one-way fiber connection, Li-Fi, light-based communication);
- Very short distance (e.g. smaller than 10 cm);
- Highly controlled environment, thus very low environment noise;
- Error correcting code.

Journey of a Data Block from Sender Device to Receiver Device. Every data block sent from Sender to Receiver will be identified by a sequence number[5], which is unique among all data blocks within a proper time period. When a data block is split into two smaller data slices by Sender, the two smaller data slices will have the same sequence number as the original data block. The sequence number will have two roles:

- Ensure correct order among data blocks at the Receiver device;
- Allow Receiver to match a data slice from Repeater 2 and a data slice from Repeater 4, and merge the two data slices to restore the original data blocks.

We remark that: (1) To differentiate from TCP sequence number, we may refer the sequence number for data block as "VIN sequence number". (2) VIN sequence number should not be encrypted. (3) When a large data block with VIN sequence number i is divided into multiple IP packets, each of the resulting IP packet should be labeled as (i, j), $j = 0, 1, 2, \ldots$, where the first index i helps to distinguish them from other VIN data blocks and the second index j, helps to maintain the correct order among themselves.

1. Sender encrypts a given data block m with VIN sequence number i using secret key K, and splits the resulting ciphertext c into two ciphertext shares c_0 and c_1. Optionally, Sender may encode c_0 and/or c_1 using error correcting code (ECC).
2. Sender device sends data c_0 (c_1, respectively) with VIN sequence number i via UDP protocol to Repeater 1 (3, respectively).

---

[4] https://en.wikipedia.org/wiki/Multipath_routing.

[5] This could be simply a 32 bits count number and the number will loop back after 2^{32} blocks.

3. Repeater 1 (3, respectively) generates a TCP packet based on the received UDP packet, where the VIN sequence number is set to i and the payload is identical to the payload of received UDP packet. Repeater 1 encapsulates this TCP packet into a standard IP packet with Repeater 1's (3's, respectively) IP address as source address and Repeater 2's (4's, respectively) IP address as destination address, and sends this IP packet to Repeater 2 (4, respectively).
4. Once receiving an IP packet from Repeater 1 (3, respectively), Repeater 2 (4, respectively) will generate a UDP packet with the same VIN sequence number, where the payload of UDP packet is identical to the payload of the received TCP packet. Repeater 2 (4, respectively) sends this UDP packet to Receiver device.
5. Once receiving the UDP packets from Repeater 2 (4, respectively), the Receiver device will retrieve the payload c_0 (c_1, respectively), from a group of UDP packets with the same VIN sequence number i.
6. Receiver device will match ciphertext share c_0 from Repeater 2 with cipher-text share c_1 from Repeater 4 according to their VIN sequence number, then decrypt ciphertext (c_0, c_1) using the shared secret key K, to obtain the message block m. If required, Receiver device will decode c_0 and/or c_1 using ECC.

Communication Delay. The communication latency of the proposed hybrid network will be the encryption/decryption time plus the maximum of the network latency time in the two communication channels. The speed of our proposed encryption method is estimated as at least a half of speed of the underlying block cipher (e.g. AES). Both the isolated network and Internet can run SSL protocol with acceptable network delay. Therefore, the total network delay in our proposed hybrid network will be only marginally longer than the two communication channels.

Unidirectional Network and Bidirectional Network. Compared to bidirectional network, there is an inherited theoretical limitation for unidirectional communication network: *Sender cannot get any feedback from Receiver or Repeaters, and thus cannot adjust its sending speed according to the network congestion status. Furthermore, Sender cannot know which data packet may be lost, and will not re-send the lost packet.*

Fortunately, in practice, this limitation can be reduced to minimum. From Fig. 2, we can find that UDP protocol over unidirectional link is only used to connect Sender/Receiver device with Repeaters, and TCP protocol over bidirectional link is employed to connect Repeaters. As we discussed in Sect. 3.2, the unidirectional link could achieve extremely high reliability, and the TCP connections between Repeaters can recover possible data loss using standard ACKed-Resend mechanism. Therefore, as long as Repeaters have a sufficiently large buffer storage and sending speed of Sender device is set to a proper value according to the long-term network statistics of the Internet and the isolated network, the unidirectional VIN could achieve practically reliable end-to-end communication in most of time.

3.3 Security Features Guaranteed by Hardware Architecture

The existing isolated network is still physically disconnected from the Internet. More precisely, in our setting in Fig. 2, there is still no physical network path from the Internet (in light red color in Fig. 2) to the existing isolated network (in light green color in Fig. 2), and no physical network path from the existing isolated network to the Internet either.

Two VINs can be combined to provide bidirectional communication. In this case, theoretically, there will be a physical link between the Internet and the existing isolated network. This physical link could be effectively cut-off by cryptographic protection and software method (like firewall) in the Sender/Receiver device.

Note that, the existing isolated network is assumed to be well disconnected from the Internet and the physical site of the isolated network is also well protected from any physical attack. However, the computer/network devices inside the isolated network might potentially have vulnerabilities or even trapdoors and malwares, possibly embedded by vendors or distributors.

4 Our Proposed Encryption-then-Secret-Sharing Method

In the VIN network, Sender will encrypt every data block and split the ciphertext into two shares. The smaller share will be sent to the isolated network and the larger share to the Internet.

4.1 Our Secret Sharing Method

Let positive integers ρ and τ be system parameters. We define our secret-sharing (or information dispersal) scheme (KGen, Split, Merge) with help of two secure hash functions $h(\cdot)$ and $H(\cdot)$ as below.

- KGen$(1^\lambda) \rightarrow k$: Randomly choose a λ-bit string $k \in \{0,1\}^\lambda$ and output k.
- Split$(k; u) \rightarrow (x, y)$ where $u \in \{0,1\}^{\rho(\tau+1)}$, $x \in \{0,1\}^\rho$ and $y \in \{0,1\}^{\rho\tau}$.
    1. Divide the bit string u into a prefix v and a suffix w such that $u = v \| w$ and $|w| = \tau |v|$, i.e. the bit length of w is τ times of v. Here τ is a system parameter (e.g. $\tau = 10$ or 20).
    2. Compute $\bar{v} := h_k(v)$ where $h_k(\cdot)$ is a secure length-preserving keyed hash function. Note that in our application, the length of u is typically a few times of 256.
    3. Compute $y = w \oplus (\bar{v} \| \bar{v} \| \bar{v} \| \cdots)$.
    4. Compute $x = v \oplus H_k(y)$, where $H_k(\cdot)$ is a proper secure keyed hash function with fixed output length.
    5. Output (x, y).
- Merge$(k; x, y) \rightarrow u$.
    1. Compute $v = x \oplus H_k(y)$.
    2. Compute $\bar{v} := h_k(v)$.
    3. Compute $w = y \oplus (\bar{v} \| \bar{v} \| \bar{v} \| \cdots)$.
    4. Output $v \| w$.

4.2   Our Novel Encrytion Scheme

Let (KGen, Split, Merge) be as defined in previous subsection. Let (KG, E, D) be a given encryption scheme (e.g. AES in a proper mode of operation). Our proposed encryption scheme (KeyGen, Enc, Dec) is defined as below

- KeyGen(1^λ) $\leftarrow$ (k_0, k_1):
    1. Compute key $k_0 \leftarrow$ KG(1^λ).
    2. Compute key $k_1 \leftarrow$ KGen(1^λ).
    3. Output (k_0, k_1).
- Enc($k_0, k_1; M$) $\rightarrow$ (C_0, C_1)
    1. Encrypt plaintext M to obtain $\bar{C} \leftarrow$ E($k_0; M$).
    2. Split $\bar{C}$ into two shares (C_0, C_1) $\leftarrow$ Split($k_1; \bar{C}$).
    3. Output (C_0, C_1).
- Dec($k_0, k_1; C_0, C_1$)
    1. Merge C_0 and C_1 as $\bar{C} \leftarrow$ Merge($k_1; C_0, C_1$).
    2. Decrypt $\bar{C}$ as $M \leftarrow$ D($k_0; \bar{C}$).
    3. Output M.

4.3   Security Analysis

It is easy to see that, under the standard setting of encryption scheme, if the adversary knows both C_0 and C_1, our proposed scheme is at least as secure as the underlying encryption scheme (KG, E, D), which we can instantiate with any existing well-known encryption scheme (e.g. AES in practice, or some theoretical semantic secure ciphers).

Theorem 1. *Let* (k_0, k_1) $\leftarrow$ KeyGen(1^λ) *and* (C_0, C_1) $\leftarrow$ Enc($k_0, k_1; M$). *Then we have*

$$\mathbf{H}(M|C_1, k_0, k_1) = |C_0| \tag{1}$$
$$\mathbf{H}(M|C_0, k_0, k_1) = |C_1|. \tag{2}$$

Proof. Recall the definition of function Split and Merge in Sect. 4.1. We have the property that

$$(x, y) = \mathsf{Split}(k_1; u) \iff u = \mathsf{Merge}(k_1; x, y), \tag{3}$$

where $x \in \{0, 1\}^\rho$ and $y \in \{0, 1\}^{\rho\tau}$, $u \in \{0, 1\}^{\rho(\tau+1)}$.

So for a given value of k_0, k_1 and C_1, $M = \mathsf{Dec}(k_0, k_1; C_0, C_1) = \mathsf{D}(k_0; \mathsf{Merge}(k_1; C_0, C_1))$ is a injective (i.e. one-to-one) function of C_0. Therefore, Equality 1 holds. Equality 2 can be proved in a similar way.   □

5   Experiment

5.1   Physical Unidirectional Network Link

Physical Unidirectional Network link[6] has been used to prevent sensitive information leakage from secure network to insecure network for a decade. It is also known as "Data Diode". "Air gap"[7] is another similar term. Commercial unidirectional network links are available on the market, e.g. Waterfall gateway and Fox DataDiode. But prices of those devices are very expensive. In theory, it is easy to construct a unidirectional network link using cheap consumer level fiber network communication device. As quoted from Wikipedia page[8],

> *"The most common form of a unidirectional network is a simple, modified, fiber-optic network link, with send and receive transceivers removed or disconnected for one direction, and any link failure protection mechanisms disabled. Commercial products rely on this basic design, but add other software functionality that provides applications with an interface which helps them pass data across the link."*

However, some subtle issues have to be addressed before we could DIY a unidirectional network link successfully:

– In TCP/UDP protocol level, only UDP is applicable, because no returning route provided for TCP acknowledgement mechanism.
– In IP protocol level, automatic IP configuration service (e.g. DHCP) should be disable and IP addresses for each PC node should be configured manually.
– In MAC protocol level, the ARP protocol should be disabled and the mapping between IP address and MAC address should be manually inserted into the ARP table in each PC node.
– In each fiber device, link fault pass-through (LFP) feature should be disabled.
– Add a third fiber device and connect its outgoing port (Tx) with the incoming port (Rx) of the sender fiber device, where all incoming ports (e.g. Rx and Ethernet port) of the third fiber device remains empty. This third dummy fiber device will send carrier signal to the sender fiber device, so that the sender fiber device can send out data as expected. We remark that, in our experiment, this step is essential, even if we have already disabled link fault pass-through feature.

Using the above method, we manage to construct a single unidirectional network link using 3 fiber transmitter devices at a cost less than 100 US dollars.

---

[6] https://en.wikipedia.org/wiki/Unidirectional_network.

[7] https://en.wikipedia.org/wiki/Air_gap_(networking).

[8] https://en.wikipedia.org/wiki/Unidirectional_network.

5.2   Our Experiment

We setup a testbed with 6 PC (Intel i7 CPU, SSD hard disk, multiple network interfaces in a PC) and 4 unidirectional network links, as in Fig. 2. We set our Internet communication channel bandwidth as 60 times larger than the isolated network bandwidth. We generate random test files of size ranging from 1 MB to 100 MB, and achieve throughput about 7 MBps (i.e. 56 Mbps) with no errors. Our result shows that, with high quality hardware support, we could be able to achieve about 60 times expansion in bandwidth of secure (isolated) network at low cost (See details in Tables 2 and 3).

Table 2. VIN experiment data. In this experiment, the size of larger share is 60 times larger than the smaller shares, which means our VIN network bandwidth could be 61 larger than the isolated network bandwidth.

File size (megabytes)	Transmission speed (kilobyte per sec)
1	6898.923
10	7128.661
50	7178.287
100	7187.595

Table 3. Our VIN technique can effectively boost the bandwidth of secure isolated network. In the experiment, our VIN network only utilizes a small portion (45%) of isolated network bandwidth capacity to eventually constitute a hybrid network with about 7 MBps throughput, where the security of this hybrid network is closer to the isolated network and could be much more secure than the Internet if the isolated network is properly isolated from outside.

Isolated network capacity	Small channel of VIN	Large channel of VIN	VIN
2 Mbps	0.9 Mbps	54 Mbps	54.9 Mbps

Note that the unit "Mbps" denotes megabit per second.

6   Conclusion

In this paper, we proposed a hybrid network, called as "Virtually Isolated Network". In this hybrid network, an isolated network and the Internet are connected using unidirectional network links in a way that the isolated network remains physically isolated. All data in this hybrid network will be encrypted and then split into two (possibly unequal) shares using secret-sharing approach. The smaller share will be delivered via the isolated network and the larger share will be delivered via the Internet. Due to the physical isolation property, any adversary cannot obtain both shares at the same time. Consequently, our method achieves unconditional security by hiding partial ciphertext from adversary.

References

1. Ben Othman, J., Mokdad, L.: Enhancing data security in Ad Hoc networks based on multipath routing. J. Parallel Distrib. Comput. **70**, 309–316 (2010)
2. Daemen, J., Rijmen, V.: The Design of Rijndael: AES - The Advanced Encryption Standard. Springer, Heidelberg (2002). https://doi.org/10.1007/978-3-662-04722-4
3. Ho, T., Medard, M., Koetter, R., Karger, D.R., Effros, M., Shi, J., Leong, B.: A random linear network coding approach to multicast. IEEE Trans. Inf. Theor. **52**(10), 4413–4430 (2006)
4. Koetter, R., Médard, M.: An algebraic approach to network coding. IEEE/ACM Trans. Netw. **11**(5), 782–795 (2003)
5. Krawczyk, H.: Secret sharing made short. In: Stinson, D.R. (ed.) CRYPTO 1993. LNCS, vol. 773, pp. 136–146. Springer, Heidelberg (1994). https://doi.org/10.1007/3-540-48329-2_12
6. Li, S.Y., Yeung, R.W., Cai, N.: Linear network coding. IEEE Trans. Inf. Theor. **49**(2), 371–381 (2003)
7. McEliece, R.J., Sarwate, D.V.: On sharing secrets and reed-solomon codes. Commun. ACM **24**(9), 583–584 (1981)
8. Rabin, M.O.: Efficient dispersal of information for security, load balancing, and fault tolerance. J. ACM **36**(2), 335–348 (1989). https://doi.org/10.1145/62044.62050
9. Resch, J.K., Plank, J.S.: AONT-RS: blending security and performance in dispersed storage systems. In: Proceedings of the 9th USENIX Conference on File and Storage Technologies, FAST 2011, pp. 14–14 (2011)
10. Shamir, A.: How to share a secret. Commun. ACM **22**(11), 612–613 (1979)
11. Zhang, S., Liew, S.C., Lam, P.P.: Hot topic: physical-layer network coding. In: Proceedings of the 12th Annual International Conference on Mobile Computing and Networking, MobiCom 2006, pp. 358–365 (2006)

Fingerprinting Crowd Events in Content Delivery Networks: A Semi-supervised Methodology

Amine Boukhtouta[1]([envelope]), Makan Pourzandi[1], Richard Brunner[2], and Stéphane Dault[3]

[1] Ericsson Security Research,
8275 Trans Canada Route, Saint-Laurent, Montréal, QC, Canada
`{amine.boukhouta,makan.pourzandi}@ericsson.com`
[2] Ericsson Universal Delivery Network,
8275 Trans Canada Route, Saint-Laurent, Montréal, QC, Canada
`richard.brunner@ericsson.com`
[3] Ericsson Business Area Digital Services, R&D Security Operations,
8275 Trans Canada Route, Saint-Laurent, Montréal, QC, Canada
`stephane.dault@ericsson.com`

Abstract. Crowd events or flash crowds are meant to be a voluminous access to media or web assets due to a popular event. Even though the crowd event accesses are benign, the problem of distinguishing them from Distributed Denial of Service (DDoS) attacks is difficult by nature as both events look alike. In contrast to the rich literature about how to profile and detect DDoS attack, the problem of distinguishing the benign crowd events from DDoS attacks has not received much interest. In this work, we propose a new approach for profiling crowd events and segregating them from normal accesses. We use a first selection based on semi-supervised approach to segregate between normal events and crowd events using the number of requests. We use a density based clustering, namely, DBSCAN, to label patterns obtained from a time series. We then use a second more refined selection using the resulted clusters to classify the crowd events. To this end, we build a XGBoost classifier to detect crowd events with a high detection rate on the training dataset (99%). We present our initial results of crowd events fingerprinting using 8 days log data collected from a major Content Delivery Network (CDN) as a driving test. We further prove the validity of our approach by applying our models on unseen data, where abrupt changes in the number of accesses are detected. We show how our models can detect the crowd event with high accuracy. We believe that this approach can further be used in similar CDN to detect crowd events.

1 Introduction

CDNs are the global networks delivering content from different content providers to cope with the increasing demand for the QoE required by the commercial

© IFIP International Federation for Information Processing 2018
Published by Springer International Publishing AG, part of Springer Nature 2018. All Rights Reserved
F. Kerschbaum and S. Paraboschi (Eds.): DBSec 2018, LNCS 10980, pp. 312–329, 2018.
https://doi.org/10.1007/978-3-319-95729-6_20

content providers. To address the ever increasing demand for content in the Internet, CDNs turned out to be the de-facto solution to cache content, including video streaming, news, and social media [5]. CDNs are meant to accelerate the delivery of content on the Internet to cope with the business-grade performance. As such, their importance increased within the cyberspace ecosystem over time. A recent report stipulates that 70% of all Internet traffic will cross CDNs by 2021 [4].

Among the key players in networks deployment, CDNs have been facing many challenges from the complexity and versatility of emerging online services. Thus, CDNs are exposed to benign events such as crowd events and cyber-threats like DoS, DDoS and harmful crawling of cached assets. The CDN operators are therefore increasingly interested in the prediction of faulty events in CDNs result-ing from misconfigurations, unpredictable networking conditions, or the result of cyber-attacks. In recent years, sophisticated malicious artifacts are used by attackers to take advantage of any vulnerability to conduct sabotaging CDN itself or target critical infrastructures to cause service unavailability. By meta-morphosing CDNs to support security as a built-in asset to counter different cyber-threats have become then of a paramount importance to operators. As part of this effort, there is a keen interest shown operators to investigate events logging data for identifying misbehavior of CDNs. Crowd events (flash crowds) are simultaneous and huge access to web or media based content from legitimate users. There have been several efforts to predict the DDoS attacks based on analyzing the event logs. However, few works targeted to distinguish between the benign crowd events from DDoS attacks. However, this distinction is of high importance to avoid false positive DDoS attacks and better planning of resources to address legitimate users during crowd events. To this end, we aim at address-ing the problem of framing crowd events in CDNs and differentiate them from unsolicited/malicious activities by exploring CDN's data obtained from a large operator. In this research effort, we aim to provide an answer to the follow-ing questions: (1) What are the key indicators identified in CDNs ecosystem? (2) Given observable crowd events, how to profile them and isolate them from normal events? (3) By considering profiles, how to use engineered features to distinguish between crowd events and anomalies?

To answer these questions, we shape the contributions of this paper as fol-lows: (1) We draw upon 169 GB of logging data collected from a large CDN operator to characterize access events in a hybrid CDN, where web and media assets are cached. The number of events is more than 452 million events (more than 386 million access events, whereas the rest are routing events). We present different perspectives to engineer features, namely, delivery, cache, IP and HTTP based features. (2) We propose a semi-supervised methodology to identify crowd events with high detection rate on the training dataset (99%). The methodol-ogy is driven by the number of requests to profile patterns in a timely manner (time series). By using a density clustering algorithm (DBSCAN), we manage to create profile normal and crowd accesses. The clustering plays the role of a first filter layer towards crowd events fingerprinting. The resulted labeling is then used for classification (XGBoost) which subsequently identifies the crowd events. We manage to identify two patterns of crowd accesses patterns that can be considered as a ground truth to potentially identify anomalies. (3) To test further our methodology, we used anomalous unseen data to test classifiers. We showed that our methodology allowed to discern crowd events and anomalies. Thus, we believe our methodology can be used to create multi-level time series classification system to identify anomalies in CDN's deployment.

The remainder of this paper is as follows: In Sect. 2, we explain the methodology used to discern crowd and normal accesses, as well as the features set used to characterize. Section 3 puts forward a description of the dataset and experiments layout as well as results obtained from them. In Sect. 4, we expose the different related works as well as how they compare with our work. In Sect. 5, we conclude with a few observations and future directions of our research.

2   Methodology

2.1   Overview

The reason behind showing an interest to crowd events, lies in the fact that they tend to be frequent over time, therefore, prone to be fingerprinted in comparison with cyber-attacks like DDoS, where data needs to be recorded during an on-progress attack (e.g., [6]), or inferred from network telescopes (e.g., [10,11]), or even simulated through attacking tools (e.g., [12]). Our strategy is to characterize thoroughly crowd events through number of accesses, then differentiate them from anomalies based on attributes collected from different perspectives (delivery, IP, cache, HTTP). Figure 1 depicts our approach. We pre-process the input logs and events to extract patterns representing aggregated counters collected during a time window. We then use them to train a first model to discern between the normal and crowd accesses (fingerprinting component in Fig. 1). Subsequently, the

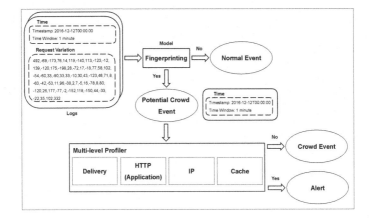

Fig. 1. General approach.

potential crowd events are subject to a more in-depth multi-level profiling to check whether the event is a real crowd event or an alert (Multilevel profiling component in Fig. 1). In our approach, we use different perspectives to aggregate several features (attributes) into new features allowing to detect crowd events. Then, we use collected aggregates as a downstream outcome to fingerprint crowd events. We refer readers to Sect. 2.3, where we describe the different features considered in our work.

2.2   Fingerprinting Crowd Events

Figure 2 illustrates the fingerprinting methodology, which is a semi-supervised approach, where we use empirically a density clustering algorithm to label crowd and normal accesses. Based on that, we create a detection model to identify labeled patterns. As such, we apply a data-driven approach based on logs collected from CDN's operator. The logs are used to compute different attributes indexed per time. Given a time granularity and aggregation window, we create patterns, which are fed to a density clustering algorithm to segregate between normal and crowd events. However, obtained solution does not allow to balance between normal and crowd accesses cardinalities. Therefore, we employ data augmentation technique to increase the number of crowd accesses patterns. This is done to balance the number of normal access patterns with crowd access patterns. Afterwards, we label the balanced data to create a ground truth for classification. The latter's result is a model that represents a decision system that discerns crowd events from normal events. It is important to mention that all these steps are done offline. In the sequel, we detail different components.

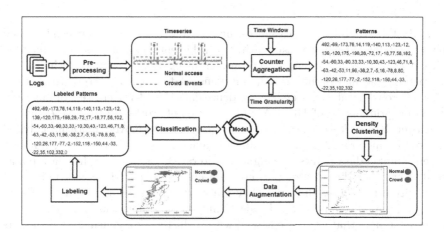

Fig. 2. Detailed view of the fingerprinting approach.

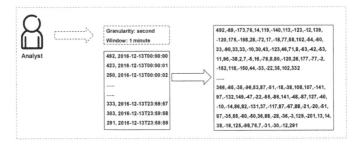

Fig. 3. Aggregation example.

Aggregation. By aggregation, we mean encompassing observed raw values during a granularity time unit (e.g., 1 s) into one value observed during a time window period (e.g., 1 min). As such, the result of the aggregation is a data point that reflects a statistical view of raw values, which can be a count, sum, average, etc. In the context of our work, we consider initially the number of access requests to CDN, indexed per second. It is important to mention that the aggregation period ca be adjusted, but, needs to be selected carefully to obtain a rich set of patterns to fingerprint crowd events. In this work, as a first attempt, we consider two aggregation time windows, namely, 1 min or 5 min. Other aggregation periods can be considered, although the aggregation period is longer (e.g., 10 min), less is the number of collected patterns. Figure 3 illustrates an aggregation pattern recorded for 1 min aggregation time window. A pattern is represented by a starting and an ending value, as well as, differences (shifts) between values observed every second.

Density Clustering. Density clustering is meant to segregate between high and low density data, thus, we assume that crowd events happen less in comparison with normal events. As such, we consider using this clustering technique to characterize normal events as a highly dense data (highly dense core cluster), whereas crowd events are seen like low dense data (low dense clusters or outliers). Based on prior usage of DBSCAN [3] in different works [13–15], we exploit it to cluster data collected from accesses aggregates. DBSCAN algorithm is based on two parameters, namely, the radius distance and the minimum core number. Given sampled data points, the algorithm iteratively looks for other data points located within radius distance to create a cluster. If two data core points are close within the radius distance, they are merged into the same cluster. Based on the minimum core number, the algorithm sets a minimal cardinality to create a cluster. Points that are not enclosed within clusters, are considered as outliers or singletons. In our case, we target mainly to group normal accesses in a core cluster and crowd accesses in low density clusters or singletons. Thus, we set the minimum core number to 1, to find data points representing crowd events as singletons. As a distance function, we use Euclidean distance between points. We use the silhouette score to evaluate the quality of clustering solution.

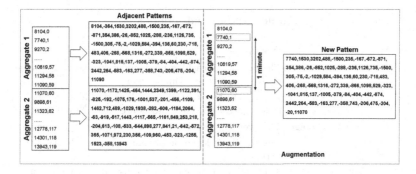

Fig. 4. Augmentation example.

Data Augmentation. Being inspired by works from [16–18], we employ data augmentation on time series. The main reason behind doing so, lies in the fact of unbalance between normal accesses and crowd accesses. With this intent, low density clusters and singletons representing crowd access patterns are used to create new patterns. Timely adjacent patterns are used to extract new patterns to create a balanced dataset between normal accesses and crowd accesses. We use a sliding window (e.g., 1 s) to extract a new pattern, Fig. 4 depicts an example of two adjacent patterns aggregated during 1 min and used to obtain a new pattern by utilizing a sliding window of 1 s.

Labeling and Classification. As a downstream outcome from clustering solution and data augmentation, we label the core cluster patterns representing normal accesses with 0, whereas singleton and augmented patterns are labeled with 1. Thus, a labeled dataset is created, and used as an input for a binary classifier. The latter is built by applying the XGBoost algorithm [1], which is based on optimization through tree models [19,20] and boosting [21]. It supports many learning and boosting parameters that can be used to build classification models. XGBoost has three loss functions to control prediction, namely, Mean Square Error for regression, Log-Loss for binary classification and mLog-Loss for multi-classification. XGBoost uses regularization functions to control the complexity of the model to avoid over-fitting. Both loss function and regularization terms to define the objective function. The latter is optimized by using the gradient descent algorithm to compute gradients. XGBoost builds the boosting tree by computing predictions of leaves and greedily finding splitting points optimizing the objective function. In [22], the authors enumerated the advantages of XGBoost: (1) Tree models have rich representational abilities. (2) The boosting is adaptive, thus, models are flexible to determine neighborhoods in different parts of the input space. (3) Bias-Variance trade-off control, XGBoost starts with low variance and high bias model and reduces the bias accordingly by decreasing the size of neighborhoods in the input space.

Table 1. Features description.

Perspective	Feature	Description
Delivery	Hit ratio	The number of caching hits divided by the total number of requests during a time period
	Volume sum	The sum of bytes saved by caching during a time period, it is negative if content assets are fetched from the origin
	Volume average	The average value of volume records during a time period
	Volume deviation	The standard deviation of volume records during a time period
	Volume minimum	The minimum value of volume records during a time period
	Volume maximum	The maximum value of volume records during a time period
	Duration average	The duration average for content assets delivery during a time period
	Duration deviation	The standard deviation of content assets' delivery duration during a time period
	Duration maximum	The maximum value of delivery duration records during a time period
IP	Number of requests	The total number of requests observed during a time period
	Number of distinct IPs	The total number of requesting unique IPs during a time period
	Maximum requesting IP	The maximum number of requests issued by the most accessing IP during a time period
	IPs entropy	The number of unique IPs divided by number of requests issued by IPs during a time period
	Average request per IP	The average value of requests issued per IP during a period of time
	Deviation request per IP	The standard deviation value of requests issued per IP during a period of time
Cache	Number of distinct caches	The total number of unique caches serving requests during a time period
	Maximum requested cache	The maximum number of requests observed on the most serving cache during a time period
	Caches entropy	The number of unique caches divided by number of requests served by caches during a time period
	Average request per cache	The average value of requests served by a cache during a period of time
	Deviation request per cache	The standard deviation value of requests served by a cache during a period of time
HTTP	Ratio status	The HTTP status ($20X$, $40X$, $50X$) observed requests divided by the total number of requests
	Ratio HTTP method	The HTTP method (GET, POST, HEAD, DELETE, PUT) observed requests divided by the total number of requests

2.3   Features Engineering

The features engineering aims to the creation of attributes from the domain knowledge, namely, log traces collected from CDN deployment. Based on internal experts' inputs, we define four perspectives based on field attributes: delivery perspective, IP perspective, cache perspective, and HTTP perspective (see Table 1). We consider these metrics as an increase in the delivery duration metrics indicates a bandwidth saturation indicating a possible crowd event. From a delivery perspective, we are interested in: (1) the hit ratio through counting how frequent the content assets are found in caches, (2) the cached volume through computing saved bytes (content objects' size) as well as different statistical metrics, and (3) the delivery duration of different content assets as well as the average, the standard deviation and the maximum values. As the delivery perspective asses the effectiveness of CDNs, we propose to use those features for fingerprinting.

The IP perspective is meant to monitor clients requesting content from CDN. The metrics associated with IPs help to describe the dynamics of accessing content, thus, they are potential indicators for DDoS attacks or massive contents' crawling. From IP perspective, we are interested in: (1) the total number of requests produced by clients (IP addresses), (2) the total number of distinct IP addresses observed during aggregation time, and (3) the maximum number of requests generated by the most occurring IP address, (4) IPs entropy score, which represents the total number of distinct IP addresses divided by the total number of requests, (5) the average of requests' number generated per IP, and (6) the standard deviation of requests' number generated per IP.

The cache perspective represents how cached content is served to clients instead of accessing the content from origin servers. As such, being aware how content is distributed can help detection of caching anomalies. For instance, the distribution of requests through caches pinpoints to how fairly or unfairly requests are distributed to caches. Low cached volume metric indicates potential high number of requests to unpopular content indicating possible DDoS events. From cache perspective, we are interested in: (1) the total number of distinct caches serving requests during aggregation time, (2) the maximum number of requests observed on the most serving cache, and (3) caches entropy score, which represents the total number of distinct caches divided by the total number of requests, (4) the average of requests' number served by a cache, (5) the standard deviation of requests' number served by a cache.

The HTTP perspective is meant to be aware of the application protocol used to request content from CDN. A drastic change in the number of POST or GET can indicate the presence of a flooding attack; thus a misuse of HTTP protocol. From HTTP perspective, we are interested in: (1) the ratio of HTTP status codes (e.g., 200 or 404), and (2) the ratio of HTTP methods (e.g., *GET, POST*). At the end, we discard some constant features: (1) the minimum delivery value since it tends to 0, (2) the number of requests from the less requesting IP addresses since it tends to 1, and (3) the number of requests observed on less accessed caches, which tends to 1.

3   Experiments

3.1   Experiments Setup

We run the experiments on a virtual machine deployed on Intel Xeon CPU E5-2060 2 GHz, consisting of 12 virtual CPUs and 32 GB of memory. The experiments are done on a dataset collected from the 12th to 19th of December 2016. It represents Web access logs collected from a large operator hosting a sport league website. The size of the data is 169 GB of logs, which corresponds to $386, 396, 885$ access events. We enumerate $1, 268, 160$ IPs spanning over $200, 634$ "/16" subnets, geo-located in 219 countries and $15, 646$ cities. The crowd events were observed on 14th and 15th of December 2016, whereas anomalies were observed the 12th of December 2016. Figure 5 represents the distribution of requests' number between 13th to 19th December 2016. We notice two peaks of the request number in the 14th and 15th of December, these peaks represent crowd accesses during games. We consider then data collected from 13th to 19th December 2016 to cluster normal and crowd accesses. The clustering is done on the patterns as described in Sect. 2.2. Once the clustering is done, we augment the patterns collected from the original data, then, label different patterns to create the classifier. To build the latter, we use a 10 rounds' classification process with a 5-fold cross validation. To test our approach, we apply the classifier on the anomalous day (12th of December 2016, not used for the training) to check, if the model detects abrupt changes. As such, we can use patterns extracted from other features, to see which ones can segregate between crowd accesses and anomalies.

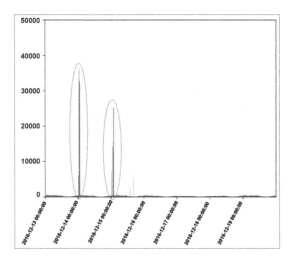

Fig. 5. Number of requests (13th to 19th December 2016).

3.2   Clustering and Augmentation Results

We apply DBSCAN algorithm on patterns extracted from two aggregation periods (1 min and 5 min). The intent is to find empirically a core cluster grouping normal accesses, and discerning crowd accesses. To do so, we tweak the distance parameter of DBSCAN and check the quality of clustering solutions through silhouette scores and how many patterns are enclosed in the core cluster. The intent is to find a distance parameter that produces a good quality of clustering, meanwhile segregating crowd accesses from normal ones. For each distance, we compute clustering execution time, silhouette score and core clustering coverage. Figure 6 depicts clustering running time, silhouette score and core cluster coverage with respect to distance parameter, which varies from 5 to 65 for 1 min patterns, and from 5 to 110 for 5 min patterns. The running time to build clustering solutions spans from 10.7 to 28.25 s for 1 min patterns, and from 2.69 to 5.01 s for 5 min patterns. The clustering running time average is 14.2 s for 1 min patterns and 3.71 s for 5 min patterns. Regarding silhouette scores, we observe that it tends to 1, which means that clustering quality is good and therefore no need to increase the distance beyond the current distances used for our experiments. The core cluster is discernible, since the majority of patterns are grouped together (core cluster covers the majority of patterns). We observe that the silhouette scores increase when the distance gets higher, but we need to monitor a trade-off between high silhouette scores and missing patterns representing crowd accesses. To illustrate this trade-off, we consider two clustering solutions for both 1 min (distances equal to 25 and 65, silhouette scores equal to 0.855 and 0.931, coverage values equal to 9965 and 10055) and 5 min (distances equal to 80 and 110, silhouette scores equal to 0.877 and 0.909, coverage values equal to 1995 and 2002) patterns (see Fig. 6).

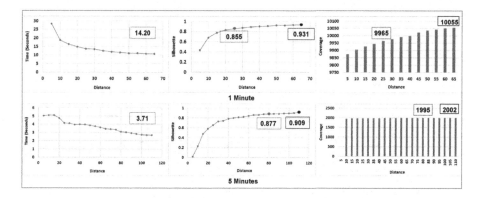

Fig. 6. Clustering: running time & silouhette scores & core cluster coverage.

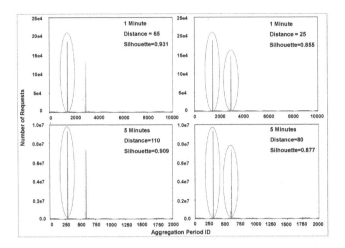

Fig. 7. Silhouette & distance vs. Crowd events identification.

We refer to Fig. 7 to depict the trade-off between solutions for different patterns. Based on observations inferred from aforementioned illustration, we select two solutions, meaning a distance equals to 25 for 1 min patterns and a distance equals to 80 for 5 min patterns. Despite the fact that these distances do not output the best silhouette score, their values manage to segregate better between core cluster patterns (normal accesses) and singleton patterns representing crowd accesses (see circled peaks in Fig. 7). In the second case observed in Fig. 7, where distance values are respectively 65 and 110 for 1 min and 5 min patterns, the silhouette scores are slightly better, but the clustering solutions do not segregate effectively between normal and crowd accesses. We can observe

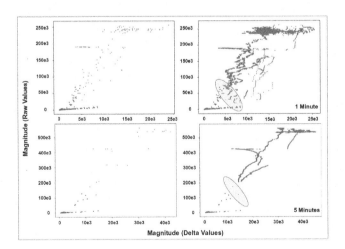

Fig. 8. Patterns augmentation (1 min & 5 min).

that some peaks are not distinguishable from normal accesses (the peaks that are not circled in Fig. 7).

We apply augmentation to balance between the patterns belonging to the core cluster (normal accesses) and other patterns (crowd accesses). The motivation behind doing so, is to infer more crowd access patterns from existing patterns and scale their cardinality with normal access patterns in order to label them for classification. Figure 8 illustrates the plotting of magnitude values of raw values and difference values within patterns. Data points at the bottom of both plots represent the core cluster, whereas data points in the middle up to the top of plots represent crowd accesses. Augmentation of crowd accesses can be observed in the right hand side, where new patterns are created to balance classification dataset.

Table 2 shows the number of patterns before and after augmentation. In this experiment, we randomly select some adjacent crowd access patterns and infer augmented data. For 5 min aggregation period, data augmentation is used for both normal and crowds accesses to increase the number of samples to more than 5, 000; whereas for 1 min aggregation, we consider increasing the number of crowd accesses patterns since we already have more than 9, 000 patterns for normal accesses. However, the data augmentation process is to subject for refinement, since we can infer more normal access and crowd patterns, thus, increasing number of patterns in the classification dataset. Moreover, we need to carefully label patterns in the border between normal and crowd accesses. This is depicted in the grey zone illustrated within the right hand side of Fig. 8, where normal and crowd accesses can be mixed, therefore a potential over or under fitting of the classification model can take place.

Table 2. Number of patterns before and after data augmentation.

Patterns	Normal access (before)	Crowd access (before)	Normal access (after)	Crowd access (after)
1 min	9, 965	115	9, 965	7, 015
5 min	1, 992	24	5, 893	5, 409

3.3 Classification Results

We apply the XGBoost algorithm by considering its default execution layout. We use first and second order gradients (*grad* and *hess*) by applying logistic transformation (sigmoid) [2] on *LogLoss* function. To evaluate trained models, we consider *stacking*, an ensemble learning technique, where the predicted value is computed from cross validation. The number of learning rounds is 10, where the number of folds within the dataset is 5. The evaluation metrics are: (1) the Area Under Curve (*AUC*) of Receiver Operating Characteristic (*ROC*) function, which represents the trade-off between sensitivity (fall-out) and specificity (recall), and (2) the accuracy average for both training and testing.

Table 3. 10 rounds of 5 fold cross validation results (Tr. Training Phase, Te. Testing Phase).

Period	AUC Mean (Tr.)	AUC Std (Tr.)	AUC Mean (Te.)	AUC Std (Te.)	Acc. Mean (Tr.)	Acc. Mean (Te.)
1 min	%99.9128	%0.0144	%99.7489	%0.0766	%99.8274	%99.6370
	%99.9552	%0.0168	%99.8066	%0.0964	%99.8542	%99.6489
	%99.9814	%0.0075	%99.8740	%0.1108	%99.1070	%99.6608
	%99.9831	%0.0048	%99.9125	%0.1063	%99.9137	%99.6371
	%99.9838	%0.0050	%99.9200	%0.1187	%99.9420	%99.6906
	%99.9861	%0.0037	%99.9442	%0.0773	%99.9509	%99.7144
	%99.9861	%0.0037	%99.9665	%0.0528	%99.9524	%99.7263
	%99.9872	%0.0033	%99.9661	%0.0536	%99.9628	%99.7203
	%99.9945	%0.0040	%99.9667	%0.0529	%99.9673	%99.7204
	%99.9980	%0.0026	%99.9663	%0.0533	%99.9702	%99.7322
5 min	%99.9915	%0.0217	%99.9739	%0.0214	%99.9911	%99.9735
	%99.9915	%0.0217	%99.9739	%0.0214	%99.9911	%99.9735
	%99.9915	%0.0217	%99.9739	%0.0214	%99.9911	%99.9735
	%99.9915	%0.0217	%99.9739	%0.0214	%99.9911	%99.9735
	%99.9915	%0.0217	%99.9739	%0.0214	%99.9911	%99.9735
	%99.9915	%0.0217	%99.9739	%0.0214	%99.9911	%99.9735
	%100	%0.0217	%99.9738	%0.0214	%99.9911	%99.9735
	%100	%0.0217	%99.9738	%0.0214	%99.9911	%99.9735
	%100	%0.0217	%99.9736	%0.0216	%99.9911	%99.9735
	%100	%0.0217	%99.9736	%0.0216	%99.9911	%99.9735

Table 3 depicts classification results for both 1 min and 5 min patterns. Each row contains a round of 5 fold cross validation, where we consider AUC mean and standard deviation, as well as accuracy mean. These metrics are computed for both training and testing phases. From results observed in the table, we notice that for each round, AUC statistics are maintained, since the mean tends to 1, whereas the standard deviation tends to 0. We also observe that the accuracy is high and tends to 1 for both training and testing. Regarding 5 min patterns classification, the results are constant; consequently, any round can be considered. Regarding 1 min patterns classification, the results change slightly from a round to another. Usually, the model with the highest accuracy rate, or with the lowest difference between AUC mean and standard deviation (best sensitivity and specificity trade-off), can be selected. As such, we can consider models obtained from the 10th round, which has the best AUC and high accuracy rate metrics. To test their detection of abrupt changes, the models are then tested on unseen data (12th of December). Figure 9 illustrates patterns detected by models as abrupt changes in the number of requests for two training days (14th and 15th of December 2016) and unseen data (12th of December 2016).

Regarding crowd accesses, we notice 2 types of patterns illustrated in the top and bottom plots within Fig. 9 (dashed ellipses). The first crowd accesses' patterns illustrate a continuous periodic access to a sport event, whereas the second ones illustrate some crowd accesses at the beginning of the game, then, another set of crowd accesses during up to the end of the game. This can be explained as people followed up the first game continuously at the opposite of

Table 4. Classification runtime (milliseconds) per pattern.

Patterns	Minimum	Maximum	Average	Deviation
1 min	0.715971	3.186941	0.749865	0.103742
5 min	0.961065	2.573013	1.008195	0.123094

the second one. In the latter, people were more interested to know what is the issue of the game than following it continuously. The abrupt changes present in the middle plot are different than the aforementioned crowd accesses' patterns. As such, we will consider studying other attributes during the period, where we observed crowd accesses and suspicious patterns. Regarding the classification runtime, we compute the time taken to predict each pattern. Table 4 illustrates different statistics observed on classification runtime expressed in Milliseconds. We notice that the average time to classify 1 min pattern is in the range of

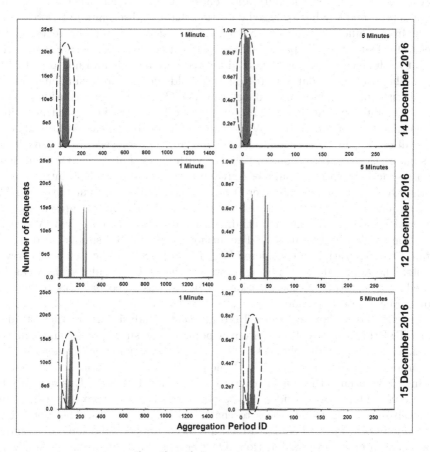

Fig. 9. Prediction on 12th 14th 15th December 2016 Patterns (1 min & 5 min).

0.75 ms, whereas it is in the range of 1 ms for 5 min pattern. The standard deviation is in the range of 0.1 ms for both 1 min and 5 min pattern.

4   Related Work

Several works considered studying abnormal access patterns to the web sites in order to detect DDoS attacks. In [23], authors analyzed IBM Olympic Games Web site, and developed models to predict seasonal patterns based on peak request rates and traffic variation. The study did not consider the implication of CDNs, or DoS attacks. In [24], authors studied a peak workload analysis of the football World Cup 1998 Web site [9]. They focused on the reference of few extremely popular webpages, where clients inter-session time were short. The authors considered the workload observed on the world cup website as an initial characterization of how future workloads look like. They profiled HTTP server response codes, type of content, unique file distribution and, files' reference behavior (temporal locality and concentration of references). In [28], the authors proposed a behavior based detection that can discriminate DDoS attack traffic from traffic generated by real users. Their detection method relies on the repeatable features of the packet arrivals. They used Pearson's correlation coefficient to define a segregation threshold between predictable and non-predictable data. They used [8,9] datasets to test thresholds defined from simulated inter-arrival time data. This work did not consider CDNs' logs and consider traffic flows. The inter-arrival time can be subject to other networking constraints like congestion, type of content (e.g. Video) and cached and non-cached web objects. In addition, as any correlation analysis, an error metric needs to be considered to support threshold decision. In [29], the authors used also Pearson coefficient on users' activity through number of requests. In [30], the authors introduced a method to detect application-layer DDoS attack based on the entropy of HTTP GET requests per source IP address. They used adaptive auto-regressive model to transform time series into a multi-dimensional vector, then, applied SVM classification to identify the attacks. The authors utilized NS-2 simulator to create attacks ground truth and considered World Cup 1998 Web dataset [9] for crowd events. The approach is promising, however, the use of simulated data can be biased or noisy. None of the mentioned studies considered patterns to build a crowd events detection model.

In [25], the authors considered crowd events analysis, where they studied two HTTP log traces collected from a popular TV show (24 h) and Chilean election site (approximately 33 h). They showed that number of clients was in the proportion of request rate. They studied also the number of clients' clusters during crowd events, the clusters overlap, and request rate, as well as reference to files access. They also considered datasets representing password cracking and five web servers disabling traces to characterize DoS attacks. They looked at the same perspectives, clients and files, and drew upon results some differentiation between crowd events and DoS. They proposed an enhancement to CDNs, namely, adaptive CDN, by using collected trace-driven simulation to study their enhancement. Despite the fact the study considered clustering clients, it has not investigated temporal aggregation of counters to create a crowd event detection model. In [26], the authors examined usage patterns, files' characteristics (popularity and referencing), transfer behaviors of YouTube, and compare them to traditional Web and media streaming workload. The data were collected from a university network, where staff and students accessed two Youtube's points of presence. This work focused more on usage patterns and file referencing without elaborating predictive tasks. In [27], the authors differentiated DDoS and crowd access flows by considering the fact that generated flows from DDoS tools can be fingerprinted (high level of similarity), whereas crowd accesses are randomly distributed (low level of similarity). The authors used Jeffrey distance, Sibson distance, and Hellinger distance to measure the similarity among flows. They concluded that Sibson distance is the most suitable, after applying experiments on two distinctive datasets, Aukland VIII [7] representing crowd events and Lincoln Laboratory DDoS scenario [8]. Despite the fact that the approach is interesting, they used old datasets (collected on 2003 and 1999 respectively). As explained above, none of the previous works, consider using a temporal set of patterns as we use in our approach to detect crowd events.

In [31], the authors applied a discrimination algorithm based on a similarity metric, namely, entropy variations to identify suspicious flows. They formulated the problem in the Internet with botnets, and presented theoretical proofs for the feasibility of their method. In this work, the authors relied on simulations to prove their approach. For our work, we used a recent dataset collected from a major operator, and applied a semi-supervised approach to profile crowd accesses.

5   Conclusion and Future Work

The distinction between crowd events and DDoS attacks is difficult, making it of an increasing interest to CDN operators. In this paper, we applied a semi-supervised approach on a sport league dataset collected from a major operator to identify normal and crowd access patterns. The patterns are represented by number request shifts during 1 and 5 min. We first used DBSCAN to group normal accesses into a core cluster, a crowd accesses into low dense clusters and singletons. By applying data augmentation, we balanced classification vectors representing 1 min and 5 min patterns. Then, we utilized XGBoost to fingerprint crowd and normal accesses. The results of the classification (99% accuracy) showed the great potential of our approach. We tested our approach by applying it to unseen data. The approach detected abrupt changing patterns, even though these change patterns do not have the same shape like the ones identified in the training dataset. We believe our approach can be successfully used to detect crowd events in other CDN environments. Despite of our initial good results, the diversity of CDN environments would necessitate more investigation. We frame our future works to consider other features described in Sect. 2.3 to distinguish anomalies (e.g., DDoS) from crowd events. We will rely on patterns found on unseen data to carry on this research. In addition, we plan to tweak XGboost models to study the trade-off between their complexity and performance. Moreover, we want to thoroughly test the classification model on additional data, as well as deploy it in online mode.

References

1. Tianqi, C., Guestrin, C.: XGBoost: a scalable tree boosting system. In: Proceedings of the 22nd ACM SIGKDD International Conference on Knowledge Discovery and Data Mining. ACM (2016)
2. Chen, T., He, T., Benesty, M.: xgboost: Extreme gradient boosting, pp. 1–4. R package version 0.4-2 (2015)
3. Ester, M., Kriegel, H.P., Sander, J., Xu, X.: A density-based algorithm for discovering clusters in large spatial databases with noise. In: KDD, vol. 96, no. 34, pp. 226–231 (1966)
4. Cisco, Cisco Visual Networking Index: Forecast and Methodology 2016–2021. http://www.cisco.com/c/en/us/solutions/collateral/service-provider/visual-networking-index-vni/complete-white-paper-c11-481360.html
5. Stocker, V., Smaragdakis, G., Lehr, W., Bauer, S.: The growing complexity of content delivery networks: challenges and implications for the internet ecosystem. Telecommun. Policy **41**, 1003–1016 (2017)
6. The CAIDA UCSD "DDoS Attack 2007" Dataset. http://www.caida.org/data/passive/ddos-20070804_dataset.xml
7. WITS: Waikato Internet Traffic Storage. https://wand.net.nz/wits/auck/8/
8. Lincoln Laboratory MIT. DARPA Intrusion Detection Evaluation. https://www.ll.mit.edu/ideval/data/2000/LLS_DDOS_1.0.html
9. The Internet Traffic Archive, WorldCup98. http://ita.ee.lbl.gov/html/contrib/WorldCup.html
10. Fachkha, C., Bou-Harb, E., Debbabi, M.: Fingerprinting internet DNS amplification DDoS activities. In: The 6th International Conference on New Technologies, Mobility and Security (NTMS), pp. 1–5. IEEE (2014)
11. Rossow, C.: Amplification hell: revisiting network protocols for DDoS abuse. In: Proceedings of the 21st Network and Distributed System Security Symposium (NDSS) (2014)
12. Moustis, D., Kotzanikolaou, P.: Evaluating security controls against HTTP-based DDoS attacks. In: 2013 Fourth International Conference on Information, Intelligence, Systems and Applications (IISA). IEEE (2013)
13. Erman, J., Arlitt, M., Mahanti, A.: Traffic classification using clustering algorithms. In: Proceedings of the 2006 SIGCOMM Workshop on Mining Network Data. ACM (2006)
14. Manh, T.T., Kim, J.: The anomaly detection by using DBSCAN clustering with multiple parameters. In: 2011 International Conference on Information Science and Applications (ICISA). IEEE (2011)
15. Shahaboddin, S., Amini, A., Anuar, N.B., Kiah, M.L.M., Teh, Y.W., Furnell, S.: D-FICCA: a density-based fuzzy imperialist competitive clustering algorithm for intrusion detection in wireless sensor networks. Measurement **55**, 212–226 (2014)
16. Le Guennec, A., Malinowski, S., Tavenard, R.: Data augmentation for time series classification using convolutional neural networks. In: ECML/PKDD Workshop on Advanced Analytics and Learning on Temporal Data (2016)

17. Howard, A.G.: Some improvements on deep convolutional neural network based image classification. arXiv preprint arXiv:1312.5402 (2013)
18. Krizhevsky, A., Sutskever, I., Hinton, G.E.: Imagenet classification with deep convolutional neural networks. In: Advances in Neural Information Processing Systems, pp. 1097–1105 (2012)
19. Hastie, T., Tibshirani, R., Friedman, J.: The Elements of Statistical Learning. SSS. Springer, New York (2009). https://doi.org/10.1007/978-0-387-84858-7
20. Murphy, K.P.: Machine Learning: A Probabilistic Perspective. The MIT Press, Cambridge (2012)
21. Breiman, L.: Arcing classifier (with discussion and a rejoinder by the author). Ann. Stat. **26**(3), 801–849 (1998)
22. Nielsen, D.: Tree Boosting With XGBoost-Why Does XGBoost Win Every Machine Learning Competition? MS thesis. NTNU (2016)
23. Iyengar, A.K., Squillante, M.S., Zhang, L.: Analysis and characterization of large-scale web server access patterns and performance. World Wide Web **2**(1–2), 85–100 (1999)
24. Arlitt, M., Jin, T.: A workload characterization study of the 1998 world cup web site. IEEE Netw. **14**(3), 30–37 (2000)
25. Jaeyeon, J., Krishnamurthy, B., Rabinovich, M.: Flash crowds and denial of service attacks: characterization and implications for CDNs and web sites. In: Proceedings of the 11th International Conference on World Wide Web. ACM (2002)
26. Phillipa, G., Arlitt, M., Li, Z., Mahanti, A.: Youtube traffic characterization: a view from the edge. In: Proceedings of the 7th ACM SIGCOMM Conference on Internet Measurement, pp. 15–28. ACM (2007)
27. Yu, S., Thapngam, T., Liu, J., Wei, S., Zhou, W.: Discriminating DDoS flows from flash crowds using information distance. In: Proceedings of the 3rd IEEE International Conference on Network and System Security (NSS 2009), 18–21 October 2009 (2009)
28. Thapngam, T., et al.: Discriminating DDoS attack traffic from flash crowd through packet arrival patterns. In: 2011 IEEE Conference on Computer Communications Workshops (INFOCOM WKSHPS). IEEE (2011)
29. Chuan, X., Du, C., Kong, X.: An application layer DDoS real-time detection method in flash crowd. In: IACSIT Hong Kong Conferences, pp. 68–73 (2012)
30. Ni, T., Gu, X., Wang, H., Li, Y.: Real-time detection of application-layer DDoS attack using time series analysis. J. Control Sci. Eng. **2013**, 4 (2013)
31. Prasad, K.M., Munivara, K., Reddy, A.R.M., Rao, K.V.: Discriminating DDoS attack traffic from flash crowds on internet threat monitors (ITM) using entropy variations. Afr. J. Comput. ICT **6**(2), 53 (2013)

Assessing Attack Impact on Business Processes by Interconnecting Attack Graphs and Entity Dependency Graphs

Chen Cao[1(✉)], Lun-Pin Yuan[1], Anoop Singhal[2], Peng Liu[1], Xiaoyan Sun[3], and Sencun Zhu[1]

[1] The Pennsylvania State University, Harrisburg, USA
caochen11@mails.ucas.ac.cn, lunpin@psu.edu, pliu@ist.psu.edu,
szhu@cse.psu.edu
[2] National Institute of Standards and Technology, Gaithersburg, USA
anoop.singhal@nist.gov
[3] California State University, Sacramento, USA
xiaoyan.sun@csus.edu

Abstract. Cyber-defense and cyber-resilience techniques sometimes fail in defeating cyber-attacks. One of the primary causes is the ineffectiveness of business process impact assessment in the enterprise network. In this paper, we propose a new business process impact assessment method, which measures the impact of an attack towards a business-process-support enterprise network and produces a numerical score for this impact. The key idea is that all attacks are performed by exploiting vulnerabilities in the enterprise network. So the impact scores for business processes are the function result of the severity of the vulnerabilities and the relations between vulnerabilities and business processes. This paper conducts a case study systematically and the result shows the effectiveness of our method.

1 Introduction

Although enterprises and organizations have been paying ever more attention to cyber defense, today's cyber-attacks towards enterprise networks often undermine the security of business processes. The reason is directly related to several main limitations of existing cyber-defense practice, because the security of business processes heavily relies on the deployed cyber-defense measures and procedures.

Although a fundamental limitation of existing cyber-defenses is that zero-day attacks cannot be prevented, this limitation is clearly *not the only reason* why cyber-attacks can undermine security. In many, if not most, real-world cyber-security incidents, the security of business processes is actually undermined by known attacks.

© IFIP International Federation for Information Processing 2018
Published by Springer International Publishing AG, part of Springer Nature 2018. All Rights Reserved
F. Kerschbaum and S. Paraboschi (Eds.): DBSec 2018, LNCS 10980, pp. 330–348, 2018.
https://doi.org/10.1007/978-3-319-95729-6_21

Regarding why known attacks could significantly undermine the security of business processes, the following main reasons have been recognized in the research community. First, enterprises and organizations do not have the resources needed to patch all the known vulnerabilities. As a result, although the security administrators are working hard to patch as many vulnerabilities as possible and as soon as possible, many vulnerabilities are actually in the "not yet patched" status when cyber-attacks happen. Another contributing factor to the result is that the time a vulnerability becomes known is *not* the time the corresponding patch becomes available.

Second, when cyber-attacks are happening, even if the intrusion detection system accurately detects the intrusions, the intrusion alerts and alert correlation results are still not able to directly tell "what should I do?" in terms of intrusion response. (In real-world enterprises new intrusion alerts keep on being raised, and the security administrators are already fully loaded.) It has been widely recognized in the research community [8,18,20] that there is a wide *semantic gap* between the information contained in intrusion alerts and how the cost-effectiveness of intrusion response is evaluated. On one hand, the cost-effectiveness of intrusion response is usually evaluated based on business process-level metrics (e.g., the number of customers affected by a cyber-attack, the number of tasks that need to be undone) and measurements. On the other hand, business process-level metrics are not really measured by intrusion detection systems.

Therefore, to achieve cost-effective intrusion response, this semantic gap must be bridged. To bridge the semantic gap, impact assessment is necessary. Although researchers have found the necessity of using entity dependency graphs [8] to assess the impact of attacks on business processes for quite a few years, the existing impact assessment techniques still face a key challenge. The challenge is two-fold: (1) impact assessment results cannot be automatically used to make recommendations on taking active cyber-defense actions; and (2) existing active cyber-defense techniques cannot be business-process-aware. That is, these techniques will not be able to directly state their effectiveness using business process-level measurements such as how much of what tasks will be accomplished by when.

In [19] it has been perceived that attack graphs and entity dependency graphs could be interconnected to address the above key challenge; however, no realistic case study has been conducted to validate the perceived method. As a result, the intrusion response research community still lacks essential understanding about (a) how to efficiently implement the perceived method; (b) whether it really works; and (c) how well it works.

The goal of this work is to efficiently design and implement the perceived method and conduct a realistic case study to assess the impact of attacks on business processes using not only system-level metrics (e.g., how many files are corrupted, which processes are compromised) but also business process-level metrics. We believe that this case study is a solid step forward towards bridging the aforementioned semantic gap.

The main contributions of this work are as follows.

– We propose the first efficient implementation of the method perceived in [19]. We extend the perceived method to make use of CVSS scores. We invent an algorithm to prune the raw interconnected graph. Through logic programming, the implemented tool can automatically generate an interconnected graph, which interconnects an attack graph and an entity dependency graph, and calculate the impact scores of an attack on tasks in a business process.
– The first realistic case study is systematically conducted to show how the perceived method and our implementation can assess the impact of attacks on business processes using not only system-level metrics but also business process-level metrics.
– Through the case study, we also evaluate our implementation in several aspects such as scalability and running time.

2 Background

2.1 CVSS Score

The Common Vulnerability Scoring System (CVSS) provides a way to measure the impacts of vulnerabilities and produce a numerical score for the attack impact [9]. The current version of this score system is version three, which is released in 2015. The system contains three metric groups: base score metrics, temporal score metrics, and environmental score metrics. A base score ranging from 0 to 10 is assigned to a vulnerability according to the base score metrics. The temporal score metrics and environmental score metrics can be used to refine the base score to better reflect the risks caused by a vulnerability to the user's environment. However, the temporal score metrics and environmental score metrics are optional. Therefore, in this paper we only use base score for impact analysis and still refer it as CVSS score. The National Vulnerability Database (NVD) provides a CVSS base score for almost all known vulnerabilities. A higher CVSS base score of a vulnerability implies that: (1) the vulnerability is easier to be exploited due to more vulnerable components and available technical means for exploitation; or (2) more impact on the availability, confidentiality, and integrity upon successful exploitation. Therefore, the base score can be leveraged to assess the impact of vulnerability exploitation on business processes in terms of both exploitability and impact.

2.2 Attack Graph

To analyze the impact of attacks on business processes, it's necessary to first understand how the vulnerabilities in an enterprise network can be used to compromise the host machines. Attack graph [1,7,10,12,17] is a very effective way to generate potential attack paths. Given the vulnerabilities, the attack graph is able to show the possible attack sequences to the final attack target.

MulVAL (Multihost, multistage Vulnerability Analysis) is an attack graph generation tool that models the interaction between software vulnerabilities and the system and network configurations [11]. It leverages Datalog [14] to model network system information (such as the vulnerabilities, configurations of each machine, etc.) as facts and the interaction of various network components as rules. With these facts and rules, MulVAL can generate an attack graph showing the potential attack paths from the vulnerabilities to the attack goal. In the attack graph, facts and rules are represented by nodes with different shapes. There are two types of fact nodes: primitive fact nodes and derived fact nodes. The primitive facts nodes are denoted with boxes, which represents host and network configuration information. The derived fact nodes are denoted with diamonds, which are generated according to certain rules. The interaction rules are denoted with ellipses.

Figure 1 shows a very simple attack graph containing only 5 nodes. In Fig. 1, if the conditions in node 1, 2 and 3 are satisfied, then the rule in node 4 can be applied. The eventual consequence is that the attacker is able to execute arbitrary code on the host machine (shown in node 5).

Fig. 1. An example attack graph

The attack graph is essential for business process impact assessment, as it shows how the vulnerabilities can be leveraged to compromise the host machines. If the host machines are involved in the business processes, the impact of vulnerabilities on business processes can then be further analyzed.

2.3   Entity Dependency Graph

In an enterprise network, a business process is supported by a number of entities at several abstraction layers: asset layer, service layer and business process task layer. At the asset layer, an asset is (part of) a persistent disk and the file stored on the disk, a computer (hypervisors, desktops or servers), or a peripheral device. At the service layer, services represent the functionalities provided by hosts, such as web services, database services, etc. At the business process task layer, a business process is composed of one or more tasks.

An entity dependency graph [2] can be established due to the dependencies between the abstraction layers and the dependencies on each individual layer. Generally, the higher layer depends on the function of the lower layer. The business process task layer depends on the functionality provided by the services at service layer. One task may even depend on several services. The services further depends on the assets at the services layer. In addition, dependencies also exist at an individual layer. For example, at the business process task layer, a task may depend on another task.

3 Approach Overview

The primary goal of our paper is to assess the attack impact on business processes. Since attacks essentially exploit vulnerabilities in the enterprise network, the attack impact heavily relies on the intrinsic characteristics of each individual vulnerability. Considering that the characteristics of vulnerabilities have been measured using the CVSS scores, the impact towards a business process can also be measured based on the scoring system. That is, an impact score can be generated for a business process to indicate the impact of attacks towards the business process. Therefore, the key problem need to be addressed is how to generate the impact score for a business process given the CVSS scores of involving vulnerabilities.

In this paper, we propose an three-step approach for business process impact assessment. The general idea is to generate an interconnected graph by analyzing the dependency relationships between vulnerabilities and attacks on hosts, between services and hosts, and between tasks and services. The approach takes three sets of knowledge units as the inputs and generates the business impact score as the output.

The three sets of knowledge units are respectively (1) Common Vulnerability and Exposure (CVE) system that provides information of publicly known vulnerabilities and their CVSS scores, (2) the vulnerability information generated by the vulnerability scanner, and (3) the business process dependency graph. The business impact assessment approach mainly involves the following steps:

Step 1: Instantiate the knowledge units with Datalog as facts and rules in MulVAL. Utilize MulVAL to generate an interconnected graph which consists of impact paths from the vulnerabilities.

Step 2: Prune the interconnected graph to get a more clear relationship between business processes and vulnerabilities.

Step 3: Calculate the impact score based on the CVSS scores of the vulnerabilities exploited in this attack.

3.1 Instantiate Knowledge Units

CVE system refers to the vulnerability database which contains all information about publicly known vulnerabilities. From this system, we can get the CVSS score of each vulnerability. The vulnerability information generated by vulnerability scanner contains the exact CVE IDs of each vulnerability and where these vulnerabilities are located in the enterprise network. By combining these two sources of knowledge, we can easily get the whole picture of these vulnerabilities, including CVSS score, CVE ID, and location in the enterprise network, etc. Such vulnerability information can be used to analyze the potential attacks that

Listing 1.1. Example Interaction Rules Describing Three Dependency Relationships

```
interaction_rule(        /* And depends */
    (nodeImpact(Task):-
        node(Task, and, Task1, Task2), nodeImpact(Task1)
    ),
    rule_desc('An impacted child task affects an And task')
).
interaction_rule(        /* Or depends */
    (nodeImpact(Task):-
        node(Task, or, Task1, Task2),
        nodeImpact(Task1), nodeImpact(Task2)
    ),
    rule_desc('Both impacted child task affects an Or task')
).
interaction_rule(        /* Flow depends */
    (nodeImpact(Task):-
        node(Task, flow, Task1, Task2), nodeImpact(Task2)
    ),
    rule_desc('A flow node is impacted from its flow')
).
```

might happen, which may further impact the business processes. As the information represents facts about vulnerabilities in the network, we crafted fact nodes in MulVAL to instantiate the information.

Business process dependency graph describes how entities in the network depend on each other. Sun et al. [19] summarizes and bridges the semantic gap between the attack graph generated by MulVAL and the business process dependency graph. Hence, in this paper, we extend MulVAL to craft new fact nodes and new rule nodes to interconnect the attack graph and the business process dependency graph.

First of all, entities in a business process dependency graph become primitive fact nodes or derived fact nodes. Primitive fact nodes usually represent already known information, such as host configuration, network configuration, etc. Derived fact nodes are computed information by applying interaction rules towards primitive fact nodes.

Secondly, rule nodes are added to model the causality relationships among fact nodes. For example, if a service S runs on a machine H and an attacker has exploited a vulnerability to *execute arbitrary code on the machine*, then this service S can be impacted by the attacker. This relation can be interpreted as a rule "A compromised machine impacts a service running on it". In other words, when two fact nodes "S runs on machine H" and "attacker executes arbitrary code on the machine" are both present, this rule node will take effect and the derived fact node "S is impacted" will become present. In this example, machine H has a vulnerability. The attack graph generated by MulVAL can only tell "attacker executes arbitrary code on the machine," but it is not able to tell "S is impacted". Therefore, interconnecting the attack graph and the business process dependency graph can help infer the impact of attacks on business process.

Thirdly, the dependency relationships among entities in the business processes become rule nodes. There are three dependency relationships in the business process dependency graph: Or-depends, And-depends and Flow-depends. Listing 1.1 shows a set of example interaction rules crafted to depict the impact propagation among tasks when different types of dependency relationships exist among these tasks. That is, if a task *and-depends* on task 1 and task 2, then this task is impacted by the attacker when either of the two tasks are impacted. if a task *or-depends* on task 1 and task 2, then this task is impacted only when both tasks are impacted. if a task *flow-depends* on task 1 and task 2, then this task will be impacted when task 2 is impacted. In this case, task 2 can be completed only after task 1 is completed. So if task 1 is impacted, then task 2 is impacted. We will explain more about the dependency relationships in Sect. 5.1.

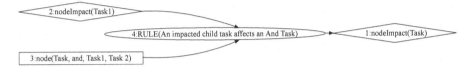

Fig. 2. And-dependency in the graph

With all the fact nodes and rule nodes set up, MulVAL can be used to generate the interconnected graph. For example, Fig. 2 shows the first and-depends example in Listing 1.1. In the interconnected graph, different nodes are represented by different shapes, i.e., box, ellipse and diamond. The ellipse shape represents rule node, which is applied only if all needed precondition fact nodes are present. Hence, the ellipse shape represents AND-relation for all precondition fact nodes. The diamond shape represents derived fact node, which is generated as long as one deriving rule node is present. Therefore, the diamond shape represents OR-relation between the deriving rule nodes. In other words, the interconnected graph reflects the relationship between vulnerabilities and the business processes. However, the interconnected graph is too complicated for generating the impact assessment score for a business process. To enable computation of the impact score, we prune the graph to reduce the complexity.

3.2   Prune Raw Interconnected Graph

Impact score is a function result of CVSS scores of the vulnerabilities involved in the interconnected graph. When we prune the graph, we must preserve the vulnerability node and the impacted business process node. We apply all the five rules below to prune the graph. The entire process of pruning may take several rounds by applying different rules in each round. In addition, based on different circumstances, we also deal with the edges connecting to the reduced nodes correspondingly.

Prune all the Non-vulnerability Leaf Nodes. In this interconnected graph generated by MulVAL, derivation nodes (rule nodes) imply AND relations and derived fact nodes imply OR relations. The primitive fact node in this graph represents the facts in this network, such as the vulnerabilities and deployment configuration. They are represented as leaf nodes in the graph with a shape of box. These non-vulnerability leaf nodes do not participate in the function of CVSS scores. So if a node is not a vulnerability node and is not an AND or OR node, we can prune it. Then each edge derived from these nodes can also be pruned.

Prune the Nodes That Have Only One Ancestor Node. If a node has only one ancestor node, no matter how many child nodes it has, it does nothing but directly deliver impact from its ancestor node to its child nodes. This node is an intermediate impact deliverer for its ancestor node and can be directly pruned without information loss. This kind of nodes is usually the derivation nodes which have only one ancestral vulnerability node, or derived fact nodes which have only one rule to be generated. By pruning one node, the edges from the ancestor node to this node and from this node to the child nodes are removed. A new edge is added directly between the ancestor node and the child node. This operation of pruning one-ancestor nodes may be done several times in the graph-pruning process, as more of them may be produced in other rounds of pruning.

Prune the Nodes, Except the Vulnerability Nodes, Which Have No Ancestors. Because all left nodes are relation nodes, vulnerability nodes, and the impacted business process nodes. If a node has no ancestor node and is not a vulnerability node, it is a relation node and does not contain any valuable information. This kind of nodes are produced by pruning their ancestor nodes that are usually non-vulnerability nodes. As their ancestor nodes have been pruned, no impact information is delivered to them. Therefore, they can be pruned without impact information loss. The edges from these nodes can also be pruned.

Find the Shortest Path from One Vulnerability Node to the Target Impacted Business Process Node and Merge These Paths. The impact assessment for an attack is to find the relationship between vulnerabilities and the target impacted business processes. If a vulnerability can be exploited in an easy way to affect a business process, there is no need to make it more complex. The assumption in our paper is that attackers always choose the easiest way to achieve the attack goal. Based on this assumption, if there are different paths between a vulnerability node and the impacted business process node in the interconnected graph, the shortest path that has least nodes should be chosen. As a result, each vulnerability node has a shortest path to the target business process node. All other nodes and edges that are not on these paths should be pruned. In some cases, one vulnerability node may have more than one shortest paths to the target business process node. In this case, these paths should also be preserved. To simplify these circumstances, if there are two or more equal shortest paths between one vulnerability node and the impacted business process node, we convert this interconnected graph to two or more interconnected graphs to ensure there is only one shortest path for a vulnerability in one interconnected graph. Finally we calculate each graph's impact score to get the average score.

Leave Only One Edge for Linked Nodes and Prune the Other Edges Between Them. In some cases, there are more than one edges between two nodes. The extra edges could be produced by the previous rounds of pruning. They are not needed and thus should be removed too.

These five ways are applied sequentially to the raw interconnected graph generated by MulVAL until the graph does not change again. Two or more graphs could possible be generated as one vulnerability may have two or more equal shortest paths to a target business process node.

3.3   Calculate Impact Score

Step 2 can prune the raw interconnected graph to the simplified graph which contains only the vulnerability nodes, the target business process node and their relations. The impact score of the vulnerability node and the target business process node can be represented by V and M respectively. The impact score calculations based on AND-relations and OR-relations are called AND-calculation and OR-calculation. We take the following steps to generate the impact score.

First, we value V by a number between 0 and 1, i.e.,

$$V_i = \frac{CVSS_i}{10}. \tag{1}$$

Second, we define AND-calculation as:

$$V_i \ AND \ V_j = V_i \times V_j. \tag{2}$$

and OR-calculation as:

$$V_i \ OR \ V_j = V_i + V_j - V_i \times V_j. \tag{3}$$

Finally, M can be easily calculated by above mentioned calculation methods. For example,

$$M = FUNC(V_1, \ V_2, \ V_3) = (V_1 \ OR \ V_2) \ AND \ V_3 = (V_1 + V_2 - V_1 \times V_2) \times V_3 \tag{4}$$

In this paper, we use the above definitions of AND-calculation and OR-calculation to compute the impact score. However, the administrators of an enterprise network can change the definitions of AND-calculation and OR-calculation based upon different situations and scenarios.

The results of AND-calculation and OR-calculation are directly influenced by the CVSS score of the vulnerabilities. Higher CVSS score usually leads to higher impact score towards the business process, which implies more impact the attack can bring to the business process.

4   Case Description

To demonstrate the method for attack impact assessment, we describe a concrete case in this section. We will illustrate the application of our method to this case in Sect. 5.1.

Business Process Scenario. This case is a travel reservation system supporting a business process of "providing customers with a web interface for reserving tickets and hotel". This business process consists of seven tasks: T_1: Search travel information; T_2: Reserve tickets and hotel options; T_3: Prompt for signing in or signing up; T_4: If signed in, load preference and promotion code; T_5: If signed in, reserve a hotel and tickets as a member; T_6: If not signed in, reserve a hotel and tickets as a guest; T_7: Prompt for payment and confirm the reservation.

From T_1 (start of the business process) to T_7 (end of the business process), the business process may be executed through four different workflows (i.e. execution paths) as shown in Fig. 3a: P_1: $T_1T_2T_3T_4T_5T_7$; P_2: $T_1T_3T_2T_4T_5T_7$; P_3: $T_1T_2T_3T_6T_7$; and P_4: $T_1T_3T_2T_6T_7$. The difference between P_1 and P_2 and between P_3 and P_4 is the order of T_2 and T_3. The customer can either first make reservations (T_2) and then be prompted to sign in (T_3), or first sign in and then make reservations. If the customer chooses not to sign in during T_3, she is recognized as a guest. The difference between P_1 and P_3 and between P_2 and P_4 is whether the customer has signed in. If signed in, the system loads customer preference and promotion code (T_4) for reserving a hotel (T_5). Since T_5 depends on the information obtained from T_4, T_5 should come after T_4.

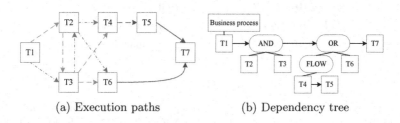

(a) Execution paths   (b) Dependency tree

Fig. 3. Inter-task dependency

This travel reservation system can be viewed as a complicated business-process-support enterprise network shown in Fig. 4. The services provided by the network are hosted on different hosts. VM 1, VM 2 and VM 3 are three virtual machines. Web service 1 is hosted in VM 1 which runs in Hypervisor 1. Web service 2 is hosted in VM 2 which runs in Hypervisor 2. VM 3 also runs in Hypervisor 2.

Database service runs in Container 1 which is hosted by Docker 3. Ticket service, which processes ticket-related business, runs in Container 2 which is also hosted by Docker 3. Hotel service, which processes hotel-related business, runs in Container 3 which is hosted by Docker 1. Payment service, which is

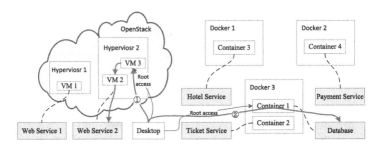

Fig. 4. Software architecture

responsible for monetary transaction, runs in Container 4 hosted by Docker 2. These dockers run in different workstations. A developer's desktop can access the VM 3 and has a root account credential. It can also access Container 1 as a root user. This desktop has a dashboard which displays through HTTP protocol, i.e. it runs a web service. It can also be accessed through SSH protocol from Internet.

Table 1. Vulnerability information

Vulnerability	CVSS score	Exploited result
CVE-2016-0777	6.5	Privilege escalation
CVE-2016-7479	9.8	Privilege escalation
CVE-2016-6325	7.8	Privilege escalation
CVE-2014-3499	7.2	Container escape
CVE-2016-6258	8.8	Virtual machine escape

Attack Scenario. We assume this network has five vulnerabilities and their related information is displayed in Table 1. CVE-2016-0777, CVE-2016-7479 and CVE-2016-6325 locate in the developer's desktop and allow attackers to escalate privilege. CVE-2014-3499 locates in the docker software and can enable an attacker to escape from the container. CVE-2016-6258 locates in the Kernel-based Virtual Machine (KVM) software and can also be used to break the virtual machine.

There are two attack paths in Fig. 4. One attack path is denoted as red line 1 in Fig. 4. The attacker firstly exploits the vulnerability in the web application or the SSH application to compromise the developer desktop, which has the log-in credential for VM 3. By leveraging the vulnerability in the KVM software, the attacker can directly access the host, i.e. Hypervisor 2, by breaking the isolation between the virtual machine and the host. The attacker can then access VM2 which hosts Web service 2 and execute arbitrary code on this virtual machine. Once Web service 2 is compromised, all tasks depend on this service are impacted. The other attack path is denoted as red line 2 in the Fig. 4. As the developer's desktop has the log-in credential for Container 1, the attacker can also access this container. With the database running in this container, the attacker can execute arbitrary code in the database process and then affect all tasks depending on the database.

5   Case Study and Evaluation

5.1   Case Study Results

In this section, we applied the impact assessment method to the case described above and demonstrate the experiment results.

First, we obtained the CVSS scores for the five vulnerabilities in this case according to their CVE IDs.

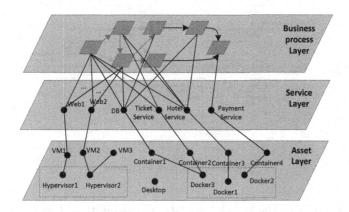

Fig. 5. The entity dependency graph

Second, we constructed a entity dependency graph for this network, as shown in Fig. 5 (as web services are depended on by each task, some edges from the tasks to Web1 and Web2 are ignored in this figure). The entity dependency graph contains three layers: asset layer, service layer and business process task layer. Among these tasks, T_1 and-depends on the web services, database service, ticket service and hotel service. T_2 and-depends on web services, ticket service and hotel service. T_3 and-depends on web services, and database service. T_4 and-depends on web services, and database service. T_5 and-depends on web services, database service, and hotel service. T_6 and-depends on web services, and hotel service. T_7 and-depends on web services, and payment service.

At the business process layer, we specified the dependency relationships among tasks. To better understand the relationships, we firstly define three special tasks: T_{or}, T_{and} and T_{flow}. As the name implies, these tasks represent three relationships: Or-dependency, And-dependency, and Flow-dependency. That is, if a task T_{or} or-depends on sub-tasks T_i and T_j, then T_{or} is impacted only when T_i and T_j both are impacted. If a task T_{and} and-depends on sub-tasks T_i and T_j, then T_{and} is impacted when T_i or T_j is impacted. If a task T_{flow} flow-depends on sub-tasks T_i and then T_j, then T_{flow} is impacted when T_j is impacted. In addition, the impact on T_i will cause an impact on T_j, which leads to an impact on T_{flow}. The relationships of the seven tasks of this business process can be depicted in Fig. 3b. In other words, this business process viewed as one T_{flow} flow-depends on T_1, T_{and}, T_{or} and then T_7. T_{and} and-depends on T_2 and T_3. T_{or} or-depends on T_6 and T_{flow}, which flow-depends on T_4 and then T_5.

Fig. 6. Interconnected graph

After instantiating the knowledge units, we can get the interconnected graph as shown in Fig. 6. In this graph, the ellipse represents AND-calculation and the diamond represents OR-calculation. By applying the five pruning rules described in Sect. 3.2 against the raw graph, we generated the pruned graph, as shown in Fig. 7, to show the relationship between vulnerabilities and the target business process. The expression "nodeImpact(X)" means "X" is impacted, e.g. "nodeImpact(business process)" means the target business process is impacted. The CVSS scores of these vulnerabilities are shown in Table 1. Therefore, the final impact score of this attack can be calculated as:

$$M = (((V_{CVE-2016-0777} \ OR \ V_{CVE-2016-7479}) \ AND \ V_{CVE-2016-6325})$$
$$AND \ V_{CVE-2016-6258}) \ OR \ V_{CVE-2016-3499}$$
$$= 0.91.$$

Apart from the impact score calculated from the pruned interconnected graph, there is more information about whether the services and tasks are impacted or not from the raw interconnected graph. By searching through the raw interconnected graph showed in Fig. 6, we can get that all tasks are

$$M = (((V_{CVE-2016-0777} \ OR \ V_{CVE-2016-7479}) \ AND \ V_{CVE-2016-6325})$$
$$AND \ V_{CVE-2016-6258}) \ OR \ V_{CVE-2016-3499}$$
$$= 0.91.$$

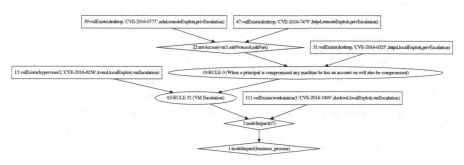

Fig. 7. Pruned interconnected graph

impacted by this attack. Three services including Web service 2, Ticket service and Database service are also impacted. All tasks are impacted as they all and-depend on Web service 2. These three services are impacted as they can be accessed by the developer's desktop which can be controlled by the attacker. That is, the impact on these services match the attack path described in Sect. 4. Moreover, we can also get the impact score for each task through the same process: pruning the graph and calculating the score based on the AND-calculation and OR-calculation. The impact score for each task is 0.992 for task 1, 0.91 for task 2, 0.973 for task 3, 0.973 for task 4, 0.973 for task 5, 0.682 for task 6, and 0.91 for task 7. We can see some scores are higher than the impact score for the whole business process. This is because some task are easily attacked by the attacker from the Internet. For example, task 3 and-depends on web service 1, web service 2 and database service. The attacker can impact task 3 without exploiting the vulnerability "CVE-2014-3499", which lowers the requirement for the attacker.

There are three services that are not impacted by the attack, including Web service 1, Hotel service and Payment service. They cannot be found as the impacted nodes in the raw interconnected graph. This is because they are not involved in the attack path. Therefore, the raw interconnected graph can precisely present the attack path in the real world.

5.2 Analysis of Different Cases

Section 5.1 has shown a successful application of our impact assessment method to the case described in Sect. 4. However, in the real world, the enterprise network is not static. For example, a vulnerability can be patched or a host can be removed. In this section, we will show that our method can still handle the dynamic changes in the enterprise network and generate new impact scores for the business processes by re-running the analysis after changes to the system.

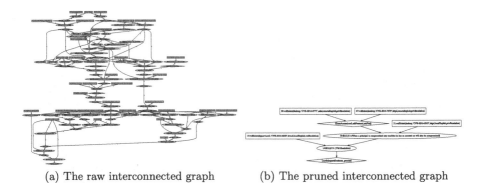

(a) The raw interconnected graph   (b) The pruned interconnected graph

Fig. 8. Interconnected graphs with a vulnerability is patched

A Vulnerability is Patched. When a vulnerability is patched, it means a fact node should be deleted. As a consequence, the interconnected graph will be different and so is the pruned graph. For instance, we assume the vulnerability "CVE-2014-3499" is patched as this vulnerability is the oldest one in these five vulnerabilities. Figure 8 shows the new raw interconnected graph and pruned graph without "CVE-2014-3499." By analyzing this pruned graph, the new impact score towards the business process is 0.682, which is much smaller than 0.91.

Whether a task or a service is impacted can also be acquired through the raw interconnected graph. By searching this graph, we can see all tasks are still impacted. Two services including Web service 2 and Database service are impacted. The other four services, including Web service 1, Hotel service, Payment service and Ticket service, are not impacted. Compared with Sect. 5.1, ticket service is not impacted in this case. This is because patching the vulnerability "CVE-2014-3499" prevents the escape from Container 1. The attacker cannot access Container 2 any more so that the ticket service running in Container 2 is free from the impact.

The Developer Desktop is Removed. When the developer desktop is removed, several fact nodes should be deleted. For example, three vulnerabilities in this desktop no longer impact the network, so these vulnerability nodes are deleted. When generating the interconnected graph with MulVAL, we found no graph was generated. This means although there are vulnerabilities in this network, the attacker located in the Internet cannot impact this business process. The reason is that all attack paths start from this desktop as the entry point. Removing this desktop prevents the attacker from exploiting the vulnerabilities inside the network. Therefore, the interconnected graph can precisely reflect the real-world impact circumstances.

5.3   Evaluation of Scalability

Section 5.1 illustrates how to leverage our impact assessment method to calculate the impact score for an attack targeting a particular business process.

Table 2. Time consumed to generate interconnected graphs according to different Number of Units (NoU) and different Connectivity Level (CL)

CL	NoU			
	100	200	400	600
5	1 m 2.45 s	7 m 44.71 s	67 m 55.64 s	228 m 42.53 s
10	1 m 0.33 s	7 m 49.49 s	65 m 4.48 s	253 m 9 s
100	0 m 59.67 s	7 m 48.85 s	65 m 18.60 s	224 m 33.49 s

The key idea is to extend MulVAL to generate an interconnected graph and calculate the impact score based on the pruned graph. In this process, generating the interconnected graph is the most time-consuming part. It directly affects the scalability of our impact assessment method. Therefore, in this section, we evaluate the scalability of our method in terms of how fast interconnected graphs can be generated for different scopes of network.

In order to get different scopes of network, we view the small network of the aforementioned case in Sect. 4 as one unit and duplicate it. These units are then combined on the basis of different connectivity levels. Because different connectivity levels differ the network complexity, which may affect the time used to generate the interconnected graph. We define connectivity level as how widely one web server is shared, i.e., how many units share one web server. These units sharing one web server constitute one group and each group is connected by the database server of one unit in the group. Therefore, the scope of a network generated through this method can be measured by number of units and connectivity level.

Table 2 describes the time consumed to generate interconnected graphs for different scopes of network according to different number of units and different connectivity level. The first column indicates connectivity level and the first row presents the total number of duplicated units. The other grids in the table indicate how much time is used to generate one graph. For example, with 100 duplicated units in the network and every 5 units sharing one web server, generating the interconnected graph for this scope of network consumes 1 min and 2.45 s.

From Table 2, we can see the time used to generate an interconnected graph is mainly determined by the number of connected units, not the connectivity level. This is because when generating the interconnected graph, the time is mainly consumed by finding new path from one node to another node. As sharing web server does not increase paths in the graph, the consumed time does not affected by the connectivity level. Furthermore, the time increases non-linearly, i.e., the time increases faster than the number of connected units increases. In summary, our method cannot scale well in a very large network. However, it does not mean our solution is not practical in the real world. Taking a university as an example, the scope of one unit is similar to a network of a department. Therefore, for a big university with 100 departments, the time consumed to generate an interconnected graph is less than 2 min, which means our solution is feasible in practice.

6   Related Work

Little research has been done on business process impact assessment in recent years. Jakobson [8] presents a business process impact assessment that quantifies impact by using Operational Capacity (OC), and considers intra and inter dependencies between assets, services, and business processes. Dai et al. [3] propose a cross-layer Situation Knowledge Reference Model (SKRM) which considers intra and inter-dependencies between instruction layer, OS layer, app/service layer, and workflow (task) layer. Sun et al. [18] introduce a novel probabilistic impact assessment method which leverages Bayesian networks. Sun et al. [20] also propose a multi-layer impact evaluation model which includes four layers, namely vulnerability layer, asset layer, service layer, and mission layer. They measure impacts by OC and impact factor. Poolsappasit et al. [13] leverages attack graph (called Bayesian Attack Graph) and attack tree to revise the likelihoods in the event of attack incidents and identify the vulnerable points in the network system. Frigault et al. [5] use attack graph as a special Bayesian network to model probabilistic risks in a network. They also introduce Dynamic Bayesian Networks [6] with attack graphs to model the security of dynamically changing networks. Dewri et al. [4] leverage an attack tree model with multi-objective optimization to solve the problem, i.e. balance between security hardening and limited budget for an enterprise network. Ray et al. [15] also utilize an attack tree model with an algorithm simplifying the tree to locate the malicious insiders in a network. Saripalli et al. [16] present QUIRC which utilizes Microsoft's STRIDE to assess the security risk in a cloud computing environment and define risk as a combination of the Probability of a security thread event and its severity.

Our method uses the interconnected graph, which interconnects attack graph and entity dependency graph, to demonstrate the relationships between vulnerabilities and the impacted business process. By pruning the interconnected graph, we can get simplest relationships and calculate the impact score based on vulnerabilities' CVSS score. For different cases in one network, our method can handle these changes and generate related impact scores. With these impact scores, the network operator may do further security hardening for the network.

7   Conclusion

In this paper, we propose a new business process impact assessment method, which measures the impact of an attack towards a business process in an enterprise network. Our method produces a numerical score for the attack impact. We extend MulVAL, a logic-based network security analyzer, to support more fact nodes and rule nodes for business process impact assessment. With the facts and rules, our approach generates an interconnected graph for an attack and prunes the interconnected graph to show the simplified relation between vulnerabilities and business processes. In the end, the impact score can be calculated by analyzing the pruned graph and following the relation calculation rules. According to our case study, this business process impact assessment method is effective and can facilitate the cyber-defense and cyber-resilience in an enterprise network that supports business processes.

Acknowledgment. We thank the anonymous reviewers for their valuable comments. This work was supported by NIST 60NANB17D279, NSF CNS-1505664, ARO W911NF-13-1-0421 (MURI), and NSF CNS-1618684.

Disclaimer. This paper is not subject to copyright in the United States. Commercial products are identified in order to adequately specify certain procedures. In no case does such identification imply recommendation or endorsement by the National Institute of Standards and Technology, nor does it imply that the identified products are necessarily the best available for the purpose.

References

1. Ammann, P., Wijesekera, D., Kaushik, S.: Scalable, graph-based network vulnerability analysis. In: Proceedings of the 9th ACM Conference on Computer and Communications Security, pp. 217–224. ACM (2002)
2. Chen, X., Zhang, M., Mao, Z.M., Bahl, P.: Automating network application dependency discovery: experiences, limitations, and new solutions. In: OSDI, vol. 8, pp. 117–130 (2008)
3. Dai, J., Sun, X., Liu, P., Giacobe, N.: Gaining big picture awareness through an interconnected cross-layer situation knowledge reference model. In: 2012 International Conference on Cyber Security (CyberSecurity), pp. 83–92. IEEE (2012)
4. Dewri, R., Poolsappasit, N., Ray, I., Whitley, D.: Optimal security hardening using multi-objective optimization on attack tree models of networks. In: Proceedings of the 14th ACM Conference on Computer and Communications Security, pp. 204–213. ACM (2007)
5. Frigault, M., Wang, L.: Measuring network security using Bayesian network-based attack graphs. In: Proceedings of the 2008 32nd Annual IEEE International Computer Software and Applications Conference, pp. 698–703. IEEE Computer Society (2008)
6. Frigault, M., Wang, L., Singhal, A., Jajodia, S.: Measuring network security using dynamic Bayesian network. In: Proceedings of the 4th ACM Workshop on Quality of Protection, pp. 23–30. ACM (2008)
7. Jajodia, S., Noel, S., O'Berry, B.: Topological analysis of network attack vulnerability. In: Kumar, V., Srivastava, J., Lazarevic, A. (eds.) Managing Cyber Threats. Massive Computing, vol. 5, pp. 247–266. Springer, Boston, MA (2005). https://doi.org/10.1007/0-387-24230-9_9
8. Jakobson, G.: Mission cyber security situation assessment using impact dependency graphs. In: 2011 Proceedings of the 14th International Conference on Information Fusion (FUSION), pp. 1–8. IEEE (2011)
9. NIST: Cvss score (2017). https://nvd.nist.gov/vuln-metrics/cvss
10. Noel, S., Jajodia, S., O'Berry, B., Jacobs, M.: Efficient minimum-cost network hardening via exploit dependency graphs. In: 2003 Proceedings of 19th Annual Computer Security Applications Conference, pp. 86–95. IEEE (2003)
11. Ou, X., Boyer, W.F., McQueen, M.A.: A scalable approach to attack graph generation. In: Proceedings of the 13th ACM Conference on Computer and Communications Security, pp. 336–345. ACM (2006)

12. Phillips, C., Swiler, L.P.: A graph-based system for network-vulnerability analysis. In: Proceedings of the 1998 Workshop on New Security Paradigms, pp. 71–79. ACM (1998)
13. Poolsappasit, N., Dewri, R., Ray, I.: Dynamic security risk management using Bayesian attack graphs. IEEE Trans. Dependable Sec. Comput. $9(1)$, 61–74 (2012)
14. Racket: Datalog (2017). https://docs.racket-lang.org/datalog/
15. Ray, I., Poolsapassit, N.: Using attack trees to identify malicious attacks from authorized insiders. In: di Vimercati, S.C., Syverson, P., Gollmann, D. (eds.) ESORICS 2005. LNCS, vol. 3679, pp. 231–246. Springer, Heidelberg (2005). https://doi.org/10.1007/11555827_14
16. Saripalli, P., Walters, B.: QUIRC: a quantitative impact and risk assessment framework for cloud security. In: 2010 IEEE 3rd International Conference on Cloud Computing (CLOUD), pp. 280–288. IEEE (2010)
17. Sheyner, O., Haines, J., Jha, S., Lippmann, R., Wing, J.M.: Automated generation and analysis of attack graphs. In: 2002 Proceedings of IEEE Symposium on Security and Privacy, pp. 273–284. IEEE (2002)
18. Sun, X., Singhal, A., Liu, P.: Who touched my mission: towards probabilistic mission impact assessment. In: Proceedings of the 2015 Workshop on Automated Decision Making for Active Cyber Defense, pp. 21–26. ACM (2015)
19. Sun, X., Singhal, A., Liu, P.: Towards actionable mission impact assessment in the context of cloud computing. In: Livraga, G., Zhu, S. (eds.) DBSec 2017. LNCS, vol. 10359, pp. 259–274. Springer, Cham (2017). https://doi.org/10.1007/978-3-319-61176-1_14
20. Sun, Y., Wu, T.Y., Liu, X., Obaidat, M.S.: Multilayered impact evaluation model for attacking missions. IEEE Syst. J. $10(4)$, 1304–1315 (2016)

Author Index

Alhebaishi, Nawaf 3
Argento, Luciano 99
Atluri, Vijayalakshmi 51

Barshap, Guy 131
Batra, Gunjan 51
Boukhtouta, Amine 312
Bourget, Edwin 38
Brunner, Richard 312

Cao, Chen 330
Cuppens, Frédéric 38
Cuppens-Boulahia, Nora 38

Dault, Stéphane 312
Dubus, Samuel 38
Durak, F. Betül 113

Eisenbarth, Jean-Philippe 21

Fan, Liyue 148
Fernandez-Gago, Carmen 69
Foley, Simon 38
Fotopoulos, Spiros 278

Guajardo, Jorge 113
Gudes, Ehud 165

Hatamian, Majid 198
Hoang, Thang 113
Hossen, Md Zakir 232

Ignat, Claudia-Lavinia 21

Jajodia, Sushil 3
Jatain, Nivia 85
Joye, Marc 243

Kirrane, Sabrina 198
Kitkowska, Agnieszka 198

Kolar, Martin 69
Korunovska, Jana 198

Laarouchi, Youssef 38
Liu, Peng 330
Lopez, Javier 69

Mackie, Ian 182
Mannan, Mohammad 232
Margheri, Andrea 99
Mulliner, Collin 278

Narendra Kumar, N. V. 219
Neuner, Sebastian 278
Nguyen, Hoang-Long 21

Önen, Melek 263

Paci, Federica 99
Patil, Vishwas T. 85
Perrin, Olivier 21
Pourzandi, Makan 312

Radhika, B. S. 219

Salehi, Fariborz 243
Sassone, Vladimiro 99
Shyamasundar, R. K. 85, 219
Singhal, Anoop 3, 330
Sun, Xiaoyan 330
Sural, Shamik 51

Tassa, Tamir 131

Vaidya, Jaideep 51
Van Rompay, Cédric 263
Voyiatzis, Artemios G. 278

Wang, Lingyu 3
Weintraub, Grisha 165
Weippl, Edgar R. 278

Xu, Jia 299

Yavuz, Attila A.   113
Yıldırım, Merve   182
Yuan, Lun-Pin   330

Zannone, Nicola   99
Zhou, Jianying   299
Zhu, Sencun   330

Printed in the United States
By Bookmasters